Third Edition

Special Education Considerations for Multilingual Learners

Delivering a Continuum of Services

Else Hamayan

Barbara Marler

Cristina Sánchez-López

Jack Damico

Baltimore • London • Sydney

Paul H. Brookes Publishing Co.
Post Office Box 10624
Baltimore, Maryland 21285-0624
USA

www.brookespublishing.com

Typeset by Progressive Publishing Services, York, Pennsylvania.
Manufactured in the United States of America by
Versa Press, Inc., East Peoria, Illinois.

Photo of Cristina Sánchez-López by Michaela Wellems.

Library of Congress Cataloging-in-Publication Data

Names: Hamayan, Else V., author. | Marler, Barbara, author. | Sánchez-López, Cristina, author. |
    Damico, Jack, author.
Title: Special education considerations for multilingual learners: delivering a continuum of services,
    third edition / Else Hamayan, Barbara Marler, Cristina Sánchez-López, Jack Damico.
Description: Third edition. | Baltimore : Paul H. Brookes Publishing Co. [2023] |
    Includes bibliographical references and index.
Identifiers: LCCN 2022021720 (print) | LCCN 2022021721 (ebook) | ISBN 9781681256283 (paperback) |
    ISBN 9781681256290 (epub) | ISBN 9781681256306 (pdf)
Classification: LCC PE1128.A2 H288 2023 (print) | LCC PE1128.A2 (ebook) | DDC 372.65/21—dc23
LC record available at https://lccn.loc.gov/2022021720
LC ebook record available at https://lccn.loc.gov/2022021721

British Library Cataloguing in Publication data are available from the British Library.

Contents

Chapter 1
A Framework for Considering the Special Needs of Multilingual Learners. 1

Chapter 2
A Collaborative Model of Information Gathering and Service Provision 23

Chapter 3
The Learning Environment Created for Multilingual Learners 53

Chapter 4
Personal and Family Factors 73

Chapter 5
Physical and Psychological Factors 89

Chapter 6
Previous Schooling Factors. 103

Chapter 7
Oral Language and Literacy Development 117

Chapter 8
Academic Performance 149

Chapter 9
Cross-Cultural Factors 170

Chapter 10
Describing before Identifying:
When Specific Challenges Persist. 188

Chapter 11
Delivering a Continuum of Services 207

Foreword

Multilingual or English learners constitute one of the fastest-growing groups of students in the United States. This population represents over 9% of the school enrollment nationwide (National Academy of Sciences, 2017). A distinctive trait of this group is its deep heterogeneity. Some multilingual learners are born in the United States; others come from many nations around the globe, particularly from Latin America and Asia. They speak many languages, such as Spanish, Chinese, Portuguese, French Creole, Korean, and numerous indigenous languages and dialects. Compared to their U.S. counterparts, English learners have a higher level of poverty and live in households with two parents who have lower levels of education (National Academy of Sciences, 2017). Compared to monolingual-English speakers, this population has lower levels of educational attainment. However, multilingual students "have assets [e.g., cultures, languages, experiences] that may serve them well in their [development,] education and future careers. [Multilingual learners] are likely to reap benefits in cognitive, social, and emotional development and may also be protected from brain decline at older ages" (National Academy of Sciences, 2017, pp. 1–2).

English learners inhabit multiple identities related to their second language (L2): ethnicity, national origin, social class, and sometimes refugee status. Because of their academic struggles, multilingual learners may also acquire a disability identity. According to the National Center on Educational Outcomes (NCEO; 2016), about 11% of students with disabilities were designated English learners in the 2017–2018 school year. Although the population of students identified as English learners with disabilities appears to be growing, there is considerable variability in the representation of this group around the nation. To illustrate, the representation of multilingual learners with disabilities across states in the 2017–2018 academic year ranged between <1% to 29% of the special education population (NCEO, 2016). During this school year, about 80% of English learners with disabilities were distributed in three categories, namely, learning disabilities (49%), speech or language impairments (19%), and other health impairments (9%; NCEO, 2016).

The complex identities of multilingual students demand multifaceted educational responses. However, school systems tend to be organized around identity silos that compartmentalize students' multilayered needs. This structural barrier has important consequences. For instance, there is evidence that English learners tend to lose access to language supports after they get identified for special education services, in part due to the bifurcated structures of L2 and special education services (Artiles, Waitoller, & Neal, 2011). In addition, behind these structural divides are misunderstandings and deep epistemological differences in how the various identity dimensions of multilingual learners are framed and addressed. This contributes to the creation of "professional dilemmas" and myths that practitioners grapple with when working with struggling multilingual learners. A common example is: "The student is struggling because he or she is not proficient in English. Thus, I should wait at least 4 to 5 years before I refer to special education to allow time for the acquisition of English." Another pervasive dilemma: "I don't know whether this student is struggling because of a lack of English proficiency or a learning disability, but I should refer to special education because a diagnosis will at least secure some supports." And a favored myth—even among some families—is: "English learners should be taught in English only to avoid confusing them and minimize academic struggles."

Hamayan, Marler, Sánchez-López, and Damico tackle these barriers and misunderstandings in this volume. This book is grounded in a unique, urgently needed perspective. Two distinctive qualities stand out in this guide. First, the book uses what I characterize as a countercultural approach. That is, the model presented in this volume advances practices that disrupt longstanding traditions in the education of struggling multilingual students. For instance, Hamayan et al. caution practitioners against rushing to diagnose students as a prerequisite to addressing their needs. Hamayan et al.'s reframing of traditional practices compels practitioners to center their attention on the descriptive profiles of struggling English learners before committing to diagnostic labels. Of significance, these descriptive portraits help differentiate behaviors and performance patterns that may be associated with the acquisition of a second language or a disability. An important corollary is that student behaviors must be examined as situated in learning contexts. Thus, Hamayan et al.'s analytic attention focuses on both individual factors and contextual influences. Again, this represents a significant departure from the practices of a field that has been vested in the traditions of individual difference analyses inherited from medicine and psychology. The volume also diverts from orthodoxy by articulating a system of learning supports irrespective of funding sources. This is a transformational arrangement for it infuses flexibility in practitioners' work as they navigate institutional requirements and structures.

The second distinguishing quality of this book is the vital role assigned to the examination of learning environments, particularly in the contexts of multi-tiered systems of support (MTSS). This is of consequence for two reasons. Careful analyses of learning environments afford the possibility of framing interventions from a proactive stance. The authors take issue with MTSS's core assumption that all students have equitable access to the curriculum and effective interventions; they call for action before English learners fail. Research evidence shows multilingual learners are educated in school contexts with less access to resources, including well-prepared teachers (National Academy of Sciences, 2017). In this way, Hamayan et al.'s model is concerned with considerations of educational opportunity, a long-neglected aspect in the education of this population.

Furthermore, attention to learning environments requires a robust assessment system, which is a significant strength of this book. This is accomplished through comprehensive data collection via classroom observations and other methods used to craft holistic representations of a student's history and performance, including personal (physical and psychological) and family factors, educational history, profile of oral language proficiency and literacy in the first language (L1) and L2, as well as trajectories of academic performance and teaching in both languages and cross-cultural factors. Considerations of L2 acquisition and how it can mediate educational assessments and academic performance are consistently monitored. The goal is to map the configuration of potential influences in student difficulties and offer appropriate services (i.e., L2, special education) in a timely fashion within MTSS team models. This proactive model calls for an iterative approach, including cycles of data collection, implementation of supports and interventions, evaluation of their impact, and refinement of the supports. The model is designed to be interdisciplinary, it draws from theory and research from bilingualism, multicultural education, and special education. Hamayan et al.'s approach expands the paradigm prevalent in schools that relies on standardized measures, decontextualized analyses of student performance and learning environments, and limited use of bilingualism theory and research. The core purpose of Hamayan et al.'s model is to sustain a proactive team-based continuum of services in a timely fashion. This is a perspective that is urgently needed and will undoubtedly benefit the growing population of multilingual learners in U.S. schools.

Alfredo Artiles
Lee L. Jacks Professor of Education
Stanford University
Stanford, California

References

Artiles, A. J., Waitoller, F., & Neal, R. (2011). Grappling with the intersection of language and ability differences: Equity issues for Chicano/Latino students in special education. In R. R. Valencia (Ed.), *Chicano school failure and success: Past, present, and future* (3rd ed., pp. 213–234). London, UK: Routledge/Falmer.

National Academy of Sciences. (2017). *Promoting the educational success of children and youth learning English: Promising futures.* Washington, DC: The National Academies Press. doi: 10.17226/24677

National Center on Educational Outcomes (2016). *ELs with disabilities.* Retrieved from https://nceo.info/student_groups/ells_with_disabilities.

Preface

This is the third edition of a guidebook that we wrote 14 years ago; the original guide was the result of a workshop that Jack Damico and I developed in response to requests for assistance from schools. Those requests typically took the form of a question: "How can we tell whether English language learners (ELLs) have special education needs?" Initially, the workshop focused exclusively on the question of how to distinguish between long-term disabilities and normal second language difficulties that ELLs may have in school. In fact, the workshop became known casually as *the LD/L2 (Learning Disability/Second Language) Workshop*. Over the years, however, we came to understand that the question of L2 versus LD was extremely murky, and probably the wrong question to ask.

Much has changed over the years in the way ELLs are perceived and how difficulties that some ELLs face at school are interpreted. Not all changes have been positive, especially changes in the sentiments toward immigrants and refugees coming to the United States. Animosity by some sectors of U.S. society toward people from different ethnic and linguistic backgrounds has led to legislation that clearly disfavors these families. However research has continued to support the important role of students' home languages and has shown the enriching role that linguistic and cultural diversity can play within a school. In that vein, we decided to use the term **multilingual learner** in this edition to refer to students who come to school with a home language other than English, including but not limited to students officially designated as **English language learners**.

The foundational principle for our work is that support is more effective if it is provided seamlessly as part of a continuum that is integrated into the students' everyday school life rather than trying to determine whether academic challenges faced by some multilingual learners stem from a second language development issue or a long-term disability. In our work in schools over the 14 years since the publication of the first edition, we have tried to move teachers and educators away from needing to know right at the beginning whether a multilingual learner facing academic challenges has a disability that can be categorized as a special education need. Rather, we focus on providing support that uses the benefits of knowledge and experience from both fields: second language acquisition/bilingualism first and special education next. Ensuring a continuum of services within a diversity and equity context has become of utmost importance to our framework.

Over the past 14 years, three significant changes have affected multilingual learners who are facing challenges in school: (1) response to instruction and intervention (RtI) is more widely implemented, (2) testing to check whether students are meeting standards has become even more entrenched in daily school life, and (3) a multi-tiered system of supports (MTSS) that has a broader range than RtI has come into widespread use. Each of these changes has both positive and negative consequences for multilingual learners. In this third edition, we integrate discussions of these three issues throughout the chapters, and provide guidance for improvement when RtI and/or MTSS is implemented in nonsensical ways for multilingual learners, or when the pressure of testing leads to invalid conclusions about multilingual learners' academic performance.

One of the major changes in this third edition—bringing to the forefront the examination of the learning environment that has been created for multilingual learners at school—makes it more likely for support to be given to these students in a seamless way. Another significant change in this edition is that we separated the process of providing different levels of support, as suggested in RtI and MTSS systems, by moving two chapters (*Describing Before Identifying, Delivering a Continuum of Services*) that appeared early in the second edition to a later position in this book. That way, the chapters follow more closely the chronology of Tiers of support. More than anything else, our suggestion to ensure a continuum of services helps school personnel implement an MTSS approach that is more responsive and relevant to these learners' linguistic and cultural attributes.

We have identified six integral factors in the student's home and school life that provide us with general information about our multilingual learners, including: Personal and family factors; physical and psychological factors; previous schooling/performance; oral language and literacy development in both home language and English; academic performance and instruction in both, or all of the students' languages; cross-cultural factors. Based on a system of extensive information collection, we suggest changes in the learning environment and learning support strategies for the particular difficulties that multilingual learners often have in school. Some of these strategies are specific to individual students or small numbers of students, whereas others are systemic and would improve the learning context for all multilingual learners. None of these strategies stand in the way of advancing the learning of students who are not multilingual; in fact, these strategies expand all students' growth. The strategies we recommend emerge from (1) our focus on the importance of meaningfulness and a usage-based approach to language acquisition, (2) our knowledge of second language learning/bilingualism as well as from special education research and practice, and (3) our firm belief that these strategies enrich the learning environment for all students not just multilingual learners. To ensure that a broad perspective and continuum of services are provided to these students, we also recommend that a team consisting of teachers, administrators, and specialists be used. Many schools already have these teams in place if they have adopted the principles of MTSS.

This guide was written with three purposes in mind. First, we wanted to help teachers identify specific challenges that students encounter in school in a way that would lead to useful support for multilingual learners. Second, we wanted to help educators understand those challenges through extensive information gathering. Third, we wanted to help school staff identify strategies for the learning environment most likely to be effective in alleviating these academic challenges. The framework that we suggest can fit well into an already existing RtI/MTSS system.

We hope that this guide helps educators in deciding what type of support to provide for these students. Finding assistance that works for any student experiencing academic difficulty is not easy. When those students are multilingual learners, the challenge is amplified; finding assistance that works becomes much more difficult. This guide helps educators better navigate the support strategies and intervention options. We offer pragmatic and effective strategies and interventions that are rooted in the theoretical tenets of second language acquisition, bilingual development, and acculturation. They are also firmly based on research about effective educational programs for multilingual learners and they result from our work in schools. The book can be used as a professional learning tool for study groups, problem-solving teams, and action research groups.

The approach we propose would not work without a strong collaborative model in which professionals with expertise in different areas come together to solve a problem: What to do about a student or a group of students who are having unusual academic difficulty? The approach requires that individuals from different specializations collaborate and share their expertise with one another. In doing so, they must be open to perspectives different from their own. In the past we called these collaborative groups *ECOS (ensuring a continuum of services) teams*. In this edition we refer to them as *MTSS teams*, which coordinate the information gathering, the formulation of support strategies and interventions, and the support of teachers.

The way that the workshop on which this guide is based was conceived reflects that collaboration directly. Jack Damico is well versed in special education, and my expertise is in multilingual learner education. We brought our areas of expertise together and created the workshop that eventually led to this guide. Later, with the addition of Barbara Marler and Cristina Sánchez-López to the team, new perspectives were introduced. Barbara brings insights from her work as a program director in a highly diverse school district on the suburban edge of Chicago. Cristina is an educational consultant who gives us insights from a teacher's perspective. Her work with Theresa Young, a speech–language pathologist from the Toronto District School Board, added yet another perspective. Without this evolving collaboration, the ideas in this book would not be as wide ranging.

The special features in this book were designed to make it easier for schools to begin offering a continuum of services to multilingual learners who are having academic difficulties. One or more of the following special features appear in each chapter:

Chronicles: The chronicles are true stories told by different individuals, ranging from a university professor to a parent. They illustrate specific points made in the book and are accompanied by questions for discussion.

MTSS Team Activities: This feature sets up discussions, challenges, and practical activities that help MTSS teams understand and further investigate issues presented in the chapters. Many of these items are also effective as professional learning activities.

Checklists and Rating Scales: The guide offers many tools to assess aspects of the program or the way that support is provided to students, to evaluate the current situation in a school, and to develop the process of establishing a continuum of services.

Glossary: A glossary provides definitions of some of the key concepts presented in the text. Glossary terms appear in bold type at first use in the text.

Questions for Reflection and Action: Each chapter includes questions that are intended to prompt further discussion of the integral factors that need to be considered in designing support strategies and interventions for multilingual learners experiencing academic difficulties. These questions get teams to think about their own specific setting and to apply the concepts to their student population.

Online Resources: The book includes online resources, which are called out in the book and can be found on the Brookes Download Hub (see the About the Online Resources page that follows for details on accessing these materials). Teachers can use these resources to support their work at different stages in the MTSS process.

We hope that the suggestions in this guide are helpful in setting up a system in schools whereby multilingual learners receive the support they need in a seamless way. We would be gratified if the book also inspired educators to move away from the status quo and join with colleagues to do what is most effective for multilingual learners who are having more than the average share of challenges in school.

—ELSE HAMAYAN

About the Online Resources

Purchasers of this book may download and print select resources from the book for professional and educational use. Online resources include the following documents:

Chapter 3

- Key Laws and Court Cases Regarding Multilingual Learner Education

- Gathering Information and Evaluating the Adequacy of the Learning Environment

- Sample Health Education Unit

Chapter 10

- Observable Behaviors That Multilingual Learners May Exhibit in English

Chapter 11

- Generating Multilingual Learner Interventions: Listening, Speaking, Reading, Writing, and Cultural Influences

- Generating Special Education Interventions: Listening, Speaking, Reading, and Writing

- Linguistic and Cultural Resources

To access these materials:

1. Go to the Brookes Download Hub:
   http://downloads.brookespublishing.com

2. Register to create an account (or log in with an existing account)

3. Filter or search for the book title *Special Education Considerations for Multilingual Learners*.

A Framework for Considering the Special Needs of Multilingual Learners[1]

Key Concepts. *To proactively serve the needs of multilingual learners who are experiencing significant challenges in school, staff must be able and willing to take a critical look at the learning environment that has been created, and set up a process that can help prevent difficulties through a culturally and linguistically responsive multi-tiered system of support (MTSS). This will ensure that support is provided on a continuum, without interruption, in a way that is integrated into the learners' schooling experience as soon as challenges are identified.*

When multilingual learners, formerly referred to as English Language Learners (ELLs)—students who are developing proficiency in a new language and who are learning academic content through this new language—are perceived as having an inordinate amount of difficulty in school, the issue presents a tremendous challenge to teachers, special educators, and administrators. Almost immediately the question arises as to whether the challenges the student is experiencing are possibly the result of a special education exceptionality.[1] More often than not, when a teacher feels that a multilingual learner is having greater than expected difficulty at school, there is an inclination to jump to the conclusion that the student has a need for special education.

Historically, in the United States, there has been a tendency to refer multilingual learners to special education inappropriately, which in turn has led to the overidentification of multilingual learners as having special education needs and a disproportionate representation of these students in special education classes (Artiles & Ortiz, 2002; Artiles et al., 2016; Caesar & Kohler, 2007; Gottlieb & Hamayan, 2006; Peña et al., 2017). The overrepresentation of multilingual learners is particularly acute in programs for students with learning disabilities (Harry & Klinger, 2014; Rueda & Windmueller, 2006) and with students who have non-native accents (Roessell et al., 2020). The path to the special education door is well worn because it is often seen as the most efficient and fiscally feasible way of getting help for students who are experiencing significant challenges in school. Owing to the lack of other effective remedial

---

[1]The terms *exceptionality* and *disability* are used in this guide to refer to the variety of cognitive, perceptual, language, or mathematical disabilities that lead to difficulties in learning in an academic setting.

options, special education may also be perceived as the only means available to teachers to find help for these students. This may be true in cases in which the language assistance program for multilingual learners has been recently created or in which the program is not particularly well implemented and does not offer an effective continuum of support for all learners. Teachers are likely to choose special education as the source of support for multilingual learners because it does generate help, funding is still available, and even if teachers and administrators know that it may not be appropriate, it assuages their feelings of guilt and satisfies the need for accountability.

Placing an inappropriate special education label on multilingual learners often results in changed expectations for those students and often provides a convenient, if incorrect, excuse for the multilingual learners' observed or perceived difficulties (Gutierrez-Clellen et al., 2012; Kapantzoglou et al., 2012). Unfortunately, this perceived solution frequently results in negative consequences. Because most special educators who serve monolingual English-speaking students are not well trained in diversity education, second language acquisition, bilingualism, or **bilingual education** (Caesar & Kohler, 2007; Kritikos, 2003; Ozfidan & Toprak, 2020; Roseberry-McKibbin et al., 2005), their best attempts at assistance often are misdirected and may not be what is most effective for multilingual learners. Finally, if multilingual learners are served in special education, the school system may believe that the students' needs are met and may not provide the language-rich support needed by these learners. It is important, therefore, that this apparent "solution" not be employed inappropriately.

Reasons for the Misidentification of Special Needs

To ensure that misidentification does not occur, this guide proposes an approach that can help overcome many of the problems in assessment and remediation directed toward multilingual learners. Before highlighting solutions, however, we present three reasons why such misidentification is likely to occur in this population: problematic assessment practices, the influence of the medical model when addressing learning difficulties, and funding biases toward special education. Each is briefly discussed here.

Assessment Practices

The first and most significant reason for the tendency to overidentify multilingual learners as needing special education is that the assessment of proficiency and academic achievement among multilingual learners is fraught with difficulty. Assessment is a complex enterprise that requires consideration of multiple factors, including symbolic proficiency, affect, previous experience, cultural and linguistic learning and application, expectations, and contextual variables (Goldstein & Horton-Ikard, 2010; Gutkin & Nemeth, 1997; Lubinski, 2000; Müller, 2003; Tomczak & Jaworska-Pasterska, 2017; Wentzel & Wigfield, 1998). However, this complexity and the methods necessary to address it are not typically considered in school settings. In addition to the complexity of the assessment process we encounter a heterogeneous population of learners with widely diverse experiences using two or more languages. It may surprise some that the largest group of school-age multilingual learners in the United States consists of simultaneous bilingual learners—children who have been exposed to two languages from an early age and were born in the United States (Capp et al., 2005; Kay-Raining Bird et al., 2016). As a consequence, a number of biases that orient the assessment process away from the best interests of the multilingual learner become operational. These biases include a focus on superficial behaviors rather than underlying proficiency as indices of difficulty, a lack of attention to **intrinsic** versus **extrinsic** factors, the collection of inadequate data—often in the form of **norm-referenced** and standardized test results—that do not enable sufficient descriptions of proficiency, a lack of recognition of several consequences of bilingualism during assessment, and the application of inappropriate discrepancy formulas for interpretation purposes (e.g., J. S. Damico, 2019a; Hamayan & Damico, 1991; Peña et al., 2011).

- **A focus on superficial behaviors rather than underlying proficiency as indices of difficulty**: At a superficial level, the way that academic and language challenges manifest among multilingual learners is very similar to the way such difficulties manifest among students with long-term disabilities or special needs (Crago & Paradis, 2003; J. S. Damico & Damico, 1993a; Freire, 2014; Oxley et al., 2017; Salameh et al., 2004). For example, Paradis (2005) found that multilingual learners' accuracy rates and error patterns in producing grammatical morphemes in English were similar to those reported for same-age monolingual English-speaking children with specific language impairment. That is not to say that the possible sources of these difficulties are the same in the two populations. Rather, there are only so many ways that language and learning difficulties manifest behaviorally, despite the underlying causal variables (i.e., disability or difference). It is not enough to focus only on the superficial indices of difficulty; one must also determine whether deeper or more complex variables are operating (e.g., Ahlsén, 2005; Armstrong, 2005; J. S. Damico et al., 1996; Perkins, 2005; van Kraayenoord, 2010; Washington et al., 2021).

- **Intrinsic and extrinsic factors:** Language and learning disabilities are generally due to factors intrinsic to the learner, such as a neurological impairment or a problem with symbolic processing (Perkins, 2005), whereas second language learning involves a developmental process that can be influenced by factors external to the learner such as the quality of language instruction, or how supportive the learning environment is to language learning within a classroom and throughout a school community (Bialystok, 2015; Cuero, 2010; Sloan, 2007). In the case of vocabulary usage, for example, if a multilingual learner frequently forgets a common word that has been taught, it is possible that the visual aid used to represent the concept may have been culturally irrelevant for that student (e.g., the Liberty Bell representing the concept of freedom or independence, which is specific to American history); hence the visual symbol would not provide any help for that student in learning new vocabulary. For students with special education needs, the same observable behavior—that is, forgetting common words that have been taught—may result from a completely different set of reasons. The student may have oral language comprehension or production difficulties as a consequence of word retrieval problems, or the student may have memory problems. In such cases, the pedagogical needs of the two populations are different: Students with special education needs require support in creating compensations to overcome their difficulties (J. S. Damico et al., 1996; Dunaway, 2004; Paradis et al., 2021), whereas second language learners need to develop further proficiency in **academic language** (e.g., Echevarria et al., 2017; Meisuri et al., 2018).

- **Collection of data**: Another difficulty in assessment is that the data gathered as part of the referral and evaluation process or even as part of the universal screening process in response to instruction and intervention (RtI) and/or MTSS are frequently inadequate or inappropriate. Teachers tend to rely too heavily on norm-referenced and standardized test scores administered exclusively in English, which give only a very narrow and potentially quite inaccurate view of what a student is able to do (Caesar & Kohler, 2007; Flynn, 2000; Gutiérrez-Clellen & Peña, 2001; Herrera et al., 2012; Kapantzoglou et al., 2012; Laing & Kamhi, 2003; Tetnowski & Franklin, 2003; Xu & Drame, 2008). These tests typically focus on superficial aspects of language structure, have validity and authenticity concerns, provide numbers that have a differentiating function rather than an interpretive function, and focus on identifying students' weaknesses (J. S. Damico, 2019b; Horton-Ikard & Ellis Weismer, 2007). Further, multilingual learners, who are often unfamiliar with the cultural context of test items, are likely to give the wrong answers, not because they have not developed the specific skill being assessed, but because they do not understand the question. This constellation of factors promotes unreliable test results that give an inaccurate view of the student (Gunderson & Siegel, 2001; Müller, 2003; Samson & Lesaux, 2009).

- **Lack of understanding of bilingualism:** In addition, we cannot assume the validity and reliability of tests designed for monolingual students that are translated from one language to another and re-normed. Even assuming that the tests developed are valid and reliable (a dangerous assumption), factors relating to bilingualism as a process are not always carefully considered (Flege, 2019; Genesee et al., 2005; Grosjean, 1998; Matson et al., 2017; Oller & Eilers, 2002; Pacheco, 2010). For example, although numerous studies have indicated that multilingual learners' test performance should be interpreted using both languages via conceptual scoring— that is, scoring the meaning of a response regardless of the language in which it is produced (Bak, 2016; Bedore et al., 2005; Hammer et al., 2007;

Marchman & Martínez-Sussman, 2002; Oller & Eilers, 2002; B. Z. Pearson et al., 1995)—this is not typically done. Further, when valid and reliable assessments in both languages can be found and instruction through the student's home language is not provided, careful interpretation and analysis of the resulting scores is required (J. S. Damico, 2019b). Failure to take into account the complexity and dynamic nature of the bilingual process during assessment further reduces the effectiveness of traditional assessment and diagnostic tools when used with multilingual learners.

- **Application of inappropriate discrepancy formulas for interpretation purposes**: The **discrepancy model** used to identify learning disabilities, which was initially useful as a gatekeeping mechanism, does not serve multilingual learners well because it is normal for these students, who are at different levels of developing English proficiency, to have lower scores on verbal tasks in English than on tasks that do not require as much verbal processing (Barac et al., 2014; Y. Kohnert, 2004). This discrepancy may accurately indicate a special education need in monolingual English-speaking students (Sternberg & Grigorenko, 2002). However, it also reflects quite precisely a characteristic of typically developing multilingual learners! Perhaps because of these problems, the **Individuals with Disabilities Education Improvement Act (IDEA)** of 2004 has given districts permission to go beyond the discrepancy formula to embrace a model that assesses how students respond to different **interventions** and instructional activities. This moves the definition of *learning disability* out of the domain of a discrepancy between performance and potential and into the domain of RtI (van Kraayenoord, 2010). The RtI/MTSS model seeks to improve the learning environment for all students in the classroom in core instruction by supporting both teachers and students and keeps track of students who do not respond to these interventions. For this reason, we focus on the learning environment that has been created for multilingual learners as the pivotal element in interpreting and supporting challenges facing these students.

To get a better sense of what multilingual learners are able to do and what they have difficulty with, a considerable amount of information needs to be gathered. Rarely do school teams use ethnographic approaches to collect data in such a way that the information obtained is meaningful and useful. It is important to adhere to certain standards in order to collect qualitative data that are authentic and to have the conviction that these data are not inferior to data obtained through more standardized means (J. S. Damico & Ball, 2010; Freire, 2014; Kašćelan et al., 2019).

Staff cannot always collect the amount of information needed for such a determination, however. At the end of the assessment process, we are often left with something akin to a huge jigsaw puzzle with several pieces missing. Further, these data are often gathered and interpreted by school personnel who are not adequately versed in multilingual learner education issues, bilingualism, second language acquisition, or culturally responsive education and

Monica Graduated from University!

By N. B., a Parent

When my daughter Monica was in third grade, she was getting Cs in everything. Monica had been in this school since kindergarten. She arrived from Poland not speaking a word of English. The school did not do anything special for her; they didn't give her any special classes in English. Now I know there is something called *ESL* (English as a second language) for children who come with no English. I thought someone should be helping her with English, but I also didn't want her missing what the teacher was teaching. She needed a lot of help with English, but I figured the school knew best what to do. A lot of people told us to speak English at home, but my English is not so good, and besides, I wanted her to keep up her Polish. So we kept speaking Polish at home, and it was difficult for her at school. But we worked hard and I knew she was smart, so at a parent–teacher conference I asked whether the school could give Monica a test to determine her level of English proficiency. I was interested in knowing how much English Monica had acquired.

The teachers must have misunderstood. The next thing I knew, we received a "consent to test" permission form to initiate special education testing. I was shocked! I had never imagined that Monica had any kind of learning problems. Here she was learning two languages and doing OK. Sure, it took her a little longer to get things in class, but she seemed to be managing. I have a friend who is a bilingual teacher at another school, so I asked her what I should do. She said not to test her. She said that if

they tested her it would probably be in English, and even if it were in Polish, Monica would not do well on the test, but not because she had a learning problem. She said that we should talk to the teachers and see whether they would give Monica some more help with English.

The school was not happy that we were not signing the form, and they did nothing to help Monica. They told us to get her tutoring at home. We did that in English, math, and American history. I can't say that it was easy, but we worked at it, and little by little, Monica's English became better and better. When Monica finished grade 8, she graduated with high honors.

Monica is now fully bilingual; she graduated from university and is a regional director of a national corporation working with attorneys to provide financial relief to clients. I guess we made the right decision, but it was very difficult. What if Monica did have a problem? Well, I don't worry much about it. She did well, and most important, she can speak and read both English and Polish.

Questions for Discussion

1. What beliefs did the parent have that are supported by research?
2. What misconceptions does the parent have, if any?
3. What did the school do that was effective?
4. What did the school do wrong, if anything?

the implications of these factors for the assessment and instruction of multilingual learners (Goldstein, 2011; Müller, 2003; Oller & Eilers, 2002; Sox, 2009). Often the bilingual or English as a second language (ESL)[2] specialist is not involved in making sense out of the gathered information, let alone in the data collection. Chronicle 1.1 describes an instance in which language proficiency testing was overlooked completely.

Prevalence of a Medical Model

A second fundamental reason for the tendency to inappropriately identify multilingual learners as needing special education services lies in the way in which we conceptualize special education needs in the United States. In the last quarter-century, a medical model that is based on the notion that

---

[2]Many districts are using the term *English language development (ELD)* to refer to learning or teaching English as an additional language. Many multilingual learners are simultaneous bilingual learners for whom English is not a second language per se. We use the term *ESL* in this book to refer to any context in which proficiency in English is being developed in addition to another language that is used at home.

disabilities or challenges can be identified much like the list of ailments that are officially recognized as diseases in the medical field has prevailed (Conrad, 2007; J. S. Damico, 2019c; McDermott & Varenne, 1995; Skrtic, 1991). This tendency to view academic and language learning difficulties from the perspective of human pathology can be seen in the medicalization of learning problems in the *Diagnostic and Statistical Manual of Mental Disorders*, Fifth Edition (American Psychiatric Association [APA], 2013) and the eleventh edition of the *International Classification of Diseases* (World Health Organization, 2018). Whether these medical designations are defensible or not, they do function to create an explicit grounding for the discipline of special education (Lai et al., 2013; Skrtic, 1991).

As a result, this prevailing medical orientation has created a set of beliefs about the nature of special education and even about the role of multilingual learners within special education, and these beliefs inform both our perceptions of academic and language-learning difficulties and our assessment practices (J. S. Damico et al., 2021; J. S. Damico & Nelson, 2012; Klasen, 2000). This situation has falsely suggested to educators that special education needs can be easily identified in a valid and reliable manner, resulting in misidentification, because the complexity of the phenomenon and the individuality of the multilingual learner are often overlooked.

In reality, exceptionality is not an objective and easily verifiable empirical entity. Rather, it is a social construct, and the diagnostic criteria employed for various exceptional traits have been based on a number of sociocultural factors that mirror whatever ideologies are in vogue at any given time (J. S. Damico et al., 2021; McDermott & Varenne, 1995; Skrtic, 1991), or whatever set of standards are accepted as the norm. For example, the illusionary "autism epidemic" currently referred to in the media is primarily due to drastic changes in the *Diagnostic and Statistical Manual's* (*DSM-IV*; APA, 2000) decision (somewhat socially determined) to include two milder variants (Asperger's disorder and pervasive developmental disorder–not otherwise specified) with dramatically reduced (subthreshold) symptoms that have resulted in 75% of the recent autism diagnoses (Chakrabarti & Fombonne, 2001; Gernsbacher et al., 2005; Grzadzinski et al., 2013). These diagnostic categories may be further complicated by ambiguity and subjectivity, and this lack of definitional rigor may result in various types of problems that start with inappropriate diagnoses and then proceed to a cascade of other psychological and academic problems (J. S. Damico et al., 2021). Indeed, the extreme overidentification of multilingual learners as learning disabled and language disordered, when no such overrepresentation exists in categories that can, in fact, be medically validated, such as visual or hearing impairment, is a clear demonstration of the problem (J. S. Damico, 2019c; Goldstein & Horton-Ikard, 2010; Stow & Dodd, 2005).

Availability of Categorical Funding

The third reason for the misidentification of multilingual learners as having disabilities lies in the categorical status of special education. The legal status of special education gives impetus to the tendency to formally identify separate categories of disabilities. When Public Law 94-142 (The Education Act for All Handicapped, also known as *IDEA*) passed in 1975 in the United States, it provided legal support for special education and subsequently created a separately funded category within the educational system. Since then, students in the United States have had to be identified formally as having special education needs before additional funding for supplementary assistance can be received by the school for that individual student. Thus, the identification of these disabilities is connected with additional funding that gives the school much-needed resources, especially when funding for multilingual learner education remains minimal and precarious. Having additional funding attached to the categorization of students in special education may make it less objectionable for schools to identify special education needs. The gate or hurdle that would keep students from being needlessly categorized into special education is simply not there. It is too tempting to place students in special education when they are perceived to fall outside of what is considered "typical learning," regardless of the underlying reasons.

This categorization of special education could also have the opposite effect. In some districts, because of fear of monitoring agencies or potential litigation, the gatekeeping mechanisms are overused. Students have to fail or wait for an extended period before they are even referred to special education.

Developing a Multi-Tiered System of Supports

Developing a culturally and linguistically responsive and sustaining RtI/MTSS provides an alternative to the disjointed and siloed practices that have been employed in many schools in the past to support students who experience academic difficulties (Ehren & Nelson, 2005; D. Fuchs & Fuchs, 2006; E. R. Mesmer & Mesmer, 2008). These traditional practices evolved out of special education approaches and medical models that assumed academic difficulties were caused by disabilities intrinsic to the student. Once students were identified as having academic difficulties, they were referred for evaluations that were oriented toward diagnosing and labeling these students with an identifiable categorical disability, such as a learning or reading disability, specific language impairment, or developmental delay, before the student could receive the necessary remedial support.

The identification, assessment, and placement of students into such categories are problematic on all counts, however, and especially so when the students are multilingual learners. When traditional monolingual English assessment procedures are employed and then fit into the "test-score discrepancy models" that have been used for 3 decades in special education (e.g., Cummins, 2008; Flynn, 2000; Kay Raining-Bird et al., 2016; Vaughn & Klingner, 2007), several limitations to this approach to assessment and placement become obvious. First, the student must demonstrate chronic academic failure to be referred for assessment and eventual placement. Second, the decisions about identification and placement frequently depend on test scores and discrepancy formulas that provide no information on why a student is performing poorly. Finally, this approach provides little or no information to assist in determining what might be done to address the student's difficulties (J. S. Damico, 1991; Gunderson & Siegel, 2001; Washington et al., 2021). These last two limitations are especially problematic when addressing the kinds of diversity issues seen with multilingual learners, because test scores and discrepancy formulas fail to consider variables external to the child, such as experiential, linguistic, and instructional quality differences. This failure often results in misdiagnosis and inappropriate placement of these students in special education, which leads to significant underrepresentation or overrepresentation of multilingual learners in special education programs (Allington & Walmsley, 2007; Gersten & Edomono, 2006; Harry & Klingner, 2014; Peña et al., 2017; Rinaldi & Sampson, 2008; van Kraayenoord, 2010).

With the revised Individuals with Disabilities Education Improvement Act (IDEA) of 2004, however, there has been a shift in focus regarding the identification of students for special education services. Primarily, there has been a shift away from the use of discrepancy models to identify exceptionalities, particularly learning disabilities. According to federal regulations, state departments of education can no longer force school systems to use a severe discrepancy between intellectual ability and achievement as the litmus test for determining whether a child has a specific learning disability. Instead, it is suggested that the schools employ a process that determines whether the child responds to scientific, research-based intervention by using a **dual discrepancy model**—in other words, RtI/MTSS.

When the dual discrepancy model (L. S. Fuchs, 2003; L. S. Fuchs et al., 2003; Vaughn & Klingner, 2007) is used to identify problems, including exceptionalities, the student is provided with actual interventions, and changes in the student's performance are documented (L. S. Fuchs, 2004; Stecker et al., 2005). In this model, the first indication of discrepancy is the finding that the student is performing academically at a level significantly below that of his or her typical classroom peers, regardless of the suspected reasons. That is, the student exhibits a discrepancy in initial skills or performance that is important in the context of interest, the classroom. At this time, various levels of intervention or instruction may be employed, and any changes that occur are documented. If the student fails to reduce the performance gap with classmates, despite the implementation of one or more well-designed, well-implemented interventions crafted to address the difficulties, then the second and more specific discrepancy in the rate of learning relative to classroom peers is noted. This may be sufficient reason for eventual placement into special education services.

With this reorientation, the dual discrepancy model has been employed to create more recent assessment processes that have evolved from the understanding that the source of some students' academic difficulties might be the quality of the instruction they have experienced rather than an intrinsic disability (J. S. Damico, 2019a; Vaughn & Fuchs, 2003; Wright, 2005). RtI/MTSS takes a different tack to address the broad-ranging academic challenges that students face in the general education classroom. This approach is based on a tiered model of high-quality instructional support, with ongoing assessment used to determine which students respond to this specific instructional support. When the students respond to the interventions by making progress, it is assumed that the instructional support that is provided at this tier is sufficient to meet their learning needs (L. S. Fuchs et al., 2004; Kame'enui et al., 2006; Vaughn & Fuchs, 2003).

In the RtI/MTSS approach, Tier 1 is considered the level of core instructional programming and the instruction employed is available to all students. Changes in programming, use of resources, teacher capacity building, and other aspects of the learning environment are examples of what a school or district might decide to focus on to ensure high quality education within Tier 1. At the instructional level, for example, these changes would include authentic in-class reading, process writing within a writing workshop format, employing bilingual texts, providing strong models during classroom lessons, and providing additional classroom writing instruction in the form of several dedicated mini-lessons (Allington, 2009; Cloud et al., 2009; Cunningham, & Allington, 2011; Hornberger & Link, 2012). This level of instruction is provided for all students in the general education, ESL, and bilingual classrooms combined with ongoing curriculum-based assessment.

Students who do not respond or who are **resistant to instruction** are then provided with a second tier of support. In addition to curriculum-based assessment, students who are provided with Tier 2 intervention may also be identified through universal screening or benchmark testing (L. S. Fuchs & Fuchs, 2008). Because Tier 2 serves as an instructional safety net that works in concert with Tier 1 by adding both time and instructional intensity into the school day, those students provided with Tier 2 interventions are typically given more individualized intervention (Howard, 2009). This level of support may take the form of specialized, small-group, intensive instruction for nonresponsive students that extends rather than replaces the instruction in Tier 1 (Collier, 2010; Howard, 2009; Vaughn & Denton, 2008). This might involve, for example, direct one-on-one shared reading with a teacher or trained aide, providing a mini-word wall for a student in a file folder left on his desk, or supplemental peer tutoring to increase fluency during reading. As this level of intervention is employed, ongoing assessment is used to determine which students continue to resist intervention and thus require an additional third tier of support.

When required, Tier 3 is the level of intensive intervention. This level of support may entail specialized individualized interventions for students with significant needs (Fletcher et al., 2005; L. S. Fuchs, 2002; Howard, 2009). This level of support may involve reading and/or math or other instructional specialists, special education services, or may be employed as the last set of interventions before placement into special education. Tier 3 is used differently in various locales, and in some states, a four- or five-tiered model is in place (Barnes & Harlacher, 2008; Mellard et al., 2004). Throughout this entire process information obtained about students' integral characteristics serves as an indispensable context for generating additional learning support strategies for these students.

Unfortunately, much of the work that has recently been done in RtI/MTSS has not been applied within the context of multilingualism or cultural diversity. Rather than using this multi-tiered approach to address the problems of overidentification due to poor testing and teaching procedures, many of the problematic procedures have simply been repackaged under the RtI/MTSS rubric (J. S. Damico & Nelson, 2012; van Kraayenoord, 2010). Districts may use their Title I funds to support RtI/MTSS efforts; subsequently, purse strings may rest with someone unfamiliar with the needs of multilingual learners. It is imperative that any efforts to make the RtI/MTSS process more responsive to the needs of multilingual learners extend to the individual who manages Title I grants in the school or district.

The Need to Provide Relevant Services in a Timely Manner

The accurate identification of the special needs of multilingual learners is important for two reasons. The first reason has to do with the stigma of the label (Cummins, 2000; J. S. Damico et al., 2021; Goffman, 1964; McDermott & Varenne, 1995). As much as we try to make it sound as though a special education placement is within acceptable limits, the label still carries a certain stigma that remains with a student, formally and informally, for a long time (J. S. Damico, 2019c; Danzak, 2011). This stigma is especially problematic insofar as many in mainstream society perceive multilingual learners as having lower status; many in the general society do not value the languages and cultures that multilingual learners and their families bring with them. Immigrants and refugees, as well as multilingual learners born in the United States, are often marginalized and do not participate fully in what the larger society has to offer. In recent times, the stigma of a multilingual learner label has intensified for many parents who would prefer a special education label to anything that suggests any connection to individuals or groups that are targets for deportation or travel bans. So the added burden of yet another stigmatizing label is not helpful at all (Harry & Klingner, 2014).

The more compelling reason for not placing multilingual learners erroneously into special education is that we must ensure the most effective learning environment for these students. This is not only an ethical issue; it is also a requirement under IDEA 2004 when RtI is implemented in a school and it is the ultimate goal of MTSS. If a multilingual learner is experiencing significant challenges in school due to the typical process of second language development, the best support for that student would come from expanding proficiency in **English as a second language** and support in the student's home language, and not from special education interventions (e.g., Beeman & Urow, 2013; Cloud et al., 2010; D. E. Freeman & Freeman, 2001; Hodgson et al., 2007; Janzen, 2008; Meisuri et al., 2018; Paradis et al., 2021). Studies have shown that Hispanic students who were classified as learning disabled performed at a lower level after 3 years of special education placement with accompanying high failure and dropout frequencies (Wilkinson & Ortiz, 1986). Thus, these students may not benefit at all from the support they receive in that setting.

Another difficulty with the way special education services are provided to students in general is that it often takes a long time before any support is given to multilingual learners who may require assistance in addition to that which is provided through their bilingual/ESL program in school. Many school districts feel compelled to wait until a full-fledged referral has resulted in a formal categorization into special education before providing specialized support. Thus, the student remains without those specialized interventions for too long. This situation is somewhat alleviated with the implementation of RtI/MTSS, but it is still often the case that the challenges that multilingual learners face are seen as the sole responsibility of the bilingual education or the ESL department even when additional specific support from special education would benefit the student. This state of affairs is significantly influenced by some myths regarding multilingual learners facing academic challenges.

Some Myths Regarding Multilingual Learners and Special Education

Several myths prevail in the area of special education for multilingual learners. These myths can misguide us in the way we approach education in general, in the way we interpret students' behaviors, and in how we teach and assess students. The following are commonly held misconceptions regarding multilingual learners and special education, followed by an explanation that addresses that misconception.

Myth 1: If we label a multilingual learner as having special education needs, at least the student will get some help.

A special education placement when none is warranted does not serve the student well. First, we are bestowing on the student a stigmatizing label that the student does not need. Second, interventions that are specifically geared to help processing, linguistic, or cognitive disabilities often do not help children acquire second language proficiency. In fact, traditional reductionist approaches to special education implemented monolingually can limit the kind of learning that multilingual learners need (Goh et al., 2020; Kay-Raining Bird et al., 2016). Special education interventions tend to target a narrow selection of skills to enable mastery, and discrete skills are often practiced out of context (H. L. Damico et al., 2017; van Kraayenoord, 2010; Westby & Vining, 2002; Xu & Drame, 2008). This complicates the learning process for multilingual learners because they need a meaningful context in order to comprehend the language that surrounds them (Genesee, 2012; Sánchez-López & Young, 2018). In addition, special education interventions often use reading materials with controlled phonics and vocabulary and they focus on surface structures of language, which reduces the meaningfulness of the task and constricts language usage, making it more difficult for multilingual learners to understand and retain information (J. S. Damico et al., 2021).

Myth 2: We have to wait 4 to 7 years for multilingual learners to develop their English language skills before we can rule out language as a cause for the student's difficulty.

Although it takes 4 to 7 years for multilingual learners to show what they know on academic achievement tests in English (H. G. Cook et al., 2011; Cummins, 2012), there is no need to withhold any kind of support services that a multilingual learner might need in the meantime. Use of a timeline suggested by research was meant to give teachers a sense of how long it might take students to be able to learn abstract academic concepts with no special supports using a language that was not yet fully developed (B. A. Collins et al., 2014; Goh et al., 2020). Besides, if a student truly has an intrinsic difficulty, then it exists in all the student's languages and in most use contexts. The sooner these exceptionalities are identified and supported, the better opportunity the student has to be successful in school.

Myth 3: When a multilingual learner is identified as having special education needs, instruction should only be in English, so as not to confuse the student.

Children with speech, language, or learning impairment can become bilingual (e.g., Genesee et al., 2005; Goh et al., 2020; Gonzalez-Barrero & Nadig, 2018; Kay-Raining Bird et al., 2016). There is evidence that children with Down syndrome can be bilingual and that bilingualism does not hinder their language development (Kay-Raining Bird et al., 2005). The majority of people in the world are bilingual, and some of them have special education needs. Disabilities certainly do not arise from being bilingual. They manifest in all or most contexts. The decision to shift to instruction in English exclusively is usually based on lack of knowledge of the research, ignorance of students' home language, or convenience. Besides, developing students' home language can help students with specific language impairment make better progress in the second language (Cardenas-Hagan et al., 2007; B. A. Collins et al., 2014; Gonzalez-Barrero & Nadig, 2017; Gutierrez-Clellen et al., 2012; K. Kohnert & Goldstein, 2005). In addition, for multilingual learners with significant disabilities, it is especially important to maintain the home language because the students' families will continue to be a significant support well after they have left the school system and have entered adult life. It is important that parents and family be able to communicate with and have close ties to their children.

The Continuum of Services Framework

Because of the tremendous difficulties associated with identifying multilingual learners as having special education needs, an altogether different approach to providing services is needed. Three major changes must occur in the school culture for this new approach to be implemented. First, we must dispose of the urge to formally and quickly categorize a student into a special education placement. Instead, we must set up a proactive process that can help prevent difficulties through a culturally and linguistically sustaining RtI/MTSS system. In order to do this, we need to gather information as extensively as possible about the student and his or her surroundings. As more information is gathered, we introduce instruction and learning support strategies that we believe to be most effective for specific observable behaviors into students' everyday routines (J. S. Damico, 2019c, d; Sánchez-López & Young, 2003). As an added advantage of this approach, these strategies, especially if they are implemented from a sociocultural constructivist lens, would be helpful to other students in the classroom, not just the particular multilingual learners in question (J. S. Damico, 2019e; Gergen, 2015; Sánchez-López & Young, 2018). Indeed, this is the end goal of any MTSS: to improve core instruction for the vast majority of students. Second, we must be willing to take a serious look at the instructional program that has been set up for multilingual learners to begin considering possible changes to the learning environment that may be causing challenges for these learners. Third, we must circumvent the compulsion to provide only the interventions allowed by specific funding sources. Instead, meaning-based instruction and learning support strategies, both systemic and specific, must be introduced independently of the category or the specific funding program that eventually supports the students. In fact, this support must be introduced as soon as or before significant challenges are identified (Berquist, 2017).

The **continuum of services framework** shown in Figure 1.1 is supported by the current trend to use an RtI/MTSS approach when assessing the need for and providing special needs support to students who are experiencing significant academic difficulties. In this model, specific support strategies are implemented and the student's response to those strategies is used as a basis for further decision-making.

There are several advantages to using a well-implemented, culturally and linguistically responsive RtI/MTSS approach with multilingual learners (Allington, 2009; Howard, 2009). First, it encourages a proactive process that does not wait for multilingual learners to fail but instead provides enhanced instruction in a timely manner across grade levels. Second, it emphasizes high-quality, consistent, and effective instruction, linked to **authentic assessment**, for multilingual learners throughout the day. Third, it focuses on students in a very explicit way by assisting them with the specific and unique barriers to each student's learning based on the best assessment practices for this population. Finally, it requires collaboration across disciplines and creates new roles for problem-solving team members.

A Collaborative Model

The continuum of services framework and the process entailed when using it cannot be implemented without use of a strong collaborative setup within the school. First, the information gathering about the learning environment and

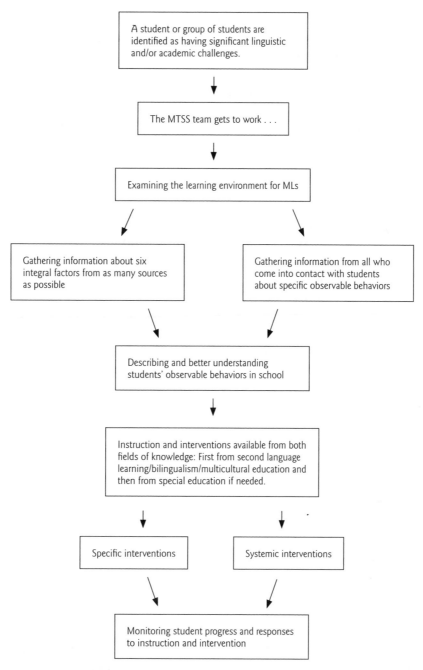

Figure 1.1. The continuum of services framework. (*Key:* ML, multilingual learner.)

about the students in question that is part of this framework, or the screening that is part of the RtI/MTSS process, requires the participation of everyone who comes in contact with the students in question. Everyone who knows the multilingual learner is a valuable source of information. It is not unusual for individual staff members to have quite different perceptions of the same student. The ESL teacher may find a student gregarious and an active participant in classroom work, whereas the physical education teachers may think that the same student is shy and reserved. Yet another teacher may perceive the same student as a troublemaker, and parents may see the student completely differently. It is important for all those individuals to contribute their perceptions and assessment of the student.

Second, because a large body of information is to be gathered from a number of people, a team of four or five individuals needs to be established to process and interpret the information. In many schools, these teams are called *RtI/MTSS teams*, *problem-solving teams*, or *strategy- development teams*. In the earlier editions of this guide we referred to these teams as ensuring a continuum of services (ECOS). Since MTSS has become a widely accepted concept whose nomenclature is common, we now use this better-known term to refer to the team that coordinates the provision of support to multilingual learners who need it. The MTSS team also manages the delivery of learning support strategies and provides assistance to the teachers, administrators, and parents in making the changes necessary in the student's daily school and home lives. In that capacity, the team suggests support strategies and helps the staff and the parents provide the help that the team has determined to be most effective for the students. The team serves as a sounding board, thought partner, and critical friend for the teachers as they try the instructional strategies suggested. It undertakes the same role with respect to the parents. The team supports administrators in their effort to make the more general systemic changes in the program or at the district level. The team also helps teachers and administrators monitor student progress and evaluate the effectiveness of the instructional strategies. Without this collaborative structure, the continuum of services framework will not be effective.

Look Critically at the Learning Environment

The first task facing the MTSS team is to take a critical look at the learning environment that has been created for multilingual learners. This is no easy task because it requires an honest questioning of the status quo and of decisions that staff or administrators made regarding the instructional program for multilingual learners. Beginning with the learning environment is essential, however, because it brings to the forefront the single most important context within which general instruction and **specific interventions** are given.

An RtI/MTSS system assumes equitable access to the core curriculum and is based on the supposition that the school provides an adequate learning environment for all students. This erroneous assumption may not accurately describe many multilingual learners' school experience, however. An effective learning environment for multilingual learners is created through use of an enriching rather than a compensatory or remedial approach. Unfortunately, many schools still see their role vis-à-vis multilingual learners from a deficit perspective, as though they are offsetting the negative effects of these students' lack of English proficiency, rather than seeing them as enriching everyone's experiences by bringing diversity to the school and by seeing the potential that these students have to become fluent in two or more languages. Critical issues to consider here are the teachers, the available resources, the type of program implemented, and the range of services offered in the school, with special attention paid to the role that students' home languages and cultures play in the learning environment. School teams learn how to identify strengths and available resources in the learning environment, and to determine areas that need improvement in the learning environment. Teachers also learn how to integrate systemic and specific learning support strategies that could benefit students into the learning environment.

Gather Information

The continuum of services framework is characterized by constant information gathering, not just about the learning environment created for multilingual learners, but about these students themselves. Rather than attempting to determine immediately whether the academic challenges that multilingual learners experience are specifically because of a long-term disability (i.e., something that would lead to a special education designation), a normal part of the second language learning process, or due to the way instruction is provided, educators must acquire extensive information about each student. This information includes: student characteristics and background, specific challenges that students exhibit in the classroom, and how they are responding to any special support strategies being used. School-based teams are encouraged to ask each other:

- What do we know about particular multilingual learner students?

- What specific observable behaviors have students exhibited in different learning environments?

- What instructional supports and interventions have been provided for these students?

- Were these supports based on multilingual learner research and evidence-based pedagogy?

Answering these questions entails gathering information about the characteristics that define those students, any specific academic challenges that students are facing while in school, and the effect that learning supports and instructional strategies have on these students' performance.

We have identified six integral factors in the student's home and school life that provide us with general information about our multilingual learners, including:

1. Personal and family factors

2. Physical and psychological factors

3. Previous schooling/performance

4. Oral language and literacy development in both home language and English

5. Academic performance and instruction in both, or all of the students' languages

6. Cross-cultural factors

This information serves two purposes. First, it provides an important context within which general instruction and specific learning support strategies are used. Having a better understanding of multilingual learners' background and their cultural and linguistic strengths and resources gives teachers some sense of how these integral factors influence learning and achievement in general. Thus, the information would be valuable for any teacher who came into contact with multilingual learners. Second, this information may also lead to more general systemic support strategies that could create more linguistically and culturally relevant and enriched learning environments for the wide diversity of learners in a school.

If we understand what these factors are and how they influence learning, the information may inform data collection and evaluation. By gathering information about these integral factors and changing the extrinsic environment, schools can anticipate and prevent a great many challenges that multilingual learners encounter. In this way, schools can be proactive about multilingual learner issues. For example, if school administrators know the school is about to receive a group of refugee students from a particular region of the world, it would help the process if they researched the refugee experience and prepared their social workers and other school staff to identify the rich experiences that these students are likely to be bringing with them to school and to anticipate possible difficulties that these students may experience at school. By planning ahead, teams can prepare a core instructional learning environment that will support these learners and help them to feel welcome and to be successful. At the same time, the school or school district can support the educators and all staff through professional learning opportunities geared toward this group of students.

It makes sense to concentrate on the factors that are focused on linguistic and cultural diversity because many second language learners experience difficulties in school when they receive instruction through a language in which they are not fully proficient. On the other hand, only a small proportion (in the United States, around 10%) of students have a long-term disability or disorder that could be diagnosed as exceptionality. Because bilingualism, or the development of proficiency in two or more languages, does not itself lead to the creation of a disability, it is much more likely that many challenges encountered by second language learners can be remedied by changing extrinsic factors. Thus, we need to eliminate the barriers that impact a multilingual learner's performance before we conclude that the student may have an intrinsic special education need.

Describe before Diagnosing

As we begin to understand the characteristics that define multilingual learners by gathering information on the six integral factors, we also need to build a clear understanding of their performance at school by observing particular aspects of learning that seem to be difficult for these students. The information about the challenges that students encounter must be as specific as possible—for example, difficulty remembering multiplication facts in English, or difficulty following oral directions in English. It is important to focus observations as much as possible on specific academic behaviors or aspects of learning that students are having difficulty with rather than to claim a more ambiguous "learning problem," as is often the case.

As specific observable academic and linguistic behaviors are identified for a student or a group of students, the MTSS team, which includes experts in both ESL/bilingualism and special education, reflects on possible explanations for those behaviors. The MTSS team then lists possible second language development explanations and possible special education explanations for each behavior that has been observed. As soon as that is done, the ESL/bilingualism and special education specialists identify the specific instructional strategies they believe will best benefit that student, or group of students, for that particular behavior. Thus, some of these strategies come from the field of ESL/bilingualism and serve the purpose of strengthening students' second language proficiency and bilingual development as well as making the academic content more accessible for multilingual learners. If needed, some interventions and support can come from the field of special education and serve the purpose of helping students with processing strategies and retention.

Up to this point in the continuum of services framework the approach falls within the realm of Tier 1 strategies. As suggestions for support emanating from needs identified in the information-gathering phases are implemented, and as their effectiveness is evaluated, students' difficulties can be investigated more specifically and more thoroughly. We also describe the first step to be taken when a teacher or another staff member continues to express concern about a student or a group of students: Identify specific observable linguistic and academic behaviors that multilingual learners exhibit. Specific areas of classroom behavior, performance, or tasks that the student has difficulty with or is likely to have difficulty with must be listed, and we include a limited list of possible observable behaviors exhibited by students with special needs. Further, we show that each of these behaviors can be attributed to either a typical second language learning process or a disability.

Thus, it is essential to describe in as much detail as possible what it is that the student is having difficulty with before rushing to identify a special education need. We also point out the importance of addressing extrinsic environmental explanations for multilingual learners' challenges first, before intrinsic explanations are considered. The information that was collected (and probably still continues to be collected) about the students' background through an examination of the six integral factors will be indispensable in interpreting the challenges that students are facing.

This information about specific observable behaviors needs to be gathered by all who come into contact with the student, and it must be gathered through a variety of formal and informal means. It is only through a collaborative approach that school staff can come close to having enough of the right kind of information to make an informed decision about the kinds of instruction and interventions that will more effectively support the student at school.

Provide Support: A Continuum of Services

Once specific behaviors that the multilingual learner has been having difficulty with have been identified and possible reasons for those behaviors have been considered, the MTSS team begins to identify possible support and interventions for each behavior based on the team's expertise; first, from the field of second language acquisition, bilingualism, and multicultural education and then from the field of special education, if needed (Sánchez-López & Young, 2003). These are the strategies that teachers believe would be most effective to cope with and address the specific observable behaviors identified. These instructional strategies are introduced as soon as they are identified for a student. We refer to these as *specific support strategies*.

As information continues to be gathered, both about the specific behaviors exhibited by a multilingual learner at school and about the integral factors that describe the multilingual learner, the support strategies that would be most appropriate to respond to any of the more general integral factors are also determined by the team. We refer to these as *systemic support strategies*. As we begin to learn more about the students, their cultural backgrounds and experiences, personal history, home life, and language and academic development, we can begin to build on the resources that the student brings to the learning process. For example, if we discover that the parents of a Spanish-speaking multilingual learner do not have reading materials in Spanish at home, we would want to ensure that the school library has a collection of high-quality books in Spanish (systemic support strategy), and begin to send home books in Spanish for parents to read with their children (specific support strategy).

Gathering information regarding these six integral factors can provide a meaningful context within which to understand students' performance in school. For example, the school social worker may find that some multilingual learners in the fourth and fifth grades have had a total of 1 year of formal schooling because of war conditions in their home country, and that fact cannot be changed. What can be changed, however, is that the school seeks to enrich the learning environment for students with limited formal schooling (a systemic support strategy). As soon as they enter school, these students could participate in a program in which they would learn about school in the United States and would acquire some of the foundation they missed by not attending school the expected number of years, while receiving cultur-ally and linguistically appropriate counseling and support for trauma they may have experienced in their home country. The support strategies, both systemic and specific, that seem to be most effective can become part of the student's daily routine.

For schools in which RtI/MTSS is in place, these specific and systemic support strategies can be applied throughout the various tiers that have been created for students with academic difficulties. Some schools may have a three-tier system, whereas others may have as many as five. Depending on the number of tiers that are in place, the intensity, length of time, and level of support of the strategies can be varied to fit students' needs.

As the factors in the student's life become clearer to teachers and special-ists, the specific instructional strategies can begin to take into account the possible conditions that may be leading to the specific behaviors exhibited by the student. For example, if a student has been observed to consistently forget words that have been taught from one day to the next, and, from the extensive information gathering that is taking place, the teacher realizes that visual materials used during instruction or as a special support strategy may not be familiar to the student, a possible instructional strategy might be to prepare students prior to the beginning of a lesson or unit by giving them key vocabulary in both languages and brief explanations in the students' home language using more culturally relevant visual supports. These explanations could be provided by peers, the parents, or the teacher. On the other hand, if, from talking to the parents, the school's parent liaison discovers that they have observed their child experiencing memory problems and having diffi-culty recalling words in the home language, the teacher might begin to help the student use cueing strategies (e.g., teaching the child to use surround-ing text, descriptions of the word and its meaning). This intervention could be provided under the guidance of a speech pathologist in consult with the teacher as to the best way to use these strategies, preferably in the home lan-guage as well as in English.

The more general systemic support and interventions would be intro-duced as soon as information emerged about an integral factor in the stu-dent's life. That same information may also lead to refining the instructional strategy in such a way that it begins to make more sense within the larger context of that student's surroundings. Thus, the two sets of interventions, one set based on specific observations of the student's behavior in the class-room and the other on information gathered about the six integral factors, would occur simultaneously and quickly.

The key to providing this support is to begin it immediately, as soon as observable difficulties are identified. In this way the services provided to these students would flow smoothly and continuously, as shown in Figure 1.1. Because this solution-seeking approach to providing a continuum of services is not without its challenges, we suggest ways to create struc-tures within the school that facilitate problem-solving and collaboration. The continuum of services framework creates an enriched environment for multilingual learners and, more broadly, is of benefit to all learners. However, it entails a major change in the way we have generally approached special education and the education of multilingual learners in schools. Advocating change in the system so that it helps all students become more successful in school is a responsibility for all of us. We hope that this handbook helps you attain that goal.

Questions for Reflection and Action

1. How does the framework presented in this chapter compare to the process that you follow in your school or school district?
2. What changes would you need to make in order to come closer to what this framework suggests?
3. What possible challenges might you face when you attempt to make these changes?
4. How can these challenges be surmounted?

A Collaborative Model of Information Gathering and Service Provision[1]

Key Concepts. *To provide a continuum of services, a team consisting of staff with expertise in different areas must collaborate to gather information about the challenges that students are encountering; student strengths, interests, and resources as well as characteristics of students' home and school life. The team then suggests learning support strategies and monitors students' progress.*

The process of developing a continuum of services to meet student needs relies on solution-seeking, strategy-development, or problem-solving teams that share their expertise and work within a strong collaborative structure in the school. In both special education and bilingual or second language education settings, when these structures have been employed, the results have suggested positive and effective innovations (e.g., Abedi et al., 2004; Allington & Walmsley, 2007; Bartolo et al., 2001; D. S. Damico & Nye, 1990; Giangreco, 2000; Miramontes et al., 2011; Orelove & Sobsey, 1996). The primary responsibility of the team is to coordinate information gathering and to help teachers and other practitioners implement learning support strategies. The team is ultimately responsible for ensuring that a continuum of services that fit identified needs as closely as possible is provided to individual students and to similar groups of students within a school.

In schools where **response to intervention (RtI)** and the broader multi-tiered system of supports (MTSS) are implemented, problem-solving teams function in a similar manner; however, they may not delve into linguistic and cultural diversity issues, and often the strategies and interventions that they choose are not the most appropriate ones for multilingual learners (Allington, 2009; Artiles, 2015; van Kraayenoord, 2010). In our version of the team approach, and in earlier editions of this guide, we called these collaborative groups *ensuring a continuum of services (ECOS)* teams. Because many schools have adopted the MTSS concept, which lends itself to supporting multilingual learners much more effectively than past systems created in special education, we have chosen the more common nomenclature, MTSS, to refer to these teams even though our approach is distinct from the

---

[1]Theresa Young, a speech-language pathologist based in Ontario, Canada, collaborated with us on writing Chapters 2, 10, and 11 of this guide.

traditional RtI/MTSS model. The team structure may exist in a school under different names, such as **teacher assistance team (TAT)** or student services team, and the team may have a different setup and set of objectives. When addressing the issue of support for multilingual learners, a new team may be formed or an existing team may be modified to fit the parameters of the continuum of services framework presented in this guide.

Getting a Head Start

One of the real advantages of our approach is that the MTSS team can be proactive by focusing on issues that are critical for multilingual learners. To get a head start, begin by considering the learning environment that has been set up, or is in the process of being established for multilingual learners. In many schools that follow a traditional RtI/MTSS system, the focus is on the students, with little or no heed paid to whether the learning environment that has been created for multilingual learners gives them the optimal opportunity to learn (Bower et al., 2015). In addition, traditional RtI/MTSS systems wait for the screening and identification of struggling students by means that are often inappropriate for multilingual learners. In our approach, MTSS teams have at their disposal a variety of options for getting a head start in addressing student needs (Cloud et al., 2010; Cunningham & Allington, 2011; Miramontes et al., 2011; Stevenson, 1995; Woodward, 1994). For example, team members could attend and facilitate spring articulation meetings for the different grade levels in their school. It is essential that these articulation meetings have a clear focus on linguistic and academic information that does not get derailed by more mundane anecdotes. A focus on academic issues can be attained through use of transparent protocols that can be followed at these meetings. After an entire year of instruction, the information presented by teachers can help the MTSS team and the teachers of the next grade anticipate difficulties that may arise and help identify student strengths and resources. It could also help in curricular planning before the start of the new school year. The team can start planning interventions and procedures to be implemented during the summer and the following school year, and can suggest professional learning activities that would help staff meet the incoming students' needs. This strategy is extremely effective for systemic learning support strategies that involve more than one teacher's instruction and plans for one classroom (Dunaway, 2021; Lucas et al., 1990). For example, if a middle school administrator knows that her school will be receiving a group of refugee students from the elementary school, it would be beneficial to find out as much as possible about this group of students, their culture, how individual students responded to their first year in the U.S. school system, and other information related to the six integral factors previously described in this guide. Why wait for difficulties to arise when they can be anticipated, especially because these **systemic interventions** will only improve the school environment, help facilitate a smooth transition for students, build cohesive learning experiences, and expand the staff's expertise?

In another situation, school administrators might review the most recent demographics on English language proficiency, home language, and academic achievement data across grade levels in their schools. They can approach the MTSS team to discuss any changes in these demographics and try to figure out ways to anticipate some of the needs of a wide range of language and socioeconomic groups. The MTSS team may recommend that a particular emphasis be placed on hiring teachers and other staff members who share the language and cultural backgrounds of the incoming students (Coelho, 1994; Echevarria et al., 2017). They might also ask library or media center personnel to order books in the languages of the students (Cunningham & Allington, 2011; Krashen, 2004). This is especially important because any young readers require interesting books they can read in all of their languages—accurately, fluently, and with strong comprehension—if they are to exhibit maximum educational growth (Allington, 2009). The team might contact a nearby university and organize university teacher education candidates to help support multilingual learners during the school day, and who receive clinical credit toward their credentials for the time they spend in the schools. This type of "university in-reach" may also help build various types of collaborative programs across academe and within the schools themselves (van Kraayenoord et al., 2011; Welch et al., 1996; Wiener & Davidson, 1990).

Another approach that the MTSS team can take is to gather information from teachers once school has been in session for a month or 2. The earlier in the school year that the MTSS team meets with groups of teachers to discuss the information they have gathered about their students through interviews, surveys, observation checklists, and student work samples, the sooner the team can generate learning support strategies, both systemic and specific, that will be effective for those anticipated difficulties (D. H. Graves, 2002; Howard, 2009; Pacheco, 2010). During these meetings, MTSS team members and teachers can view students' portfolios and see examples of progress or lack of progress from the beginning of the school year (Afflerbach, 2007; Gottlieb, 2012, 2021; Shea et al., 2005). Teachers might also share their concerns about particularly disruptive classroom behavior, and the team could help these teachers establish culturally responsive classroom procedures to engage diverse learners and to run things more smoothly (Xu & Drame, 2008). If these procedures proved successful, the teachers might, in turn, share the strategies and procedures with the rest of their colleagues in a school staff meeting. In this case, the specific strategy may become a general intervention that is implemented throughout the school, and the students will benefit by experiencing consistency throughout their day and across grade levels. The end result of such proactivity is that the teachers will be glad that a team exists in the school to listen to their concerns about how to best address multilingual learners' needs before these concerns become crises.

Another benefit of this "head-start" approach is that it allows staff to plan for ways in which multilingual learners' linguistic and cultural diversity can be used to make school life richer and more interesting for all students. For example, a school that is receiving many children from Western African countries could incorporate the strong oral story-telling tradition of many communities from that region into their study of literature. They can identify adults from the community who are storytellers and invite them to share their expertise (Bower et al., 2015; Poveda, 2003; Reyes & Azuara, 2008).

This approach is in contrast to the more traditional models that exist in many schools. The traditional models often pit one set of professionals against another and one professional's judgment against another's. This contentious environment puts professionals on the defensive and leads them to rely heavily on the results of standardized tests, which are often invalid, rather than on their own professional judgment (J. S. Damico & Nelson, 2012; Kohn, 2000; McNeil, 2000; Pacheco, 2010; Sacks, 1999). It may also put teachers on the defensive for needing or wanting assistance for their students. On the one hand, teachers feel they have to prove they have done everything possible before asking the team for help. On the other hand, the team is under great pressure to reduce the number of students served in special education and to prove definitively that the difficulties are due to intrinsic factors and not to other possible causes (Chalfant & Pysh, 1989; Gonzales-Barrero & Nadig, 2017; Gutkin, 1990).

It is very difficult to identify definitively the so-called soft diagnostic categories of special education (J. S. Damico et al., 2021), such as a learning disability or language impairment in an multilingual learner (or anyone), and to sort out which difficulties are typical manifestations of learning a second language and which are related to disabilities. These soft categories tend to stand for vague concepts that are operationalized through test scores and are more likely influenced and associated with socioeconomic indicators and cultural biases than with proficiency. In fact, there is a great deal of research suggesting that these loosely substantiated labels have far more negative consequences than positive ones (J. S. Damico, 2019c; J. S. Damico et al., 2021). In more traditional models, the system of assessment and assignment of diagnostic labels has become so cumbersome that only the most persistent teachers get instructional support in the classroom and support for their students and their families (Five, 1995; Gibbs & Elliot, 2015). Many teachers remain silent out of concern that their inability to deal with a particular student's or group of students' challenges reflects poorly on their skills as a teacher. If in addition to that pressure the system makes teachers feel even more vulnerable by questioning their motives and abilities, they are more likely to remain silent about students' difficulties in the future. We have seen many schools in which staff even avoids referring multilingual learners with significant disabilities that are clearly apparent.

If given the power to do so, the MTSS team has the ability to pull resources, ideas, and creative solutions together to support students and teachers in a timely manner. The MTSS team can also be a place where teachers come to propose ideas they have about innovative and creative programming that could be implemented in their school to address the constantly changing needs of their students. This is more likely to happen when teachers see the MTSS team as advocates for effective multilingual learner education. Once MTSS teams have gathered information about the needs of multilingual learners in their schools, they can begin the process of generating learning support strategies for those specific needs as defined by the six integral factors. This process is in some ways analogous to aspects of the RtI/MTSS approach that has become increasingly popular or, in the case of some states, mandatory. The primary difference, however, is that the MTSS process suggested in this book is typically descriptive and individualized, whereas most RtI/MTSS systems rely on a standard treatment protocol model and assessment techniques that are easy to administer but often lack critical psychometric characteristics like construct validity (Allington & Nowak, 2004; J. E. Brown & Dolittle, 2008; Kapantzoglou et al., 2012; Speece & Walker, 2007; van Kraayenoord, 2010).

Challenges to This Continuum of Services Framework

Changing perspectives and practices present challenges for professionals in all contexts, but when the changes involve the public domain (that is, public education), there may appear to be even more barriers to implementation (e.g., Menken, 2008; van Kraayenoord & Chapman, 2016). In this section we discuss several of the more salient challenges to the effective implementation of the continuum of services framework. For some of the perceived challenges, the barriers are surprisingly minimal. For others they may be deceptively complex. We discuss these potential barriers in three primary groups: barriers created by a shift in practices, barriers created by regulatory and fiscal constraints, and barriers due to inertial expectations and tendencies.

Shifting Practices

The first set of perceived barriers emerges with the need to alter one's practices to accommodate a more effective framework. Changing practices, whether it involves procedural modifications, test selection, interpretative notions, or intervention approaches, is never easy. We all have a tendency to employ practices that we are comfortable with and that appear to have met our professional needs in the past. These familiar routines and practices give us confidence and enable us to operate with less cognitive effort when we are implementing them. Once it has been shown that these practices are ineffective and not the best approaches to service delivery, however, we must strive to adapt so that we maintain our professional integrity (Arrow et al., 2015). Showing the ineffectiveness of these practices may be challenging but essential to motivate the shift in practice. MTSS team members may need to demonstrate district- or school-level data that have previously not been reviewed. Data may need to be disaggregated based on **intersectionality** by looking at subgroups of multilingual learners. This means learning new frameworks, methods, strategies, and knowledge bases if necessary (Artiles, 2019; Crenshaw, 1989). For illustrative purposes, we mention several important changes that we may be expected to make in implementing the continuum of services framework.

When school problem-solving groups, such as MTSS teams, shift their focus toward anticipating and preventing difficulties rather than taking a "wait-and-fail" attitude with the student before assessment and placement, many things must change. Most obvious, teams will have to resist the impulse to label before programming. The team—and the individuals who make up the team—must not indulge the initial temptation to try to localize the problems within the child. Rather, the immediate orientation should be to assume the child's intrinsic competence. This individual should be considered initially as a typically developing learner who is influenced by external variables that interfere with learning (H. L. Damico et al., 2017; Martin, 2009). If this shift in practice occurs, energy spent on finding definitive diagnoses can be redirected toward finding research-informed ways to intervene while identifying the explanations for the challenges that multilingual learners experience and monitoring the effectiveness of these interventions through the students' responses to them. With this shift in both perspective and practice, the localization of difficulties within the student should occur only after multiple attempts to identify the external operational variables are unsuccessful and only after reasonable and appropriate interventions to overcome external variables have failed (Maxwell et al., 2020).

Second, collaboration should increase in schools as professionals realize that no one professional perspective can address all multilingual learners' needs. These collaborative relationships require professionals to step outside their traditional roles and share their perspectives, knowledge, and experiences with their colleagues through creative programming. In fact, this is a primary focus of the MTSS teams, a primary reason for this book, and why many implementation exercises have been provided in these pages. This process, however, may not be easy to accomplish. When changing to more collaborative practices, the professional pairings that may emerge as a result of collaborative interventions may be foreign to the school setting and to the work habits of the involved individuals. Initially, a new collaboration may feel threatening to the individuals involved, and the arrangement may seem cumbersome. However, with some experience working together and with the successes obtained through collaborative efforts, any initial awkwardness can be overcome.

One reason that an honest attempt at collaboration works is because of the complexity of service delivery to multilingual learners. Any professional who has worked with this population knows that many variables and complicating factors must be addressed, and it is rarely possible to face these issues alone. As a consequence, while team building, the school personnel face challenges, but they also observe that many of these challenges and the complexities wrapped in multilingual learner service delivery are addressed more effectively and efficiently as the collaborations within the MTSS team improve. Success is typically the watchword as team members acquire new information for their professional knowledge bases in areas that may be completely outside their previous experience. Honing collaborative practices, understanding the skills and expertise of other professionals, and building trust occur over time with ongoing teamwork (Archibald & Vollebregt, 2019; Bahr et al., 1999; Chalfant & Pysh, 1989; Dove & Honigsfeld, 2018).

A third example of changing practices involves a direct collaboration of a different kind: collaboration with the appropriate administrative personnel. When modifying practice to improve service delivery, it is not sufficient that only the team members change. They must secure the assent of the classroom teachers and the parents of the students they serve if the changes are to be successful (Blosser, 1990; Bower et al., 2015; J. S. Damico, 1987; Gutkin, 1990; Marvin, 1990; Montgomery, 1990). To gain that kind of support, it is often necessary to secure administrative support. Administrative support is necessary to initiate and sustain the level of systemic change required to shift to a more proactive framework. Inadequate funding for personnel and resources to support MTSS team involvement in the classroom strains the system and sets the team up for failure if these needs are not addressed. These issues are not within the bailiwick of most team members, however. Rather, they are the purview of administrators, and therefore collaboration with principals, directors, and coordinators is needed to address these issues. Chronicle 2.1 describes a remarkable program that takes a proactive stance and involves the collaboration of professionals with different areas of expertise.

Chronicle 2.1

A Proactive Program Enhanced through Cross-Disciplinary Collaboration

By a Speech–Language Pathologist

The Toronto District School Board in Toronto, Ontario, Canada, provides a remarkable example of interdisciplinary collaboration through its Kindergarten Early Language Intervention (KELI) program. The goal of this innovative program is to provide early oral language intervention for young students from schools in low socioeconomic areas as a way of preventing or alleviating later challenges with academic, literacy, and social skills. Kindergarten teachers from general education classes nominate students who appear to be learning language differently than other students. It is important to note that the Toronto District School Board is one of the most multicultural and diverse education systems in the world. Based on the experience that these general education teachers have in working with many students from different language backgrounds, the teachers nominate students who appear to be learning language differently than other multilingual learners do as they progress through their kindergarten year.

The speech–language pathologist and KELI teacher combine information from classroom observations, language and academic screening activities, and nomination checklists from general education teachers to come up with specific criteria for selecting students for the KELI program. The selected students attend a special program that is designed to provide supplementary instruction rather than supplant the time these children spend during regular school hours. In this program, students attend school for 2 half-days in addition to the 5 half-days of their regular kindergarten program at their neighborhood schools.

In the KELI classes, a speech–language pathologist and kindergarten teacher, with special education qualifications, co-instruct classes of eight students to provide them with rich learning opportunities to use oral language, literacy, and social interaction skills. The speech–language pathologist provides interventions that are completely contextualized so that children are never given language tasks that are not meaningful and relevant. So that these students can build meaningful connections, each unit of instruction is designed around a theme, using five to seven related stories. The activities in the unit, for example, story retelling, dramatic play, and snack preparation, all relate to the vocabulary, events, and messages communicated in the stories. In this model, the expertise of the speech–language pathologist and of the kindergarten teacher is combined in ways that support students in developing their expressive and receptive language and early literacy skills.

The teacher and speech–language pathologist are presented with incredible learning opportunities on a daily basis as they blend their roles and share responsibilities through planning and co-instructing all aspects of the lessons together. Administering

(continued)

Chronicle 2.1

continued

By a Speech–Language Pathologist

assessments collaboratively and reporting results to parents and administrators offer further opportunities for these professionals to learn from one another.

Questions for Discussion

1. What would it take for your district to set up a program similar to KELI that offers intervention proactively, offers instruction to a group of students beyond the school day, and entails interdisciplinary collaboration?

2. Describe some of the potential benefits of this professional collaboration for these students.

3. What professional strengths and resources do each of these professionals bring to the classroom?

The approach described in this guide encourages all educators in a school to develop and modify their practices accordingly, to build professional bridges with others outside their field, to consult their colleagues regularly, and to work collegially to address the needs of their students. There are always students who need the very specific services of a particular professional in a particular program, but we believe that the learning environment for all students is enriched when the professionals in the school collaborate and are encouraged to consult one another outside of a formal protocol. The recognition that changing practices present opportunities rather than barriers should help overcome potential challenges.

Regulatory and Fiscal Constraints

When the continuum of services framework is discussed on school sites, especially when special education is involved, some of the challenges most frequently mentioned are the regulatory and fiscal constraints placed on school personnel. Professionals are often concerned that the various innovations suggested are inconsistent with federal regulations or guidelines and that the fiscal constraints are insurmountable (Bhat et al., 2000; Menken, 2008; Stevens, 2019). In the case of the suggestions for the MTSS team and the continuum of services framework, this is more a perception than a reality.

In remedial public education in the United States, the major regulatory instrument is the Individuals with Disabilities Education Act (IDEA). First formulated in 1975 as PL 94-142 and reauthorized several times since then, IDEA is the congressional Act that results in the Regulations Governing the Assistance to States for Education of Children with Disabilities Program and the Preschool Grants for Children with Disabilities (2006). In the most recent reauthorization of IDEA, the 2004 Individuals with Disabilities Education Improvement Act (IDEA), PL 108-466, some rather significant changes were introduced that support the need for and implementation of processes like those used by the MTSS team.

Because of continued disenchantment with the traditional approach to special education, the 2004 reauthorization of IDEA discussed several obstacles to implementing effective special education services. Among the obstacles cited were that implementation of the Act had been impeded by (1) low expectations for the students, (2) an insufficient focus on applying replicable research involving proven methods of teaching and learning for students with disabilities, (3) a disproportionately high number of referrals and placements of "minority children" in special education, and (4) the application of discrepancy models that used inappropriate tests, which often led to disproportionate placements. To address these and other concerns, the 2004 Act requires a number of innovations that provide the opportunity for local educational agencies and individual schools to implement programs like the continuum of-services approach. For example, the reauthorization requires states to submit a plan that provides assurances of policies and procedures designed to prevent the inappropriate overidentification or disproportionate representation by race and ethnicity of children as children with disabilities. In effect, this provides an opening for innovative programs like MTSS and our continuum of services framework to be suggested as ways to meet the federal plan requirements.

In addition and of significance, the document provides for more specific incorporation of "**early intervention services**" rather than the use of discrepancy models to place students in special education programs. The phrase *early intervention services* refers to exactly what our framework is designed to do: Address the needs of students and determine the need and eligibility for special education services on the basis of prereferral interventions rather than assessments. In reality, this was also the intent of the last reauthorization of IDEA, in 1997. However, the term used in that document was *prereferral intervention*, and it was merely recommended. In the 2004 version, the focus shifts from evaluation to intervention as the primary determinant of placement. Although the 2004 Act does not directly mention RtI or any other specific approach, the phrase *early intervention services* points toward such approaches. In fact, the document also authorizes the appropriation of federal special education funds to implement an early intervention process to try to bolster academic achievement before referral to special education; the monies that may be used for such an approach may be as much as 15% of the IDEA funding in some states.

The new reauthorization of IDEA and the regulations that implement it (2006) have also required other changes that provide an opportunity for innovations such as MTSS teams. For example, with regard to the category of learning disabilities, the regulations state that a local education agency may use a process that determines whether the child responds to scientifically based intervention and that state education agencies may not require the use of discrepancy models. Rather, local education agencies may use alternative research-based procedures to determine a classification of "learning disabled." Finally, the new documents (as with the 1997 reauthorization) do not require test scores to make placement decisions into special education. In fact, in the 2004 version, references to tests have been changed to "assessment material," thus downplaying the more traditional testing paradigm.

It should be pointed out that these regulatory changes reduce other concerns as well. For example, concern has often been expressed about collecting information on children with suspected difficulties. In many local education agencies, certain kinds of data cannot be collected for special education considerations unless parents sign a consent form. Although there has always been disagreement as to whether this was necessary or not, a focus on early intervention services before placement is made reduces this concern. Procedurally, then, the MTSS team does not need consent to do a formal observation or classroom-based assessment of a student under the law's new reauthorization.

The fiscal constraints suggested as reasons to refrain from implementing innovations, such as the continuum of services framework, are also more perceived challenges rather than real ones. These perceptions typically result from an inaccurate understanding of special education funding issues. For example, there is a misconception on the part of many professionals that the bulk of financing for special education comes from the federal government and that regulations governing those monies are highly restrictive. This is not the case (Menken, 2008; Vaughn et al., 2003; Zirkel, 2006). Current IDEA monies may be used for early intervention innovations (up to 15% of total IDEA Part B funds in some states). Especially in kindergarten to third grade, such expenditures are encouraged. In fact, the federal regulations require several states to use monies for early intervention services. Second, although Congress was authorized by PL 94-142 to provide as much as 40% of the average per-child expenditure for special education in public schools by 1982, this has never occurred. According to the Understanding Special Education (2012) website, the federal government provides less than 15% of the funding to states for special education, and the state and local governments provide more than 85% of the average per-child expenditure for special education in public schools. Finally, because state and local governments provide most of the funding, and because the current reauthorization of IDEA encourages innovations such as RtI and MTSS, there is an opportunity to influence state and local regulations and practices. Insofar as the average per-pupil cost of special education is estimated to be twice as great as that of regular education (Chaikind et al., 1993) and these costs are escalating, local agencies should be willing to support any innovations that provide better services at a more affordable price (Allington, 2009).

The Challenge of Inertial Concepts

The last barrier to implementation of the continuum of services framework may be the most problematic. That is the tendency toward inertia in professional matters. In physics, inertia is the tendency of a body to remain at rest or to stay in motion unless acted on by an outside force. We can employ that concept metaphorically to describe the professional tendency to resist action or change. Some refer to this inertia as the *seduction of the status quo* (De Brigard, 2010).

Although it is sometimes the case that defensible innovation is recognized and implemented, too often when innovations are suggested there is a reaction against them that may be traced to sheer inertia. That is, the resistance is determined less by the difficulties that might accompany such an innovation and more by reluctance to change. Inertia may manifest in one of two forms. The first is direct opposition to the innovation by teachers and other professionals involved in its implementation. These confrontations often take the form of objections to innovation for a variety of reasons. Often cited in this context are regulatory and fiscal constraints; refutations of the theoretical, empirical, or clinical basis for the proposed changes; or the dramatization of barriers to implementation. These arguments are advanced in such a way as to stop the innovation. However, these often are not legitimate barriers but tactics employed because of the inertial tendencies of professionals.

Another example is the frequently cited claim that the federal government allows only "scientifically based" assessment and intervention practices when discussing regulatory or funded activities or initiatives. The claimants then quickly assert or assume that this means practices based on experimental research. This is not the case. Scientific research is not limited to the experimental paradigm. Rather, scientific research includes any practices reported and documented in research articles published in peer-reviewed professional journals, and this includes all forms of naturalistic and observational research as well (Cronbach, 1957; J. S. Damico & Ball, 2010; Lum, 2002; Penn, 2014; Wright, 2005). Indeed, much of what we know about human development and learning is the result of research that is not experimental in nature (Simmons-Mackie & Damico, 2003). To presume that the demonstrations of efficacy and effectiveness must hinge on experimental research that often does not enable the appropriate investigation of real learning and meaning-making is not defensible (Agar, 2013; Bruner, 1983; Cronbach, 1975; Guendouzi, 2014; Pearson & Samuels, 1980; Strauss, 2001). Challenges to innovation based on this claim are most likely an overt reflection of the inertial tendency.

The second form the inertial reaction may take is more subtle and therefore more problematic. It involves a superficial adherence to the innovation while the agent continues to employ traditional or noninnovative components, activities, or practices that may actually subvert the innovation. A single illustration should suffice. Over the past few years, there have been many attempts to apply RtI approaches using the three tiers of intervention that quickly disintegrated into discrete, fragmented, and decontextualized interventions or tests rather than contextualized, authentic, meaning-based interventions and assessment as documentation. For example, the professional may employ decontextualized phonemic awareness drills or activities as the well-designed and well-implemented intervention in order to determine the learning responses of the students. The problem is that in the case of multilingual learners (and many other learners), such decontextualized activities are not effective teaching or intervention strategies (H. L. Damico et al., 2017; Freeman & Freeman, 2001, 2002; Krashen, 2001; National Academies of Sciences, Engineering, & Medicine, 2018; Wells, 2003). A poor RtI, then, is likely to be an indictment of the method and not the child. Further, the measures employed to assess change might also be less innovative. Documenting change by using tools that are artificial and measure only discrete skills, such as the NWEA MAP or FastBridge (Kaminski & Good, 1998), further subverts the excellent goals of the RtI/MTSS approach because these tools are not innovative and do not provide the useful information that can be gathered from authentic measures of literacy skills (e.g., H. L. Damico et al., 2021; Goodman, 2006; Manning et al., 2005). Consequently, while the framework and the emphasis on placing intervention before evaluation are positive, using the same tired, ineffectual teaching strategies and assessment procedures will significantly dilute the effectiveness of RtI/MTSS. In effect, because of the tendency toward inertia, we merely see old wine in new bottles, and the needs of the children are not met (Allington, 2009; Damico et al., 2021; Howard, 2009; van Kraayenoord, 2010; van Kraayenoord & Chapman, 2016). This seems to happen when educational innovations are packaged and popularized, especially with an acronym or a label that becomes trendy (Brantlinger, 1997; P. Brown, 1995; Damico et al., 2021).

It should be stated, of course, that the tendency toward inertia is often unconscious and the individuals who exhibit these reactions may not recognize this tendency. Tom Skrtic (1991) and others (Fullan, 2019; Fullan & Quinn, 2016; Wagner et al., 2006) have written very persuasively that the real reason for reluctance to change—that is, the tendency toward inertia—is an underlying culture in the schools that has been assimilated by the teachers and other professionals. As with other cultural knowledge systems, this cultural system creates expectations and places various boundaries on the awareness and behaviors of those who interact with it. Unless the professionals are inherently reflective or are given explicit reasons to change, the tendency is to change only superficial mechanisms, and not the underlying knowledge system. This is why the overt or subverting reactions occur. Real change, according to Skrtic, depends on changing both the superficial operational mechanisms and the underlying cultural expectations. In this guide, we have designed procedures and exercises that assist in making these changes. We also describe some efforts and discuss the tremendous need for advocacy as a catalyst for additional change.

MTSS Team Activity

Become experts in the laws that govern special education. Assign pairs of MTSS team members different sections of a law to study. Each pair's task is to scrutinize a section of the law in order to understand how a continuum of services framework could be created within legal parameters.

Responsibilities of MTSS Teams

To effectively meet the needs of each individual multilingual learner in a school, the MTSS team must obtain sufficient information to determine the needs of the various groups of multilingual learners within the school, their performance in different contexts, and the strengths and weaknesses exhibited by these students. To accomplish these objectives, MTSS teams have five major responsibilities: examining and evaluating the existing learning environment for multilingual learners, coordinating information gathering, interpreting information, suggesting learning support strategies, and helping teachers monitor students' progress.

Examine the Learning Environment

The first step in establishing a system of support for multilingual learners who are experiencing difficulties at school is probably the most difficult part of this this process as it involves self-examination and an honest evaluation of decisions that were made regarding the instructional program and approach used with multilingual learners. This is no easy task as it requires setting aside personal interests, anxieties, and political views. It requires taking an objective look at how closely the educational program for multilingual learners aligns with what the research says. Studies on the effectiveness of educational programs and instructional strategies and approaches are not lacking. Extensive research provides us with clear guidelines as to the learning environment that is most effective for multilingual learners to become proficient enough in English to be able to learn new, abstract, and sometimes complex concepts taught in English. Studies have identified key factors that make it more likely for multilingual learners to learn new concepts and to perform at their optimal level at school. In the next chapter we review the research that should form the basis for multilingual learner program design and implementation, and provide tools that can help MTSS teams identify strengths and weaknesses in the educational program for multilingual learners.

Gather Information

In schools where traditional RtI/MTSS is implemented, the part that comes closest to this step is the screening process. In our framework, the information gathering is much more extensive, includes quantitative and qualitative data on various aspects of the students' home and school lives, and goes beyond administering one screening tool as is standard in most traditional models of RtI (Barnes & Harlacher, 2008). Many school districts review screening data that are based on a standardized tool administered in English and target children whose performance falls within the bottom 20% for intervention. Districts following this practice should consider a few guiding notions:

1. When looking at data in English, teams should look at various comparison groups. Initially, multilingual learners should be compared to their cultural and linguistic peers, rather than solely to their grade-level monolingual English-speaking classmates (Flege, 2019; Peña et al., 2017).

2. When deciding on true peers within the subgroup of multilingual learners, take into account the various distinguishing characteristics: How recently did students or their families arrive in the country? Have students received academic instruction in their home languages? How mobile has

the family been? These and other characteristics are discussed in greater detail in the chapters on integral factors that follow.

3. To the extent possible, gather screening data in as many languages as possible, and then look at students' performance across their languages to develop a range of performance levels rather than a definitive cutoff point (Escamilla & Hopewell, 2010).

Failure to take into account these characteristics and to use true-peer comparisons will fill caseloads and intervention groups overwhelmingly with multilingual learners. The MTSS team ensures that all the information already available in the school is identified and available to all those who can make use of it. The work of Howard (2009) and Rinaldi and Sampson (2008) provide contextualized questions that incorporate both second language and reading considerations. The team then begins coordinating the information-gathering process, once gaps in the data have been identified. Table 2.1 presents a checklist that can be used to monitor the information-gathering process.

Table 2.1   Checklist for Determining Whether Sufficient Data Are Available about the Six Integral Factors

Please check data that has been collected and is available for review by the MTSS team.

Personal and family factors

_____ Past and current socioeconomic status

_____ Family dynamics

_____ Family's degree of mobility

_____ Student's and family's expectations of school

_____ Student's interests and motivations

_____ Student's experiential background

Physical and psychological factors

_____ Possible challenges such as trauma, impaired vision or hearing, phobias or current psychological stress, or dysfunctional family situations

_____ Social and emotional development and skills

_____ Developmental milestones

Previous schooling/performance

_____ Amount of formal schooling in the student's home language

_____ Amount of formal language assistance the student has received or is receiving

_____ Quality of previous home-language instruction and English-language assistance

_____ Amount of interrupted/consistent/sustained formal schooling in student's home language(s)

Oral language and literacy development

_____ Stages of second-language development

_____ Competence in home (and other) languages

_____ Student's literacy experiences and instruction in all their language

Academic performance

_____ Distinction between assessment of student knowledge of concepts, and of the language that is used to communicate those concepts

_____ Relationship between student's language development and academic performance

_____ Support strategies for student when learning new concepts

Cross-cultural factors

_____ Familiarity with student's home culture

_____ Potential barriers to learner's functioning in a new, unfamiliar, culture

_____ School strategies to welcome and integrate student's culture into the curriculum and general environment

MTSS team members do not actually gather all the data themselves. Rather, they contact individuals who have access to the necessary information and ensure that the information is added to the repository. Information needs to be gathered about the specific observable behaviors that multilingual learners are exhibiting in school and organized around the six integral factors described in the chapters that follow.

Interpret Information

Interpretation is a collaborative process that employs careful and disciplined analysis of data obtained from systemic and specific sources simultaneously. MTSS teams look for patterns in the data across the entire school, in particular grade levels, a classroom, or a particular student or group of multilingual learners. At this point it is important to look at how multilingual learners are performing in different settings, grade levels, and content areas. Looking for bright spots in the data is as important as looking at the areas where multilingual learners are facing challenges. Learning from these bright spots can help teams make additional improvements in the learning environment that will support many multilingual learners and perhaps other students as well. When examining data that show groups or individual multilingual learners having significant challenges, team members can turn to the six integral factors to make sense of the behaviors that have been observed. The challenges that students experience may stem from the way that the instructional program for multilingual learners has been set up, including instructional practices and the materials used in the classroom, as well as a host of elements in students' lives pertaining to any of the six integral factors, including experiential differences, second language learning processes, or a disability in processing or learning. The team starts putting the puzzle together as more information about the student or the group of students is received.

Suggest Learning Support Strategies

Rather than submit to the temptation of relying on packaged published programs that claim to fix the problems that students are facing, we suggest a more direct and focused search for instructional and learning support strategies that adheres to important principles of learning and that specifically corresponds to the behaviors observed among the students. As information is collected and the student's behavior and performance are being interpreted, the team begins to identify support strategies for each identified concern. Some of these strategies will be based on the interpretation of the reasons for the observed behaviors (Allington, 2009; J. S. Damico, 2019d; Grigorenko, 2009; Keene, 2008). For example, some of the behaviors may reflect the normal language learning developmental process, some may stem from the disconnection between the learning environment and students' background and personal characteristics, and some may be attributable to an intrinsic disability. Pooling MTSS team members' expertise, the team suggests support strategies to the teachers and all the professionals who work with the student. At this point, the learning support strategies will come from the vast body of knowledge that has been gained over the years regarding second language acquisition, bilingualism, and bilingual education. These strategies will come from all the fields of knowledge represented by the team, and perhaps from further consultation with resources outside of the school district. The MTSS team also recommends ways that teachers can implement the strategies suggested, and if possible, they support the teachers in making these aspects of instruction part of the everyday classroom activities. Because the team is considering systemic (Tier 1 or core instructional environments) as well as specific causes for the challenges students experience, the team can help administrators bring about a change at the grade level, school level, or program level that will scale up many of the supports that were successful at the specific classroom, small-group, or individual levels (Dunaway, 2021; Hamayan & Freeman Field, 2012; Miramontes et al., 2011; Winter, 2001).

Monitor Progress

The fourth responsibility of MTSS teams is to monitor the effectiveness of the support strategies and programming they suggest. It is not enough for the team to simply make suggestions, however, or to select interventions solely because they provide charts and graphs that make reporting easy during this progress-monitoring phase. As advocates for multilingual learners, and to ensure a kind of fidelity to and agency for learning strategies and cohesive instruction, it is important to determine (1) what types of professional learning teachers and other staff need in order to implement the suggested support or programming, (2) whether the teachers are able to effectively implement these suggestions in the classroom, and (3) the impact of these suggestions on multilingual learners' progress behaviorally (e.g., Chalfant & Pysh, 1989; J. S. Damico, 1987; Dunaway, 2021; Hoff et al., 2012; Linan-Thompson et al., 2007; Reid et al., 1993).

Continue Supporting Students with Ongoing Challenges

As information regarding the learning environment and characteristics of multilingual learners continues to be gathered, changes in instruction and the general learning environment will help many multilingual learners overcome difficulties at school. Some multilingual learners may continue to face challenges, however. The MTSS team will begin the second tier of support by (1) describing as specifically as possible particular behaviors or aspects of academic performance that recur in these students, (2) seeking first extrinsic then intrinsic reasons for these behaviors, and (3) determining support strategies and interventions that would help students. The cycle of monitoring progress and modifying instruction as needed continues.

Throughout this guide, we offer a variety of suggestions for accomplishing each of these responsibilities. The key to success on all four tasks—gathering data, interpreting information, suggesting learning support strategies, and monitoring student progress—is to keep the tasks manageable. For example, the methods chosen to monitor progress should not be so cumbersome that no one can implement them. In addition, methods used for assessing the effectiveness of a learning support strategy should cause few if any interruptions to instruction. Rather, the assessment practices should be embedded in best practices school-wide and should enhance and enrich rather than constrict what happens in schools. All these tasks should be done collaboratively. The cycle of brainstorming, implementing, assessing, and reflecting will be disrupted if any part of the process is repeatedly delegated to the same person. If MTSS teams suggest support strategies, they must support the implementation of those strategies. When a method for monitoring progress is suggested, a plan must be in place for those who will make the assessment to know how often the assessment will take place, under what conditions, and how the qualitative and quantitative assessment results will be reported to the MTSS team.

Makeup of MTSS Teams

An important characteristic of these school-based MTSS teams is that members represent diverse professions. Bringing multiple perspectives to the task of interpreting information about any student, as well as creating and implementing learning support strategies, is important for all students, regardless of their language background (Archibald & Vollebregt, 2019; Bunce, 2003). However, multiple perspectives are especially important for understanding how multilingual learners are progressing in school because functioning bilingually is a complex process, especially in an academic setting (Cloud, 2012; Cummins, 2012; N. Flores & Schissel, 2014; Garcia et al., 2016; Pacheco, 2010; Sloan, 2007; WIDA, 2012; Young & Westernoff, 1999).

Multilingual learners represent a varied group of students. They enter U.S. schools from countries all over the world and from many regions within those countries. They arrive with different school experiences around the United States or even within the same school district. They come from every socioeconomic category, from hundreds of language backgrounds, and with a variety of life and educational experiences. The more professionally and personally diverse the MTSS team, the more likely it is that the team will be able to generate a variety of support strategies and creative solutions for implementation. With a more homogeneous team it is less likely that the team will be able to generate the range of appropriate strategies needed to support an individual student or group of students. A homogeneous team is also less likely to expand team members' knowledge and perspectives, thus making the team less able to keep up with the needs of increasingly diverse student populations.

When a team is trying to determine whether the academic challenges that multilingual learners are experiencing are due to intrinsic causes, and trying to create the most effective support for those students, it is essential to have both the ESL/bilingual perspective and the special education perspective to sort through possible explanations of the observable behaviors and begin to craft instructional and programming strategies. Remember that the process for determining eligibility for special education services for multilingual learners can be fraught with difficulties. No one perspective or piece of information can determine if a student's difficulties are due to typical English language learning processes, to a learning disability, or to a specific language impairment. Only by sharing our professional knowledge and experience with one another can we develop a deeper and broader understanding of possible causes of students' classroom performance (Archibald & Vollebregt, 2019; Barac et al., 2014; Damico et al., 1996; Gutierrez-Clellen et al., 2012). Only then can we develop specific strategies and programming options that would be effective in supporting multilingual learners in the culturally and linguistically responsive RtI/MTSS process.

English as a Second Language/Bilingual Specialists

Although there is no normative database with which to construct a profile of the "typical" multilingual learner (Bialystock, 2001; Grosjean, 2015), most English as a second language (ESL)/bilingual specialists understand the developmental nature of the second language acquisition process. The progress that we can generally expect from multilingual learners at different levels of proficiency has been described in the literature quite clearly (H. G. Cook et al., 2011). This knowledge base may come from research and theories of learning that come from fields as diverse as applied linguistics, teaching English as a new language, social anthropology, educational psychology, and psycholinguistics. These specialists' understanding of multilingual learners also comes from their observations of students as they develop proficiency in two languages. Bilingual teachers and some ESL teachers can also draw on their own experiences in becoming proficient in a second language.

The knowledge that may be specific to the ESL/bilingual specialist includes information about characteristic stages of learning a second language. It also includes information about common patterns of linguistic errors and typical challenges that multilingual learners encounter on their way to becoming proficient in the new language. This knowledge also includes information about the **acculturation** process and how to use the students' home language and culture in instruction.

Based on their experience teaching a variety of multilingual learners at different stages, ESL/bilingual specialists also bring a sense of what can be expected from these students. They have seen a multitude of writing samples, engaged in conversations with students from all over the globe, witnessed how affective issues influence multilingual learners' performance, implemented and adapted instructional strategies at various levels of language proficiency across content areas, and developed cultural insights from interactions with multilingual learners and their families. This experience can enable astute ESL/bilingual specialists to perceive more readily unusual aspects of learning that warrant attention, especially when they instruct the same students over a period of time.

Special Education Specialists

Special education specialists—resource room teachers, learning disability specialists, psychologists, speech–language pathologists, and specifically trained social workers—bring knowledge and experience unique to their professions to the solution-seeking process. Some of the knowledge available to these professionals may be different from that of the ESL/bilingual specialist. For example, many special education specialists have knowledge about different types of special education needs, the range of severity within those disabilities, and how they manifest in both instructional and social interactions. Special education specialists typically know the meaning-making principles and instructional methods that are most likely to help children compensate for a disability. They are also familiar with the written and spoken language of students at different points in their academic development and can recognize the various compensatory adaptations that exceptional learners employ in their attempts to overcome their difficulties (Brinton & Fujiki, 2010; Damico et al., 2021; Perkins, 2005). The range of professionals who come together to serve students with special needs further diversifies the team by virtue of their professional training, unique experiences, and professional perspectives. Thus, collectively, special education personnel can offer a broad repertoire of strategies to use with a range of learners. However, it is important to note that when those strategies are suggested for multilingual learners, at times they will be implemented in the students' home language and at other times in English, a context in which students are learning concepts through a language with which they are not yet fully proficient.

These specialists typically have an academic background in child and adolescent development, learning principles, social science, and physiological psychology, and they are familiar with various working models to aid hypothesis making in the diagnostic problem-solving process (Bartolo et al., 2001; Gillam & Gillam, 2006; Kroska & Harkness, 2008). Special educators bring experience, strategies, and perspectives to the MTSS team as advocates, in that the very nature of their work is to give a voice to students with unique learning needs.

Other Professionals

MTSS teams need, at a minimum, ESL/bilingual specialists and classroom teachers, but they need to enlist other professionals at their schools as well. These include school administrators, literacy specialists, instructional coaches, social workers, speech–language pathologists, psychologists, parent liaisons, and occupational therapists. Any and all of these professionals can form part of MTSS teams. In the end, it is to the students' benefit for staff to take the time to build multi-perspective teams, which transcend the otherwise compartmentalized nature of schools.

We can no longer afford to imagine we teach in isolation or to think of some students as "mine" and others as "yours." To address the range of learning needs presented by students, we must work across disciplines and across classrooms. By looking at the school community as a whole and pooling our professional and experiential resources, we can address the needs of more students, develop a variety of creative learning environments, and share the responsibility of teaching the diverse range of learners in our schools. All of these outcomes will ultimately serve not only to deal with challenges as they emerge, but prevent difficulties in the long term.

Building Professional Bridges across Specializations

Most teachers can probably remember occasions when they informally consulted a colleague on a particular topic, teaching strategy, or concern. The professional discussions that result from such consultations enrich teaching and significantly expand teachers' ability to help students (Cloud et al., 2010; Garcia et al., 2016; Miramontes et al., 2011). Most teachers probably also remember other occasions in their teaching experience when they wished they could have consulted a colleague, but there was no structured time built into the day for these discussions to occur. Some teachers work in schools where they are not allowed to talk to a particular professional without submitting a written request or getting official permission. Many schools do not have an environment that encourages teachers to talk to one another professionally during the school day. In addition, different regulatory constraints that result in funding and auditing obligations in different professional areas make it more difficult to maintain open collaboration among departments and staff.

MTSS team meetings can become a forum for sharing expertise and experiences, asking questions, querying new developments, and clarifying problematic ideas that individual teachers may have. Time spent with the team is an opportunity for seeking innovative solutions, developing cross-professional programming, crafting instructional support and intervention strategies, and designing ways of implementing and documenting the success of these strategies. The potential outcome of effective teamwork is that strategies, scaffolds, and other supports from bilingual education, general and special education will be built into the general school environment so that more students overall gain access to learning in a timely manner (Berquist, 2017; CAST, 2018; Gibbons, 2015). This proactive approach creates access and more inclusive environments rather than waiting until students fail before they receive attention and support. The potential of these teams will be lost if professionals fall back on the familiar model characterized by gatekeeping, lengthy waiting times, and compartmentalized service delivery (Chalfant & Pysh, 1989; Stevens, 2019; van Kraayenoord, 2010).

Box 2.1

Checklist for Assessing the Effective Characteristics of an MTSS Team

Clear and Congruent Principles

___ I have a clear understanding of the principles that we believe in.

___ I am in agreement about the principles that we adhere to.

Shared Language

___ There are very few terms that we use repeatedly that are not clear to me.

___ Whenever someone uses a vague or unknown word, I ask for clarification immediately.

___ If needed, we have a glossary of terms and acronyms that I can refer to for clarification.

Loosening Disciplinary Boundaries

___ Performance on discipline-specific tests are explained and described in terms that I can understand.

___ I am encouraged and feel free to collect open-ended data on students that I can share with team members.

Respectful Questioning

___ I feel comfortable asking for clarification from any member of the team.

___ I feel respected by all the members of the team.

___ I know who to go to for questions about issues that I do not feel expert in.

___ I feel comfortable answering questions that others ask of me.

Effective Interpersonal and Communication Skills

___ I am able to communicate clearly even about topics that others on the team are not familiar with.

___ I rarely misunderstand something that someone else on the team has said.

___ If a communication breakdown occurs, we are generally able to repair it quickly.

___ When a miscommunication escalates into an emotional argument, we are generally able to step back and start over.

Characteristics of an Effective MTSS Team

In order for productive interdisciplinary discussions to occur, professional bridges must be built across areas of specialization. Building bridges requires the team to have clear and congruent principles, a shared language, a loosening of disciplinary boundaries, the freedom to pose questions to others, and effective interpersonal and communication skills (Allington & Walmsley, 2007; Archibald & Vollebregt, 2019; Chalfant & Pysh, 1989; Marvin, 1990). These characteristics combine to create positive team dynamics.

To ensure that a newly formed team is off to a good start or to assess how well an established team displays these characteristics, the checklist in Box 2.1 may be useful.

Clear and Congruent Principles

For an MTSS team to function well, members must share some basic principles and values under the guidance of supportive leadership (Marzano et al., 2005). These principles, regardless of whether they are verbalized or remain unspoken, form the foundation for interdisciplinary discussions. Box 2.2 contains a checklist regarding principles that are essential for an MTSS team to follow to function within the framework that we are suggesting.

If there is a serious mismatch among the principles that different members of the MTSS team believe in, conflict and misunderstanding are likely to occur. From our work as members of interdisciplinary teams and from our experience developing a continuum of services framework at various schools,

Box 2.2

Checklist of Basic Principles Shared by MTSS Team Members

Please check your beliefs about multilingual learners (MLs) here.

I believe that . . .

___ the presence of MLs enriches our school.

___ linguistic and cultural pluralism is positive, not a problem to overcome.

___ acquiring the academic language and literacies students need for school success is a developmental process that may take more than 5 years.

___ effective instruction is coordinated across content areas and across grade levels.

___ MLs learn from and are the responsibility of all adults in a school, not just specialists.

___ learning abstract concepts in a language that is still developing and within a cultural context that may be unfamiliar to the learner is a challenging enterprise.

___ home language development (including home language literacies) provides a solid foundation for cognitive development, academic achievement, and English-language development.

___ ML parents, including those who are not yet fully proficient in English, are a valuable resource not just for their children at home but for the classroom and the school.

___ engaging lessons are based on what teachers know about their students, their backgrounds, and culture.

Adapted from Hamayan, E., & Freeman Field, R. (2012). *English language learners at school: A guide for administrators* (2nd ed.). Philadelphia, PA: Caslon.

we have found that it is best to talk about the principles or norms that team members adhere to openly and explicitly. We have also found that it is best to have this discussion about principles before a conflict arises. That way, team members can have the discussion with minimal emotional burden. Discussion of principles will overlap somewhat with the first task set for the team, evaluation of the multilingual learner program in their school (or district), and can open the door for the critical self-examination that is so valuable.

MTSS Team Activity

Use the checklist in Box 2.2 to generate a discussion by dividing the team into two groups. Assign one group to agree with the principles and one group to disagree with them. Have each group think of arguments to defend their positions before they begin to discuss the principles. Follow up by having each member reflect privately on his or her own position regarding these principles. End the activity by affirming the importance of adhering to these principles, and invite individuals who are doubtful about their beliefs and the extent to which they are congruent with the rest of the group's beliefs to share their feelings (either privately or, if the person feels comfortable sharing in public, with the rest of the group).

A Shared Language

Conversations have a way of turning into monologues when two professionals use the same term to mean different things (Prelock, 2000). For that reason, it is essential that MTSS teams clarify the terminology that is used repeatedly in their discussions, learn what colleagues from other professional perspectives mean when they use a particular term, and then come to a consensus on shared terminology. For example, a discussion can lead to a great deal of miscommunication when, perhaps, the ESL teacher uses the term *bilingual* to mean any student who has proficiency in two languages but the general education classroom teacher understands the term to mean only those students who are in the bilingual program and who are still developing proficiency in English. The ESL teacher will likely refer to the bilingual student as being able to function in both languages, whereas the general education teacher will protest that in her class, the bilingual student is not able to do the work in English at all. In turn, the ESL teacher may interpret that remark as prejudicial to all students who come from a language background other than English, and before long the discussion can become an emotional argument.

These conversations become more complex when we consider that each MTSS team member has their own set of acronyms and professional vocabulary that nonmembers may misunderstand. Even words, such as *language*, *comprehension*, or *processing*, may cause miscommunication as each individual interprets the term from their unique professional experience and knowledge base (Afflerbach et al., 2008; Cox & Hopkins, 2006). Thus, it is essential that a common vocabulary be established among team members, and that a safe environment exists whereby individuals on the team feel comfortable at any time to ask for clarification of terms or acronyms used by other team members.

MTSS Team Activity

Have team members each bring a list of three or four terms, with definitions, that they think are essential for the team's discussions. Discuss the meanings and possible interpretations of these terms.

Loosening Disciplinary Boundaries

As mentioned previously, building bridges among professions is essential in order for effective interaction to occur. Gutkin and Nemeth (1997) and others (e.g., Chalfant & Pysh, 1989; Damico et al., 2021; Elias & Dilworth, 2003; Winter, 1999) have demonstrated how the subjective biases, professional orientations, and discipline-specific practices of the members of school-based teams often result in a lack of perspective taking and a breakdown in communication, often to the detriment of the students being considered during the teaming process. Consequently, MTSS teams should attempt to reduce the boundaries that exist between the disciplines and partner with colleagues from other disciplines to build collaborative conversations.

Perhaps the most frequent practice upholding disciplinary boundaries is the use of norm-referenced and standardized tests (Chandler et al., 2005; Damico et al., 2021; Harry & Klingner, 2014). Each of the various disciplines has typically been trained in the administration and interpretation of skill- or trait-specific tools. Thus, whether it is the speech–language pathologist holding on to a test of language ability, a resource room teacher guarding their Woodcock-Johnson, or a psychologist insisting on a concentration on cognitive or processing abilities, each tends to focus on professional turf with respect to assessment practices, interpretation, and recommendations, even when those assessments come from published benchmark and progress-monitoring systems in English that are utterly inappropriate for multilingual learners (Bak, 2016; Gunderson & Siegel, 2001; Gutkin & Nemeth, 1997; Oller, 2008; Poehner, 2007; Valencia et al., 2010). To reduce these boundaries, the team should embrace more descriptive assessment practices that focus on the actual needs of multilingual learners in their learning contexts or a standardized measure that is calibrated to language proficiency levels such as World-Class Instructional Design and Assessment (WIDA) Interim Assessments (see https://wida.wisc.edu/). In this way, each of the professionals can collect data on what the student actually does when attempting to learn, and the discussion can focus on authentic evaluations and contextualized behaviors rather than on discipline-specific test scores. Thus the team shifts away from defense of professional territory and toward enriching the learning environment for all multilingual learners and, in the process, aids the individual student (Anastasi & Urbiba, 1997; Chandler et al., 2005; Dunaway, 2021).

MTSS Team Activity

Using a shared document, team members list areas of their own expertise. The list of items is then reorganized into categories. Team members label the categories and analyze the results. Discuss the areas of expertise that are well represented and identify areas that are not well represented or not present at all that are needed to serve multilingual learners. Use this list to plan professional learning for the team.

Respectful Questioning

When building professional bridges and reducing disciplinary boundaries, team members need to feel comfortable exploring other colleagues' perspectives. They need to be able to ask questions freely about what they do not know. This can be a very vulnerable position to take as a professional. However, for productive interdisciplinary interactions to occur—and they are at the heart of the model we propose—it is vital to ask questions (Harry & Klingner, 2014; Marvin, 1990). Team members should begin with the understanding that no individual has the answer as to the best placement choice or type of support strategy for any particular student or group of students. Team members should acknowledge that the services that students need might not exist yet in the school system. Then the team can begin to develop innovative solutions to overcome this lack by blending the individual team members' expertise, knowledge, experience, and resources.

Recognizing that team members have spent a large portion of their adult lives studying and practicing in a professional field engenders a respectful approach to others' contributions and perspectives. Team members must understand that they come from differing professional backgrounds and experiences and must rely on colleagues for their perspectives and expertise. This requires each professional to use collaborative skills to learn more about their colleagues' contributions and to be open to fitting that knowledge into their existing professional schema (Archibald & Vollebregt, 2019). These sorts of exchanges are more likely to take place in an environment in which the primary disciplinary boundaries have been relaxed, where there is a focus on the students (not on discipline-specific practices and biases), where all participants listen to each member's point of view, and where team members feel comfortable seeking clarification on any given point without being viewed negatively (Archibald, 2017; Howard, 2009; Joyce & Showers, 2002; Prelock, 2000; Suleman et al., 2014). This relaxed environment allows members of the team to better understand the different needs of the students they serve and to consider different explanations for the challenges that students experience in light of the new information they receive.

MTSS Team Activity

Have team members jot down phrases and expressions that were used effectively during a discussion that reflected respect toward another person, represented a way of clarifying something someone else had said, or showed a similar positive quality. At the end of the meeting, allow 15 minutes for a team member to say the following: "I liked this phrase [*fill in the blank*] because it did the following [*fill in the blank*]. It would have been far less effective if the person had said [*fill in the blank*]." (This activity is most effective if the name of the person responsible for the particular phrase is left unmentioned.)

Effective Interpersonal and Communication Skills

For respectful questioning to occur, team members use interpersonal skills and communication strategies that lead to smooth dialogues. These skills include active listening, clarifying, refining, and summarizing information to understand other viewpoints (Archibald, 2017; Ontario Association of Speech–Language Pathologists and Audiologists [OSLA], 2005). The ability to depersonalize difficult exchanges that arise by acknowledging emotional comments as a by-product of sharing new and different perspectives is also an important characteristic of effective collaborative exchanges (Chronicle 2.2 provides an example). Making the effort to repair communication breakdowns and to adapt to others' communication styles, as well as a willingness to modify a position, contributes to positive team dynamics.

How to Form Effective MTSS Teams

In many schools, a team already exists that is responsible for special education issues, or there may be a problem-solving team that has been formed as a result of use of the RtI/MTSS process. The existing team can be transformed to

Chronicle 2.2

An Open Conversation Turns Sour

By an Administrator Member of an MTSS Team

I was sitting in on an MTSS Team meeting once and was quite impressed with how well team members were working together. The team had only started getting together a couple of weeks earlier, and it had not been a smooth start. The special education specialists had not been very open to considering the suggestions and ideas put forth by the ESL and bilingual teachers. But that day, the conversation was very balanced—until the ESL teacher started to talk about the merits of an ESL strategy she used frequently and she thought would be helpful for all teachers to know about. The strategy is called the total physical response (TPR). Although it is limited in scope, TPR is quite useful for introducing new vocabulary.

The complicating factor for the team was that the ESL teacher kept using the term *TPR* without explanation, until one of the special education teachers ventured to ask, "What's TPR?" The ESL teacher seemed surprised and said, "You don't know what TPR is?" As soon as the words were uttered, something changed in the group dynamics. The special education teacher, who had been leaning forward, moved back in her chair, crossed her arms, and said, "Obviously not." The conversation went downhill from then on.

It took a lot of mediating to get the group back to functioning smoothly, but I could see that we had to be very careful with how statements were made and how questions were asked.

Questions for Discussion

1. What assumptions did the members of the team make during the meeting described?
2. How would one go about "mediating to get the group back to functioning smoothly"?
3. What type of activity would be good as a follow-up to this event?

work as a team that focuses on multilingual learners by following the framework suggested in this guide. As an alternative, the school staff may decide to start at the beginning and form a new team. In that case, the following steps are likely to occur:

Step 1: The bilingual/ESL director, the special services (special education) director, and the district curriculum administrator meet to develop a common vision. Administrative support and involvement are essential to tailor the format of the team to meet existing needs and to function well within existing structures.

Step 2: The idea of the MTSS team and the philosophy underlying the framework of a continuum of services for multilingual learners are introduced to school staff.

Step 3: Staff members begin to consider the following questions: Who will take the initiative to form a (or modify an existing) team? Who will constitute the members of the team? What kind of support will the school provide?

Step 4: Each school suggests that a representative group of professionals form the MTSS team. The following professionals are typically members: classroom teacher, bilingual/ESL educators, a social worker, a school administrator, and someone with a special education background.

Step 5: Other professionals are encouraged to attend meetings.

Step 6: The MTSS team is introduced to the rest of the school.

Step 7: The team decides on regular meeting times: before the school year begins, regularly at a convenient time while school is in session, and in the spring to attend articulation meetings to anticipate needs that might arise during the next school year. Meetings are scheduled when all members can attend with ease and regularity.

Step 8: MTSS team members determine their professional learning needs in both professional content areas (such as language learning and the impact of cultural diversity on learning) and procedural aspects (such as problem-solving procedures and interpersonal communication). They make a plan for professional learning in those areas.

Step 9: The team plans a schedule for meetings when there are no students to be brought up for discussion and when there is time to share expertise and to brainstorm possible explanations and learning support strategies for typical difficulties that arise each year.

What MTSS Teams Can Accomplish

Several benefits arise from establishing MTSS teams as part of the everyday workings of the school. One of the most important benefits is the change that occurs in the general school ambiance. A school where MTSS teams meet regularly is likely to be a more collegial place where teachers support each other. Having MTSS teams as part of the everyday functioning of the school also has specific benefits, as described in the sections that follow.

Professional Reflection

A specific benefit of establishing MTSS teams within a school is that it leads teachers to reflect on their work with students. Teacher reflection has been shown to enhance a teacher's performance and, as a consequence, student achievement (DuFour, 2004; Schön, 1991). Because the main purpose of MTSS teams is to focus on the needs of students, teachers become accustomed to questioning the nature and origin of students' learning challenges. In addition, because MTSS team meetings attempt to provide support to teachers by suggesting instructional and program strategies that might help improve students' classroom performance, teachers are likely to develop the habit of asking why they teach the way they do or why a program is set up the way it is. By asking these questions, teachers begin to reflect on their practice and on the theoretical bases that define that practice. By taking the time to ask, "What worked? What didn't work?" and "What can I do differently next time?" (Schön, 1991) educators and other professionals within a school become more innovative in their practice and more sensitive to the needs of diverse learners.

Capacity Building

Another specific benefit of having MTSS teams is that teachers learn from one another. By collaborating with one another within the comfortable context of team meetings, practitioners with different specializations can learn about each other's skills. This capacity building in both content knowledge and collaborative skills works to the benefit of the team and the students. Thus, the continuum of services framework allows teachers to generate unique professional learning opportunities for themselves when they pair up with another educator with a different area of specialization. For example, if a speech–language pathologist co-teaches a unit with an ESL teacher in which graphic organizers are used in oral or written retelling, both professionals are likely to learn something new. The speech–language pathologist may see the value of contextualizing interventions, and the ESL teacher may discover ways to increase students' oral language expression within that meaningful context. A bilingual teacher might co-instruct with a classroom teacher to implement a year-long strategy aimed at activation of students' semantic networks across their two languages so that the students' conceptual knowledge of important terminology in one language can be employed to assist processing in the students' other language(s) (Dove & Honigsfeld, 2018; Sheng et al., 2012).

Redefining Roles

Cross-professional interactions among MTSS team members can lead to another significant benefit: a redefinition of traditional roles in delivering instruction and implementing support strategies. Members of MTSS teams may soon realize that their traditional roles—as general education classroom teachers, speech–language pathologists, or ESL teachers—will begin to change (Archibald, 2017; Swenson & Williams, 2015). They may see that by changing the way they practice their professions they can better meet the needs of students by coming up with new and innovative programming for them. For example, through discussions with teachers, the MTSS team may have found that many students were having difficulty keeping up with the literacy demands of their science, social studies, and mathematics classes in the intermediate and middle grades. The literacy specialist and the ESL teacher may decide to pool their professional resources and expertise and open a literacy enrichment center in their school that would allow grade 3 through grade 8 students to receive additional literacy support to complement what they are doing in their subject area classes throughout the day (Janzen, 2008). Another component of this project might be that the literacy and ESL/bilingual specialists develop a series of workshops to teach classroom teachers literacy strategies that could be used across the curriculum (Keene, 2008).

The Big Picture

The more members of the MTSS team extend their knowledge base beyond their own area of expertise and the more teams collaborate, the more they are able to understand each other's perspective. The more teachers and other practitioners cross professional bridges and add new information and skills to their repertoires, the more likely they are to see how their specific area of specialization fits into the larger context of education and schooling. Thus, another benefit of MTSS teams is that educators will better understand how their work fits in with everyone else's work. This is true of all the components of instruction that a student gets in one year, but it also applies to how students progress from one year to the next as well as assuring that instruction is well coordinated and cohesive during the year.

Catalysts for Change

One last important point to make about the MTSS teams is that they can become a catalyst for changing how we allocate and distribute human, physical, and fiscal resources. All the programming we design requires equally innovative methods of resource use. Proposed changes cannot be implemented if the budget cannot support them. An MTSS team can challenge this situation by suggesting that those with budgetary authority examine whether or not resources have been allocated equitably to the multilingual learners in the school and in the district. On close examination it is common to find that resources can be redistributed to implement the innovation on behalf of multilingual learners. Developing a culturally and linguistically responsive MTSS process designed to address the needs of multilingual learners will likely benefit all students.

An Innovative Approach

This team approach to gathering information, developing instruction, and implementing both systemic and specific learning support strategies stands in contrast to the traditional gatekeeping model, which can pit one professional against another. In a traditional model, teachers and families may find themselves on the defensive, trying to prove that they have done everything humanly possible to help the students, and only after the situation has significantly deteriorated is the student referred to the team for help. Conversely, school teams may be under pressure to discuss only the most severe cases to decide who qualifies for a full case study. In a more collaborative model, the goal is to help many more students in a timely manner.

Team members know that students' needs and abilities are not neatly organized in distinct categories. These teams recognize that there is a broad range of learner needs in our schools that call for an even broader range of instructional strategies and methods for implementing them. Through this collaborative solution-seeking approach, in which the goal is to prevent academic and linguistic difficulties, students ultimately benefit. Students no longer have to fail and be identified as qualified for special education services before receiving support. Teachers benefit from the collaborative teams because they need not wait for issues and concerns to become overwhelming in their classrooms before getting support for themselves and for their students.

The processes within the continuum of services framework briefly discussed in this chapter are superficially similar in some respects to the RtI/ MTSS system. The screening phase appears similar to the gathering of information done by MTSS teams: Both employ a kind of multi-tiered approach to progressive interventions, and both employ data to inform decision-making. In reality, however, our framework is much more oriented to true solution seeking and to a synergistic collaboration across several involved disciplines. Further, the hallmark of our model is meaning-based individualization in terms of description, assessment, support, and intervention. To some extent, these characteristics are potentially viable for RtI/MTSS, but this potential has not been fulfilled (Allington, 2009; Carhill et al., 2008; Chapman et al., 2015; Troia, 2005; van Kraayenoord, 2010). The principles in our framework are more similar to the early work of Clay (1993) and of Allington and Walmsley (1995) than to RtI. Indeed, the multi-tiered aspects of RtI/MTSS have their origins in some of these same earlier innovative practices (Gersten & Edomono, 2006; Jaeger, 2019; McEneaney et al., 2006).

The differences between our model and RtI/MTSS are more clearly described in the upcoming chapters. This description—and the positive results touted in this chapter—must begin by examining the foundational context of our work: the learning environment that has been created for multilingual learners. That is the topic of the next chapter.

Questions for Reflection and Action

1. In the section entitled "Challenges to This Continuum of Services Framework," three types of barriers are discussed. How do these relate to your context? What other barriers do you perceive, and how can they be overcome?
2. What are the benefits of the setup suggested in this chapter to individuals on the MTSS team?
3. How can these benefits be extended to staff members who are not members of the MTSS team?
4. Our professional identities are defined to a large extent by the specialization that we have; how does that identity influence the way we perceive and process information?
5. Can you identify bright spots in your team's collaboration thus far?
6. What is one area of collaboration that your team could work on improving this school year?

The Learning Environment Created for Multilingual Learners

Key Concepts. *As multi-tiered system of supports (MTSS) teams begin to consider how to support multilingual learners who are encountering challenges at school, they first need to think about the learning environment that has been created for these students. Learning environment is a broad term that encompasses teachers' preparation and presentation of materials, the resources available, the program design, the range of services offered, the value placed on students' home languages and cultures, and characteristics of instruction and assessment. Any changes to the learning environment that are deemed necessary are systemic and likely to improve instruction for all students.*

The learning environment created for multilingual learners is the critical context that needs to be evaluated to make sure that multilingual learners are being given the best opportunity to learn in the most equitable and effective way possible. Opportunity to learn is the most important factor that predicts a student's knowledge of subject areas (Berliner & Biddle, 1995). An effective learning environment can be evaluated through consideration of aspects of a school such as teacher qualification, quality of materials, availability of resources, and long-term program design. It also encompasses more intangible qualities, however, such as school climate or ethos (Wang & Degol, 2016). A school environment should have an enriching rather than remedial or compensatory quality and the mark of enrichment will be apparent and experienced in every aspect of school life. Multilingual learners should feel supported both affectively and cognitively (e.g., Tomczak & Jaworska-Pasterska, 2017). There are few places as exciting, hopeful, or motivating as a supportive and culturally sustaining academic environment (Gibbons, 2015; Grant & Gillette, 2006; D. Paris, 2012; D. Paris & Alim, 2017). Academic success requires this supportive learning environment. Students in such an environment can focus on acquiring new ideas and skills that also enhance their understanding of the world and their confidence in dealing with it. It is important to consider this context first, because school staff can systematically attempt to improve the learning environment for multilingual learners as soon as or, preferably, before a challenge is identified. When we become aware that learning is challenging for a particular group of students it is our responsibility to first question the efficacy of our praxis. This is the first task that faces the MTSS team. We describe this program and instructional design evaluation as a self-assessment process, but, of course, it can also be accomplished with the help of an external evaluator.

Key Factors in the Learning Environment

A number of factors have a demonstrable impact on the creation of a strong, responsive, and supportive learning environment for multilingual learners. Each of these factors should be considered important to structuring an academic environment that supports rather than conflicts with the goals of academic success for multilingual learners: teachers, available resources, the design of the instructional program (in terms of implementation and configuration), the range of services offered, the role of home language and culture in instruction and assessment, and characteristics of instruction and assessment. We believe that these aspects of education help determine the kind of climate that characterizes the physical and affective community that is school, and a healthy school climate is associated with a healthy learning environment for all students, inclusive of multilingual learners (Freiberg, 1998, 1999; B. Johnson & Stevens, 2006; Koth et al., 2008; Ozfidan & Toprak, 2020). Each of these items is discussed separately in the sections that follow.

Teachers

Qualified and engaging teachers are essential to multilingual learners' academic and linguistic success, yet two conditions relevant to personnel matters threaten this success. First, although the percentage of multilingual learners among school-age students is increasing across the United States, unfortunate social and governmental pushback that affects multilingual learner education (e.g., English-only legislation, anti-immigrant policies) has occurred in some regions. As a consequence, some language assistance programs are no longer available or are no longer as robust and rigorous as they once were and many general education teachers are now responsible for the academic success of these students (Kaplan & Leckie, 2009). Unfortunately, given their already overburdened class ratios and administrative mandates and lack of professional expertise in this particular area of education, these teachers may not be well prepared and do not necessarily have the inclination to address the unique profile of multilingual learners (Baltaci, 2017; Ceasar & Kohler, 2007; Sox, 2009; Xu & Drame, 2008). Second, the schools with the greatest needs are often staffed by teachers who are either novices or unskilled in this area of instruction (Darling-Hammond, 2013; Haycock, 1998; Janzen, 2007; Xu & Drame, 2008). Low-resourced schools and schools with high numbers of minoritized students may be assigned to novice and out-of-field (without a major or minor in the subject area) teachers almost twice as often as schools that are highly resourced and have fewer minoritized students (Bettini & Park, 2021; Jerald, 2003). Multilingual learners need to be instructed by teachers who know how to teach linguistically and culturally diverse students.

Teachers of multilingual learners must have working knowledge of second language acquisition (Hill & Flynn, 2006), the process of acculturation, instructional and assessment methods that are effective for these students, and culturally and linguistically sustaining pedagogy, in addition to acquiring basic instructional competency and subject-area expertise (Calderón et al., 2011; Janzen, 2008; Palmer & Martínez, 2013).

General education teachers without specialized training in English as a second language (ESL)/bilingual education cannot provide by themselves the enriching instructional learning environment multilingual learners need. In some cases they may make the learning environment worse for the multilingual learner by teaching content without considering the academic language that is required to access that content, not knowing how to differentiate instruction to address the wide range of English development levels of multilingual learners, or using teaching strategies that do not benefit multilingual learners because they were designed and implemented with monolingual English speakers in mind (Gibbons, 2015; Sleeter, 2012; Xu & Drame, 2008). Without this information and training, teachers may misinterpret multilingual learners' performance and arrive at flawed judgments of these students' progress. On the other hand, ESL/bilingual teachers may understand second language learning, but without subject-area expertise in the intermediate grades and at the middle and secondary school level; they also are unable to provide the needed enriched learning environment by themselves (Janzen, 2008). Chronicle 3.1 describes the dilemma many teachers of multilingual learners face at the middle or secondary school level (Ruiz-de-Velasco & Fix, 2000). Most ESL/bilingual teachers are language development experts, not content-area specialists, whereas most middle and secondary school teachers are content-area specialists, not language development experts (Janzen, 2008; Marshall & Toohey, 2010). The school district can remedy this situation by providing opportunities for collaboration among the teachers who serve multilingual learners. Sharing their expertise with one another can support the development of all educators and benefit multilingual learners across grade levels and content areas. In this way school administrators create an environment in which there is a shared responsibility for the education of multilingual learners.

Chronicle 3.1

Comparing the Roles of Content and Language Teachers

By a Junior High Bilingual/ESL Teacher

Initiating a transfer from the elementary level to the middle school level was something I wanted to do to widen my teaching experience to include more grade levels after being a bilingual/ESL teacher at the elementary level for 7 years. I certainly widened my experience, but not in the way intended. I found myself trying to teach multilingual learners (MLs) biology without specimens, chemistry without chemicals, and U.S. history without original source documents. In addition, I tried to help students study for vocabulary tests in elective courses, for example, in sewing class without benefit of access to sewing machines and in computer drafting and design class without benefit of access to computer drafting/

(continued)

continued

By a Junior High Bilingual/ESL Teacher

design software. The materials unique to core and elective content areas were not available to me as a bilingual teacher either on a sign-out basis (because there was always a section of the course running) or in my classroom (because I was not assigned to a science lab or the darkroom or the life skills room).

My multilingual learners were assigned to one team at each grade level. Fortunately, I worked with a great group of teachers who were willing to collaborate with me. My teaching responsibilities were made clear: They were restricted to the realm of home language literacy instruction, ESL instruction, and literacy development, particularly vocabulary development, within the content area. The core academic teachers were obligated to obtain training in ESL methodology and assessment, foundations of language minority education,

and issues in cross-cultural education (the ESL approval/endorsement). Additional staff members were recruited with target language fluency and/or bilingual endorsement/approval and content area endorsement to provide math, science, and social studies classes in the native language.

Questions for Discussion

1. Did the school do the right thing and improve the learning environment for MLs?
2. Is the new arrangement more manageable for staff?
3. Do ESL/bilingual teachers face a higher burnout rate than other teachers?
4. Are other student population groups subject to similar configurations?

If teachers lack the necessary depth and breadth of subject-area knowledge, multilingual learners will get a watered-down version of the curriculum at best, and little or no access to the academic curriculum at worst. In either case, learning gaps are created, and these gaps are harder to address later and increasingly difficult to distinguish from intrinsic learning disabilities as the student continues in school (Crago & Paradis, 2003; Harry & Klingner, 2014; Klingner et al., 2007; K. Kohnert & Goldstein, 2005; McDermott & Varenne, 1995; van Kraayenoord, 2010). Most states in the United States offer separate endorsements for ESL/bilingual education, in some cases for preservice teachers and in other cases for in-service teachers.

Because of the importance of having the right mixture of knowledge and experience in both general education and language diversity education, a focus on the professional development and employment of both types of teachers might be expected. If the district cannot recruit teachers with ESL/bilingual licensure, it must strive to provide existing staff with incentives to enroll in graduate programs, supplemented by in-service professional development opportunities and by setting up professional learning groups within the school or district. For a detailed description of the knowledge and skills that teachers and staff need to qualify to work with multilingual learners, see Crandall et al. (2012). Box 3.1 presents a checklist based on that document.

School administrators can establish co-teaching partners (Dove & Honigsfeld, 2010, 2018) pairing content-area teachers with ESL/Bilingual teachers. In addition, the district can establish mentoring and coaching programs, pairing veteran and novice staff and ESL/bilingual and classroom teachers. Another possibility is to organize the teaching staff into grade-level or cross-disciplinary teams. That is, groups of teachers are configured into teams that include ESL/bilingual teachers. This approach establishes a natural context

Box 3.1

Checklist for Assessing the Qualifications of Teachers Who Serve Multilingual Learners (MLs)

Monolingual English Classroom Teachers

___ Know how MLs acquire and develop their first and second languages (oral language and literacy).

___ Know how to find out about students' cultures.

___ Can distinguish between social and academic language.

___ Can differentiate instruction according to students' English-language proficiency levels.

___ Can plan for making connections to the students' home languages.

___ Can provide appropriate instruction for different learning styles.

___ Know how to have a conference with parents who may not speak English and who may have different expectations about the appropriate roles and responsibilities of parents and teachers in the education of their children.

___ Can determine the independent reading level of individual MLs and choose appropriate texts for language arts and all content areas.

___ Participate with colleagues in designing units of study that implement principles of Universal Design for Learning (UDL).

___ Can work collaboratively with bilingual/ESL educators, interpreters, and cultural liaisons.

___ Can design units of study and lessons that address both academic content standards and English-language proficiency standards.

___ Know how to assess by providing MLs with an opportunity to demonstrate their understanding in a variety of ways.

___ Know the types of ESL or bilingual programs and services offered to students and can work collaboratively with these teachers in co-planning or co-teaching lessons.

ESL Teachers

___ Know the structure of English and how to teach that structure to MLs in contextualized and meaningful ways.

___ Know how to help MLs develop oral and written proficiency in English.

___ Know the processes of first- and second-language acquisition.

___ Know sheltered instruction approaches and strategies and can implement them to develop academic language appropriate for the curriculum being taught.

___ Know about potential difficulties in cross-cultural communication and how to mediate when miscommunication leads to misunderstanding.

___ Collaborate with colleagues in designing units of study that implement principles of UDL.

___ Know the basic laws and regulations governing the education of MLs.

___ Know the policies and procedures related to MLs in the school and district.

___ Know state or district curriculum and standards related to MLs as well as academic-content-area standards.

___ Know the content of the core curriculum and can integrate academic concepts, texts, tasks, and assessment into the ESL classroom.

___ Can work collaboratively with classroom teachers in co-planning, co-teaching, or previewing/reviewing content in ESL instruction that effectively integrates academic content into the language focus.

___ Know the resources available to MLs and their families and how to access these resources.

___ If in a middle or high school with MLs who have limited prior schooling or literacy, can teach initial literacy in English.

Bilingual/Dual-Language Teachers

___ Know the policies and procedures related to MLs.

___ Know state or district curriculum and standards related to instruction of bilingual students.

___ Know and are able to implement bilingual instructional methodology.

___ Collaborate with colleagues to design units of study that implement principles of UDL.

___ Know how to make connections between MLs' home language(s) and English so that students use their languages as an integrated communication system.

___ Can work collaboratively with ESL and other classroom teachers, especially in transitioning students from bilingual classes to ESL, sheltered, or general education classes.

___ Know bilingual resources available in the community and can help families, the school, and the district to access these resources.

___ Can help serve as a cultural interpreter for other school personnel.

___ Can manage classes of students with diverse backgrounds, including differences in proficiency in the home language and English.

for educators to share their expertise; plan, learn, and prepare instruction together; get to know all the students on their team; and provide input on how to address individual student's needs. The MTSS team, working within the framework described in this book, is geared toward the construction of these types of service delivery options. However, ongoing professional learning is also needed to ensure that all staff working with multilingual learners stays abreast of developments in the field and changes in the law.

The practice of assigning program assistants to provide initial instruction to multilingual learners is all too prevalent and results in a weak, ineffectual education program. Multilingual learners whose instruction has been initiated predominantly by paraprofessionals are at considerable risk for academic difficulties (Gerber et al., 2001; Gray et al., 2007; Haycock, 1998; Youngs et al., 2011). Class and group size in secondary and tertiary interventions also make a difference: Self-contained classes for multilingual learners should be at 90% of the average district class size to ensure that teachers are able to differentiate instruction according to both content-area skill levels and language proficiency levels as needed. Caseloads for pullout and resource ESL/bilingual teachers should be comparable to those of teachers in other pullout and resource programs in the district, where daily instruction is expected. Some administrators' tolerance of large class sizes for language minoritized students and heavy caseloads for pullout and resource ESL/bilingual teachers results in an unproductive learning environment for multilingual learners (Miramontes et al., 2011). To be equitably included and have access to the curriculum it is essential that multilingual learners receive linguistically and culturally appropriate instruction across all settings in Tier 1. In addition, more intensive supports will be required for some students in Tiers 2 and 3. The size of learning support groups for struggling learners varies widely across the United States (Vaughn et al., 2003) and numerous research studies indicate that very small groups of one to three students at a time are most effective for specific interventions for native speakers of English (Allington, 2006; Denton et al., 2003; McEneaney et al., 2006; Swanson & Hoskyn, 1998). Therefore, if multilingual learners are provided with any types of specific intervention, small groups of three or fewer are preferred.

When multilingual learners receive instruction from unqualified or inappropriately certified teachers, there is a negative cumulative effect on their educational experience that isolated instances of good instruction cannot overcome. Multilingual learners must receive enriched, engaging, and rigorous content-area, language and literacy instruction from highly motivated and talented teachers over their entire school experience to keep pace with and even outperform English-speaking peers. If this does not occur, a host of potential reactions may result. First, and critically, they may never close the gap between themselves and their mainstream peers (Thomas & Collier, 2002; Echevarria & Short, 2003). Second, students may simply become less responsive to the teaching strategies and the acceptable expectations of the classroom. Because they have not been able to receive effective assistance from teachers and educational support staff, they may create other types of strategies that result in marginalizing them within the classroom context, and multilingual learners may simply opt out of the process (Hammond, 2014). Third, students may be inappropriately placed in special education, where their needs cannot be met effectively and their potential is greatly reduced (Cummins, 1984; J. S. Damico & Damico, 1993a; Damico et al., 2021). Finally, multilingual learners may simply drop out of school when that option becomes available. No individual chooses to remain in a situation of struggle or failure when other options are available.

Resources Available

A combination of high-quality, age-appropriate academic-content-area materials, technology, connectivity, mathematics manipulatives, and science resources is essential for an effective learning environment for multilingual learners. Studies conducted on the most important features of effective learning support strategies used with struggling readers show that the single most critical factor is matching the readers with texts they can actually read (Allington, 2006, 2009; Arrow et al., 2015; Ehri et al., 2007; R. E. O'Connor et al., 2002; Swanson & Hoskyn, 1998). This matchup is defined by Allington (2006) as the use of texts with which students experience high-success reading. That is, comprehension of 98% of the words in the text they are reading, fluency when they read, and understanding what they read.

Consequently, reading material and academic content materials should be available at a variety of language proficiency and reading levels. In addition to English, academic materials in the languages and cultures of the students in the school are essential. Later in the book we present ideas on how to integrate these multilingual and multicultural materials throughout the curriculum. Sufficient teacher resource materials, including teacher manuals for any series the district has adopted, must be provided. Curriculum guides in all content areas and copies of content-area standards are also needed. Additional teaching materials, such as current technology, tablets, audio and video editing software, microphones, trade books (in both the home and second languages), realia, mathematics manipulatives, software, and access to all materials and technological support available to every teacher in the district, should also be part of this environment. An abundance of leisure reading materials should be available to students in the classroom library, the school library, and the community library (Krashen, 2004). Instruction without sufficient academic and leisure reading materials in both languages renders the instruction less accessible for multilingual learners and therefore compromises the learning environment. The wide range of multilingual resources that are currently available could be useful for setting up libraries of multilingual materials in school, as well as for parents and children at home.

Multilingual learners need to interact with other students using oral language, both social and academic, in order to practice newly learned language skills and increase their understanding of content (Sánchez-López & Young, 2018). Multilingual learners also need to have access to peer language models in both nonacademic classes (such as physical education, music, and art) and planned academic activities. One-on-one or small-group instruction, which is often offered during Tier 2 or 3 intervention time for multilingual learners as part of response to intervention (RtI)/MTSS, does not provide the rich and varied opportunities for multilingual learners to communicate with peers and adults when it is the sole instructional situation created for multilingual learners (Coelho, 1994; Genesee, 2012). The district should provide physical classroom space sufficient to accommodate group sizes of two to 20 students. Within the scheduling process, the school must provide opportunities for multilingual learners to attend nonacademic classes with their English-speaking peers. In addition, schools must provide opportunities for the integration of multilingual learners with peers in carefully designed academic activities by providing time to ESL/bilingual teachers and classroom teachers for collaborative planning and co- teaching (Dove & Honigsfeld, 2018). Chronicle 3.2 provides the account of an ESL teacher who not only works under dire conditions, but also provides instruction while isolated from the classroom teachers. Multilingual learners who have had the bulk of their language assistance in a one-on-one configuration or who have not experienced integration in

Chronicle 3.2

Dealing with Heavy Caseloads

By an ESL Teacher

Last year was chaotic, and given the bumps in enrollment, this year promises to be even more chaotic! I am an ESL teacher in a small, rural school district. The school board tells us that money is tight, but I feel that in my efforts to serve multilingual learners, I am actually doing them a grave disservice. I have teaching responsibilities at four different schools—two elementary, one middle school, and one high school. My caseloads at each school range from six to 30 multilingual learners. The students range in English-language proficiency from the preproduction level to nearly fluent.

There is no way I can be at each school each day—the schools are at least 10 miles apart, and because my schedule is so unpredictable I cannot participate in grade-level teams at any school. The physical space I have to teach in varies at each building, depending on how much space the principal can spare. In some buildings I have to work at a table in the library; in others I may be given be a small classroom. Most of my teaching materials are in the trunk of my car.

I cringe when I hear that a student needed my help with a project or a parent dropped by the school to speak with me and I missed the opportunity to clarify, explain, or reassure because I was at another school. There is no continuity in my instruction. Pretty much, I can only manage to help multilingual learners with their homework or projects, many of which are linguistically and culturally inappropriate. I feel that I am not providing the high-quality instruction I know my students need. More important, my body and my mental health may not withstand yet another chaotic year.

Questions for Discussion

1. What assistance do you imagine is in place for multilingual learners when this teacher is at another building?

2. What does this learning environment communicate about the value the district places on the multilingual learners it serves? What assumptions are being made?

3. What must be done to improve the learning environment for multilingual learners in this school district?

nonacademic classes are less likely to develop their language and academic skills at the same rate as those who have had many opportunities for group interaction in an instructional setting.

In the interest of equity and protection from discrimination, classrooms for multilingual learners should not be isolated in a remote location or differ in quality from the classrooms the school provides for English-speaking students. These students often face problems fitting in with their peers. Creating supportive and inclusive school and classroom environments for all should be a goal for administrators and educators who support multilingual learners. Ensuring that no student feels isolated or set apart promotes a smooth acculturation experience (Chhuon & Hudley, 2010; Freire, 2014; Grosjean, 2015b; Monz & Rueda, 2009; Morita, 2004; Toohey, 1996). Instruction in the hall, on the stage, in mobile units on the playground, or in the lunchroom is not acceptable. Student desks, classroom furniture, and other equipment should be on par with what all other children in the school are using. Multilingual learners should have equitable access to all resources that are available to every other student in the building, even providing those resources in the students' home languages. Multilingual learners and their families are very aware of substandard room assignments, lack of connectivity and technology tools, poor-quality equipment, and barriers to educational programs that preclude their participation. Such situations send a clear message that often results in lower self-esteem and pessimism, which in turn influence academic and linguistic achievement negatively. Table 3.1 can be used to rate the adequacy of resources for multilingual learners.

Table 3.1 Rating the School's Resources

For each sentence below, rate the degree to which the item is true in your school.

1 = Hardly 2 = Somewhat 3 = Mostly 4 = Very much so				
Sufficient age-appropriate content-area materials are available in students' home languages and English.	1	2	3	4
Sufficient student materials that correspond to students' levels of English proficiency are available.	1	2	3	4
Sufficient teacher resource materials and technology are available.	1	2	3	4
Adequate and useful curriculum guides are available in all content areas for all teachers who serve MLs.	1	2	3	4
Sufficient supplementary books are available in home languages and English.	1	2	3	4
Supplementary materials, manipulatives, and other visual and technological resources are readily available to MLs and their teachers.	1	2	3	4
The library has sufficient leisure reading materials in MLs' home languages and English.	1	2	3	4
Classrooms are set up in such a way that MLs have opportunities (social and academic) to interact with English-speaking peers.	1	2	3	4
Classrooms provide comfortable space for the number of students they hold.	1	2	3	4
Classrooms for MLs are in the midst of all other classrooms.	1	2	3	4
ML classrooms are equipped equitably when compared to classrooms for English-speaking peers.	1	2	3	4

ML, multilingual learner.

MTSS Team Activity

Assign students and teachers from each grade level and each classroom the task of taking four photographs of their rooms and the interior of the school, two of spaces or things they like, and two of those they do not like. Include common spaces such as the library, the lunchroom, and central office. Make copies of the list in Table 3.1, and rate each classroom and area of the school as to the quality of resources it offers. The photographs serve as reminders of how different classrooms look, but they also give the team a sense of students' perspectives of their own environment. You can make the activity more interesting by not indicating which photographs were positive and which were negative. Ironically, this activity will be much more difficult for schools that do not have adequate resources. Taking photographs and making prints or slides on the computer will be more complicated than in a school in which resources are abundant.

Design of the Instructional Program

The creation of an effective instructional program is no small endeavor. It requires an understanding of the law (to establish minimum requirements), a needs assessment (to establish the needs within the district), and a review of the research (to establish which pedagogical practices would be most effective for the specific population of multilingual learners). Many districts maintain a language assistance program for multilingual learners that was formally established years ago and may now be based on outdated research and practices. Just as demographics change (through changes in immigration patterns, numbers of newly enrolled students, and home language backgrounds), so do new research findings, and laws or regulations to meet new needs. Often the basic instructional program design is kept, with small changes made to meet immediate needs on a short-term basis. Over time, staff members realize that the current way instruction is provided no longer works efficiently and effectively and begin to modify it to fit new contexts (N. Flores & Schissel, 2014).

State and federal legislation and court cases set the minimum standard for the learning environment of multilingual learners. At the very minimum, the instructional design for educating multilingual learners must conform to statutory demands delineated in both federal and state laws as well as court case precedents (see Online Resources: "Key Federal and State Laws and Court Cases Regarding Multilingual Learner Education"). Ignorance of the law is no excuse for a school's failure to meet the requirements of the law. However, simply meeting legal requirements does not result in the most effective plan for teaching multilingual learners. An evaluation of the program design, from the perspective of different constituent groups, not only serves as the foundation for our framework but may also indicate where other systemic learning support strategies are warranted. Addressing the needs of different constituent groups at the beginning of the process of program design ensures that the design has broad-based appeal and remedies missing components or services identified by ESL/bilingual teachers, classroom teachers, administrators, parents, and multilingual learners.

Research on program effectiveness, along with the minimal requirements of state law, should inform decisions regarding the suitability of the instructional program design. Miramontes et al. (2011) assert that crucial decisions should be made to ensure that students are (1) developing proficiency in English; (2) learning what the academic curriculum offers; and (3) as much as possible, continuing to develop their home language. As Nguyen (2012a) and de Jong (2012) suggest, decisions regarding program design should be made by administrators and staff based on the real needs of the population and the long-term goals of the students. Districts and schools need to take a flexible approach in their program design to be able to meet the diverse needs that exist in the community that the school serves (Palmer & Martínez, 2013).

MTSS Team Activity

Have team members reflect on the existing program model used to serve multilingual learners in their school or district. Ask team members to respond to the following questions: "What is the educational theory (or experimental strategy) that is reflected in the way we teach our multilingual learners? To what extent are the multilingual learners in our district/school making academic and linguistic progress? Do they have good mental health and well-being?" Have individuals write down their thoughts, discuss these with a partner, and then hold a group discussion.

We have strong evidence regarding two general aspects of the program for multilingual learners: the use of the home language and culture, and the approach to developing proficiency in English as a second or new language. As far as the first aspect is concerned, there is a considerable body of research that points to the crucial role of the home language in the academic achievement of multilingual learners (August & Shanahan, 2008; Collier & Thomas, 2017a, 2017b; Genesee et al., 2006; K. Kohnert et al., 2005; Lindholm-Leary, 2012; Piasta & Wagner, 2010; Roberts, 2008; Soltero-González, 2009; Thomas & Collier, 2017). The International Literacy Association advises educators to teach initial literacy skills in students' home language whenever possible to prevent reading difficulties in the future (International Literacy Association, 2019). Children who never learned to read or who have not received subject-area instruction in their home language are at a distinct disadvantage when compared with multilingual learner peers who did. More is said regarding the importance of the home language and culture later in this chapter.

As for ESL instruction, since the early 1990s, research-based instructional approaches that integrate language and content to foster the academic progress of multilingual learners have been widely advocated (Echevarria et al., 2017; Genesee & Hamayan, 2016). Studies (Collier & Thomas, 2017a, 2017b) show that multilingual learners who received traditional ESL instruction, as opposed to content-based ESL instruction, are likely to experience more academic difficulty.

Although program design is important and necessary, it alone is not sufficient. Consideration must also be given to the actual program configuration. That is, one must consider the manner in which the teachers and students are organized within the classroom so that the actual interactions and teachable moments may occur (e.g., Flege, 2019; García & Kleifgen, 2010). This consideration is essential because it helps specify the actual implementation of the program design. Examples of the different configurations that may be chosen include self-contained classes, pullout programs, and resource rooms. All of these configurations may produce solid results, but they must be implemented properly. If not implemented properly, multilingual learners may have insufficient amounts of comprehensible instruction and insufficient peer interaction; consequently, they experience academic and linguistic difficulty.

In addition, if school districts are engaged in some other type of building or district-wide innovation or initiative, such as comprehensive school reform, implementation of professional learning communities, adoption of a **Universal Design for Learning (UDL)** approach (CAST, 2018), or another systems model, care must be taken to ensure that multilingual learners are considered from the outset and their strengths and needs are incorporated into the action plan. Regardless of the specific program design, Commins (2012) suggests seven critical features that can guide educators' efforts to address the needs of multilingual learners adequately. These critical features are included in the checklist in Box 3.2.

Range of Services Offered

Once the program design has been determined and the instructional emphasis decided, the range of services—that is, the frequency and duration of instructional services offered to multilingual learners at all levels of academic English language development—must be considered. The possibilities extend from the minimal to the optimal. Some language assistance programs offer a minimal amount of services: one period of ESL instruction each day or allowing multilingual learners to participate in language assistance programs for only 1 year. Other programs provide a full day of comprehensible instruction and allow multilingual learners to participate at all levels of English language development until they are able to compete academically in a general education classroom with their English-speaking peers. Multilingual learners whose only comprehensible instruction occurs during short periods when they are with their ESL/bilingual teacher are more at risk for academic difficulty than multilingual learners who are provided language support services designed to meet the students' academic and linguistic needs across all settings and during the 5 to 7 years they are acquiring academic English (Carhill et al., 2008; Collier & Thomas, 2017a; Cummins, 2012; Genesee et al., 2006; Hoff et al., 2012).

Role of the Home Language

In quality programs for multilingual learners, the role of the home language(s) in instruction is never left to chance. When multilingual learners have the opportunity to acquire literacy in their home language, the probability of future academic and linguistic difficulties diminishes (August & Shanahan, 2008; Beeman & Urow, 2013; International Literacy Association, 2019; Krashen, 2003; Reyes & Azuara, 2008; Roberts, 2008). In addition, planning for use of the home language in instruction is essential for building on

Box 3.2

Checklist for Assessing Programs for Multilingual Learners (MLs)

We have created a climate of belonging by . . .

___ Using materials that value students' home languages and cultures

___ Reaching out to parents and community members

___ Encouraging parents to interact with their children in their home language

___ Bringing the value of bilingualism for all students to the forefront

___ Encouraging parents to help develop and participate in school activities

We have implemented standards-based instruction by . . .

___ Organizing instruction around a common body of knowledge, with attention to differentiation in the methods of delivery

___ Addressing language proficiency as well as academic content standards in every lesson and unit of study for MLs

___ Identifying enduring understandings and essential academic language and highlighting them in instruction

___ Gathering curriculum materials at a wide range of reading levels

___ Obtaining adequate materials for meeting state standards

We use data to inform and shape instruction by

___ Finding out who the learners are and what strengths and experiences they bring to instruction

___ Assessing students' academic and literacy skills in their home language

___ Using multiple forms of assessment to document students' progress as well as attainment of benchmarks

___ Taking into account the time that it takes MLs to acquire the academic language that is needed for school success

We elevate oral language practice by . . .

___ Providing constant opportunities for interaction in order to increase peer-to-peer interaction

___ Using well-planned cooperative structures integrated throughout a unit of study and within each lesson

___ Determining the language structures required for participation in instructional activities, and providing students with opportunities to practice them aloud

We deliver meaning-based literacy instruction by . . .

___ Using text to represent ideas and concepts that students understand and can say

___ Incorporating language experience approaches

___ Making conscious connections between the big ideas from the content areas and what students will read and write during literacy instruction

___ Making clear connections across content areas

___ Preparing all teachers to make or to encourage students to make cross-linguistic connections that strengthen learning

We prepare the physical environment to tie meaning to text by . . .

___ Using every inch of the classroom as a resource for students in their independent work

___ Making it apparent through words and pictures posted on the walls what students are learning about

We collaborate with our professional colleagues by . . .

___ Taking a school-wide perspective on meeting students' needs

___ Working in grade-level or content-area teams

___ Finding time to articulate across grade levels: topics and genres, enduring concepts, shared resources, expectations, and assessments

___ Involving practitioners—not just the ESL and bilingual staff—in decisions regarding the instruction of MLs

Adapted from Commins, N. (2012). What are defining features of effective programs for English language learners? In E. Hamayan & R. Freeman Field (Eds.), *English language learners at school: A guide for administrators* (2nd ed., pp. 98–99). Philadelphia, PA: Caslon.

multilingual learners' strengths, activating prior knowledge, and assisting with the **transfer** of knowledge to the second language (O. García & Kleifgen, 2010; O. García et al., 2016; Genesee et al., 2006; Gibbons, 2015; Hamayan et al., 2013). Articulating how home language(s) will be used across grade levels helps administrators and educators purchase sufficient content and literacy materials. It is also important to support educators with professional learning opportunities to develop units, lessons, and materials that integrate the students' home languages.

We must guard against the two extremes of using the home language in instruction: (1) token use of the home language in instruction and (2) relying heavily on the home language simply as a short cut to convey meaning. We must understand that the home language supports the development of academic English for typically developing multilingual learners as well as those who experience language impairment or learning disability (K. Kohnert et al., 2005; Paradis et al., 2021). For example, offering multilingual learners simultaneous translation of instruction or bringing in a teaching assistant whenever possible to translate the English classroom instruction in small groups of students is not effective home language instruction. This short-term and haphazard approach limits language proficiency and skill development (Miramontes et al., 2011). While students appear to be receiving support in their home language, concurrent translation and other such approaches result in an uneven learning experience from year to year. At the same time, we must beware of the home language taking precious time away from opportunities to use expressive language and to comprehend in English. Multilingual learners with such uneven experiences in instruction are likely to experience both short- and long-term academic and linguistic challenges (Genesee, 2012; Harry & Klingner, 2014).

Role of the Home Culture

A culturally sustaining curriculum delivered in a culturally responsive way is critical to multilingual learners' academic and linguistic success because learning is an interaction between individual learners and an embedding context (Bruner, 1996; H. L. Damico et al., 2017; Hammond, 2014; Lantolf & Thorne, 2006; Rogoff, 2003; Watson-Gegeo, 2004; Wells, 1986). We often forget that in addition to the challenge of learning new and abstract concepts in a language they are not yet proficient in, multilingual learners have to overcome the hurdle of learning in sometimes unfamiliar contexts. As Hammond (2014) suggests, multilingual learners process information in culturally familiar and comfortable ways, and that is how they learn best. These culturally specific information processing strategies may be at odds with the way that information is presented in the classroom, which can make learning challenging. This is true even for multilingual learners who were born in the United States if their home culture is not represented in the cultures that the school values or that are represented in the textbooks that are being used. It is more difficult for multilingual learners to reach optimal levels of achievement in the content-area curriculum when a school does not have a culturally responsive environment (Hammond, 2014).

When students' home cultural contexts are integrated into teaching and learning experiences, multilingual learners will have relevant and familiar contextual and information processing scaffolds on which to build new knowledge and skills in the new language (Gibbons, 2015; Hammond, 2014). With the familiarity of their home cultural contexts seen in the materials and activities used in the classroom, school becomes a truly inclusive and sustaining environment. Curricula can be culturally responsive and sustaining in many different ways (Banks, 2005; D. Paris & Alim, 2017). A good foundation includes infusion of the history and culture related to students' native countries into the social studies curriculum as well as a curriculum that centers on the experiences of First Nations, immigrants, refugees, and African Americans (Marshall & Toohey, 2010; Sleeter, 2012). Instructional teaching strategies, student learning activities, and assessment tasks should be carefully chosen in all content-area subjects to build on and activate prior knowledge and to illustrate concepts and skills in multiple ways that are familiar to the participating multilingual learners. Resources integral to instruction, as well as those selected to provide enrichment or extension, should be reflective of multilingual learners' background and previous experiences to promote optimal learning and reduce cultural bias.

Meaningful cultural learning begins with allowing all students to view the curriculum from multiple perspectives. This enriches the school experience for everyone, not just multilingual learners. Presenting history, science, literature, and mathematics from multiple viewpoints opens a window for all students and allows students to be better prepared to live in the world they will encounter when they leave school (Gilbert, 2005). Making certain that multilingual learners see themselves reflected in the curriculum is critical in keeping these students motivated, in affirming their multicultural identities, and involving them in school (Bak, 2016; Calderón et al., 2011; Cloud et al., 2009; de Jong, 2011). Stereotypical cultural experiences presented in school that promote caricatures of different ethnic groups make students ashamed of their ethnic identity, language, families, and community. This separation may lead to other difficulties (Chhuon & Hudley, 2010; Darling-Hammond, 2013; Freire, 2014; Monz & Rueda, 2009; Morita, 2004; Ozfidan & Toprak, 2020; Toohey, 1996). Cultural relevance goes beyond school and into the extracurricular activities. Multilingual learners may not take advantage of all the activities that the school offers if they are excluded, not invited, or if the activities do not seem relevant to them. As Chronicle 3.3 illustrates, a little effort goes a long way toward increasing the integration of multilingual learners in all aspects of school life, including extracurricular activities.

Chronicle 3.3

A Small Effort Has a Long-Term Effect

By an ESL/Bilingual Junior High Teacher

My principal called me into his office one day and said that he was bothered by the fact that multilingual learners were not participating much in extracurricular activities. He asked me why the multilingual learners were not attending the basketball games and the dances and said that he wanted to increase their participation in these and other extracurricular activities. I asked him the following: How many multilingual learners were on the team or support the team? How many songs played at the dances appealed to multilingual learners? How many of these multilingual students are on the planning committees for school activities and events?

Clearly, these questions had never crossed his mind. And this principal was someone who was very committed to helping students. He was a true advocate of preteens. He just had never contemplated the situation from the perspective of these students. He and I hatched a plan to begin working with all the coaches and club sponsors to be sure the gatekeeping mechanisms did not exclude multilingual learners and that they were actively recruited to help plan and participate in extracurricular activities. We also made sure that the school provided support for multilingual learners who wanted to participate but did not have adequate resources (such as money for

(continued)

Chronicle 3.3

continued

By an ESL/Bilingual Junior High Teacher

uniforms, transportation, and someone to help the kids practice before tryouts). All the staff members were enthusiastic about the endeavor. Slowly, we saw participation increase. I left the school at the close of the school year to take another position.

About 10 years later, I was sitting in a conference session on the topic of extracurricular involvement when a man sitting behind me raised his hand and shared with the group the incredible statistics he had regarding extracurricular participation of cultural and linguistic minorities at his middle school. Everyone in the audience wanted to know the name of the school that had achieved such tremendous success. It was the same school in which the

principal and I had hatched our plan. It is gratifying to know that even with changes in personnel and leadership (the principal had since retired) the goal of multilingual learner participation in extracurricular activities was still being implemented and pursued.

Questions for Discussion

1. Many changes that are made at the program level do not survive beyond the tenure of the individuals who initiated the change. What could have contributed to the long life of this change?

2. How would you approach coaches, club sponsors, and volunteers who help with extracurricular activities with a challenge like this one?

Characteristics of Instruction

The quality of instruction influences the learning environment for multilingual learners. As there has been a greater orientation to sociocultural aspects of second language acquisition, the actual instructional interactions and contextualization have come under greater scrutiny (Lantolf & Thorne, 2006; Swain & Deters, 2007). This should come as little surprise because the impact of teacher interaction and instruction has proven to be a crucial variable to successful learning in many other aspects of education (Allington, 2002b; Cunningham & Allington, 2011; H. L. Damico et al. 2017; Geekie et al., 1999; Langer, 2001; Lave, 1988; Maxwell et al., 2017; Pressley et al., 2001; B. M. Taylor et al., 2000; Ullucci & Howard, 2015). Regardless of the specific instructional strategies or approaches used in the classroom, three principles of effective instruction for multilingual learners must be applied: increased comprehensibility, increased interaction, and the promotion of higher-order thinking skills (H. L. Damico et al., 2017; Miramontes et al., 2011). Approaches that increase comprehensibility of content-area material, language, and literacy include sheltered English instruction (Echevarria et al., 2017) and content-based ESL (Cloud et al., 2010; Genesee & Hamayan, 2016; Janzen, 2008). Approaches that increase peer interaction for multilingual learners include cooperative learning, cross-age and peer tutoring, opportunities for integration with English-speaking peers, and use of hands-on manipulatives and other physical models (Brown-Jeffy & Cooper, 2012; Hill & Flynn, 2006; Klingner et al., 2004; Lesaux & Harris, 2015; Schall-Leckrone, 2018).

Multilingual learners should be exposed to higher-order thinking skills instruction from the very beginning of their schooling; there is no need to postpone this instruction until they are fluent in English. There have been a number of strategies that have been used to promote higher-order thinking skills in multilingual learners (Callahan & Gandara, 2014; Connor et al., 2009; Dufva & Alanen, 2005; Janzen, 2008). By using speaking and writing to mediate cognitively complex activities, what Swain and Deters refer to as "languaging" (2007, p. 822), complex concepts can be understood and internalized (H. L. Damico et al, 2017; Licona & Kelly, 2020; Swain, 2006). Similarly, engaging students in cross-linguistic reflection and making cross-linguistic connections (Genesee & Hamayan, 2016) by using bridging strategies (Beeman & Urow, 2013) and translanguaging (Garcia et al., 2016) also engenders higher-order thinking. Hadjioannou (2007) advocates for more authentic, dialogue-oriented interactions in the multilingual learner classroom in order to increase perspective-taking and higher-order skills. A focus on content-area skills and concepts with an emphasis on academic language development contained within thematic and integrated units of instruction is essential. Familiarity with the process of second language acquisition and English as a new language standards (also known as *English language proficiency standards*), language development standards of the students' various home languages, and content-area standards allows teachers to align these standards, and in the process set high yet reasonable expectations for multilingual learners (e.g., Meisuri et al., 2018). All teachers—not just ESL or bilingual teachers—should be encouraged to differentiate their instruction to meet the range of academic and linguistic skills found in the groups of multilingual learners they serve.

Multilingual learners exposed to poor instruction or instruction that does not incorporate best practice as outlined in the research on ESL/bilingual education are likely to have their academic and linguistic growth stifled and hindered.

Characteristics of Assessment

For an assessment to be comprehensive enough to serve its purposes, it should involve both formative and summative measures and should include qualitative and quantitative data. This ensures that both the process and the product of meaning-making are addressed and that both rich descriptions of strengths and areas of difficulty and numerical data for comparison purposes are available. Assessment should be student centered and embedded in instruction. Assessment should span all four language domains—listening, speaking, reading, and writing—and should measure progress in all content areas. Self- and peer review should be integral components. Evaluations of student work samples should be made against clear and understandable criteria. For multilingual learners specifically, assessment should be conducted in the home language and in English (Boerma & Blom, 2017; J. S. Damico, 2019a, 2019b; Gottlieb, 2021; Gutierrez-Clellen et al., 2012; Hammer et al. 2007, 2012; Kapantzoglou et al., 2012; Oller & Eilers, 2002).

Traditional assessment practices administered in English only do not provide a full picture of what multilingual learners know and can do. Standardized and multiple-choice tests tend to have several problems that make them ill-suited for multilingual learners (Ivey & Broaddus, 2007; Menken, 2008; Neill, 2012). First, these tools typically focus on superficial aspects of language structure (e.g., vocabulary, verb tenses) and learning (e.g., informational comprehension that only requires repeating brief facts) rather than on more complex and authentic aspects of texts (J. S. Damico, 2019d; Wells, 1998). Second, they are language dependent, making it difficult to ascertain whether the student does not know the content being assessed or does not know the language needed to express knowledge of the content. Third, they are primarily dependent on acquisition and use of knowledge within a particular cultural context—one that does not incorporate the multilingual learner's cultural knowledge system. Authentic assessment is often promoted in the field of ESL/bilingual education as a mode of assessment that must be paired with traditional assessment measures to obtain valid and reliable student profiles. Authentic assessment for learning consists of any method of finding out what a student knows or can do that is intended to show growth and inform instruction and is an alternative to traditional forms of testing (J. S. Damico & Nelson, 2012; Gottlieb, 2016, 2021; Heritage & Harrison, 2019). Educators should be wary of drawing conclusions about student progress based on standardized test scores in English. The use of dynamic assessment, curriculum-based assessment, authentic and descriptive classroom-based assessment administered bilingually provides a better profile of what students know and can do. The characteristics of effective assessment are discussed in greater detail in the remaining chapters.

Evaluating the Adequacy of the Learning Environment

An accurate and comprehensive picture of the learning environment that has been created in school must be assembled to determine whether multilingual learners are being given the best opportunities to learn (Gee, 2008). The current learning environment must be evaluated, but in addition, for older students, some information must be obtained about the learning environment that surrounded them in the past. Previous schooling is one of the integral factors, and will be described in a later chapter.

Qualitative information about the learning environment can be collected informally by interviewing and surveying teachers and administrators. Teacher observations and anecdotes may also provide insight into how multilingual learners are responding to different aspects of their school environment (J. S. Damico, 2019d; Dunaway, 2021; Ivey & Broaddus, 2007; van Kraayenoord, 2010). In addition, MTSS team members may choose to use a more standard tool or protocol to obtain evaluations of the different aspects of the learning environment (see Online Resources: "Gathering Information and Evaluating the Adequacy of the Learning Environment"). Regardless of how information is obtained about the learning environment, it is essential that different types of school staff give their opinions because we often find that teachers, students, parents, or administrators may assess the same learning environment differently (Archibald, 2017).

Enhancing the Learning Environment

Box 3.3 lists some suggestions for interventions that would have a system-wide impact at the school or district level. Because the MTSS team is intended to serve an advocacy role in addition to its pedagogical one, it is important to

Box 3.3

Policies, Practices, and Strategies for Creating an Effective Learning Environment for Multilingual Learners (MLs)

Teachers

- Use a plan for the recruitment, hiring, and retention of teachers that reflects the student population based on historical and projected demographics.
- Post job vacancies in publications that ESL/bilingual teachers read.
- Partner with universities that have preservice requirements in ESL/bilingual programs.
- Work with local high schools and Future Teachers of America to help "grow your own" teacher candidates.
- Start a graduate level cohort of teachers who receive training that leads to ESL/bilingual certification.
- Design and implement a long-term professional learning plan that includes all staff that interact with MLs and focuses on ML education.
- Institute a mentoring and/or coaching program.
- Reduce large class sizes and ESL/bilingual teacher caseloads.

Resources

- Ensure that MLs receive an appropriate allocation or percentage of the entire district/school budget.
- Incorporate the resources needed to teach MLs in all grant budgets, not just those that are focused on ML education.
- Inventory the number of home language materials in the school library, classroom libraries, and classrooms (students can do this as a project) and ensure that they are at par with materials in English.
- Inventory all teaching materials to be sure everyone has what they need.
- Audit use of space in the building and make changes to assure that MLs have instruction in equitable instructional areas.
- Revamp the building scheduling process to allow MLs to participate in nonacademic classes with their monolingual English peers.

Program Design

- Have individuals who play different roles in the school evaluate the effectiveness and efficiency of the existing program design.
- Gather information on long-term academic achievement and high school graduation rates of your MLs.
- Investigate clustering MLs into mainstream homerooms.
- Make sure that the various programs established in the school flow into one another and are coordinated with one another rather than having separate programs that students enter and exit.

Range of Services Offered

- Increase the weekly frequency of specialized support that MLs receive.
- Extend specialized support that MLs receive for a longer period of participation.

- Ensure that the support that MLs receive is cohesive and connected to what is being taught in the content area classrooms.
- Avoid pulling MLs out to work on decontextualized, splinter-skill tasks out of context that will not transfer to real learning contexts.

Role of Home Language

- Provide home language instruction. In cases where formal instruction in the home language is not possible (e.g., having only two students in the entire school with the same home language), ensure that teachers create opportunities for students to use their home language in school and that home language support is set up outside of school.
- Help teachers plan how they can integrate students' home language(s) into their lessons by bridging and translanguaging strategies.
- Create a district and curricular plan for language allocation.
- Examine the home language support that is given to each group of students over the entire range of grades to ensure that it makes developmental sense.
- Ensure that the support that is given in the home language is well integrated with the rest of instruction that the student receives.

Role of Home Culture

- Complete a cultural responsiveness audit of the existing curriculum.
- Evaluate the extent to which the cultures represented within the school are visually and orally reflected in the daily functioning of the school.

Characteristics of Instruction

- Ensure that all teachers who work with MLs are using sheltering strategies that make the language of instruction more comprehensible.
- Assess the extent to which there is interaction among students in the classroom that helps MLs reach curricular goals.
- Evaluate the curriculum and classroom activities to make sure that they promote high levels of thinking skills.

Characteristics of Assessment

- Make sure that performance-based assessment is used and that results of such assessment play a significant role in the evaluation of the student.
- Ensure that teachers embed assessment into instruction.
- Assess in both students' home language and English whenever possible.
- Distinguish between assessment of language proficiency and academic achievement.
- Distinguish between social or conversational language proficiency and academic language proficiency.

build capacity at a level broader than the individual student, specific classroom, or school. Without such capacity building, the same procedures will likely have to be reestablished over and over again at different locations or with different multilingual learners. This results in inefficiency at best and a systemic failure at worst. These systemic interventions are likely to take time and need extensive planning to ensure their implementation and success.

Reflecting on the Six Integral Factors

While school-based MTSS teams work on the introspective assessment of the learning environment that has been created for multilingual learners, the school district as a whole must take time to study and reflect on each of the six integral factors presented in this guide. The explanation for many of the challenges that multilingual learners experience can generally be found when we examine the following:

1. Personal and family factors

2. Physical and psychological factors

3. Previous schooling/performance

4. Oral language and literacy development in both the home language and English

5. Academic performance

6. Cross-cultural factors

When considering multilingual learners who are experiencing difficulties, we are too quick to ask, "Is it a second language difficulty or is it a learning disability?" A more productive conversation can begin once you start to consider a broader range of explanations for these challenges and attempt to provide support on the basis of explanations that you propose as experienced professionals. To have this type of conversation we need to understand who these students are by paying attention to how the six integral factors laid out in this book can influence student learning.

Questions for Reflection and Action

1. What are the strengths and needs in the learning environment for all multilingual learners in our school?

2. How does the school learning environment support multilingual learners in achieving high academic expectations? How are these expectations communicated?

3. What data have been gathered through program monitoring and evaluation?

4. What systemic interventions are needed to enrich the learning environment for multilingual learners and give them the best opportunity to learn?

5. What changes to our policies and practices should we seek to implement?

6. What teacher/administrator professional learning opportunities are needed?

Chapter 4

Personal and Family Factors

Key Concepts. *The first integral factor to be considered is personal and family characteristics, including socioeconomic status, family dynamics, expectations, students' interests and motivation, experiential background, and parental engagement. It is important for multi-tiered system of support (MTSS) teams to learn about and understand the community and home contexts that impact learning for all students, including those who are experiencing challenges at school.*

Personal and family characteristics have a tremendous influence on every aspect of our lives, including success in school. For this reason, when students are experiencing challenges at school, we need to find out as much as we can about their lives outside of school. Learning something about students' personal and family backgrounds can help educators understand better and identify the strengths that these students bring with them from their homes and communities. Intentionally centering on and incorporating these strengths into instructional planning can enrich everyone's learning. Information about these characteristics can guide educators to find culturally and linguistically sustaining ways to support the students during instruction and assessment. Gathering information about students' home life and personal circumstances can also aid in evaluating students' progress more accurately by revealing the larger context within which the student functions (Bialystok et al., 2014; Bradley & Corwyn, 2002; DaSilvia-Iddings, 2009; Dudley-Marling, 2000; Durán-Cerda, 2008; Nieto, 2010).

In this chapter we discuss the personal and family characteristics that are likely to play a significant role in the academic performance of multilingual learners. The list is by no means exhaustive, but it is a good start. The chapter ends with suggestions for gathering information about these aspects of personal and family life, as well as suggestions to help build on the skills, resources, and talents that students bring with them (Cuero, 2010; Moll et al., 1992; D. Paris & Alim, 2017). These suggestions also offer ways to support multilingual learners as they navigate complex cultural norms and experiences that are similar or different from their own (Gursoy & Ozcan, 2018; Ladson-Billings, 2006).

Key Factors in the Student's Personal and Family Background

Multilingual learners and their families are shaped not only by the fact that they belong to an ethnic or linguistic minority that has immigration or refugee status as a result of their recent arrival in the United States, but are also shaped by the interaction of other social and political categorizations. This has been referred to as *intersectionality*, a term originally coined by Crenshaw (1989) and points to the complexity of factors that can affect multilingual learners and their families (Artiles et al., 2016; P. H. Collins & Bilge, 2016; Crenshaw, 1989; Harris & Leonardo, 2018; McCall, 2005). Among key personal and family variables that play an implicit or explicit role in orienting students toward learning are socioeconomic status (SES), family dynamics, expectations, the student's interests and motivation, experiential background, and parental engagement.

Socioeconomic Status

Considerable research has focused on the impact of SES on academic achievement (e.g., Arnold & Doctoroff, 2003; Carhill et al., 2008; Cheadle, 2008; Harris et al., 2008; Isaacs, 2012; Kalil, 2015; A. Portes & Fernández-Kelly, 2008). SES has a dramatic impact on school performance. In general, the higher the SES of the student's family, the higher the student's academic achievement is likely to be. Although SES is a complex and fluid construct whose actual influence is quite variable (Bassok & Galdo, 2016; Bolger et al., 1995; Bradley & Corwyn, 2002), this relationship has been demonstrated in countless studies and seems to hold no matter what measure of status is used—occupation of the principal breadwinner, family income, parents' education, or some combination of these (S. Brown & Souto-Manning, 2008; Ollendick et al., 1992). The most recent investigations of the impact of SES provide similar data to these earlier studies but with a bit more interpretive sophistication. Cheadle (2008), for example, employed Lareau's (2011) concept of "concerted cultivation" wherein parents of higher SES promote the deliberate cultivation of cognitive and social skills in institutions like schools to provide their children with advantages. Parents of lower SES, however, typically engage in a collection of practices to encourage children's spontaneous, rather than guided, development. As a consequence, according to Cheadle, children from higher SES are provided with various skills and expectations that are not always available to lower SES children, but that are advantageous in the academic context. These "educational investments" by the higher SES parents are an important mediator of disparities. According to Cheadle's and others' research (e.g., Bachman et al., 2020; Harris et al., 2008), socioeconomic background is the primary factor in gaps in academic performance.

Coming from a family with a lower SES almost always also means going to a school that does not meet high standards with regard to teacher turnover rates and the quality of instruction (Bettini & Park, 2021; Carhill et al., 2008; Haycock, 1998). Thus, the issue is muddied by the fact that students from lower SES levels typically end up in ineffective schools and therefore show lower academic achievement (Darling-Hammond, 2013; Sirin, 2005).

In the case of multilingual learner families, the family's current SES may have nothing to do with their SES in their home country. Many immigrant parents who were professionals in their home country and enjoyed a high level of income may find themselves working in blue-collar jobs in the United States. Educators should keep this in mind when obtaining information about the SES of a student's family (A. Portes & Fernández-Kelly, 2008; Sirin, 2005). Although the family might be experiencing economic difficulties currently, they would have benefited from the advantages of economic comfort in the home country such as high levels of education for the parents and access to good nutrition, healthcare, books and technology.

Meeting the families' physiological needs depends on employment and income. Many immigrant families are employed in lower-paying jobs, and therefore the immigrant family striving to meet the physical needs of all its members must expend significant effort at this lower level of the hierarchy of needs (Kozol, 1988; Ladd, 2012; Lareau, 2011; V. E. Lee & Burkham, 2002; Maslow & Lowery, 1998), at least for an initial period of time. This can be true of some culturally and linguistically diverse families whose children are born in the United States. In some families both parents work long hours; in other families parents stagger their shifts in order to have one parent at home when the other is at work, and in many families older children are expected to work and contribute a paycheck. Often the work is physically exhausting or even dangerous, and sometimes meeting the family's basic needs can be so all consuming that other needs go unmet.

Safety needs also figure prominently for multilingual learner families, particularly those in lower SES groups. Newly arrived immigrant families often first settle in poorer neighborhoods, many of which have a high crime rate. Safety concerns can interfere with children's ability to concentrate on their studies. Some multilingual learner families live in close quarters, where it may be difficult to find a quiet space for the children to do their homework. In general, children from lower SES homes do not have easy access to resources such as crayons, glue, books, a printer, or a reliable Internet connection (Bassok et al., 2016). Having all these resources at home gives higher SES children a tremendous advantage over their peers, who have to share the few crayons, one device, or other resources with siblings in order to complete an assignment and who cannot look up information they need for a report right in the comfort of their home.

Family Dynamics

Immigration, especially when it is by limited choice, can wreak havoc on the family structure. Children's separation from their parents, grandparents, or other caregivers and the change in family dynamics because of immigration can play a big role in multilingual learners' academic success by adding to the anxiety level that many students experience when they enter a new school.

The family's degree of mobility can play a role. Current anti-immigrant laws and attitudes can add tremendous anxiety and trauma to the family's resettlement experience (Blitz et al., 2016; Brunzell et al., 2019). Chronicle 4.1 describes one school district's response to the trauma caused to teachers, students, and their parents by the travel ban signed into law in 2017. As a result of the ways that immigration unfolds, many multilingual learners may have been separated from their parents for long periods. Parents may have left their children in the care of grandparents or other relatives while they immigrated to the United States, with the intention of sending for their children once they secured jobs and housing. In other situations, one parent may come to the United States with older offspring while leaving younger children back home with the other parent. In still other situations, parents may send their children to live with relatives already established in the United States. Parents' work schedules once they get to the United States may preclude much contact

Chronicle 4.1

Battling the Effects of Toxic Political Rhetoric and Policy

By a School District Administrator

The 2017 travel ban that mainly targeted Muslims wreaked havoc in my school district. Muslim staff, students, and their parents felt as though they had targets on their backs as a result of the ensuing anti-Muslim rhetoric that accompanied this executive order. One English-as-a-second-language (ESL) teacher had family on their way from Iraq when this order took effect. It was days, moving into weeks, before she knew where they were and whether they were safe. A bilingual teacher confided that she was afraid to go to the grocery store alone because she felt that her hijab singled her out for abuse in the community where she lives and shops. Her understandable fear persisted for weeks. As for students, social workers noted a distinct uptick in acting out, crying, and distractibility in class as children struggled to understand where en route family members were, why their parents were fearful to venture outside their homes, and whether they would be the next victims of bullying as they were seeing on broadcast news.

The school took immediate action both at the smaller scale school level and banded with the community for larger scale action. We wanted to remediate the noxious environment surrounding both students and teachers regardless of whether the trauma was primary or secondary. I believe that the large-scale response that our community had as a result of the travel ban had the greatest impact on those suffering from it, which is why the schools in our district participated fully in all of the related activities held in our community. The feeling of assault was so overwhelming, so encompassing, and cut so close to the bone, that the remedy could not be a Band-Aid (something I might have

implemented) or a large bandage (something the superintendent might have implemented). Rather, the remedy had to be so enveloping, so massive, and so unprecedented as to convince students and teachers that we would shelter them from the assault. Fortunately, we were poised to respond well and quickly; the superintendent and I have a close collegial relationship with the principal of the Muslim Day School across the field from our district office. We had been building a supportive infrastructure for several years before the travel ban: For example, in addition to the holy days observed in Christianity and Judaism, the holy days celebrated in Islam are also holidays on our school calendar.

Having worked for the past 3 years on a research project concerning this specific topic, I conclude that (1) to have sufficient impact and counter-effect, a coalition must be formed with the community to combat the racist, anti-immigrant political rhetoric and accompanying policies; (2) the coalition must involve more than just the teachers, the school, or even the district; (3) the coalition's efforts cannot just be window dressing, done piecemeal, or based on individual good intentions; and (4) it must reach deep into the school infrastructure to feel authentic, meaningful, and genuine.

Questions for Discussion

1. In this response to the crisis at hand, what is being gained beyond the immediate solace for students and teachers by the school fully supporting the Muslim community?

2. How would the scenario described in the chronicle differ if the community itself was divided by the political rhetoric and policy?

with their children during the workweek. The lack of regular and routine parent contact over months and even years may prove stressful for some students and may devastate the family dynamics.

Upon arrival in the United States, families may experience outside cultural and linguistic influences that also change the family dynamics. For example, as children acquire English proficiency at a faster rate than their parents, the school and, in some cases, the parents themselves tend to rely on the children to provide translation services. Whether children are translating for their parents in a doctor's office, to help purchase a car, or at a parent–teacher conference, such situations can affect the balance of power in the family structure, yielding more power to the child and less power to the parent. Schools must be diligent in providing trained translators or interpreters for all official meetings with families.

MTSS Team Activity

In many schools, teachers may not live in the neighborhood around the school, and thus do not know the comings and goings of the community. How familiar is the MTSS team with the school's neighborhood? For those team members who are not residents of the school neighborhood, assign a simple everyday errand to each staff member, such as borrowing a book from the local branch of the public library, buying a carton of milk from the local grocery store, and mailing something from the local branch of the post office. Have each person jot down notes so that they can tell others about their experience and about their impressions of the neighborhood.

In addition, if children have been discouraged in school from continuing to develop their home language, they begin to lose fluency in that language. Besides the negative effect that home language loss has on cognition and academics (Cummins, 2000; Gonzalez-Barrero & Nadig, 2018; K. Kohnert et al., 2005), the ties that bind parents to their children weaken (Harding-Esch & Riley, 2012). This has a significant effect on the strength of the family unit and certainly affects the students' well-being and positive identity formation.

The family may also have a gender role structure that is different from that of the community to which it has immigrated. The original family structure may change once the family immigrates, and this might result in added stress. For example, the original family structure may have been more patriarchal in the native country, but in the United States, mothers may feel pressured to have a stronger voice in decision-making. Shifting family dynamics can create conflict in the family.

Possibly as a result of tenuous employment status and strained family ties, families of multilingual learners may also move frequently. These moves may interrupt the children's instruction, whether they move across the United States following agricultural crop schedules or industrial plant openings or move between neighboring school districts in pursuit of more affordable housing or higher wages. Feelings of homesickness and a desire to stay connected to the home language, culture, and friends and relatives left behind can fuel the desire to return to the native country for long trips. Such trips, if not handled properly by the school, can exacerbate the effects of the family's mobility and the amount of interrupted education the student experiences, and thereby may hinder the multilingual learner's progress in school. Schools do well to recognize the transnational nature of many multilingual learners' lives, which carry deep connections to the native country as well as their new country. With that recognition, schools can develop policies and strategies to help students maintain continuity in their schooling experience even as they move between schools and school experiences (Jiménez et al., 2009; Nieto, 2010) instead of castigating them for their absences.

High levels of stress are not atypical in the families of multilingual learners. Even when parents are able to secure employment, such employment may be erratic or undependable, causing stress in the family. Many parents may not have access to the resources necessary to deal with such stress, and this situation can lead to depression, verbal abuse, physical abuse, or substance abuse. When these symptoms of stress emerge, parents may have little knowledge of support systems within the community they can turn to for help. Community and school support systems may or may not be culturally and linguistically responsive, thereby limiting the effectiveness of treatment.

Although the discussion so far has considered the negative effects of the family stressors associated with immigration, many immigrants are able to situate themselves in supportive and safe communities, get the help they need, and adapt quite well to their new surroundings (Ascenzi-Moreno, 2018; Stanton-Salazar, 1997; Trueba, 1988). However, school staff must be aware of the stressors that may be affecting some families of multilingual learners, and must be sensitive to the issues that may be causing a challenge for these multilingual learners at school. Because the presence or lack of support seems to be one of the major determinants of how well culturally and linguistically diverse families adapt to their environment, the school needs to work diligently to create that support for its students and their families as best as it can.

MTSS Team Activity

Have team members think about their expectations for their own children (hypothetically, if they do not have children). Have each person write down what those expectations are. Share those expectations with other members of the team, and discuss how they might be similar to or different from those of the parents of multilingual learners.

Expectations

Parents' and their children's expectations of education and their attitudes toward school influence multilingual learners' school success (N. Flores et al., 2015). Few parents would argue that education is not valuable for their children. Exactly why it is valued may differ among families and from the school's perspective. Parents from different cultural backgrounds may view education as the path to upward economic mobility and a way to gain entry into the workforce as soon as possible. Others may view education as a top priority for their sons but of less importance for their daughters. Still others may push the oldest child to pursue higher levels of education, with younger siblings expected to help support the eldest in this endeavor. Parents, students, and educators may find themselves at cross-purposes if the views of the parents and children are not in accordance with those of the school system. Even when families have high expectations for their children's education they may support their child in ways that are not acknowledged by the school. E. Garcia and Miller (2008) found that the vast majority of Hispanic families of young children believed that the experience of going to school would make their children's lives better. It is up to the school to create learning environments where all students can make academic progress and reach their academic, personal, and professional goals.

Student Interests

Students' interests come from their past and current lives outside of school, their hobbies, and their passions. Much has been said about the importance of a culturally responsive curriculum that taps into multilingual learners' interests in academic areas and extracurricular activities (Banks, 2005; Brown-Jeffy & Cooper, 2012; Gutiérrez & Larson, 2007; Ladson-Billings, 2014). These curricula incorporate the students' cultural backgrounds and interests as integral elements during learning activities rather than trivializing or negating them. As a result, culturally sustaining curricula are developed with multilingual learners' interests, talents, experiences, and strengths in mind. When students are provided with tasks and activities that are inherently engaging, their motivation rises (Callahan & Gándara, 2014; Hadjioannou, 2007; Janzen, 2008; Marzano, 2003; Swain, 2006). Schools should pay close attention to the interests of multilingual learners to create thematic topics, instructional and assessment tasks, and school activities that extend beyond the school day that are connected to the interests of the multilingual learners they serve (Milner, 2010).

Multilingual learners contribute the added advantage of bringing with them interesting and often dramatic experiences that monolingual English-speaking students can only read about in stories or see in documentaries or movies. When the curriculum integrates these different perspectives and experiences into the everyday working of the classroom, it gives the multilingual learner a sense of importance, value, and belonging. It is not only the multilingual learner who benefits from this culturally reciprocal approach to schooling (Harry et al., 1999; Kalyanpur & Harry, 1999; Lesaux & Harris, 2015); all students are enriched by this exposure.

Student Motivation

The link between student motivation and achievement is straightforward. If students are motivated to learn the content in a given subject, their achievement in that subject is most likely high. If students are not motivated to learn the content, their achievement is limited (Marzano, 2003). Although there are many theories that attempt to explain how motivation works, it would be wise to use these theories with the specific needs and wants of typical multilingual learners in mind (Jurado & Garcia, 2018; Möller, 2018; Suarez-Orozco,

1995). For example, according to attribution theory (Heider, 1958), success is attributed to one or more of the following four causes: ability, effort, luck, and task difficulty. The perception of one's ability is tainted for multilingual learners by a constant struggle to express what they know in their second or new language and constantly making mistakes and not being understood by others. As for effort, when multilingual learners spend hours each night doing homework that takes monolingual English students a fraction of the time, it gives them a skewed concept of what level of effort is rewarded and produces results. Student motivation wanes when teachers give multilingual learners assignments that are beyond their linguistic capabilities in English. When students are given engaging and interesting inquiry-based units of study that connect to their lives, they are more likely to talk about what they learned at school with their families and friends and will look forward to going to school. Students who are provided interesting, relevant, and challenging academic tasks in a nurturing and supportive environment will be motivated to learn.

MTSS Team Activity

Have each classroom gather statistics about students' hobbies and then graph the number of students participating in each hobby (relate to mathematics), and perhaps find the most popular hobby in the entire school (relate to social studies, science, art, or music). In addition to connecting content areas to an authentic everyday purpose, this list can inform teachers of their students' interests so that they can organize instructional themes around those interests. This will not only be useful to the teacher but will show students that they are heard and that their teachers paid attention to them.

Self-worth theory is based on the premise that the search for self-acceptance is one of the highest human priorities (Marzano, 2003; Stanton-Salazar, 1997; van der Putten, 2017). Self-acceptance or acceptance into one's peer culture can be very hard to come by for a multilingual learner. If academic achievement in English is a criterion for acceptance, multilingual learners may not experience that acceptance for years on end. If adeptness in social interactions is a criterion for acceptance, multilingual learners may also wait years to experience the English language proficiency and fluency such social interaction demands. Vitanova (2005) uses the work of Bakhtin (1981) and his dialogic philosophy to explain motivation and the construction of one's self. In effect, one can employ both internal and external dialogue to increase affective reactions and to create oneself through dialogue. As Swain and Deters put it, "Thus, to speak is to create oneself" (2007, p. 830).

Mawi Asgedom, a young man who emigrated from Africa as a child, says that while growing up in suburban Illinois as an multilingual learner, he sat through many awards ceremonies and never received any kind of acknowledgment for his efforts or his successes in learning English (Asgedom, 2002, 2003). Many awards were given—for perfect attendance, for honor roll achievement, for sports performance, for volunteering—but because he had limited English proficiency he was precluded from being considered for those awards (except for perfect attendance). Many U.S. states have put in place a process for students who reach high levels of literacy in two languages to acquire a Seal of Biliteracy upon graduation from high school. Teachers and families can work together toward the goal of incorporating bilingualism and biliteracy into the award system in place.

Experiential Background

When multilingual learners experience difficulty in understanding content area concepts, school team members often comment that they "lack the background knowledge essential to academic success." It is possible that a multilingual learner's background knowledge differs from the school's expectations. Many teachers and other school staff may come from backgrounds where everyone has had access to field trips to pumpkin farms, museums, or zoos. Team members may assume that everyone is familiar with indoor supermarkets, post offices, drive-through pharmacies, and banks (King & Fogle, 2013). Multilingual learners may enter school with a whole other set of experiences that give them a wealth of knowledge as varied and unique as those of monolingual English-speaking students. Families of multilingual learners may have had many varied firsthand experiences teaching school, building complex irrigation and other water systems, designing renewable energy systems, raising chickens to sell at a market, running a small business, building the family home with adobe bricks, or designing intricate patterns for textiles. Multilingual learners coming from war-torn areas or extreme poverty may have developed street smarts in their struggles to survive in their native country or in refugee camps. These **funds of knowledge** can prove to be a valuable resource in instruction (González et al., 2005; Moll et al., 1992). Grade-level teams can develop units of study that incorporate these skills and knowledge that would help students use them as contexts and bridges for academic learning; Chronicle 4.2 illustrates how a group of students were able

---

Chronicle 4.2

Is That What She's Talking About?

By an ESL Teacher

I was trying to teach about vertical and horizontal axes and points on a grid (typically taught in sixth-grade math) to my ESL students. My three students were boys from Vietnam. They spoke limited English and I spoke no Vietnamese. I had tried everything to make the concepts comprehensible—visuals, games, simulations, and manipulatives—all to no avail. After many excruciating attempts and failures to get the concept across, I had just about given up. All of a sudden, one of the students said to me, "Oh, I know—same you drive a boat!" This child had helped his uncle navigate a raft, using the stars, when they were fleeing Vietnam trying to make it to the refugee camps in Thailand.

He began explaining to the other two boys in Vietnamese, using gestures and drawing on the board. I could see that the two boys also knew what he was talking about. I felt so humble. These boys knew a lot more about math than I had given them credit for. I had failed to activate their prior knowledge, and in the process had almost given up.

Questions for Discussion

1. How can a teacher learn about her students' previous experiences?
2. How can the teacher connect these experiences to the curriculum?

to tap into their funds of knowledge about boating and, using Vietnamese, helped each other learn key concepts in math.

> **MTSS Team Activity**
>
> Begin keeping an inventory of interesting experiences students in the school have had. Be sure to include multilingual learners in the list. The inventory can be built by word of mouth or by students themselves contributing essays about their experiences. The inventory can serve as a "speakers' bureau" type of resource, where students can be called on to showcase their knowledge through vlogs, poetry, song, news reports, and other means. This can be done in the students' home languages and English even when educators only speak English.

Parental and Family Engagement

Parents' expectations of what their role should be in their children's formal education may vary among families who are used to educational systems other than those in the United States (King & Fogle, 2013). In their childhood or as parents of a schoolchild in their native country, they may have experienced a clear divide between home and school, with the school system actually discouraging their involvement in their children's schooling. They may see their roles and that of school staff as clearly divided, with parents responsible for providing children with love and nurturing, safety, the necessities of life, and moral education. They may see the teacher as responsible for providing instruction in the basic subject areas. When their children enroll in a U.S. school, some parents of multilingual learners may find the school's requests for input into decision-making, volunteering in the classroom, fundraising assistance, and field trip chaperoning quite perplexing. Some parents may even view the school's requests for the parents' help as an indication that the schools have abdicated their responsibility to educate children. Thus, if parents of some multilingual learners are not seen as being "involved" in their children's education, it may be because of divergent expectations (Verdon et al., 2014).

Parents' ability to participate in the education of their children can also be affected by their employment. The jobs that some parents of multilingual learners have may be quite restrictive in allowing workers time off. Even a phone call from the school that pulls a parent away from work can result in a disciplinary action initiated by the employer. If, in addition to these two factors, instruction in school happens primarily in English and parents of multilingual learners do not feel comfortable in that language, they may simply opt out of having a presence inside the school building. The good news is that these hurdles can be overcome, as we see in Chronicle 4.3.

However, lack of parent participation inside the school building does not preclude the support that they can give to their children inside the home. In fact, this support may influence student achievement even more significantly than parent participation at school (Chappell & Faltis, 2013; Epstein, 2001). School staff can communicate to parents and families that they are their children's most important teachers. When parents and family members talk with

Chronicle 4.3

Cutting into My Weekend

By the Director of a Bilingual Program

I had to get creative. Attendance at my parent meetings was abysmal. A handful of parents were attending meetings intended for the parents of 2,000-plus multilingual learners. I surveyed parents as to when they wanted to meet, willing to forgo my preferred times if it meant greater attendance. The parents asked for meetings on Friday nights and Sundays after church. Although these times certainly cut into my weekend, I realized I was getting nowhere fast by scheduling meetings on Thursdays at 7 p.m.

I implemented the new schedule, which alternated between Friday nights and Sunday afternoons. I was astounded—attendance was over 90%. Trying something so unconventional as weekend meetings emboldened me. I began to try new things: substituting the never-touched cookies and coffee with potluck suppers, incorporating opportunities for adult socialization into the meetings, offering door prize items deemed desirable by the families (such as 25-pound turkeys right before the holidays, gift certificates to indoor playgrounds and amusement parks), scheduling meetings in apartment community rooms rather than always on school grounds, establishing a crew of fathers who worked the swing shift to serve as field trip chaperones, and creating a drop-in parent center with a computer lab for parents. By doing all those things, I had the most supportive and active set of parents I had ever imagined.

Questions for Discussion

1. Why is it important to think nontraditionally about parent involvement?
2. Why is it important to think about what parents need in addition to what the schools need from parents? How does one do that?

their children in their home language about what they are learning at school, students' learning is reinforced. When teachers make instruction meaningful, exciting and engaging, students will naturally feel compelled to talk about school with their families (Sánchez-López & Young, 2018).

Schools that place their emphasis on finding ways to engage families and helping parents support their children's formal education (in their home language and in culturally comfortable ways) rather than demanding that parents be physically present through volunteering during school hours on school premises will likely see more return on their efforts (Bassok et al, 2016).

Information Gathering

How should educators go about gathering information about multilingual learners' personal and family factors? In two words: very carefully. We should be sensitive to multilingual learner families' need for privacy, just as we are with all families in our school communities. Note that if this information gathering is the first extensive contact with multilingual learner parents, they may be taken aback at the "invasion of their privacy" or they may be reluctant to give the information needed. We must first establish a milieu within the school in which parents feel welcome and see the staff as having a personal connection with at least their child if not with the parents themselves. It must be totally clear to the family that their customs, norms, and traditions are valued and are not in any way less prestigious than those of the monolingual English-speaking families (Cuero, 2010; Freire, 2014). In fact, family members must see evidence in every conversation with school staff, during every school activity, in classroom assignments, in enrollment processes, and in all communication sent home that their customs and ways of daily life are highly valued for what they can contribute, not only to their child's upbringing but to the school community in general.

We need to be clear to parents and children what kind of information we want and why. We must assure parents that the information is used to create a better learning environment for their children, and we need to show them the specific aspects of everyday school life that change as a result of the information gathered. We need to be aware of the fact that parents, especially those who have an undocumented status in the United States, may be extremely reluctant to give any kind of information that they perceive as threatening to their existence in the country. If an interpreter is used to obtain information in the parents' home language, that person must be carefully chosen. The interpreter must be someone with whom the parents feel comfortable and someone they can trust.

Both historical and current information are important in understanding the student's personal and family background. Information gathering in this area likely requires staff to have extensive conversations with the student and the student's family, siblings, teachers, and community members who interact with the student, such as coaches and ministers. Because much of the information obtained is of a sensitive nature, schools should build trust, establish a relationship with the family, and seek the cooperation of the parents at the very beginning of the process, keeping in mind the precautionary notes in the preceding paragraph.

Because parents of multilingual learner may not be proficient speakers of English, an interpreter can talk to the parents in their home language and can participate in the conversation. How to conduct the interviews has to be determined on an individual basis, depending on the relationship the staff and the interpreter have with the student and the family. Box 4.1 lists a series of questions that may be used to guide the conversations that take place with students and family members. It is not recommended that questions be posed one after the other. Rather, an informal, open-ended conversation can take place in a low-anxiety setting. Only if the interviewees are reluctant to say much or are silent can the questions be used to begin the conversation. The questions in Box 4.1 can serve not only to generate conversations but also to organize the information that is being gathered by various means. These interviews can take place preferably in the home or in the school district "family room" (school districts in Ontario, for example, have "Family Reception Centres" in the schools that serve multiple purposes). Staff can determine, again depending on the level of comfort with the family, whether to write notes on the spot or to do so later.

Another way to gather information is by using teaching strategies that inform us about students' lives while serving an instructional purpose. One of the most effective ways of finding out about students' lives is through dialogue journals (Peyton & Stanton, 1993). Dialogue journals are written conversations that take place between student and teacher. The teacher writes a brief

Box 4.1

Questions for Gathering Information on a Student's Personal and Family Background

Socioeconomic Status

- What job(s) does the father hold?
- What job(s) does the mother hold?
- What shift(s) does each work?
- What job did father or mother hold in the home country?
- How safe is the block on which the family lives?
- What kind of living space did the family have in the home country?
- Does the student have a quiet space at home to do homework or someplace else to go in the neighborhood?
- What magazines, other forms of print, and paper and writing tools are available in the home?
- Is there a computer or other device with an Internet connection in or near the home?

Family Dynamics

- What is the family's immigration story?
- Which family members emigrated together?
- Which family members are still in the native country?
- Who is at home when the student returns from school?
- What responsibilities do the children have at home?
- How do the children help their parents?
- Do the parents need a translator to communicate in English? If so, who translates for them?
- How well and how comfortably do the children communicate with elders in the home language (if that is the parents' and grandparents' more proficient language)?
- What evidence of stress is there on the family dynamics? If any, is it a result of one or both parents working outside of the home?
- How often has the family moved?
- What type of a formal support network—such as a religious center or a social services organization—does the family have? How about an informal support network—such as relatives or close friends or neighbors?

Expectations

- What do the parents want and hope for regarding their children's education?
- What role does a formal education play in the family's long-term plans?

- What is the highest level of education that parents would like for their children to attain?

Student's Interests

- How does the student spend his or her free time?
- What hobbies or interests does the student have?
- What curricular or extracurricular activities does the student enjoy?
- What talents and gifts does the student possess?
- Which of these talents and gifts was identified by the school? By the student? By the parents?

Motivation

- How enthusiastic is the student about going to school?
- How often does the student talk at home with family about what is being learned at school?
- How clear is it to the student that his or her advances in English and in academic performance are something to be proud of and to celebrate?
- How clear is it to the student that his or her advances in the home language are something to be proud of and to celebrate?
- Does the student have a sense of agency and self-advocacy?
- How clear is it to the student that his or her efforts to complete assignments are well appreciated?

Experiential Background

- What interesting experiences has the student had before arriving in the United States?
- What kinds of home and community experiences and expertise does the student have?

Parental Engagement

- What is the parents' understanding of their role vis-à-vis the school?
- What was the parents' role within the school in their native country?
- How comfortable do parents feel playing an active role within the school?
- How welcome do the parents feel in the school?
- How easy is it for parents to come to school during school hours?
- What are some examples of things that parents do at home to support their children's learning?

message to the student and the student writes back; the teacher responds to the content of the student's response without correcting grammatical errors but modeling correct writing for the student, and this exchange goes on. The "conversations" reveal much about the student, but a significant added bonus is that the language proficiency of multilingual learners' blossoms through use of these dialogue journals (Hamayan, 1994).

Schools may also review past school records. However, the parents may have left the records behind, or the previous school may not have provided them. Calls to the student's previous school or the teacher may prove fruitful. Some information may be gleaned from the district's database, such as lists of students eligible for free and reduced-fee lunch, though most districts have placed restrictions on who can and cannot view those lists. For families who have just arrived in the United States, it may be difficult to come by any kind of records, but this should not be perceived as the parents' fault. Even under the best of circumstances, if the family had time to prepare for their journey, immigration is a confusing process that could easily result in lost or misplaced papers (Bachman et al., 2020).

While information is being gathered, educators should consult with someone who can serve as a cultural liaison. This person may or may not be the same as the interpreter who conducted the interviews in the home language. If it is a different person it is advisable to keep the family identity anonymous. This cultural liaison assists with the explanation of the gathered information. This person should be someone who is familiar with the home culture of the student, the immigrant experience in the local community, and the culture of the school. Educators who know and understand the factors of SES, family dynamics, mobility, expectations, student interest, student motivation, experiential background, and parent engagement as they appear in the student's life in the native country can then compare and contrast how those same factors play out in the family's experience in the United States (Deming, 2009; Kalil & Mayer, 2016). With the insight of the cultural liaison, the ability to make accurate comparisons is enhanced, providing context to the educator's assessment of the student's situation and clarifying which personal and family factors are currently playing a role in the multilingual learner's success in school.

Systemic Support Strategies

If the school or district notes that significant numbers of their multilingual learners are affected by one or more of the previously mentioned personal and family factors, systemic support strategies are warranted. Systemic support strategies address the needs of current students and may serve to proactively prevent similar needs in future students coming to your school. Box 4.2 provides a checklist that includes some systemic strategies that districts can use to mediate potential challenges from personal and family issues, including SES, family dynamics and mobility, expectations, student interest and motivation, experiential background, and parental engagement.

Specific Support Strategies

If the school determines that some of these factors affect only a handful of students, the school can implement nearly all of the previously mentioned

Box 4.2

Systemic Strategies to Mediate Potential Challenges from Personal and Family Issues

Socioeconomic Status

- Establish some type of a family reception center with links to information provided by community agencies.
- Collaborate with families to create a toy, book, or software lending library.
- Open a computer lab that is available for parents and students during accessible public transportation times.
- Operate a food pantry and a clothes closet that accepts donations and allows parents to select needed clothing and food for their families.
- Offer adult ESL and General Educational Development (GED) courses; community job-training sessions; job searches and career planning; training on the topics of budgeting, insurance, financial planning, effective parent involvement; and avenues for financial assistance for postsecondary education.
- Start breakfast and lunch programs as well as in-school snack programs.
- Run after-school homework centers and district/state sponsored early childhood programs.
- Make refurbished school computers available for parents to purchase or lease.
- Open a school store selling school supplies at wholesale cost.
- Establish a scholarship fund for school field trips.
- Provide safe transportation for after-school programs.
- Work with a translation/interpretation training institution to provide an opportunity for parents and other community members to obtain credentials as an interpreter.

Family Dynamics and Mobility

- Set up a network of culturally and linguistically responsive counseling services.
- Establish a group of trained translators and interpreters, at least for the languages with the highest numbers of speakers in the school.
- Craft a district-wide policy for making up assignments when students take long trips back to the home country.

Expectations

- Maintain ongoing communication with all the communities the school serves to incorporate parents' expectations into policies and practices designed and implemented by the school.
- Offer parent-training workshops that demystify the school's expectations of parents.
- Offer workshops that suggest clear and pragmatic strategies to parents for supporting their children's formal education.
- Establish explicit strategies to honor and value the parents' perspective.
- Consult with parents when making any recommendations regarding the student's academics,

extracurricular activities, scholarship opportunities, and out-of-school activities.

Student Interest

- Design interest surveys to be included as a part of the registration process.
- Carry out a summer project to incorporate student background, culture, and interests into the curriculum and instruction for all students.
- Have all older students complete surveys that help them learn about their individual learning styles, strengths, and interests.
- Monitor artifacts of student interest such as attendance sheets in school clubs and intramurals.
- Periodically throughout the year, ask students to complete attitudinal surveys or hold focus groups about how they feel at school and in their classes.
- Analyze lists of students trying out for different sports, theater productions, and other competitions, and if multilingual learner (ML) participation is disproportionately low, promote outreach that targets these students.
- Note ML attendance at school dances and sporting events, and if ML participation is disproportionately low, promote outreach that targets these students.
- Encourage teachers to sponsor clubs and activities that they enjoy personally and invite MLs to participate.

Student Motivation

- Develop a checklist or rubric by which teachers can evaluate the appropriateness of the assignments they give MLs.
- Develop a checklist for the students to use to evaluate the appropriateness and comprehensibility of the assignments they receive.
- Develop a rubric by which teachers can assess elements of an engaging, interesting, and culturally relevant classroom lesson or unit of study.
- Develop a survey or checklist for students about the kinds of things they would like to learn or questions they have about the world.
- Tailor incentive programs to variables over which MLs have control.
- Institute celebrations and awards for accomplishments unique to MLs.
- Implement mechanisms that ensure MLs receive meaningful and personal feedback from the teachers on their academic and linguistic progress.

Experiential Background

- Build prompts (simulations, surveys, and peer conversations that explicitly connect to home language and cultural experiences of MLs) to activate students' experiential background and then incorporate these into the curriculum.
- Budget for field trips to provide students with interesting out-of-school experiences.
- Provide more instances that build necessary conceptual and experiential knowledge through

(continued)

Box 4.2 (*continued*)

the use of shared activities (e.g., using visuals, hands-on instruction, demonstration, simulations, experiments).

Parent Engagement

- Create policies and practices that emphasize and value parental support over parental participation.
- Create a school environment in which MLs' home language and culture are visibly present and valued.
- Provide resources for teachers to incorporate the students' home languages and cultures into the curriculum.
- Make the school more welcoming to ML parents.
- Provide professional learning opportunities to all who work with MLs, including parent–teacher association/parent–teacher organization board members.
- Establish a buddy system for newly arrived students and their parents.

- Establish a friendship network that pairs immigrant parents with other ML parents and with parents from the monolingual English parent group.
- Help parents to establish a carpool or bus transportation to school events.
- Provide childcare at school events.
- Help parents establish a cooperative for childcare needs.
- Host some school events in the community rooms of the home/apartment/condominium complexes where MLs live.
- Provide a line item in the budget for district training and payment of translators and interpreters.
- Establish a preference in hiring procedures for individuals within the immigrant community the school serves or at the very least include the ability to speak more than just English as a qualification for employment as a school clerk.

strategies on site, but on a more limited scale. For example, instead of providing a clearinghouse of information to all parents, one staff member could sit down with family members and direct them to linguistically and culturally responsive community agencies that can help the family with specific concerns. A teacher could help one family resolve transportation issues by providing a bus schedule for the area or connecting the family with another parent who lives nearby and is willing to carpool or provide a ride.

Questions for Reflection and Action

1. What additional information do we need regarding the personal and family factors affecting the multilingual learners we serve?
2. How are we responding to the personal and family needs of multilingual learners?
3. What are some steps we can take to make certain that information from multilingual learners and their families is gathered in a culturally and linguistically responsive manner?
4. How will the information gathered about students and their families be used so that it increases multilingual learners' engagement in school and supports their academic achievement?

5. Analyze the degree of correspondence between multilingual learners as a subgroup and the majority student population. Are there any mismatches between the two groups? If so, do school policies and practices help to mediate or exacerbate these mismatches?
6. Investigate the experiential background of the students in your school, both as a large group and as socioeconomic, linguistic, and cultural subgroups. What role do these backgrounds play in the way instruction is planned and delivered?

Physical and Psychological Factors

Key Concepts. *The second integral factor concerns physical and psychological considerations, including medical conditions, impaired vision or hearing, malnutrition and chronic hunger, effects of recent trauma, fear, psychological stress, social and emotional well-being, and feelings of belonging. If challenges arise related to these factors, physical and psychological support needs to be offered.*

Good (or at least neutral) physical and psychological states are the foundation on which the ecology of an individual's development and knowledge acquisition is constructed (Blackburn, 1991; Jack, 2000; Kagan, 2013; Manuck & McCaffery, 2014; K. G. Noble et al., 2005; Werner & Smith, 1992). Learning requires a physical readiness void of illness and pain and an affective context that is relatively free of intervening variables (Tomczak & Jaworska-Pasterska, 2017). The presence of a physical malady or too many affective barriers—such as stress, apathy, anxiety, and perplexity—results in inefficiency or even inability to learn (Lareau, 2011; Pietarinen et al., 2014). The relationship between physical and psychological factors and academic achievement becomes even more complex when working with multilingual learners. This complexity must be taken into account and addressed from the outset (Elo, 2009).

Educators are undoubtedly aware of the influences of physical and psychological factors when they are working with monolingual English students. However, if they have limited training in English as a second language (ESL)/bilingual education or cross-cultural education, they may not be able to identify how these influences and the resulting dynamics may play out in the lives of multilingual learners they teach. Similarly, ESL/bilingual specialists may not realize how closely some physical and psychological factors may produce effects that look like physical disability (K. P. Smith & Christakis, 2008). Knowledge of these factors and of the learning and performance dynamics that can result helps educators with assessment by permitting more accurate data collection and interpretation so that effective diagnosis and support strategies can occur. As with personal and family factors, the role of physical and psychological factors in academic success is highly variable, and their influence changes with each individual student's circumstances and ability to meet challenges (e.g., Cheadle, 2008; Noble, 2017).

In this chapter we describe some variables in multilingual learners' physical and psychological contexts that can affect their performance at school. We then present ideas for gathering information about these variables or factors. Finally, we suggest systemic and specific support strategies to help students with physical or psychological issues that might be impeding optimal learning.

Key Physical and Psychological Factors

The following physical and psychological factors can play key roles in the way multilingual learners learn in school, so any consideration of behavioral data and their interpretation must also closely consider the role of these factors. Although there is a wide range of factors to consider, the following seem especially important in working with multilingual learners: disease or medical condition, impaired vision or hearing, malnutrition and chronic hunger, effects of recent trauma, fear, current psychological stress, social and emotional well-being. These factors can interact with language and learning processes in unpredictable ways.

Disease or Medical Condition

Because stress and other living conditions affecting health (e.g., poor nutrition, close living arrangements, and poor health practices) tend to co-occur with immigrant, refugee, and other diverse situations, the possibility of disease or a medical condition that leads to poor cognitive performance is much more likely in multilingual learners than in individuals in the general population who are less likely to have experienced trauma or significant change in their lives (Artiles, 2015; Carhill et al., 2008; Luby et al., 2013; A. Portes & Fernández-Kelly, 2008; Smaje, 1995; Stern et al., 1982; Weissbourd, 1996). In addition, because there is also a possibility of little or no access to healthcare in immigrants' native countries or in the transitional neighborhoods in the United States that are often home to immigrants and refugees, medical considerations should be closely scrutinized. As verification for the need to carefully scrutinize health, reports indicate a higher level of obesity (Centers for Disease Control and Prevention [CDC], 2012) and diabetes (National Institutes of Health [NIH], 2017) among Hispanic children than among non-Hispanic White children (see also Cousins et al., 1993). Records also show that more than 25% of students in the Other Health Impaired (OHI) category who are covered under special education regulations are from "culturally different" groups. Insofar as the percentage of culturally different students was about 20% of the total school population in 2001, this figure suggests a greater number of identified OHI students in the culturally different population than in the general U.S. population.

Not only is the incidence of disease and other medical conditions likely to be higher in culturally diverse populations, the reactions to these health problems are often different in the families of multilingual learners (e.g., Bachman et al., 2020; Harry & Klingner, 2014). These differences appear to reflect unique cultural beliefs and practices. In some cultures, for example, retaining personal control over one's treatments or placing control in the hands of another, having a distrust of Western medicine or believing in shamanism, may result in a disinclination to seek Western-style medical help (Cousins et al., 1993; Fadiman, 1997; Lau, 1982). In such cases it may be difficult to identify a medical condition and gain compliance with a physician-recommended course of treatment (Bussing et al., 1998).

Medical conditions may also go undiagnosed among multilingual learners who may have an illness that ends up extending beyond the limits of tolerance. When this occurs, the existing disease state or medical condition is greatly exacerbated by the overlay of unremitting pain, which serves as a harbinger of more serious medical status. For example, some children may suffer from chronic mouth pain resulting from untreated dental caries. Other children may suffer from lead poisoning or from exposure to contaminated well water. Still others may experience the side effects of exposure to chemicals such as dichlorodiphenyltrichloroethane (DDT), N, N-diethyl-meta-tolumide (DEET), and dioxin. School nurses and health aides need to get involved and work side by side with ESL/bilingual teachers to learn the hazards and conditions many immigrant families face.

For the purposes of the multi-tiered system of supports (MTSS) team, the fact that many multilingual learners are at greater risk for disease or a medical condition has a practical impact that must be considered. In academic contexts, students learn best when their physical status is unproblematic. When poor nutrition, fatigue, pain, illness, or other noxious physical conditions exist, learning takes a back seat to resolving these problems. It is necessary for the MTSS team to try to account for the possibility of a disease or medical condition that is not always obvious and to try to help eliminate or reduce the impact of this health condition.

Impaired Vision or Hearing

Many immigrant children may not have had the benefit of periodic and sustained medical attention. In such circumstances, allergies, middle ear infections, and diseases caused by exotic pathogens, like bacteria and parasites, may be present during development and may cause medical conditions leading to visual or auditory impairments. Even when these conditions occur, the limited access to medical care means that the necessary screenings for these conditions may not occur. Consequently, multilingual learners may arrive in U.S. schools with undiagnosed vision or hearing problems. Chronicle 5.1 tells the story of a child who would have been misplaced into special education for the want of a vision test.

Chronicle 5.1

Autism? No! Blind!

By a Case Manager at a School with a Large Population of Multilingual Learners

I was called in by the ESL teacher to provide my "rubber stamp" of approval to what she described as a classic case of some type of behavioral disorder. On the phone she described Igor's behaviors as problems with buttoning and zippering his clothes, inability to retain information from one day to the next, severe problems with reading, and very inappropriate social behaviors, such as being too close to peers and teacher (to the point of irritation). Igor was a fifth-grade student from Ukraine.

When I entered the room for the meeting, there were 12 building staff members (from the child study team) and an English-speaking psychologist from the district. The team members and the psychologist had reputations of superior professionalism and attention to detail. This was a wealthy suburban district with all sorts of resources at its disposal.

To start the meeting, one person read a report of Igor's current functioning and restated the behavioral descriptors the ESL teacher had previously shared with me. I listened until she finished reading. Then I asked whether anyone had checked Igor's vision. Jaws dropped around the table. No, they replied, they had not because his English was too limited and they did not have anyone who spoke Ukrainian. Fortunately, the decision was unanimous: Igor's vision had to be checked before we could proceed any further. I suggested that the

nurse give the vision test with help from the ESL teacher, who would use ESL sheltering strategies to make the test more comprehensible. As it turned out, Igor was legally blind! Even his mother did not know this, as they had lived in rural Ukraine and Igor had not attended school regularly.

We connected Igor with a teacher of the blind and sought to find him large-print materials and glasses. Igor began to make progress after that. In fact, in sixth grade he was recommended for placement in the district's gifted and talented program. I read about Igor 6 years later in the local paper. He had graduated from high school with honors and had been given a 4-year scholarship to a prestigious university!

Questions for Discussion

1. What preliminary work had this team failed to do?

2. How can your school/district update vision and hearing screening procedures so that all students get a checkup?

3. How can you feel comfortable asking a question of the team that on the surface may insult team members' professionalism yet is essential to ensure that a student's needs are accurately diagnosed?

4. What might happen if no one on the team had expertise in the area of bilingual/ESL education?

There may be several explanations for this situation, including scarcity of medical personnel in refugee camps or during wartime, lack of insurance, or inability to pay for services. Regardless of the cause, it is important for educators never to assume that a multilingual learner who is experiencing significant challenges in school has perfect hearing and vision. Sometimes these students fall through the cracks of our own system. Nurses may be unable to communicate sufficiently with a child to complete the vision or hearing test accurately, a child may enroll in school after the school-wide vision or hearing screenings are completed, or a child may have been diagnosed with a vision or hearing problem, but fails to wear the corrective glasses or hearing aid.

MTSS Team Activity

Have the nurse or health aide do a vision/hearing screening test on a member of the MTSS team, but without using language of any kind. Can gestures be used to replace the words *yes* and *no*? Can pictures that are free of cultural bias be incorporated? Discuss ways to make screenings friendlier and yield more valid results for multilingual learners.

Malnutrition and Chronic Hunger

In a country as rich as the United States, we are often unaware that so many children suffer from malnutrition and chronic hunger. However, this problem is evident in all industrialized countries (Bassok et al., 2016; Jack, 2000; Kalil, 2015; Seccombe, 2002), particularly among immigrant families (Schiller, 2001; Smaje, 1995). Immigrant children may experience malnutrition and chronic hunger because of poverty or a paucity of fresh fruits and produce in their neighborhood market. Some immigrant families struggle to prepare healthy foods in the cuisine of their new country or have to travel great distances to purchase foodstuffs used in their native cuisine. Some children must prepare food for themselves while their parents are at work, and children may not make the healthiest of choices. Malnutrition and chronic hunger should be taken into account during assessment. Any resources that are available in the community and appropriate to the multilingual learner's family circumstances should be employed to break this cycle—a growling stomach, low blood sugar, or nutrient deficiencies influence a student's academic success.

MTSS Team Activity

Assign team members to visit a grocery store that caters to a target ethnic group. The task is to purchase treats or ingredients to make treats for the next MTSS team meeting that are healthy and new to the group. Perhaps a parent could be asked for advice in preparing the treat. Have the team members report to the group on their shopping and treat preparation experiences and have the group discuss the nutritional aspects of the treats provided. Relate these conversations back to the experiences immigrant families might have when they arrive in the United States.

Effects of Recent Trauma

Some multilingual learners come from countries that have seen much violence. They may deal with aspects of stress that can occur following the direct experience with, or witnessing of, life-threatening events such as military combat, natural disasters, terrorist incidents, prolonged violence, serious accidents, or violent personal assaults (Freedman, 2006; Halligan, 2009; Suárez-Orozco et al., 2011). Given time and a different perspective on their experiences, many trauma survivors return to normal. However, some people have stress reactions that do not go away on their own or that may even worsen over time (Freedman, 2006). In some cases, the symptoms can be severe and last long enough to significantly impair the person's daily life (Day et al., 2016; Evans & Kim, 2013; Henry, 2006; Uchendu, 2007; U.S. Department of Veteran Affairs, 2006).

The existence of a disorder known as post-traumatic stress disorder (PTSD) was initially applied to veterans returning from the Vietnam, Iraq, and Afghanistan wars (Jones et al., 2010). However, a growing number of Southeast Asian refugees were reported to be suffering from severe mental health problems, including what appeared to be PTSD. In 1987, L. R. August and Gianola likened the growing number of refugees and their symptoms to the experiences of Vietnam War veterans.

Educators throughout the United States report that many more newly arrived immigrant students have borne witness to military conflicts than in previous years (Garbarino et al., 1991; Macksoud & Aber, 1996; Magid & Boothby, 2013; Potocky-Tripodi, 2002). Still others report that many more newly arrived immigrants coming from the lowest socioeconomic groups in some rural areas of Mexico have experienced stress because of extreme poverty and violence (Potocky-Tripodi, 2002; Quinn, 2001; Ruiz-de-Velasco & Fix, 2000). Many immigrants, such as the Sudanese, Darfurians, Somalis, Central Americans, Mexicans, Syrians, Burmese and Iraqis, arrive having been exposed to both war and extreme poverty, and may have spent time in a refugee camp before coming to the United States (Degloma, 2009; Potocky-Tripodi, 2002; see also Parmar et al., 2010; United Nations International Children's Fund [UNICEF], 2011). Chronicle 5.2 presents an account of an almost undiagnosed case of PTSD in a young child.

Chronicle 5.2

Post-Traumatic Stress Disorder Almost Misdiagnosed

By an ESL Teacher

Hue was a little 7-year-old girl from Vietnam. She arrived one day in my ESL classroom in the middle of winter, speaking no English and looking forlorn in her thin coat, unsuitable for Chicago winters. Hue was quiet and shy in my room and appeared terrified to leave the room for other classes like gym, music, and art. I decided to postpone that type of integration until she had a bit more English and a bit more self-confidence. She was staying with relatives in the United States. No one could find out what had happened to her parents.

One day, while the children were doing independent work at various centers around the room, Hue began screaming at the top of her lungs. She stood in the middle of the room screaming and twirling in circles with her arms outstretched. The rest of the class, all multilingual learners, simply stopped what they were doing and watched. Afraid that Hue would get dizzy from twirling and might fall and hit her head on the desk, I went to her on my knees (at her height) and approached her with my arms outstretched. As I got close to her, she fell into my arms. The minute I closed my arms around her, she started thrashing her arms and kicking. I began to rock her in my lap. The other students in the room were wonderful: They said nothing and did nothing. Gradually, Hue calmed down, snuggled in on my lap, and began to suck her thumb.

The buzz traveled all around the school and staff were unanimous in their unofficial diagnosis: The child had severe behavioral disorders and was emotionally disturbed. Fortunately for Hue and for me, the social worker did not accept the unofficial diagnosis. He worked with me to find out more about Hue's background. After much sleuthing and several interviews with Hue's relatives, we found out that Hue's mother was Vietnamese and her father was American. The father had been an American soldier and his whereabouts were unknown. Hue had been living with her mother in a small Vietnamese village, where they endured discrimination and racism because Hue's father was an American. Unable to tolerate being a pariah in the village, Hue's mother committed suicide. Hue had walked in on her mother while she lay dying from a gunshot wound to her head.

The social worker and I were able to apply a diagnosis of PTSD, rather than emotional disturbance or behavioral disorder, and we secured the services of a Vietnamese social worker through a Vietnamese community agency in Chicago to begin treating Hue for PTSD. Although things were not easy for Hue for several years, each year she made more progress emotionally, linguistically, academically, and socially. By the time Hue was in fifth grade, she was well on her way to managing her memories in a healthy way, had made many friends, and was progressing quite nicely in her studies.

Questions for Discussion

1. How might some behaviors exhibited in the classroom or on the playground be misinterpreted or misunderstood?

2. What can you do if you are the only staff member who disagrees with the consensus of the group?

Undiagnosed, untreated stress due to trauma definitely influences academic achievement (Day et al., 2016). Trauma-informed pedagogy and learning environments are now an essential component of most school district plans. The school or district should provide professional learning opportunities to support all staff in culturally and linguistically sustaining practices to address trauma-based stress, to prevent triggers in the learning environment, and to support practitioners as they address the complex needs of students and their families. Systemic or specific support strategies will be required, depending on the immigrant enrollment patterns throughout the school or district. However, we must be very careful to put the interpretation of PTSD and its treatment in a cultural context that is relevant to multilingual learners. Treatment has traditionally had a distinct Western tilt and when offered to non-Westerners can create additional problems (Ngo & Lee, 2007; Pipher, 2002; Watters, 2010).

MTSS Team Activity

Have team members contact various cultural or community associations and support networks to determine whether any illnesses, diseases, or conditions are prevalent among immigrant groups in their area. Obtain information as to how such instances are dealt with in the home country and relate that information to the current situation in the local community.

Fear

Trauma and other experiences related to immigration can result in the development of fearful reactions based on the recall of trauma that may have paralyzing effects (Dombo & Sabatino, 2019; K. L. Freedman, 2006). However, fear may arise from other less severe sources as well. In a discussion of the vulnerabilities of childhood, Weissbourd (1996) observes that many less traumatic circumstances may cause various forms of apprehension, even in psychologically healthy children. This apprehension can be broadly classified as social anxiety (Leary, 1990) and can result in affective experiences such as uneasiness, perplexity, and even fear (Kokkinos et al., 2016; Whitmore, 1987). The consequences of these reactions—especially fear—are that the individual may have feelings of tension and discomfort, a tendency toward more negative self-evaluations, and a tendency to withdraw in the presence of others (K. L. Freedman, 2006). Among the documented cognitive effects of this fear and anxiety are problems in learning a second language (MacIntyre & Gardner, 1991), a decrease in cognitive processing ability (Wine, 1980), inhibited actions, and attempts to escape the situation (Halls et al., 2014; Levitt, 1980).

When these extenuating circumstances are linked with variables, such as cultural diversity, linguistic differences, relocation or resettlement, social or cultural isolation, and other issues that must be addressed by many multilingual learners (Fozdar & Torezani 2008; P. R. Portes, 1999), then it is little wonder that fear and anxiety may be present and interfering with learning in these students (K. G. Noble et al., 2005). A new school environment that is perceived as hostile by the student can cause a multilingual learner to experience panic and can create affect and mood problems. The lack of a welcoming and nurturing learning environment can also cultivate anxiety about school attendance that may grow into chronic avoidance of school or certain learning situations (Cheadle, 2008; Dombo & Sabatino, 2019). Fears resulting from the environment can influence students' academic success. It is not possible to learn to one's full potential in an uncomfortable environment; rather, we learn to escape an uncomfortable environment as quickly as possible.

Current Psychological Stress

Stress influences the ability to learn and retain information (Alsop & McCaffrey, 1993; Education Alliance at Brown University, 2006; K. G. Noble et al., 2005; F. Smith, 1998). All students experience some degree of stress in their lives. However, as newcomers to a culture that is unfamiliar and sometimes inhospitable, culturally and linguistically diverse students, immigrant students, and their families may find many daily situations particularly stressful (P. R. Portes, 1999; A. Portes & Fernández-Kelly, 2008). For example, multilingual learners may experience anxiety or panic when struggling to navigate the new, non-native culture, and this may be in addition to any disorders, such as depression, that the students may already be experiencing. They may feel additional stress as a result of being unable to communicate with peers and adults. As social creatures, we are constantly trying to see how we fit within our social sphere (H. M. Collins, 1998). When communication is reduced for multilingual learners who are already different, they may view themselves as more different than they truly are, resulting in greater isolation (A. Portes & Fernández-Kelly, 2008). When this occurs, stress often ensues.

Given their lack of familiarity with the new culture and language, multilingual learners may suffer from their inability to do even basic everyday tasks. Like all other students, multilingual learners face pressures about grades and peer interactions. However, for multilingual learners, these pressures may be compounded by feelings of diminished status, overly taxed coping mechanisms, insufficient support systems, and acute homesickness (Weisner, 2009).

The extent to which stress affects an individual depends largely on the individual's access to effective resources and strategies to deal with that stress (Garmezy, 1991). Multilingual learner families may not have access to support systems, and culturally sensitive social, psychological, and psychiatric services may be inadequate or unavailable especially in their home language (Jurado & Garcia, 2018; Lareau, 2011; Magnuson & Waldfogel, 2005; Miech et al., 2001). Educators should be knowledgeable about how stress and circumstances in the lives of multilingual learners interact and how the interaction can potentially help or hinder the students' success in school. As is the case with many of these psychological or emotional factors, the cultural context in which behavior is interpreted and support given is of extreme importance (Geva & Wiener, 2014). The Western orientation to typical therapies offered in U.S. schools and clinical settings—for example, treating children and young adults as individuals separate from their families and communities—is incongruent with those from some non-Western cultural backgrounds (Watters, 2010).

Social and Emotional Development

The timeline for social and emotional development is quite different among families from various countries and social strata (Cowie, 2019; Weininger et al., 2009). What one family considers precocious may be perceived as developmentally late in another family. Developmental milestones are culturally specific. For example, the expectation that a child will sleep alone by about age 13 months in Anglo families in the United States is quite different from the expectation of sleeping alone by about age 39 months in Filipino families, for example. In U.S. Anglo families, children are expected to play alone at 25 months of age, whereas in a Filipino family the expectation is that this is achieved at about 12 months (Carlson & Harwood, 1999). Of course, these expectations are significantly affected by the family's socioeconomic level, their geographical location, and many other factors (Calkins, 2015; Cowie, 2019; Harris et al., 2008).

Thus, the inability of some young immigrant children to perform many self-care tasks, such as buttoning, zippering, and tying shoelaces, could generally be indicative of a child-rearing practice that emphasizes parental control over the dressing of the child, rather than a developmental delay. This child-rearing practice reflects a cultural norm that a child's appearance reflects back on the parents and the family. In another example, many immigrant children at the preschool level have difficulty using scissors. Some educators may erroneously conclude this is because of delay in the development of fine motor skills. It may well be because the children have had little or no experience with scissors.

These different cultural expectations make it essential for educators to become familiar with the characteristics of the immigrant culture and of the specific student's family. These characteristics are likely to influence a student's social and emotional development and significantly inform the observer's opinion of the student's development. Without this understanding and knowledge, educators may jump to wrong conclusions about the student's progress.

MTSS Team Activity

Have team members view a film together that shows some of the reality of the problems faced by immigrants or individuals who are outsiders trying to acclimate to a new culture. Pick out five problems that occurred for these individuals and note the responses to these problems by the characters in the film. Several films that might be viewed are *Bread and Chocolate*, *El Norte*, *In America*, and *Born in Syria*.

Feelings of Belonging to the School and Wider Community

Alienation is often cited as a significant contributing factor to many multilingual learners' decision to drop out of school (Entwisle et al., 1997; Fan & Wolters, 2014; Grosjean, 2010; Katz, 1999; A. Portes & Fernández-Kelly, 2008; Ruiz-de-Velasco & Fix, 2000). Feelings of alienation persist beyond the first generation of immigrants in a family, often extending into the second and third generations. These feelings of alienation can be accompanied by a sense of purposelessness stemming from a lack of standards, values, or structure—something akin to the state of anomie described by Durkheim (Durkheim & Coser, 1984). Multilingual learners are likely candidates for these feelings because of their struggle to enter into a new culture that often rejects their participation through government policies or discrimination (TenHouten, 2016). Together with their parents and family, they may be navigating the new cultural norms in which they are immersed. Multilingual learners may also experience dissonance when they feel conflict between the norms of their native and non-native cultures (Cheadle, 2008; TenHouten, 2016).

Educators should carefully examine the school and classroom climate to ensure that all learners are meaningfully included. Educators need to ask themselves tough questions. Do teachers plan instruction with multilingual learners in mind? Does the school's curriculum integrate the perspectives and contributions of multilingual learners' native cultures? Does the staff welcome and promote multilingual learners' participation in all aspects of schooling and extracurricular activities? Are students' multicultural identities affirmed in the classrooms and wider school communities? Do staff and the student body celebrate and honor multilingual learners' unique and varied successes in an equitable manner? Does the school acknowledge and facilitate multilingual learners' bilingualism and biliteracy development?

MTSS Team Activity

Team members are asked to recall an instance during which they felt terribly out of place and unwelcomed. Perhaps they have experienced ostracism by a clique, the oppression of the glass ceiling or gender discrimination, or other instances in which they were on the outside looking in at another group that was unwelcoming. Team members should then attempt to remember and write down as many details as possible: their emotional response to feelings of alienation, the strategies they chose to use in those situations, the success or failure of those strategies, and lessons learned from the experience. Team members then discuss ways their own experiences with these situations can build empathy for their students and then work together to make school and their classrooms more welcoming by removing barriers and building support for all students.

Information Gathering

The same prudence that we suggested be taken in gathering information about personal and family background must apply to gathering information about physical and psychological factors. We need to (1) adhere to strict privacy standards, (2) be careful in our choice of interpreters, (3) tread very carefully and with the utmost respect for the student and family, and (4) verify information as both relevant and potentially impactful. Once again, historical and current information regarding physical and psychological factors should be considered when gathering information in order to understand the student more completely and accurately. A cultural liaison can provide insights into the cultural context of these factors. Educators may have to get training in the factors discussed in this chapter from a professional to better understand how these factors might play out in the lives of multilingual learners. This knowledge and understanding provide a context to the educator's assessment of the student's situation and recommendation for meaningful and appropriate support strategies (Nieto, 2010; Pietarinen et al., 2014). Professional learning of this sort can only refine a teacher's skill in helping not just multilingual learners but students in general. Box 5.1 lists a series of questions that may

---

Box 5.1

Questions to Evaluate a Student's Possible Physical and Psychological Issues

Disease or Medical Condition

- Is there any indication of a possible medical condition?
- Has the student had the expected level of medical care for his or her age?
- When did the student's most recent checkup take place?
- Is there any suspicion of chronic pain?
- Could the student have been exposed to toxic chemicals?

Impaired Vision or Hearing

- When were the most recent vision and hearing tests administered?
- What records have been kept of previous screenings?

Malnutrition and Chronic Hunger

- Does the student show signs of hunger frequently?
- Does the family have food preparation routines that are comfortable for them?
- Who is responsible for preparing food in the family and how does it happen?

Effects of Recent Trauma

- Did the student experience military combat or a terrorist incident?
- Did the student witness a natural disaster?
- Did the student experience a serious accident or violent personal assault?
- Did the student come from extreme poverty?
- Did the student spend time in a refugee camp?
- Does the student show any signs of recurring nightmares or flashbacks?
- Does the student show any signs of having difficulty sleeping?
- Was the student separated from family at any point in his or her life?

Fear

- How comfortable does the student seem at school?
- Does the student show any signs of avoiding certain situations at school? What would be an example?

- Does the student seem to be particularly anxious in certain contexts at school? What would be an example?

Current Psychological Stress

- Does the student show signs of higher than expected levels of stress (such as headaches, nervous tics, trouble sleeping)? What would be some examples?
- Has the student formed a network of friends in school? Describe it.
- Under what circumstances has the student seemed to experience excess pressure?
- Within what aspect of school life does the student enjoy a high status among his or her peers and teachers?
- What are some examples of the student expressing feelings of homesickness?
- How connected is the student or his or her family to a support network, formal or informal?

Social and Emotional Development

- Has the student reached the developmental milestones that are expected within his or her family?

Feelings of Belonging to the School and Wider Community

- Does the student keep to him- or herself or does the student have a group of friends to spend time with both in and out of school?
- How is the student dealing with possibly conflicting norms and values in the monolingual English and home cultures?
- What are some examples of the student adapting to the acculturation process?
- How is the student's new bicultural identity developing?
- What does the student express in terms of feelings of belonging to the school and wider community?

be used to guide the conversations that take place with students and family members. These questions can also serve to guide and organize all the information gathered in the area of physical and psychological factors.

As with personal and family factors, information gathering in the area of physical and psychological factors requires staff to interview the students, their families, their siblings, their teachers, and the community members who interact with the students. As with interviews used to gather information on personal and family background, we do not recommend that questions be posed one after the other in a formal manner, but rather to let the interviewee take control of the conversation. A trusting relationship must precede such interviews. Confidentiality needs to be maintained because much of the information gathered is sensitive. Dialogue journals can also be a source of considerable information about the students, as can previous school records.

Systemic Support Strategies

If the school or district realizes that more than a few students are experiencing academic difficulties because of one or more of the physical or psychological factors discussed in this chapter, systemic support strategies are warranted. Some examples of these strategies are listed in Box 5.2.

Box 5.2

Systemic Support Strategies Used to Overcome Issues from Physical and Psychological Challenges

Disease or Medical Condition

- Make teachers and other staff aware of the possibility of medical conditions.
- Share culturally and linguistically appropriate community health and medical resources with school social workers, teachers, students, and families.
- Promote physical wellness and healthy choices as part of the curriculum, incorporating approaches from the culturally diverse communities that the school serves.
- Partner with mobile health-screening services.
- Establish collaborative partnerships with medical and dental agencies within the community to provide families with affordable access to diagnostic and treatment services.
- Connect families with free/reduced-fee vaccination clinics, school physicals, and dental clinics.

Impaired Vision or Hearing

- Implement culturally and linguistically responsive vision and hearing tests beginning in preschool and extending through grade 12.
- Provide for the administration of vision and hearing screenings for multilingual learners (MLs) who enroll after school-wide screenings have occurred.
- Cultivate partnerships with agencies that advocate and provide for those with visual and/or hearing impairments.

- Establish a process for obtaining vision and hearing assistive devices, materials, and services at reduced cost for those families with lesser means.

Malnutrition and Chronic Hunger

- Provide education for those parents who are unfamiliar with the existing community, including connecting them with grocery stores that cater to members of their community.
- Run breakfast/lunch/snack programs.
- Establish school or community food pantries.
- Promote good nutrition and healthy eating that incorporates the cuisine of the culturally diverse communities around the school into the school lunch program.
- Cultivate a school community garden/greenhouse with produce that can be used in the school breakfast, snack, and lunch program.
- Partner with organizations that develop community gardens in students' neighborhoods.

Effects of Recent Trauma

- Implement a multi-method screening tool used upon enrollment to identify stress due to recently experienced trauma.
- Create a continuum of services ranging from one-on-one counseling to support-group activities for students suspected of having some level of PTSD.

Box 5.2 (*continued*)

- Implement trauma-informed practices and pedagogy into all aspects of teaching, learning, and student support.
- Familiarize staff with the causes, characteristics, and treatment of PTSD.
- Provide professional learning and parent education opportunities.

Fear

- With the help of a cultural liaison, analyze aspects of the school that may be perceived by someone from another culture as hostile and change those aspects to lessen that perception.
- Set up a buddy system in which students are paired with an older peer who has adapted successfully to the school milieu.

Current Psychological Stress

- Implement educational programs that teach children coping and cultural navigation skills.
- Ask students school-wide to complete periodic surveys of their well-being and feelings of belonging. Look for trends and patterns across grade levels and across times of the year.
- Cultivate partnerships with community agencies that provide resources.
- Provide easy access to resources (such as reading material, retired volunteers, tutors) that are culturally and linguistically responsive.
- Ensure that resources used by ML families are culturally and linguistically responsive and sustaining.
- Incorporate a school-wide initiative that provides students with safe environments in which to discuss their mental health and well-being concerns on a regular basis.
- Promote mental health and well-being for all school staff with accompanying professional learning.
- Ask the school psychologist to work closely with the bilingual parent liaison to implement a culturally responsive school-wide program of mental health services.

Social and Emotional Development

- Provide professional learning opportunities that facilitate the integration of information specifically related to immigrants into what educators already know about social and emotional development within the general student population.
- Provide professional learning opportunities that help staff to understand how culture influences child-rearing practices and parental expectations.

Feelings of Belonging to the School and Wider Community

- Provide time for teachers to research the linguistic, cultural, and historical contexts of the MLs they teach.
- Encourage all teachers to develop units of study that represent multiple perspectives, include students' languages and cultures, and provide a wide range of instructional materials that reflect all students and their views throughout the school year.
- Develop a rubric to ensure that the school and classroom climate incorporates diverse cultural norms and values.
- Provide teachers with a self-assessment checklist to be aware of optimal learning environments for their MLs (arrangement of room, desks, and tables; level of participation of MLs in classroom activities; integration of MLs into the classroom experiences).
- Check to ensure that the school's curriculum meaningfully incorporates the perspectives and contributions of MLs' native cultures and develop units of study that include global perspectives (in social studies, mathematics, literature, and so forth).
- Provide workshops for the staff on ways to welcome and promote ML participation in all aspects of schooling and extracurricular activities.
- Develop school-wide programs to honor MLs and all students who demonstrate admirable behaviors (evidence of kindness, cooperation, good judgment, independent thought, divergent thinking) throughout the year, or behaviors that lead to successful futures—not just academic grades or test scores.
- Plan events during which the value of MLs' bilingualism and biliteracy development is acknowledged.

Physical and psychological aspects are delicate issues that need to be dealt with carefully. Families may have very different attitudes regarding physical and psychological challenges. For some of us, having a problem, especially in the psychological domain, may elicit denial responses or attempts at concealment. It is important, then, to implement any of these strategies in such a way that families and students feel comfortable and at ease.

Specific Support Strategies

If the school or district notes that the physical and psychological factors are affecting only a few students or if multilingual learner enrollment is no more than a few students, the systemic strategies previously mentioned can be implemented in a more focused manner with individual students. The need for discretion, complete transparency, and candor is crucial. In addition, if these strategies are to be used with individual students, rather than at the school or district level, the need for discretion is even more significant. Students cannot be allowed to feel singled out in any way.

Questions for Reflection and Action

1. Does the school's intake protocol for gathering information need to be changed to make it more responsive to multilingual learners' health issues?
2. Has the school instituted ongoing and periodic screening of multilingual learners' sense of well-being? If so, how is it doing that?
3. What can social workers, cultural liaisons, multilingual learner families, psychologists, and other school and community partners do to support the mental health and well-being of all students, including multilingual learners?
4. Different cultures hold diverse views of healing, mental health, and well-being. What steps can school staff take to support students in more culturally and linguistically appropriate ways?
5. Select one of the physical or psychological elements described in this chapter. Research this element thoroughly to understand the factor completely and its potential impact on multilingual learners' academic achievement and linguistic and social–emotional development. What systemic and/or specific strategies can mitigate the impact?
6. Does your school's anti-bullying and/or social–emotional learning program need to be modified to make it more linguistically and culturally appropriate?

Previous Schooling Factors

Key Concepts. *The third integral factor to be considered is the amount and quality of previous formal schooling in both English and the student's home language, as well as the congruence of educational approaches that the student has experienced. Support strategies developed from examining this factor build on prior knowledge from formal and informal educational experiences, as well as make up for gaps in students' previous formal schooling.*

The third integral element to be considered when a multilingual learner seems to face academic challenges is the student's previous schooling. Knowledge of this factor is crucial in interpreting the student's current performance because the ability to perform an academic skill or demonstrate a knowledge set is highly dependent on whether the student has had the opportunity to form the necessary foundation to learn that skill or knowledge set. Understanding which mediations were attempted when difficulties arose is also vital. Research has shown that opportunity to learn is the single factor that best predicts one's knowledge of specific subjects (Berliner & Biddle, 1995; Callahan, 2005; Klingner, 2014; National Academies of Sciences, Engineering, and Medicine, 2017; Ortiz & Artiles, 2010). In fact, this principle of prior exposure has been described as Berliner and Biddle's *Student Achievement Law.* Thus, the multi-tiered system of supports (MTSS) team should have some idea as to whether and how multilingual learners were taught the foundations for the skills and concepts they are experiencing difficulty with and how successful the teaching practices were in those instances of instruction. More generally, it is important to look at longitudinal information to determine whether these students' education followed a plan that makes developmental sense (e.g., B. A. Collins et al., 2014; Cummins, 2007; S. Paris, 2005; van Kaayenoord, 2010) or whether it coincided with the long-term plan to which the student's current school adheres.

This focus on previous schooling to determine opportunities to learn seems logical, but assessment teams all over the country routinely make placement decisions without adequate data on previous formal schooling factors. For example, if an assessment team focuses primarily on achievement and English language test scores and does not incorporate the prior teaching and curricular content that a student has had into the interpretation of the numbers, it is not observing Berliner and Biddle's *Student Achievement Law*. Teachers should try to determine whether a multilingual learner's performance can be traced back to insufficient, interrupted, infrequent, inconsistent, or inferior previous schooling the student had in the United States or in the home country. Such information can help educators explain the challenges that the multilingual learner is experiencing in school by providing answers to the question: Is the multilingual learner's progress and classroom performance less than would be expected because of learning environments that lacked:

- Sufficient instructional exposure to particular skills or concepts that form the basis for learning new skills and concepts?

- Repeated and sustained practice?

- High-quality instruction or sufficient rigor?

- A clear plan for transitioning students to new and unfamiliar educational approaches?

- The opportunity to learn foundational skills?

- Culturally and linguistically responsive and sustaining instruction?

Answers to these questions can help educators develop a more comprehensive picture of the student's educational career to date and can inform decision-making as to appropriate support strategies.

In this chapter, we discuss key factors related to previous schooling, illustrate examples of common situations hinging on schooling history, provide suggestions for information gathering and evaluating the adequacy of previous formal schooling, begin a list of possible systemic strategies to make up for lags and differences in schooling, offer recommendations for applying systemic support strategies to individual multilingual learners experiencing significant challenges, and present questions for discussion.

Key Factors in Previous Schooling

The amount and quality of instruction in both the home language and English and the extent to which cohesion and continuity existed in the educational approaches are key factors of the schooling history to consider (Harry & Klingner, 2014). School teams should examine the educational system and programming the students received in their home country, in any other countries the family has passed through en route to the United States, as well as students' experiences in other U.S. schools prior to arrival in the current school. Although such data may be difficult to obtain, a complete and sufficient picture of the multilingual learner's learning aptitude and how to proceed with support or remediation is impossible without it (Fine et al., 2007; N. Flores et al., 2015; Hodgson et al., 2007; Suárez-Orozco et al., 2011).

The amount of instruction multilingual learners have received refers to both the frequency and the duration of instructional services. How many years of formal schooling? On average, how many instructional days occurred within those years? Were there patterns of absences because of issues such as work or inclement weather? Did events, such as fighting or strikes, reduce instructional time? The quality of instruction includes the level of rigor (in terms of difficulty and thoroughness) of the teaching and curricular content, staff qualifications, utilization of effective teaching strategies, and the scope and sequence of the curriculum. If the student has had any type of bilingual education, the type of language allocation the student has experienced is important when assessing both the quantity and quality of instruction (Brown-Jeffy & Cooper, 2012). How much access to all of their languages at both program and curricular levels do students experience? Students whose families escaped from dire situations in their home country may also have spent some time in another country, immersed in another language, before settling in the United States. These students may have had their home language development interrupted without having sufficient time to build up concepts and knowledge through this temporary additional language. Assessing what knowledge and skills students have in each of their languages is crucial in order to get a complete profile of each student's achievement.

The consistency among educational approaches that the student has been exposed to is important to consider as well. Too often, inconsistent methods and approaches to instruction can hinder a student's ability to learn because these methods often operate at cross-purposes (Damico et al., 2021; J. S. Damico & Nelson, 2012).

As with any element that involves what multilingual learners bring with them from the past, it is essential to gather information about what students learned and experienced in their previous formal schooling even if the educational systems may have been very different from the U.S. system. In many countries the approach to learning and schooling may be different from what is expected in the United States (Anderson-Levitt, 2003; Calderón et al., 2011; Carhill et al., 2008; Janzen, 2008; Sleeter, 2012; Spindler, 1997; Tavares, 2015); however, the objectives and the accomplishments may be similar. Multilingual learners may have gone to a very different kind of school than the one they attend in the United States. Some multilingual learners and their families find U.S. schools to be less rigorous than what they experienced in their home countries. In other situations, multilingual learners may be missing years of formal schooling, but perhaps they learned through a more informal setting, such as an apprenticeship with an expert or an internship with a mentor. It is important to find out just what skills the student has and not to write off past experiences that can be used as building blocks for learning additional skills and a new body of knowledge (e.g., J. S. Damico & Nelson, 2012; Milner, 2010).

Amount of Formal Schooling in the Home Language

The amount of formal schooling in the student's home language is a strong predictor of their English language development and the leading factor in multilingual learners' success in U.S. schools (Collier & Thomas, 2017b;

Genesee et al., 2005). Students who have had the benefit of formal schooling in the home language beginning with kindergarten or preschool and continuing without interruption up to and including the period of time during which they immigrated to the United States have a strong foundation on which to build (e.g., Bialystok, 2018; Licona & Kelly, 2020; Ryu, 2019; Taylor-Leech, 2013). This is especially true for those students who have achieved literacy at grade level in their home language (Cloud et al., 2009).

Unfortunately, not all multilingual learners arrive in the United States with the expected number of years of formal schooling. There are many possible explanations for less than optimal frequency and duration of instructional services in a student's home country. The family's socioeconomic status may have limited the number of years the student had access to public education. Family poverty may have necessitated the children leave school and enter the workforce at a young age (Ladd, 2012; Lareau & Conley, 2008). Civil war or foreign occupation may have interrupted schooling, an administrator or teacher may have cancelled school sessions, students may have been afraid to attend school, or children may have been drafted into military service at a young age (Halligan, 2009; Uchendu, 2007). Community agricultural needs, such as planting and harvesting, may have taken precedence over school attendance. Discrepancies in the quality of public education afforded to students in remote locations as a result of difficulty recruiting teachers to serve there may have led to interrupted schooling as well. Differences in gender expectations may have led to girls stopping schooling to stay home and care for younger siblings. Some students may arrive at adolescence not having had any formal education because of extreme disruption in their lives. These students may not have basic literacy skills that are taken for granted, given their age. Chronicle 6.1 provides an example of an extremely clever child who still needs to learn some basic literacy.

There are also many possible explanations for less than optimal frequency and duration of instructional services in the home language in U.S. schools. Some of those explanations may arise from variances within the U.S. educational infrastructure; others may come from family circumstances (Chudgar & Luschei, 2009; King & Fogle, 2013; Marshall & Toohey, 2010). Not every U.S. school offers bilingual education (instruction and instructional support in the home language and English). In some cases this is because the low number of students in a particular target language group does not economically support the employment of a bilingual teacher. In other situations, even where numbers of students in the target language are sufficient to support the employment of a bilingual teacher, school officials may decide not to offer any instruction in the students' home language (Bialystok, 2018). This decision is based on the misconception that it is better to immerse students in English rather than to allow them to learn new concepts through their stronger language and to continue developing in that language so that it forms a firm base on which English proficiency is built (Ascenzi-Moreno, 2018; O. Garcia et al., 2016; Kaplan & Leckie, 2009). In U.S. schools, there is a prevalence of site-based management, which allows building administrators to set the parameters of

Chronicle 6.1

A Picture Is Worth a Thousand Words

By an ESL Teacher

I was teaching a group of Southeast Asian refugee students who were being prepared at a school in a refugee camp in the Philippines to be resettled in the United States. This was a group of adolescents from Vietnam and Cambodia who spoke very little English. On average, they had had a total of 2 years of formal schooling over their 7 to 9 years of school life.

I had set up a library in our classroom, and among the many projects involving literacy that we did, one involved each child producing a book of his or her own, which would then be added to our collection. Some children were able to write original books themselves. Others, like Lathikhone, would adapt the story in the big book we had read as a group, copying some of the words and phrases, and draw pictures in the blank space above the writing. The children enjoyed finishing books and seeing them in our library. Even the students who adapted a story would be listed as an additional author by saying "Rewritten by." Lathikhone, who had never been schooled, finally finished a story that took place in a jungle. He was very excited to start drawing pictures in the space allocated for illustrations. Each page had a sentence or two to be illustrated. The story that Lathikhone had chosen was one we had read and acted out, so he was quite familiar with the content and clearly understood the story. Out of the corner of my eye, I saw him go over to the library, pick a book, and bring it to his desk. He was completely engrossed in the drawings, looking up at the book he had borrowed once in a while as though checking his work.

When I passed by his side a little while later, I was dismayed to see that the book he had picked and was copying was about the Inuit! The beautiful drawings he was making had nothing to do with the text he had written! I had surrounded this student, who had not had a chance to learn about different aspects of literacy (such as the structure of illustrated children's books) naturally, over the years, with a literacy-rich environment. I had assumed that he would naturally pick up the notion that illustrations "illustrate" the text that they accompany. But I realized that this was still a foreign notion to him. It was one of the aspects of literacy, school life, and books that probably needed to be taught more explicitly. It was an aspect that does not have to be taught explicitly to children who are introduced to books early on, and who, naturally and gradually, go from books that are primarily picture books to books that have illustrations for every one or two sentences, to books that have an illustration every chapter, and finally to books that have only one illustration, on the cover.

Questions for Discussion

1. How could teachers build on Lathikone's notion of books and literacy?
2. What types of genres would you introduce that use only illustrations to convey meaning?
3. How would you help capture this student's voice using technology, bilingualism, illustrations, beginning writing, and then shift to more text-dense genres?

educational programming according to local community needs or personal ideology (Baltaci, 2017; Caesar & Kohler, 2007; Smeeding, 2005). This means that even if students stay within the same school system, district, parish, or corporation but change schools, the educational programs they encounter may be substantially different from school to school.

If multilingual learners have received instruction only in English for most of their early schooling, then it is possible that most of what was taught in prekindergarten through grade 2 was not comprehensible to them. Gaps in academic concepts and skills may develop because of this lack of comprehensible input, the results of which are likely unnoticeable until grade 3 (Boyd & Goldberg, 2009). The research is strong: Lack of sustained bilingual education can hinder both academic and linguistic/literacy development for multilingual learners (Lindholm-Leary, 2012).

Even when a school or school system does offer bilingual education to multilingual learners, instruction may be delivered in ways that do not ensure optimal duration and frequency. Students who participate in late-exit bilingual or developmental bilingual programs are more likely to experience academic success than those who participate in early-exit bilingual education programs (Genesee et al., 2005; Thomas & Collier, 2017). This is true regardless of whether or not students have achieved academic English fluency before they exit the program.

In other cases, multilingual learners may participate in a bilingual education program in which no one has addressed the issue of long-term language allocation. In such cases multilingual learners may experience inconsistent distribution of the home language and English instruction. This inconsistency may compound as they advance through the grade levels. Multilingual learners in this situation may attend a kindergarten where most of the instruction is in the home language, with only a small portion of the instruction time allotted to English as a second language (ESL) instruction, then advance to first grade and face an abrupt switch to instruction mostly in English, with little instruction in the home language. The second-grade teacher may see gaps in knowledge and skills due to the English-only instruction in first grade and revert to teaching mostly in the home language. Switching the language of instruction back and forth from year to year is especially problematic for the large number of simultaneous bilingual learners. These students benefit from instruction in both of their languages every day from the beginning of their schooling. Any student would be confused by such inconsistencies in instruction. This change and inconsistency often cause multiple problems—not only confusion regarding comprehensibility, but confusion regarding the sociopolitical and psychosocial considerations of the two languages and those who speak them (Cardenas-Hagan et al., 2007; Chappell & Faltis, 2013; Janzen, 2008; G. Noble, 2017).

In still other cases, parents may refuse bilingual education services because they may not have been provided accurate or sufficient information regarding its benefits. The family may be under the misconception that the sooner the children begin to receive instruction only in English, the better off they are. There is strong evidence to the contrary (Bialystok, 2018; B. A. Collins et al, 2014; Genesee, 2012), which is why parents are encouraged to use the home language with their children as much as possible (N. Flores & Schissel, 2014; Yturriago, 2012a), especially if that home language is not being supported at school. It is important for district and school personnel to develop a clear plan that they share with parents indicating the important role that the home language plays in developing proficiency in the second or new language. Presentations and publications for families should be available showing the benefits of bilingualism and how bilingual instruction is at least as effective as or more effective than English-only programs (O. Garcia et al., 2016; Menard-Warwick, 2007; National Academies of Sciences, Engineering and Medicine, 2017; Rolstad et al., 2005).

In terms of frequency of home language instruction, multilingual learners may only be offered a single period each school day or, worse, only one period per week. In resource programs, time spent with the bilingual teacher may not be valued and is therefore not protected. Students may miss instruction because the homeroom teacher chooses not to release them to the resource teacher because the homeroom teacher considers homeroom instruction more important.

Family circumstances that contribute to a lower or disrupted rate of occurrence of home language instruction in U.S. schools typically arise from conditions of poverty, when parents are struggling to make ends meet (Evans & Kim, 2013; A. Portes & Fernández-Kelly, 2008; Reyes & Azuara, 2008; Ullucci & Howard, 2015). Changes of residence can mean that multilingual learners are moving from school to school. Children of migrant workers are the most obvious example of this situation. They may travel in a predictable pattern, from state to state, based on the schedule of planting and harvesting certain crops. However, many families may move from residence to residence within the same general geographic area because of rent increases, job changes, or the purchase of a new home. Multilingual learners may need to help with childcare responsibilities or secure some type of employment to help with the family's expenses. Parents of multilingual learners may need their older children to watch younger siblings who are sick if the parents cannot take time off work to care for them. Others may work long hours after school helping in family businesses, which in turn may lead to increased school absenteeism.

Another example of "interrupted schooling" arises when students have attended U.S. schools in which a great proportion of time in the early years is spent focusing on reading instruction to the exclusion of content-area instruction. As a consequence, the teaching of mathematics, writing, science, and social studies is diminished significantly (Dee et al., 2010). This can result in multilingual learners who develop basic reading skills and some oral English proficiency but who lack content-area knowledge and academic language and literacy.

Quality of Formal Schooling in the Home Language

Quality of instruction is at least as important as the language of instruction (Calderón et al., 2011; Slavin & Cheung, 2003; Taylor-Leech, 2013). The quality of formal schooling in the home language can vary significantly among multilingual learners, depending on what the student's current school offers and what the child has experienced in the native country as well as in previous U.S. schools. It is not enough that the student has had continuous instruction in the home language. It is important to know the level of rigor in previous schooling experiences when compared to that of the current learning environment. This information allows us to better understand expectations and level of ease or difficulty that the student might be having.

In addition to level of rigor, educators should consider the scope and sequence of the curriculum in the student's previous schooling. In mathematics classes, for example, fractions may be introduced later in the previous curriculum than the current one. Other skills and concepts may have not been introduced at all. Failure to master skills and concepts before they have been taught is no fault of the student but rather a mismatch in the scope and sequence of the two curricula.

The qualifications of staff delivering home language instruction are another important consideration when assessing the quality of the education that the student received (Janzen, 2007; Rodríguez-Mojica et al., 2019; Tedick, 2009). In U.S. schools, teachers working in bilingual education programs may have been hired provisionally to remediate chronic teacher shortages. In these cases, the teachers are in the process of completing their basic teaching credential and the specialty courses in bilingual/ESL education while teaching multilingual learners. In some schools, bilingual education teachers are not hired at all. Instead, noncertified staff, namely, professionals and volunteers who happen to be bilingual in English and the home language of the students, provide instruction through that language. Instruction of this type should not be expected to yield the same results as that provided by certified bilingual teachers.

Some of the strategies and approaches that are currently used may not be the most conducive to learning for multilingual learners (Janzen, 2008; Pesco et al., 2016; Reese & Goldenberg, 2006). Educators familiar with the research as it relates to multilingual learners are better able to judge the effectiveness of approaches and strategies that the student has been given. For example, the recent trend of using scripted programs and small skill-oriented instructional strategies, along with an overemphasis on phonics to the detriment of comprehension instruction, is not very effective with multilingual learners. In fact, we may be creating a generation of proficient decoders who have low comprehension skills (Cunningham & Allington, 2011; H. L. Damico et al., 2021; Edmonds et al., 2009; Keene, 2008; Kendall & Khuon, 2005; Lai et al., 2009; Lesaux & Harris, 2015; Pacheco, 2010).

In addition, educators should determine multilingual learners' home language with accuracy. Many countries use a multitude of indigenous languages. Thus, the fact that a student comes from Mexico, for example, does not necessarily mean that the student speaks Spanish fluently. The United Nations Educational, Scientific and Cultural Organization (UNESCO) has identified 62 living indigenous languages in Mexico, 56 indigenous languages in China, and 65 in India (UNESCO, 2012). Thus, many students from various states in Mexico arrive at school in Mexico speaking their native indigenous language and participate in bilingual education programs in which Spanish is their second language. According to the *Instituto Lingüistico de Verano*, 2,563,000 speakers of Nahuatl, 1,490,000 speakers of Maya, 785,000 speakers of Zapoteco, and 764,000 speakers of Mixteco reside in Mexico (Gordon, 2005). When these children enter U.S. schools, English is their third language. The same may be true of children from many other countries.

After considering both the amount and quality of previous instruction in the home language, educators should be able to answer with more accuracy the following questions: Is it reasonable to expect that the child should have attained grade-level competency in literacy and core academic areas in the home language? How can we build on what multilingual learners have gained from previous educational experiences in their home languages?

Amount of Formal ESL Instruction

Multilingual learners who enter U.S. schools with English foreign language instruction that was provided either by their country of origin's school system or by private tutoring have an advantage over those multilingual learners who have not had the benefits of such instruction. Multilingual learners who transfer into a new U.S. school from another U.S. school may or may not have had the benefit of formal ESL instruction, as the availability of such programs varies greatly across the nation and even in neighboring districts (Bachman et al., 2020; Chappell & Faltis, 2013). The frequency and duration of ESL instruction are as important as the frequency and duration of instruction in the student's home language. Multilingual learners who receive only a period a day of ESL instruction are at considerable risk for academic failure (Collier & Thomas, 2017a, 2017b).

Less than ideal second language instruction means that students are not getting sufficient exposure to either a comprehensible learning environment or the opportunity to develop their language through teaching strategies that are geared to their language needs. Similarly, multilingual learners who exit ESL instruction prematurely, before they have achieved academic proficiency in English, are at risk for academic failure because of diminished duration of service. An inconsistent or ineffective language allocation plan can also hinder English language acquisition, as there is no consistent plan for the development of proficiency in the second or new language over a period of time.

Quality of Formal ESL Instruction

Exemplary ESL instruction is based on the notion that individuals learn a language when using it to communicate rather than by studying it in isolation (Genesee et al., 2006; Genesee & Hamayan, 2016; Nakatani, 2010; Swain, 2006). This implies that the methods and curriculum used to develop proficiency in the second or new language must incorporate the functional uses of language in meaningful contexts (McLaughlin & McLeod, 1996; National Academies of Sciences, Engineering and Medicine, 2018). When meaning and function are the basis of instruction, it follows that the topic of lessons is something other than language itself. Language is best developed when the focus of instruction is on topics such as history, science, or social studies—that is, academic content areas (Cloud et al., 2010; Genesee & Hamayan, 2016; Hamayan et al., 2013; Janzen, 2008; Mehisto et al., 2008). Research strongly suggests that content-based ESL instruction produces greater student growth in English language acquisition than ESL instruction utilizing a traditional approach that focuses exclusively on aspects of language such as grammar and vocabulary (Collier & Thomas, 2017a). Likewise, multilingual learners must not receive the majority of their English instruction or support strategy working on English grammar skills out of context. Students need to use their new language in authentic communicative contexts in order to develop the oral language and literacy associated with different disciplines and used for different purposes.

Exemplary ESL instruction is flexible because it has to meet the needs of multilingual learners with different levels of academic English development. The teacher needs to be able to adjust the curriculum and to be cognizant of the students' home language. In addition, the transition from home language or sheltered language classes to monolingual English classes is gradual, carefully planned, and augmented with support activities to ensure students' success (Cloud et al., 2010; Echevarria & Short, 2003; Fairbairn & Jones-Vo, 2019; Westernoff et al., 2021). While they are often neglected in diversity education, the transition periods between one type of instruction or support to another is a crucial consideration in successful language planning.

MTSS Team Activity

Invite someone who knows about the educational system of another country to have an informal chat about how schools work in that country. Preferably, the country of choice would be one that many multilingual learners come from. The guest could be a teacher who has recently come from that country, a school administrator from that country who serves as a virtual guest speaker, a parent who has recently had a child in a school in that country, or a multilingual learner who has recently arrived from a school in that country. Ask the person to talk about what children learn, how the grade levels are set up, what grading system is used, how students are assessed, what role parents play in the school, and how classrooms are set up. Discuss differences and similarities with the current school system.

Congruence of Educational Approaches

Another key question for the MTSS team to consider is how the educational experiences of the multilingual learner fit together to create the student's educational ecology. Just as it is crucial that we advocate for a services model that takes into account students' social and psychological development (Bronfenbrenner, 1979; Gee, 2008; Möller, 2018; Pietarinen et al., 2014), we should also view the educational experience of the student from a systems model. That is, we should ask whether the approach to education in the country of origin or previous U.S. school was similar to or different from the approach the student is currently experiencing. Some approaches may be radically different. Chronicle 6.2 provides an example of how one school dealt with this challenge.

In some schools instruction is highly teacher directed, whereas in other schools students manage activities that are set up and simply guided by the teacher. When students move from one approach to another, they may have trouble with the transition. Thus, a student who has spent 6 years in an educational system that emphasizes learning through observation and apprenticeship may feel overwhelmed with an educational approach that stresses hands-on learning and student-to-teacher interaction. In another example,

Surprisingly Traditional

By a Teaching Coordinator

I was interviewing for a coordinator position at a primary school with a large Arabic-speaking population. The principal was giving me a tour of the school, which was in a very modern building that had wonderful open spaces. The classrooms were also very modern, with circular tables for the children. I could see a lot of group work, with children working independently on projects on the floor. "Heaven," I thought. Then, we passed a classroom, and the principal casually said: "Here's our introductory classroom." I was surprised to see what I would think of as an extremely traditional classroom, with wooden desks, arranged in rows. In fact, in the image that is left in my memory everything was brown, in contrast to the multiple colors used in the other classrooms! But the children were all paying attention to the teacher standing in front of the room, talking at them.

When I expressed my surprise at finding this very traditional classroom in the middle of all the openness and the activity-centered instruction, the principal laughed and said that this "introductory classroom" emerged after a couple of years of trial and error. When children arrived in grades 2 or 3 directly from an Arab country, they would be immediately placed with their peers. But many of these newly arrived children would soon start misbehaving, running around, playing loudly, and not paying attention. At the same time, their parents began to complain that there was no real teaching going on at the school.

Then, a couple of the bilingual bicultural teachers figured out that the setup at this school was so unfamiliar to these families that they couldn't recognize it as an effective learning environment. To the children, being allowed to sit on the floor and work on an interesting project meant "playtime" and this led to the inappropriate behaviors—inappropriate for instruction time—but perfectly appropriate for playtime! And so, the school began to experiment with placing the newly arrived children into a learning environment that met their and their parents' expectations of the more traditional schools found in their home country. And after a short time, the children would begin the gradual integration into the more activity-centered environment of their acculturated peers. At the same time, the school added an introduction to the philosophy behind this activity-centered way of teaching to the orientation that was given to new parents.

Apparently, this strategy worked and the children entered their modern classrooms and functioned much better than their predecessors had done.

Questions for Discussion

1. How would you prepare the rest of the school for the presence of this "atypical" classroom?
2. What elements from this more "traditional" classroom could be integrated across the grade levels?
3. How would you plan "the gradual integration into the more activity-centered environment" for these newly arrived multilingual learners?

students who have participated in an educational approach that emphasizes rote memorization and strict absorption of the teacher's opinions may not have developed the independent skills necessary to function well in an environment that gives students more choice in how to build their knowledge base.

Information Gathering and Evaluating the Adequacy of Previous Schooling

Getting any information about the student's past can be difficult. Records and documents regarding previous schooling provide useful information; however, such records may not be available. An interview with the student and the family (parents and siblings) may yield more useful information and result in a better picture of what previous schooling looked like. Box 6.1 offers some questions that may be used to structure the conversation. However, the questions should not be posed one after another. Rather, an informal conversation should take place.

Box 6.1

Questions Used to Assess a Student's Previous Schooling Experiences

Amount of Instruction in the Home Language

- How often were school sessions scheduled? How often did the child attend school? Did any circumstances prevent the child from attending school (e.g., farm work, employment, childcare responsibilities, natural disaster, fear, or illness)?
- How consistent was the teacher's attendance (e.g., strikes, itinerant subject-area teachers)?
- How much instruction in the home language was available?
- What language(s) were used for instruction? In which subjects?
- If two languages were used, what was the allocation plan for their use in instruction?
- How long did the child receive instruction in the home language?
- What grades did the child receive in classes in which home language instruction was provided? What assessments are available?
- Was age-appropriate literacy development achieved?
- Was age-appropriate subject-area progress made?

Quality of Instruction in the Home Language

- What academic subjects were taught in the previous school?
- What was expected at each grade level?
- How would you evaluate the quality of learning materials such as books, technology, and so forth?

- What is the typical level of training for teachers at the previous school?
- How do you think the new school compares with the previous school? Do you think it is very different or similar? Do you think it is harder or easier?

Amount of ESL Instruction

- How long did your child receive specialized ESL instruction?
- How often were ESL classes scheduled?
- What types of ESL classes were offered? Were they connected with content-area instruction?
- Did anything prevent your child from attending ESL classes?

Quality of ESL Instruction

- Who provided ESL instruction—a teacher with specialized training and coursework in ESL pedagogy, a general education teacher without specialized ESL training, a volunteer or a paraprofessional?
- What were the expectations?
- What grades did the child receive in previous ESL classes? Are there work samples available from those classes?
- What was your child's performance level in previous English-language classes?
- How do you feel about the quality of projects, writing, and other activities completed in the English-speaking portion of your child's day?

Educators must be aware of the need for privacy with multilingual learner families and the need to explain how the information is used to improve the educational services for the student who is experiencing significant challenges in school. It should be clear to the family that this type of questioning is by no means an evaluation of schooling in the home country. The importance of protecting the family's privacy should be explained to and understood by the cultural liaison and interpreter who are part of the process. The MTSS team can enlist the help of a staff member knowledgeable about the previous education systems in which the multilingual learner has participated to provide context for the gathered information.

Systemic Support Strategies

If educators notice that a significant number of multilingual learners in their school have had similar previous schooling experiences, systemic support strategies should be implemented to address the needs of current students and those likely to arrive in the future. Older students who enter U.S. schools having had their formal schooling interrupted need special attention because their needs are significant. These students may not have had the opportunity to develop basic literacy skills in their home language, let alone in English. In fact, for many of them, literacy may not have played a major role in their lives. This is quite a drastic difference from life in a U.S. school (Y. Freeman & Freeman, 2002; Neokleous et al., 2020).

Like other multilingual learners, students with limited or interrupted formal education need to be taught social and academic English as well as the content of the curriculum, but they also need to develop basic literacy skills, preferably through their home language, and they need to learn the culture of school (Cloud et al., 2009; Hamayan, 1994; WIDA, 2015). Some of these students may not have much experience with writing utensils, scissors, or staplers. They may not understand the use of lockers or how cafeterias work. Many districts establish Newcomer Centers for students with limited formal schooling. Students receive intensive instruction in identified areas for a limited period of time, typically before they join their peers in the main section of the school (Aldana & Martinez, 2018; Marler, 2012). Some examples of other systemic support strategies are listed in Box 6.2.

Specific Support Strategies

If factors related to past schooling are not influencing the academic and linguistic progress of groups of children, but are of concern for only a few multilingual learners experiencing difficulty, the support strategies listed in Box 6.2 can

---

Box 6.2

Systemic Support Strategies

Strategies for Insufficient, Interrupted, or Poor Quality of Instruction in the Home Language

- Newcomers' programming
- Before- and after-school tutoring
- Cross-age peer tutoring
- Professional learning opportunities in the area of task analysis
- Professional learning opportunities in the area of differentiation for multilingual learners (MLs)
- Professional learning opportunities in the area of building on and incorporating MLs' prior knowledge, interests, talents, and experiences
- Professional learning opportunities in the area of discerning student learning styles and increasing repertoire of teaching styles
- Curriculum alignment and/or backward mapping that considers the scope and sequence of the curriculum used in other countries
- Implementation of linguistically and culturally sustaining pedagogy
- Establishment of appropriate expectations and benchmarks
- Providing resources to meet students' needs
- Providing dedicated time and personnel who can support students' home language, literacy, and concept and content development (e.g., community members, university students, professors, and bilingual teachers)

Strategies for Insufficient or Poor Quality of ESL Instruction

- Provide additional ESL instruction that is more closely aligned with content-area material and taught in a meaningful context.
- Provide targeted ESL instruction to remedy gaps in previous language instruction.
- Allow students more time to acquire English.
- Abandon traditional ESL approaches in favor of using sheltered instruction strategies that are standards based, make content comprehensible, and teach content-related language (listening, speaking, reading, and writing) objectives.
- Provide professional learning opportunities in the area of effective instructional strategies and academic English-language development standards for MLs.
- Offer professional learning opportunities to enable teachers to integrate ESL strategies into curriculum and lesson development that better address content and language objectives.

be implemented on a more limited scale. For example, a scaled-down version of a Newcomers Program could be offered to the individual multilingual learner whose formal schooling has been interrupted and who is not at grade level in core academic areas (DaSilva Iddings, 2009). Practices to welcome and prepare newcomer students can become part of the everyday functioning of the school, some of which could be initiated and led by students (see Schecter & Cummins, 2003, for ideas). As well, arbitrary deadlines for exiting language assistance support or programming can be modified to provide the multilingual learner who is not progressing more time to acquire English.

Questions for Reflection and Action

1. Do we know enough about the previous school factors influencing multilingual learners who are currently facing academic challenges? If not, how can we identify specific gaps in academic competency and literacy development among multilingual learners across grade levels and content areas?

2. Focus on the largest language group from your school or district's multilingual learner population. Investigate the educational system from their native country or countries, taking into account local variations such as rural versus urban. How does that system compare with your own system? How does the congruence of approaches, or lack thereof, impact multilingual learners' achievement?

3. If you have visited or know about a school in another part of the United States or in another country, how does its approach to multilingual learner education compare to what you know to be the approach used at your school?

4. How can data related to multilingual learner students' previous school experience be most efficiently organized? What categories would you develop?

5. What are a range of service delivery models that might emerge from the data (both qualitative and quantitative) you collect? How would this information be shared with school staff?

Oral Language and Literacy Development

Key Concepts. *The fourth integral factor to be considered is the student's oral language and literacy development in both the home language and English. To understand challenges that some multilingual learners may face at school, we must understand the level of language proficiency that these students have attained. Knowledge about bilingual development is also essential in designing learning support strategies: language-focused instruction must be contextualized in a way that is meaningful to the student, make developmental sense, make use of the student's resources in all of their languages, and be implemented in a manner that supports the student's dynamic language development.*

The fourth integral element to be considered when multilingual learners experience linguistic or academic challenges is their oral language and literacy development. In this chapter we look at the characteristics of oral language and literacy for multilingual learners in both (or multiple) languages in social and academic settings. We describe principles for appropriate multilingual learner language and literacy instruction and discuss the external factors that may impact optimal language and literacy learning for these students. We discuss the importance of gathering information about language use patterns and how this information helps the multi-tiered system of supports (MTSS) team and others assess oral language and literacy across various contexts in all of the multilingual learners' languages (Gottlieb, 2021). We look at the advantages of promoting multilingual learners' home language(s) in the larger context of school for their own benefit and as a critical diagnostic resource, and we provide suggestions for learning support strategies throughout.

Oral language is discussed separately from literacy so that we can focus attention on specific issues relevant to each of those areas; however, the separation is artificial, because the two areas of language are interdependent (Beeman & Urow, 2013; H. L. Damico et al., 2021; Geekie et al., 1999; F. Smith, 2004; Street, 2009). In fact, children who show difficulties expressing themselves orally or understanding oral language in either their home language or the second language will often have difficulties when they engage with print. If teams could focus more attention early on in supporting students with their oral language development along with literacy instruction, many difficulties related to reading and writing could be alleviated (Allington, 2002a; Chapman et al., 2015; Cloud et al., 2009).

Key Factors in Oral Language Development

Oral language development is a critical factor in multilingual learners' long-term success in school. Because oral language proficiency involves a complex configuration of abilities (Alves, 2019; Bialystock, 2001; Perkins, 2005), there are many aspects of oral language learning to consider. We start by examining briefly the processes of first and second language development to note similarities and differences between the two, as well as to focus on potential areas of concern.

Home Language Acquisition

Children develop their home language from highly contextualized interactions that they have with their caregivers and immediate family members (Bachman et al., 2020; Bruner, 1981; Harding-Esch & Riley, 2012; Kuhl, 2010). By age 4, young children have acquired a great deal of vocabulary and grammar in their home language (Bialystok et al., 2010). They understand many more words than they can produce orally and are able to process adult grammatical structures, although they still make errors in producing them. Though there is some variation in the ages at which children pass through the linguistic developmental stages, these stages seem to be universal (R. W. Brown, 1973; Cowie, 2019; Hoff et al., 2012; Pinker, 1994): Children babble, they utter one word at a time, they move on to include two-word sentences, and gradually their productions begin to approximate adult grammar and vocabulary.

Multilingual learners who begin their lives with a single language are no different than anyone else with respect to acquisition of their first or home language. They go through the same process as their monolingual English-speaking peers, so that by the time they enter prekindergarten or kindergarten, these students have gone through the expected stages of acquisition in their home language. Multilingual learners who enter U.S. schools at a later age have developed the expected skills in their oral home language unless they have had significant disruptive experiences such as war or extensive migration.

Even if schools have not formally instructed multilingual learners in their home language, there is much insight to be gained from looking at oral development in that language (Paradis et al., 2021; P. Smith, 2012). Because all children go through similar stages of acquisition regardless of the language they are born into, we can learn about any unexpected developments during those early years even if there are no specialists at school who speak the multilingual learner's home language. Although allowances must be made for individual and experiential variation, finding out when multilingual learners reached certain linguistic milestones in acquiring their home language may provide insight into any possible underlying language or cognitive difficulties or early hearing loss. On the other hand, children may be quite advanced in development of their home language and only begin having difficulties upon entering school taught in English. While exposing children to a new language early on is a positive thing for any child, the difficulty arises when multilingual learner parents are erroneously told by school staff to stop using their home language. Schools should do the opposite: by encouraging parents to use their proficient language, the home language, as extensively as possible with their children (Genesee et al., 2006; Hakuta, 1986; Harding-Esch & Riley, 2012; King & Fogle, 2013; K. Kohnert et al., 2005; Yturriago, 2012a), a rich and solid foundation is established on which to build the new language.

The importance of the home language as a crucial base for the development of an additional language has encouraged teachers to make fundamental connections between multilingual learners' two languages in a planned way throughout lessons and units of study: for example, consider the work on translanguaging (O. Garcia et al., 2016; Licona & Kelly, 2020), bridging (Beeman & Urow, 2013) and making cross-linguistic transfers (Genesee & Hamayan, 2016).

MTSS Team Activity

Have team members complete a survey about multilingual learners' home languages. Here are some sample questions to consider:
1. What are the languages spoken by the multilingual learners in your school?
2. Approximately how many students, teaching staff members, nonteaching staff members, and parent volunteers speak and read each of these languages?
3. What proportion of multilingual learners have had exposure to English from birth?
4. Have school staff members developed language surveys to use in class to highlight the different languages students speak?
5. Does the team regularly ask about home language development when discussing multilingual learners who are experiencing difficulties?

Acquisition of a Second or Additional Language

Just as in the process of acquiring the home language, children who learn a new or additional language go through predictable stages of language development (Genesee, 2003; Grosjean, 2015a; Peña et al., 2017). And just as in first language acquisition, learners pass through the different stages at very different rates. Some may spend months in the first stage, whereas others work through this stage in only a few weeks or even days. The typical stages of second language acquisition that most learners go through, along with the proficiency levels that are generally expected for each stage, are summarized in Table 7.1.

At the beginning of the process of second language acquisition, most learners say very little in the new language. This is known as the *preproduction stage*. Students remain in this silent period for varying lengths of time, depending on individual personality, how safe they feel in taking risks and making mistakes, how comprehensible the new language is to them, and

Table 7.1   Expected Stages in New/Additional Language Development and English Language Proficiency Levels

Stages in Developing a New/Additional Language	WIDA English Language Proficiency Level
Silent/Receptive or Preproduction Phase MLs may have up to 500 words in their receptive vocabularies, but they are not yet speaking. Some students repeat everything you say; however, they may be imitating, not really producing language. These new English learners listen attentively, and they may even be able to copy words from the board. They are able to respond to pictures and other visuals. They can understand and duplicate gestures and movements to show comprehension.	**Level 1—Entering** MLs process, understand, produce, or use: • Pictorial or graphic representation of the language of the content areas • Words, phrases, or chunks of language when presented with one-step commands; directions; who/what/where, choice, or yes/no questions; or statements with sensory, graphic, or interactive support • Oral language with phonological, syntactic, or semantic errors that often impede meaning when presented with basic oral commands, direct questions, or simple statements with sensory, graphic, or interactive support
Early Production Phase Early production can last an additional 6 months. Students have usually developed close to 1,000 receptive/active words (i.e., words they are able to understand and use). During early production, students can usually speak in one- or two-word phrases and demonstrate comprehension of new material by giving short answers to simple yes/no, either/or, or who/what/where questions. They can use short language chunks that have been memorized, although these chunks may not always be used correctly.	**Level 2—Emerging** MLs process, understand, produce, or use: • General language related to the content areas • Phrases or short sentences • Oral or written language with phonological, syntactic, or semantic errors that often impede the meaning of the communication when presented with one- to multiple-step commands, directions, questions, or a series of statements with sensory, graphic, or interactive support
Speech Emergence Phase Speech emergence can last up to another year. Students have usually developed approximately 3,000 words and can use short, simple sentences to communicate. Students begin to use dialogue and can ask simple questions, such as "Can I go to the restroom?" and are able to answer simple questions. Students may produce longer sentences, but often with grammatical errors that may interfere with their communication. MLs also initiate short conversations with classmates. They understand easy stories read in class with the support of pictures. They also are able to do some content work with teacher support.	**Level 3—Developing** MLs process, understand, produce, or use: • General and some specific language of the content areas • Expanded sentences in oral interaction or written paragraphs • Oral or written language with phonological, syntactic, or semantic errors that may impede the communication, but retain much of its meaning, when presented with oral or written, narrative, or expository descriptions with sensory, graphic, or interactive support
Intermediate Language Phase Intermediate proficiency may take up to another year after speech emergence. Students have typically developed close to 6,000 words and are beginning to make complex statements, state opinions, ask for clarification, share their thoughts, and speak at greater length. They are beginning to use more complex sentences when speaking and writing and are willing to express opinions and share their thoughts. They ask questions to clarify what they are learning in class. These MLs are able to work in grade-level math and science classes with some teacher support. Comprehension of English literature and social studies content is increasing.	**Level 4—Expanding** MLs process, understand, produce, or use: • Specific and some technical language of the content areas • A variety of sentence lengths of varying linguistic complexity in oral discourse or multiple, related sentences or paragraphs • Oral or written language with minimal phonological, syntactic, or semantic errors that do not impede the overall meaning of the communication when presented with oral or written connected discourse with sensory, graphic, or interactive support
Advanced Language Phase Achieving academic language proficiency in a new or additional language can typically take from 5 to 7 years or more. By this stage, students have developed some specialized content-area vocabulary and can participate fully in grade-level classroom activities if given occasional extra support. Students can speak English using grammar and vocabulary comparable to that of same-age native English speakers. Students at this stage are nearing parity with the average monolingual English speaker in performance on content-area assessments. At this stage, most MLs have been removed from language and other support programs.	**Level 5—Bridging** MLs process, understand, produce, or use • Specialized or technical language of the content areas • A variety of sentence lengths of varying linguistic complexity in extended oral or written discourse, including stories, essays, or reports • Oral or written language approaching comparability to that of English-proficient peers when presented with grade-level material **Level 6—Reaching** MLs process, understand, produce, or use • Specialized or technical language reflective of the content areas at grade level • A variety of sentence lengths of varying linguistic complexity in extended oral or written discourse as required by the specified grade level • Oral or written communication in English comparable to English-proficient peers

ML, multilingual learner; WIDA Consortium. (Adapted from WIDA Resource Guide. [2012]. *Developing a culturally and linguistically responsive approach to response to instruction and intervention [RtI2] for English language learners: Connecting to WIDA standards, assessments, and other resources.* Copyright © 2016 Board of Regents of the University of Wisconsin System, on behalf of WIDA - wida.wisc.edu) other reasons related to the affective environment. Teachers often worry that the silence of their newly arrived multilingual learners indicates a selective mutism. They should be reassured that most learners need to spend quite a bit of time processing the new language without having to perform in it (Christiansen et al., 2016; Goldstein & Horton-Ikard, 2010; Schütze, 2017; Stow & Dodd, 2005). If teachers, school staff, or parents say that the student is also not speaking in the home language either, then it is important to consider other explanations. It would also be reasonable to conduct a screening of the student's hearing or to find out whether the student has shown signs of excessive anxiety in various settings.

The next stage is the *early production stage*. During this stage multilingual learners may begin to use one- or two-word utterances, "no more," "thank you," and "go now?" They can understand more of their friends' conversations on the playground, at lunch, and in the school corridors. *Speech emergence* is the third stage; this can be an exciting time for multilingual learners as they realize that they can understand a great deal more of what their peers are saying and see that their own oral language is much more developed. Peers may begin to interact with them more, and adults may praise their English production. At this stage, multilingual learners can string together a list of words or say short phrases. Though exciting, this can also be a frustrating time for these students. They are not fully proficient in their new language but are very eager to converse with their English-speaking friends and classmates, especially in social settings (Cho, 2016; Kheirkhah & Cekaite, 2018). When they realize they do not have the exact words or enough words in English to express everything they want to say, they may get angry or withdraw from interaction.

Another cause of frustration is that multilingual learners at this stage of proficiency rehearse and practice their utterances before they try them out with their peers or teachers. This constant practice and rehearsal require a great deal of effort, concentration, patience, and persistence. If after all that effort their message is not fully understood, multilingual learners may get discouraged. At this stage, multilingual learners' oral productive language in English typically does not correspond to their receptive language in English. This situation can be frustrating for students, because after they produce a rehearsed phrase or sentence, they may not understand what the other person says in response. In Chapter 9 we discuss the culture shock that often corresponds to this stage of second language acquisition and how it may add even more frustration and emotional stress to multilingual learners' experience.

Eventually, multilingual learners reach the *intermediate fluency stage*. At this level of proficiency they have much more oral fluency, and produce fewer telegraphic-type utterances. Students still need more time and a great deal of vocabulary to engage in conversations with their friends or to understand subtleties of their new language, such as humor or figurative language. This development leads to the *fluent stage* of second language acquisition. It is important to keep in mind that it can take more than 6 years of constant exposure to and instruction in English for multilingual learners to develop sufficient proficiency in the language to participate fully in an academic setting (Carhill et al., 2008; Cummins, 2012).

Proficiency in social and academic contexts.   One often overlooked aspect of oral language is that it can be described along a kind of continuum. As we see in the following text, oral language is used in different contexts for different purposes, some more social in orientation and others more formal or academic (Cummins, 2000, 2012). As Figure 7.1 shows, students can develop this range of oral language proficiency in their home language and English (Gottlieb, 2006, 2021; Gottlieb & Ernst-Slavit, 2014). The social language end of this continuum could include the language of everyday interactions with peers, affiliation, joking and apologizing, and speaking with strangers. In language used in academic settings we can distinguish the language of mathematics, science, social studies, language arts, fine arts, and physical education (Cloud et al., 2009; Janzen, 2008; Licona & Kelly, 2020; Ryu, 2019) from the language needed to negotiate with others, make formal presentations, problem-solve with others, work through a problem individually, and to conduct interviews, among other situations.

In English, the multilingual learners' new language, it may take about 2 years to become proficient in the everyday language of social conversations, whereas it might take multilingual learners 5 or more years to develop the academic English needed to show what they know on standardized tests in English (Cummins, 2000, 2012). Social fluency can develop more quickly than academic language because it is often contextualized in meaningful real-life communication. For example, with the visual context of a television program, multilingual learners are better able to understand the language; in oral exchanges with classmates on the playground and at lunch, multilingual learners have the added support of facial expressions and gestures as clues to what is being said. This comprehensible context allows multilingual learners to understand some of the language they hear, and it helps them make themselves understood as well. That being said, developing social language may be challenging because students may not yet understand the nuances of humor, cultural references, unspoken social rules, or timing in the new language. Spending time supporting students' social language proficiency in English can be a great help to them as they navigate uncertain territory.

Academic oral language, on the other hand, is often highly decontextualized and becomes more abstract as students progress through school. Over the last few years, there have been many efforts to develop guidelines (or standards) to help teachers figure out what kind and level of language proficiency

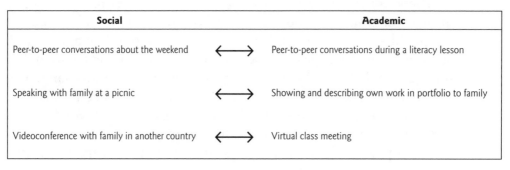

Figure 7.1.   Range of language use in social and academic contexts.

to expect from multilingual learners at different grades. An example of such a set of standards was developed by the WIDA Consortium (see https://wida.wisc.edu/teach/standards/eld). These standards are organized around Key Language Uses (argue, narrate, inform, explain) that all students need to develop in order to access academic content.

A common misconception is that once multilingual learners are speaking English, they should begin having success in school. As we understand the difference between social and academic oral language, we are less likely to make such statements. Proficiency in social fluency is not necessarily a good predictor of academic language proficiency or academic success (Bialystok, 2018; Calderón et al., 2011; Cardenas-Hagan et al., 2007). It is a place to begin for multilingual learners as they use their social language to navigate communication in their academic classes. But if they are not given guidance on the English needed to communicate or to understand mathematical or scientific ideas, for example, they may continue to use their social fluency to talk about topics that require more technical or content-specific phrases, vocabulary, and procedural language (Janzen, 2008; Licona & Kelly, 2020). Chronicle 7.1 shows the importance of the academic language and how it can be promoted in the classroom.

Chronicle 7.1

"The Glass Thing": When Conversational Language Just Won't Do

By a Consultant Who Observed a Grade 6 Classroom

I was observing a grade 6 science class and saw a teacher do a brilliant job getting the multilingual learners to use academic language. In the following exchange the teacher engaged the students' conversational language to share their ideas and then connected these to the specific academic language required for a science lab report. Consider the following exchange between the teacher and a multilingual student in Group 1:

Teacher:	After you have summarized the procedure we used in this experiment, we will share them with the class.
Group 1:	(After about 10 minutes) We're ready!
Teacher:	Let's have your first step.
Student:	We put some water in the glass thing.
Teacher:	Good. How much water? (She writes the student's sentence on the overhead projector, beginning with the word *First*.)
Student:	This much (showing the amount by the distance between his fingers).
Teacher:	How much is that in scientific language?
Student:	(Turning to a neighbor) 50 milliliters.
Teacher:	Correct. Fifty milliliters.
Student:	Milliliter (he practices pronouncing the word softly to himself). That's the same in my language!

The exchange continued as the teacher asked for clarification as to what "the glass thing" was called. She found that many students in the class had used an informal term rather than the actual name of the object, *graduated cylinder*. She also modeled writing procedural language about every specific step that was taken and each piece of equipment that was used and why. She emphasized that scientists need to be very specific and accurate in what they write so that others can replicate their experiments.

The teacher gave many examples and honored all of her students' utterances. The students themselves realized that if they wanted to write like scientists, then using "the glass thing" would not allow the reader to know what they meant. This was a very receptive and motivated group of students. They did not have to be asked to repeat the word to internalize it and to make it part of their linguistic repertoire. Many students could be seen practicing saying *graduated cylinder*, some of them even writing it down in their notebooks.

Questions for Discussion

1. What does it take for students to make something like the term *graduated cylinder* part of their language repertoire?

2. What are other ways you can honor students' social language in different content areas and then use this language as a bridge to academic expression?

Multilingual learners who have opportunities to engage in academic conversations at school and who have access to books in their home languages and in English at school, at home, and in community libraries, find it easier to use academic language. Later in the chapter we discuss the connections between multilingual learners' home language and English (or new language) that allow such cross-language development to occur.

MTSS Team Activity

Team members can experience a simulation of the speech emergence stage. Ask pairs to chat with each other for about 2 minutes about something they did the past weekend. The only stipulation is that they may not use the letter "t" in any of the words in their speech. For example, they are not allowed to say, "I went to my friend's house to eat dinner on Saturday." Rather, they could say, "I go my friend's house for dinner on a day before Sunday." After the 2 minutes are up, ask each pair to discuss how they felt. What communication strategies did they use? What would have made the task easier? What are the implications for multilingual learners at this stage of English acquisition for assessing their language proficiency? their knowledge of academic content? the role of the home language?

Evidence of Instruction in Oral Academic Language

For most children, the opportunity to develop academic oral language comes primarily at school. Assuming that instruction is optimal, how easily and how quickly the multilingual learner develops academic language proficiency depends on factors such as level and quality of previous formal schooling, and how physically and psychologically fit they are (e.g., Alami et al., 2014; Janzen, 2007; Xu & Drame, 2008). But, ultimately, it is the learning environment and the way we prepare these students linguistically to make instruction comprehensible and relevant that determines to a large extent how well multilingual learners do in school (Bruner, 2006; Callahan & Gándara, 2014; Echevarria et al., 2017; Gibbons, 2015; Hadjioannou, 2007; F. Smith, 1998; Watson-Gegeo, 2004). We need to ask ourselves how well has the school or district curriculum team integrated academic language across the content areas and grade levels? Are there opportunities for all students to learn academic language during content-area instruction?

Teachers need to integrate the specialized vocabulary, particular phrases and sentences, as well as the discourse structure and patterns (Bailey, 2007) that are essential for the topic being presented in class. As Snow et al. (1989) point out, multilingual learners not only need content-specific language, such as the words *renewable, propeller* in a unit on alternative energy (what Snow et al. call *content-obligatory language*), they also need language that is not essential to a particular text, such as the future tense, words such as *energy* and *wind* (what Snow et al. call *content-compatible language*). Examples and a discussion of how to incorporate academic language instruction into a lesson can be found in Chapter 8. In addition, teachers need to use sheltering strategies when using academic language so that meaning can be constructed without having to depend solely on language (see Echevarria et al., 2017 for a detailed description of the Sheltered Instruction Observation Protocol [SIOP]).

It is also important that multilingual learners have opportunities to engage in oral academic language practice throughout the day across various contexts. Because learning is a social process, multilingual learners co-construct meaning when they engage in dialogue with others (Lesaux & Harris, 2015; Sánchez-López & Young, 2018; Swain, 2006; van Lier, 2004; Vygotsky, 1978; Wells, 2003). When gathering information about multilingual learners who may be experiencing difficulty progressing in their oral language (e.g., not talking during collaborative literacy activities, not wanting to present in science class), it is important to determine how much opportunity students have during the instructional day to use their oral language. If the instruction multilingual learners are given consists mostly of doing silent work at their desks, if they are in groups in which one or two students dominate the discussion, or if they are passively watching a video, they are not getting the opportunity to learn and use academic oral language. The checklist in Box 7.1 may be useful to gauge the extent to which groupings, activities, and environments that promote oral language use by students are evident in the classroom. Teachers may either use this checklist for self-assessment or pair up with a colleague to observe each other's classrooms.

Teachers must create activities and circumstances that motivate students to use their academic and social oral language with one another. Typically, one does not hear students at lunch, recess, or in the hallways using academic oral language, so it is imperative that teachers orchestrate these opportunities

---

Box 7.1

Checklist of Classroom Activities That Promote Oral Language Practice

Flexible Grouping

___ Interest groups
___ Pairs
___ Grouping by language proficiency levels
___ Grouping by language background
___ Expert groups
___ Long-term project groups
___ Research teams
___ Triads

Instruction

___ Use small-group presentations/work on shared documents.
___ Prepare students for group work by introducing sentence frames to support the group interaction and have students practice them.
___ Use thematic content-area word banks.
___ Engage in active learning.
___ Engage in partner sharing and conversations.
___ Use project-based learning.
___ Use service learning.
___ Use problem-based learning.
___ Use product-based learning.
___ Shared experiences (video clips, simulations, activities with manipulatives, experiments, viewing an image or photograph, a play, field trip) are used later as a springboard for shared reading and writing.
___ Have individual conferences with students on their reading and writing.
___ Students talk at home about what they learn in school.

Affective Environment

___ Students are encouraged to collaborate with one another.
___ Students' languages are actively engaged within the classroom, including use of bilingual content-area word banks; previewing materials in home language; use of written displays of different home languages represented in the classroom; availability of multilingual welcome signs, bilingual announcements, and books in different home languages in the school and classroom libraries.
___ Ongoing team building occurs.
___ Students and teachers learn each other's languages.
___ Collaborative structures are used.
___ Materials and responsibilities are shared.
___ Procedures are established for group work and presentations.
___ Students share their own experiences.
___ Students are given time to think and plan.

within the classroom. Throughout this guide, we introduce ideas for how to design lessons and units that allow multilingual learners to develop their academic listening, speaking, reading, and writing across the curriculum.

> **MTSS Team Activity**
>
> This activity is a follow-up to the previous one during which team members experienced a simulation of the speech emergence stage when talking about a concrete social event. For this activity, show team members a visual aid from a science or social studies textbook. Again, ask team members to talk about the concept represented in the visual without using any words that contain the letter "t." To make this activity most effective, choose a topic that requires a word with a "t," such as "climate change" or "the water cycle." This simulates what multilingual learners might experience when using their oral language in an academic context.
>
> After the 2 minutes are up, ask each pair to discuss how they felt. What communication strategies were they using? What would have made the task easier? How was this experience different from the activity using language in a more social context? What are the implications for multilingual learners at this stage of English acquisition for assessing their language proficiency? their knowledge of academic content? the role of the home language?

Reinforcing Academic Language at Home

In addition to considering the quality of instruction that develops academic language among multilingual learners, we also have to take into account what happens in this domain outside of school. Multilingual learners' families and communities can provide a rich opportunity for oral academic language development when the communication occurs in a language the adults are proficient in, which for most students is the home language (B. A. Collins et al., 2014; Hoff et al., 2012). Multilingual learners' home language serves as a very important base on which students build their identities, develop their concepts, connect to their families, and establish their cultural notions. Students' home language(s) are also a firm foundation on which to build English language proficiency (Bialystock, 2001; Carhill et al., 2008; Genesee, 2012; King & Fogle, 2013; Smith, 2012). Moreover, much of the proficiency that develops in the home language has the potential to transfer to the new language. Thus, students who have their academic language reinforced in the home language(s) are better able to tackle new concepts in English.

Many cognitive, academic, linguistic, and socioemotional benefits result when multilingual learners are encouraged to talk with family members in their home language about what they are experiencing and learning at school (Bachman et al., 2020; C. J. Flores & Delgado, 2012; E. García, 2005; Watson-Gegeo, 2004; Wells, 2003). Children learn about the adults in their lives, and this fosters respect and admiration among family members for what they know and have experienced. Thus, it is critical that schools do all they can to elevate the prestige of multilingual learners' home languages and to encourage parents and other caregivers to continue using their home language with their children as long as possible (Harding-Esch & Riley,

2012; Marshall & Toohey, 2010). The following are ways in which academic language development can be encouraged in the home:

- Inform the parents in the home language, through either a bilingual teacher or bilingual aide, translator, or volunteer, what students are studying, in a way that allows parents to support the learning at home in their language(s).

- Encourage students to review at home the events of the school day and what they understood from the day's learning; suggest to parents that they ask questions and ask their children to describe and explain what activities and projects they participated in.

- Encourage parents to make connections between the home language and English; when the child uses a term or talks about a concept learned at school, ask "What is that in English/(the home language)?"

- Encourage students to generate questions at home to ask their teachers the next day.

- Work with grade-level teams to develop engaging, interesting, relevant, and comprehensible units of study so that students will feel compelled to share what they are learning about with their families.

- Encourage parents to provide their own perspective on the topics students are studying that could be shared in class the next day (such as different historical perspectives, home language equivalents of academic terminology, personal experiences, or expertise with the topic in question).

- Provide parents with guidelines they can use to model the procedural language of sequencing, cause and effect, predicting, elaborating, asking questions, storytelling, and so forth, in their home language.

When the home language is used freely and extensively by the family, not only does it help build language proficiency in general, it also gives staff another opportunity to confirm whether a difficulty that a multilingual learner is having goes beyond the challenges of learning in a new language. As will be discussed in Chapter 10, we must have access to various contexts to be able to validate the explanation for a multilingual learner's difficulty. If we notice that a group of multilingual learners is having difficulty using oral narratives effectively, we must validate whether this challenge occurs only in English at school or whether it occurs at home as well.

Key Factors in Literacy Development

Many of the challenges that students encounter in school can be attributed to hurdles faced in reading and writing grade-appropriate texts (Allington, 2009). Literacy is one of the strongest predictors of academic achievement and, therefore, of success in school (Clay, 1991; Cloud et al., 2009; Cunningham & Allington, 2011; H. L. Damico et al., 2021; Krashen, 2004; F. Smith, 2004). We often jump to the conclusion that these difficulties with literacy occur because of reading disabilities, especially if the multilingual learners have gone through a school system and received the same literacy instruction as their native English-speaking peers. To read and write efficiently and well while developing proficiency in two languages, however, multilingual learners need specialized instruction that takes into account specific issues pertaining to bilingual literacy development (Beeman & Urow, 2013; Cloud et al., 2009; Soltero-González et al., 2016). To receive exactly the same reading instruction in the same way as the monolingual English-speaking students is not sufficient to support multilingual learners in developing English literacy (August & Shanahan, 2008). We need to remember that the language practices of bilingual or multilingual persons reflect one integrated system rather than two or more autonomous side-by-side systems (Bialystok, 2018; O. Garcia & Woodley, 2015). It is important then to note that literacy instruction developed exclusively for monolingual English speakers may not have the same outcomes when implemented with multilingual learners learning to read in English.

The issues in literacy development as they relate to academic challenges encountered by multilingual learners are similar to those already discussed for oral language development. These issues include how literacy develops in students' home languages and English; the opportunities to engage in literacy for both social and academic purposes; the quality and amount of literacy instruction students have received previously, and are receiving presently, in the home language and English (Gonzalez & Artiles, 2015).

Literacy Development in the Home Language and English

Three principles embody what is most important to remember about literacy development in multilingual learners.

Literacy principle 1.   The most important outcome of engaging with reading and writing is comprehension, not just the ability to decode letters or call out words on a page (Beeman & Urow, 2013; J. S. Damico, 2019f; G. G. García, 2003; Goodman et al., 2016; Keene, 2008; 2012; Paris, 2005; F. Smith, 2004; Soltero-González et al., 2016).

The first thing we need to keep in mind in literacy development is that reading and writing are complex processes that go far beyond decoding words, copying letters, or calling out words on a page. Whether it is in the student's home language or English, the purpose of any literacy act is to either get or send meaning (H. L. Damico et al., 2021; F. Smith, 2003, 2004). For any student, it is far more important to understand what a text says rather than only to be able to decode the same passage aloud. For a multilingual learner, it is even more essential that reading and writing in English (the new language) be focused and based on meaning, because it is easier to read and write something one understands when using a language one is not yet very proficient in.

This literacy principle has implications for schools and the classroom. Any interactions multilingual learners have with print, whether in reading or writing, must be embedded in meaningful contexts to be useful to these students (Cloud et al., 2009; Dudley-Marling & Paugh, 2004; Goodman & Goodman, 2014; Lucariello et al., 2016). Thus, phonics instruction or instruction that focuses on any literacy skill taught in isolation that is devoid of meaning is ineffective for young multilingual learners who are in the process of acquiring English (Dahl et al., 1999; H. L. Damico et al., 2021; Goodman, 2014; Paris, 2005; Sánchez-López & Young, 2018). Although some multilingual learners do receive explicit instruction in foundational literacy skills (Cirino et al., 2009), it is essential that this instruction occur within meaningful literacy contexts and units of study (H. L. Damico et al., 2017; Goodman, 2014; F. Smith, 2015). Students should not be repeating meaningless sounds or words without having anything meaningful with which to connect these sounds and words. Too often, teachers give multilingual learners certain literacy tasks because they have inherited a reading or writing program, were given a particular strategy or a set of materials, or because of a district or state mandate. However, it is important that whatever multilingual learners are given to read and write engages them, stimulates them cognitively, and allows them to imagine, think, visualize, and connect what they are reading and writing to other topics and to life experiences (Cloud et al., 2009; D. Freeman & Freeman, 2003; Keene, 2012; Lesaux & Harris, 2015). In fact, when carefully reviewing the most important aspects of literacy development and usage in classrooms, the single most important variable for encouraging both literacy and academic content learning is that the students (in the home language or English) have comprehensible texts to read (Allington, 2002b; 2009; Allington & Walmsley, 2007; Chiang, 2016; Niazifar & Shakibaei, 2019). This means that school leadership, literacy specialists, librarians, and teachers must seek to develop their libraries and classroom materials to include a wide range of texts that connect to the content curriculum, are written at a variety of reading levels, and include books that are of interest to students (Cunningham & Allington, 2011; Krashen, 2004). Multiple texts must be available to students that they can read fairly independently with meaning, accuracy, and fluency so that every student is given access and an entry into the unit of study. This access is possible because of the use of specialized texts available in many subjects that are appropriate for certain grades and designed to be comprehensible for lower levels of reading (Allington, 2005; Cunningham & Allington, 2011; Mesmer, 2007). In addition, multilingual learners should be able to find something to read for pleasure in the classroom library. When designing literacy instruction or special learning support strategies for multilingual learners, we must check the effectiveness of what we are asking them to do. The following questions must be asked at every opportunity:

- Are the texts that students are reading or writing about written at the level of their oral language proficiency?

- Is the student able to read this text independently with comprehension, accuracy, and fluency?

- Have we provided students with sufficient opportunities to develop content-area background information and experiences necessary for them to understand the text?

- Are students engaged in cognitively demanding literacy activities in which they are reading and writing to solve problems, to express themselves, to put forth their perspective, to communicate with others, or to effect change in their environment?

- How do we make use of multilingual learners' home languages as resources to use in literacy activities?

- Are there texts that students find fun to read?

- Do we choose materials that reflect multilingual learners' sociocultural and linguistic backgrounds, as well as those of all the students in our schools and communities?

Literacy principle 2. There is a strong connection between oral language development and learning how to read and write (H. L. Damico et al., 2021; Genesee et al., 2005; Goodman et al., 2016; Krashen, 2004).

Literacy and oral language are closely related in three aspects. First, both literacy and oral language are primary language systems that can develop naturally if the appropriate learning and usage contexts are available. Second, the development of literacy proceeds in predictable stages, much as oral language does, although, due to the lack of appropriate contextual variables, it often requires the help of instruction. Third, oral language reinforces the development of literacy and is itself reinforced by reading and writing.

What does this principle mean for the classroom? It is essential for teachers to base their literacy instruction on what they know about natural language development. Just as with oral language, literacy development is based on the principles of social constructivism and, consequently, many of the principles of oral language acquisition and development apply to literacy as well (Cambourne, 2002; Geekie et al., 1999; Goodman, 2001; Goodman et al., 2016; F. Smith, 2004; Wells, 1986). Meaningfulness of the texts, contextualization of the material, active engagement in the process of meaning construction, recurrence of mediation and opportunity, and contrasting the various ways to formulate and interpret the material are as critical to acquiring and using literacy as they are to developing and using oral language (Cambourne, 2002; H. L. Damico et al., 2021). Teachers can employ various strategies to help make connections between oral and written language (National Academies of Sciences, Engineering, and Medicine, 2017). For example, the language experience approach (LEA; McCormick, 1988; Nessel & Jones, 1981) or the scaffolding reading experiences framework (M. F. Graves & Fitzgerald, 2003) can be used across content areas to help multilingual learners use their oral language to connect to literacy. In the LEA approach, for example, students discuss a shared experience, take notes, rehearse, and then report to the class. The teacher acts as scribe to capture the students' utterances and, in the process, models writing for the students.

Literacy principle 3.　A student's home language is a resource for developing literacy in English, not a hindrance (August & Shanahan, 2008; Beeman & Urow, 2013; Cloud et al., 2009; O. Garcia et al., 2016; Genesee et al., 2006).

It is clear from the research that literacy in students' home language supports English literacy development, regardless of what that home language is (Cardenas-Hagan et al., 2007; Cheadle, 2008; Corsaro & Nelson, 2003; DaSilva Iddings, 2009; Hornberger & Link, 2012; Lightbown & Spada, 2006). Later in the chapter we look at specific areas of literacy that transfer across languages, but, in general, the meaning-making aspects of literacy—such as drawing inferences, comparing and contrasting information, understanding main ideas and details, and recognizing propaganda—transfer broadly across languages. Once students have experience being literate in one language, they have the potential to transfer those skills and approaches to literacy to any additional languages they learn (Cummins, 2008).

What implications does principle 3 have for schools and the classroom? Multilingual learners can benefit significantly from learning to read in their home language. Reading instruction in English (the new language) can begin when the student has some oral language proficiency in English (Cloud et al., 2009; D. Freeman & Freeman, 2003; Krashen, 2004). Creating school environments that elevate and celebrate students' home languages will encourage students and their families to continue to use their languages at home, in the community, and in school for social and academic purposes. Within these supportive environments, teachers can plan to activate students' home language skills and knowledge by inviting their languages into the classroom and encouraging students to think, read, plan, and strategize in their home languages and in English. The most effective way to bring in the home language during English instruction time is to use it not just for communicating and meaning- making, but to unveil connections between the two languages. This not only allows students to get a sense of how languages are related, it also gives them a chance to reinforce a concept in the other language. This strategy can be applied in the other direction as well, when instruction is in the home language and connections are revealed in English. For example, cognates or similarities in phrasing or grammar can be explored and cross-linguistic lists can be exhibited on the wall in side-by-side posters (see Beeman & Urow, 2013).

This type of cross-linguistic transfer allows students to use what they know in one language to help them develop higher levels of proficiency in the other language (Beeman & Urow, 2013; Escamilla et al., 2014). When it is not possible for a school to provide high-quality instruction to multilingual learners in reading and writing in their home language, these students' home language literacy must be reinforced in the family or community by means of a tutoring program that the school sets up (DaSilva Iddings, 2009; Reese & Goldenberg, 2006). The multilingual resources listed in Table 3.1 in Chapter 3 could help provide multilingual reading material in classroom and school libraries. When older students, parents, or volunteers read these books aloud to younger multilingual learners, they model fluent reading, help students develop pride in the home languages, and reinforce home–school connections

(Baker, 2011; Trelease, 2001). If it proves difficult initially to find volunteers to read in the different languages, there are many benefits to be had when multilingual learners read aloud to family members in English or in their home language. The impact on multilingual learners' reading is positive even when parents do not understand the language of the books or if the parents are not literate (J. S. Damico et al., 2005; Harding-Esch & Riley, 2012; Tizard et al., 1982). A guide on how to make the most out of this literacy event can be provided to the family so that parents can ask questions and engage in critical discussion with their children.

It is even more crucial that multilingual learners who do not have an opportunity to develop literacy in their home language be introduced to literacy in English through meaningful activities rather than tasks that are devoid of context and meaning (Cloud et al., 2009; Cunningham & Allington, 2011; D. Freeman & Freeman, 2003; Genesee, 2012; Keene, 2008; Routman, 2003).

An example of how schools can address these three principles successfully is the creation of identity texts (Chow & Cummins, 2005; Schecter & Cummins, 2003). Students create dual language stories, texts, and projects in their home languages and English about topics that they care deeply about and that allow them to reflect on their multicultural identities, their opinions, thoughts, and perspectives. These texts provide meaningful literacy activities that connect oral language with reading and writing (Schall-Leckrone, 2018). Not only do they allow multilingual learners to develop literacy in both languages, they raise the status of literacy in all multilingual learners' languages to a high level. Some school principals have begun similar dual language projects in their multilingual schools as a way to engage multilingual parents (Verdon et al., 2014). Some teachers have used dual language projects as a bridge to reading and writing in both the home language and English with multilingual learners who are simultaneous bilinguals and have at least some literacy in both of their languages.

Literacy Development in Social and Academic Settings

Just as in oral language development, it is important to provide multilingual learners the opportunity to use their literacy for social and academic purposes. And, just as in oral language development, social literacy may develop more easily because it deals with more concrete ideas and has referents that are usually quite accessible to the learner (Gagarina et al., 2016). The popularity of electronic devices that allow social messaging might suggest that these social literacy skills are being developed very early and used very often. A great challenge for teachers and schools is to take advantage of students' interest and skill in social literacy and use these strengths as a resource on which to build academic literacy (Vurdien & Puranen, 2018). Building on multilingual learners' ability to send emails, join chat groups on the Internet, and send text messages can be a bridge to more complex and abstract literacy tasks (Sundqvist & Sylvén, 2014). Although academic texts tend to be more cognitively demanding because of their abstractness, and they adhere to more rigid

Table 7.2 Checklist of Literacy Activities in the Home Language and English

Social Reading	Home Language	English	Social Writing	Home Language	English
• Comic books and magazines	_____	_____	• To-do lists	_____	_____
• Books	_____	_____	• Blogs	_____	_____
• Internet sites	_____	_____	• Text messaging	_____	_____
• Text messaging	_____	_____	• Emails	_____	_____
• Social media posts	_____	_____	• Notes	_____	_____
• Emails	_____	_____	• Personal journal/diary	_____	_____
• Notes	_____	_____	• Letters to friends and family	_____	_____
• Advertising	_____	_____	• Class newsletter	_____	_____
• Closed captioning on TV	_____	_____			
• Song lyrics	_____	_____			
• Blogs	_____	_____			

Academic Reading	Home Language	English	Academic Writing	Home Language	English
• Textbooks	_____	_____	• Essays	_____	_____
• Literature	_____	_____	• Research papers	_____	_____
• Biographies	_____	_____	• Learning logs	_____	_____
• Peer reviews of written work	_____	_____	• Lab reports	_____	_____
• Oral reports	_____	_____	• Reflections	_____	_____
• Encyclopedia entries	_____	_____	• Poetry	_____	_____
• Internet articles	_____	_____	• Goal sheets	_____	_____
• Magazine articles	_____	_____	• Bibliographies	_____	_____
• Math problems	_____	_____	• Question–answer text	_____	_____
• Poetry	_____	_____	• Outlines	_____	_____
• Instructions	_____	_____	• Notes	_____	_____
• Online research	_____	_____	• Summaries	_____	_____
• PowerPoint presentations	_____	_____	• Paraphrasing	_____	_____
• Scanning, skimming texts	_____	_____	• Informational brochures	_____	_____
• Texts generated by students from language experience activities	_____	_____	• PowerPoint presentations	_____	_____

rules of accuracy, teachers can use genre families to build students' literacy skills by using familiar literacy genres, such as texting, podcasts, and transcripts, to connect to more complex genres, such as plays and scripts. Table 7.2 shows a partial checklist of social and academic reading and writing practices that students should be engaging in in English and their home language.

Although most of the activity done in the name of the standards movement has not addressed multilingual learners, some organizations have sought to create English language development standards to help states and local school districts describe the language and literacy that multilingual learners use while developing English as a new or additional language. As an example, the WIDA Consortium (https://wida.wisc.edu) has produced guidelines about the types of literacy that can be expected from multilingual learners for various content areas at different grade levels (PreK–grade 12).

MTSS Team Activity

Using the list of literacy activities shown in Table 7.2, have individual teachers or pairs of teachers check off the tasks and activities that their multilingual learners engage in. Encourage them to think about ways to incorporate some of the activities that are not checked into their daily classroom routines. What are some ways that monolingual English-speaking classroom teachers can incorporate more home language literacy activities into their classrooms?

Evidence of Appropriate Literacy Instruction in the Home Language and English

At this point it is important to determine whether multilingual learners who are experiencing challenges at school are receiving appropriate literacy instruction in both their home language and in English. Even multilingual learners who have spent a few years in U.S. schools may not have received the specialized literacy instruction they need. This issue is important because the greatest predictor of a student's mastery of any skill or ability is the opportunity to learn that skill in a sufficient and appropriate manner (Berliner & Biddle, 1995; National Academies of Sciences, Engineering, and Medicine, 2017). When we provide multilingual learners with exactly the same literacy instruction at the same time in the same way that we provide native English speakers with literacy instruction, we are not offering multilingual learners the most effective path to literacy (Arrow et al., 2015; Escamilla et al., 2014).

Effective literacy practices apply the three principles discussed earlier in this chapter (summarized as follows):

- Reading and writing have to be taught in ways and contexts that are meaningful to the student. If students are given texts that are unfamiliar to them, teachers can create shared experiences that build content-specific schemas that should prepare students to better interact with that text, or careful mediation via a more competent reader should always be available to the student (Chiang, 2016; H. L. Damico et al., 2017). Strategies like shared reading (J. S. Damico, 2006), balanced literacy instruction as discussed in reading recovery (Clay, 1993), or the use of a mediational approach (Routman, 2003) are some of the ways this might be accomplished. Even further, with whatever text students read, teachers should find ways to clearly relate the theme of the text to students' daily lives (Tharp, 1999). Chronicle 7.2 provides an illustration of a lost opportunity to relate an academic text to students' lives.

- Instruction must take into account the oral language proficiency level of each student and use that oracy to build literacy. Thus, a teacher who understands that a group of multilingual learners is at the speech emergence stage of oral language proficiency encourages these students to use content-specific word banks and introduces them to key words from a lesson, a text, or a lecture on the topic (e.g., Allington, 2001; M. F. Graves & Fitzgerald, 2003; McGill-Frazen, 2006). When teaching reading and writing to multilingual learners, it is essential that every aspect of the lesson include an oral language component (D. August & Shanahan, 2008). Instruction and activities using personal narratives that are meaningful to the students within their home and school contexts can be especially effective (Altman et al., 2016; Washington et al., 2021).

- Literacy instruction in English must also be founded on whatever literacy exists in the students' home language, and for young multilingual learners embarking on the task of learning how to read, the introduction to literacy must be done in a language the students can understand—their

Chronicle 7.2

Romeo and Juliet: **A Lost Opportunity**

By a Consultant Who Observed a High-School English-as-Second-Language English Class

This was one of the toughest high schools in the city, clearly dominated by two opposing gangs. It was also one of the lowest-performing schools in the state. I was asked to observe the English-as-a-second-language (ESL) English class. I walked in just as the students were entering the classroom in pairs and small groups. The teacher was already in the classroom, organizing his papers. As I settled in at the back of the classroom, I noticed the loud banter going on between the students. Some very sophisticated insults were being exchanged in a mixture of English and Spanish, most in good humor, and all of them very clever. In fact, some of the insults were so funny I wrote them down! I guessed it was members of the two gangs who were hurling insults at each other.

The students settled in, and the class began. They were reading *Romeo and Juliet.* And, wouldn't you know it—they happened to be reading the fight scene between the Capulets and the Montagues. I found it ironic: a group of adolescents from two opposing gangs who had entered a scene "fighting" with each other were reading their actions mirrored in the same scene in a play. I was hoping that the teacher would bring the relevance of this classroom activity to the students' lives, but he didn't. (I probably would have failed to do so as well had I been teaching the class instead of just observing it!)

The teacher asked individual students to read different roles in the scene. The reading was flat and emptied of meaning, and soon many eyes, including mine, wandered away from the page, away from the rich language, and away from the tense situation unfolding in the play. If only the teacher had pointed out the irony that here was a play, written centuries ago, about something these students were still doing today! If only the teacher had brought the relevance of this scene and the whole play to students' lives, this class would have been about the students themselves, rather than about some fictitious characters in a play written by a dead poet ages ago.

Questions for Discussion

1. How would the learning have been different for these students had the teacher pointed out the relevance of the scene to the students' lives?

2. In the larger picture of school life in general, what are some likely consequences of the cumulative effect of being taught things that have little relevance to one's life?

home language (Cloud et al., 2009; D. Freeman & Freeman, 2003; Y. Freeman & Freeman, 2002; O. Garcia et al., 2016; Genesee et al., 2006). Simultaneous bilingual learners benefit from paired literacy instruction in both of their languages from the start of instruction (Escamilla et al., 2014).

It is never acceptable to establish reductionist literacy programs for multilingual learners or those that reduce reading to its smallest elements, graphemes and phonemes taught out of context. Teachers must apply these three principles to develop literacy in these students using its most extensive definition, including social as well as academic tasks.

Literacy in the Home and Community

Multilingual learners' home literacy experiences are very important, both for reinforcing the development of literacy in general and for supporting reading and writing in the home language (Gagarina et al., 2016; Kang, 2012). Multilingual learners' home languages and cultures are tremendous resources because a high level of literacy in the native language positively influences literacy in English. If multilingual learners begin to have significant challenges in school or preferably, before difficulties emerge, we need to understand the home literacy environment. It would be helpful to know, for example, whether multilingual learners' families have access to books and other written materials in the home language in community public libraries, among community members, in neighborhood bookstores, in the school library, and in their homes. This information is especially important for older students with limited formal schooling, whose exposure to literacy is typically more limited than that of students who have had the expected amount and type of schooling. It is crucial to support home–school literacy activities: Establish a lending library of audio and digital books in the home language in addition to texts, build on existing home literacy practices, and initiate other activities that support and enrich literacy experiences in the students' home languages.

Understanding the Relationship between Students' Home Language and English

The close relationship that exists between a bilingual person's two languages can be seen in the flexible way that bilingual people use their linguistic resources in both languages (O. Garcia et al., 2016; Sims et al., 2017). Bilinguals' use of a single linguistic repertoire, rather than two separate systems, makes it possible for much information to be transferred between the learner's two languages. Evidence of transfer between multilingual learners' languages can be seen in literacy as well as in oral language (Creese & Blackledge, 2010; Licona & Kelly, 2020). While multilingual learners are in the process of developing proficiency in one or both of their languages, it is normal, for example, to see instances of syntax from the home language appearing in their English speaking and writing, or for phonology from the home language to have an impact on students' English speaking and listening comprehension (Ascenzi-Moreno, 2018).

Transfer from one language to another can happen in general areas of language no matter the languages in question. The fact that both English and Spanish express the plural of nouns by adding a morpheme at the end of the noun is something that some learners automatically carry from one language to the other. Language-specific transfer also happens in aspects that are unique to particular languages. The clearest specific transfer occurs between cognates; an example is *electricidad* and *electricity*. Many low-frequency academic words in English are similar to words in other languages. For example, *biography* in English is *biografía* in Spanish, *biografia* in Polish, and *biyografi* in Haitian Creole. By making these cross-linguistic connections a part of lessons, teachers can ensure that all multilingual learners are benefitting from using all their linguistic resources and advancing the development of both languages. These cross-linguistic connections can be particularly helpful in reading in the content areas.

In literacy, research shows both general and specific transfer (Soltero-González, 2009). Examples of general transfer are seen in reading comprehension and strategy use (Reyes & Azuara, 2008). Examples of specific transfer occur in word recognition, vocabulary building, as well as meta-literacy awareness of graphophonemic cueing and spelling. Research also shows both positive and negative transfer in literacy is similar to the findings from oral language (D. August, 2012; Cardenas-Hagan et al., 2007; Nagy et al., 1997; Reese et al., 2000).

When there are similarities between the learner's two languages, the transfer is positive and is helpful to the learner, as in the example of the cognates just discussed. However, transfer can also be negative and can interfere with communication. This frequently happens with false cognates, words that sound similar in different languages but do not have the same meaning. For example, Spanish–English multilingual learners often mistakenly use the word *library* to mean bookstore because the word for bookstore in Spanish is *librería*.

Thus, it is important to be aware of typical and predictable transfer influences in English that can be expected from a group of multilingual learners of the same language background. This knowledge helps teachers recognize what is part of typical English development for multilingual learners and what might be unusual and a possible area of concern that would require further investigation and assessment (O. Garcia & Wei, 2014). In fact, what might be seen as an annoying, recurring mistake to a teacher or other practitioner is really evidence of the student doing something useful: using knowledge in one language to communicate in and navigate the other language (Baker, 2011; Cloud et al., 2009). If anything, teachers should encourage this type of crossing between languages because it is helpful to the language learner: What they know in the home language can serve as a building block for aspects of the second, or additional, language (Beeman & Urow, 2013; Escamilla et al., 2014; O. Garcia et al., 2016).

The close relationship between a bilingual person's two languages may also be observed in **code-mixing,** *code-switching,* or *code-meshing,* which is generally defined as the alternating use of two languages within the same conversational event (Paradis et al., 2021; Poplack, 1980). This can happen in the same sentence (*I washed mi mano*) or between sentences (*I did that already. Ahora voy a ir a jugar*). Although language learners may switch languages when a word or phrase is not immediately available, code switching typically shows more proficient use of both languages among bilingual speakers.

It is important to distinguish between these two contexts for use of code-mixing to understand whether the learner is alternating between languages out of necessity, as in the case of the former example, or by choice, as in the case of the latter. If multilingual learners mix codes frequently, they may be drawing words and phrases from their home language to fill in for vocabulary they do not yet possess in English. As multilingual learners become more proficient in both languages, however, it is normal to mix codes for social communicative as well as academic reasons (for further treatment of this issue, see O. Garcia et al., 2016; Hoff et al., 2012; Paradis et al., 2021).

Language Use Patterns

Gathering information on how multilingual learners use their languages and how they started learning each of them is helpful in determining any necessary learning support strategies the students might need. Whatever challenges the students may be facing, begin creating support strategies by considering the linguistic resources students bring with them in their home language and English. This foundational building block, especially in the home language, is often overlooked because most teachers are concerned with English language development.

More often than not, multilingual learners' other languages are not considered from the beginning (Rodríguez-Mojica et al., 2019). Teachers may report that multilingual learners do not like using their home language in school, so the MTSS team does not pursue it. This raises the question of why these students no longer want to use their home language in school. Once again, the learning environment can be a huge factor in students' willingness to share their language and culture at school. Does the school celebrate multilingualism? What is the sociocultural climate at school? Are students' languages and cultures valued and incorporated into instruction and the everyday functioning of the school? If not, then multilingual learners will be less likely to use their home languages as resources even if their families speak only those languages at home.

If students begin to reject their home language and culture or if they have not been instructed in that language at school, we still cannot disregard the resources students have in any languages to which they were exposed early in life (Ramirez & Kuhl, 2016). Regardless, if parents or grandparents speak only the home language, then the students have at least receptive capabilities in that language, and we need to find out about those capabilities and use them as a resource (Bachman et al., 2020). It is important to gather information about the social and sometimes more informal language that students and their parents use at home and in the community, because what they know and experience in their home language and culture are part of the students' valuable funds of knowledge (Moll et al., 1992).

Some parents and children feel a stigma associated with using a language other than English at home. In addition to the fact that this sort of climate can have a significant detrimental effect on the student's cognitive, academic, social, and affective development, it makes it very difficult to gather accurate information about students' use of their home language and

English. When school staff ask parents or other caregivers what language is used in the home, the answer may inevitably be "English," even when it is clear that the parents are not proficient in English. They have, however, somehow gotten the message that this is the "correct" answer. The cultural milieu of the school must be such that multilingual learners' home languages are not only recognized and openly valued, but also become part of the daily functioning of the school (King & Fogle, 2013).

A difficult situation emerges when parents who are themselves in the process of developing English feel compelled to use English exclusively at home because of sociocultural pressures. Someone from school or the community may have told parents they should practice their English at home if they ever want their children to learn. Instead of using their well-developed, adult home language, which carries their rich cultural heritage, these parents begin to speak to their children in their still-developing English. Not only does the quality of the language used with the children and the messages conveyed suffer, the quantity is likely to be diminished as well. Students in this kind of home environment do not have the opportunity to solidify structures in their home language and do not have a rich linguistic environment in English. Speech–language pathologists often work with these students and have to do some detective work to figure out why they are using such unusual structures in English. The mystery is solved once they interview the parents, hear their developing English proficiency, and discover that they were counseled to use only English with their children. It is important to convey to parents how important it is that they use the language(s) they feel most comfortable communicating in with their children (S. Brown & Souto-Manning, 2008). School staff should never counsel parents and other family members to do anything that would distance them from their children in any way.

Language use patterns should be looked at beginning from birth rather than from the time the multilingual learner enters school. For example, it is important to know whether a child reached the expected milestones at the expected rate. If the parents report that the child did not speak at all until after 2 years of age, it might lead us to ask further questions or to have the child's hearing checked. Another reason we want to determine multilingual learners' language use patterns prior to their coming to school is that some multilingual learners develop more than one language simultaneously from a young age. When assessed using a monolingual perspective, these students may seem to be "limited in both of their languages." Without a truly bilingual assessment process in place (Escamilla et. al, 2014; Gottlieb, 2021), teams will miss the resources that simultaneous bilingual learners bring with them to school. Since they may have some proficiency in English when they enter school, simultaneous bilingual learners may not receive the language services they are entitled to. Because they may not sound like their monolingual peers of either of their languages, they may be judged as "limited" rather than having resources in both languages. Many multilingual learners are simultaneous bilingual learners and yet many school systems still have not developed the infrastructure necessary to assess and instruct them appropriately. These

Chronicle 7.3

That Was Me!

By a University Professor

The university where I teach ran a certification program for paraprofessionals. The program would give participants the credentials they needed to work as paraprofessionals in bilingual programs around the state. The participants in the course I was teaching were all women in their early 20s who had gone back to school while working as paraprofessionals supporting multilingual learners at a high school. They were all native speakers of Spanish who had been working in different capacities in schools but did not have university training or any kind of certification.

During this class session, we were discussing the stages of ESL acquisition and the importance of knowing when the students acquired each of their languages. We were talking about how some multilingual learners manage to acquire a bit of English by the time they enter school and somehow give the impression that they are proficient in English when they are not. Over and over these young women kept repeating the same thing:

"That was me!" "I never got extra ESL help at school because I was born here." "We didn't immigrate, so people just assumed we were regular English speakers." "Me too! We never used English at home, but I learned a little from friends, so by the time I went to kindergarten I could speak some English. School was always hard and things didn't start making sense until eighth grade, but by then I had missed a lot of stuff. I think that's why high school was so hard. I'm glad I went back to school now, but it would have been nice to know what was happening to me." "Yeah! They put me in Special Ed., but then they took me out when I learned more English. I wish I had gotten some help with my English instead of being treated like there was something wrong with me."

Questions for Discussion

1. Are there multilingual learners in your school who slip by and are placed in monolingual English classrooms without any support when they actually need help in English? What needs to be changed in the system to avoid that?

2. Other than the impact on academic performance, what are some likely outcomes (emotional, social, political) of being taken for something you are not?

students may get overlooked for any kind of support and in some school districts are not even considered to be multilingual learners. Chronicle 7.3 illustrates this situation as recalled by adults who are former multilingual learners.

Information Gathering

The easiest and fastest way to gather information about multilingual learners' oral language and literacy is to administer one of the many language proficiency tests available on the market. On their own, these tests will not reflect the complex and multifaceted nature of oral language and literacy and would result in an extremely narrow view of students' ability to use oral language proficiently and their ability to read and write with meaning, especially in academic domains. Therefore, as a minimal requirement, more extensive information about multilingual learners' oral language and literacy must be collected. Some of this information naturally describes the students' proficiency levels, but other information must address the way multilingual learners use their two languages. Decisions must be made regarding what to assess and how to assess it.

What to Assess in Oral Language and Literacy

Four domains in the home language and English.   The first condition for learning about multilingual learners' oral language and literacy is that proficiency in both languages must be included in the assessment (Gottlieb, 2012, 2021). In addition, to be able to verify exceptionalities across languages, we need to gather information about the two languages in all four domains—listening, speaking, reading, and writing. If the team only gathers information in English, then we always have an incomplete picture of what multilingual learners can do, and we can only guess about how to best support the challenges that we observe in students (Antón et al., 2016; Escamilla et al., 2014; Genesee et al., 2005).

Oral language and literacy in social and academic contexts.   It is important to assess students' bilingual proficiency and biliteracy across a range of conversational and academic contexts (Gottlieb, 2021). Language for social purposes is used in order to communicate effectively with peers and within one's community, whereas academic language is essential for accessing and communicating effectively in academic content areas. Language assessment should entail talking to students about everyday social matters as well as observing how students process language in content-area classes.

Multiple contexts.   Third, a wide range of contexts in which multilingual learners use language must be assessed (J. S. Damico, 2019a; Gottlieb, 2016, 2021). Multilingual learners use language differently and show different levels of proficiency in different contexts. For example, in the English as a second language (ESL) classroom, perhaps because students feel relaxed, they may be quite talkative and communicate effectively, whereas in the monolingual English classroom they may be anxious and appear to be less fluent. Gathering information in different contexts also ensures that the home language and English are addressed and that social and academic language is included.

Discrete aspects and holistic representations of language.   Much of the language assessment that happens at school measures the processing of discrete aspects of language, especially in reading. This practice is fraught with difficulties because a focus on splinter skills often does not yield a valid or authentic picture of an individual's proficiency (Afflerbach, 2007; Afflerbach et al., 2008; J. S. Damico et al., 2021; Dunaway, 2021). In addition, this assessment is typically done with standardized tests that yield a narrow view of what the student is able to do, resulting in misidentification of students as having unwarranted difficulties and changing who counts as a reader and what counts as reading achievement (Kapantzoglou et al., 2012; Menken, 2008; Pacheco, 2010).

Thus, it is essential that holistic and authentic use of language be included in during the information-gathering process. When school staff members assess students on discrete skills in isolation, such as the ability to read blends, multilingual learners may perform well and yet not be able to do the most important thing about reading: Make meaning. As another example, students may know how to decode words on a page in English

Table 7.3   Assessing All Aspects of Oral Language and Literacy: A Checklist

	Home Language				English			
	L	S	R	W	L	S	R	W
Type of proficiency								
• Conversational fluency	—	—	—	—	—	—	—	—
• Academic language	—	—	—	—	—	—	—	—
Contexts								
• During monolingual English instruction	—	—	—	—	—	—	—	—
• During ESL instruction	—	—	—	—	—	—	—	—
• During bilingual instruction	—	—	—	—	—	—	—	—
• On the playground	—	—	—	—	—	—	—	—
• At home	—	—	—	—	—	—	—	—
• With friends	—	—	—	—	—	—	—	—
Discrete								
• Symbol/sound	—	—	—	—	—	—	—	—
• Vocabulary	—	—	—	—	—	—	—	—
• Grammar	—	—	—	—	—	—	—	—
Holistic								
• Understanding and expressing ideas and feelings	—	—	—	—	—	—	—	—
• Understanding and describing concrete things	—	—	—	—	—	—	—	—
• Understanding and describing abstract concepts	—	—	—	—	—	—	—	—
• Communicating with peers and adults	—	—	—	—	—	—	—	—

ESL, English as a second language; L, listening; S, speaking; R: reading; W, writing.

but have no idea what those words mean. They might as well be decoding nonsense words (F. Smith, 1998, 2015). The checklist offered in Table 7.3 can be used to ensure that all aspects of oral language and literacy are being assessed.

How to Assess Oral Language and Literacy

Standardized norm-referenced tests.   As long as they are used nonexclusively in conjunction with other methods, there may be a place for standardized norm-referenced tests in the assessment of oral language and literacy when assessing for comparison purposes. However, because of the many problems that occur with the use of these tests with multilingual learners (J. S. Damico, 1991; Gottlieb, 2006; Neill, 2012), certain criteria must be met:

- If a comparison group is being used, that population must be similar to the students being assessed.

- Assessment must be based on home language or English language development standards.

- Assessment must be based on grade-level, content-area expectations.

- Assessment must make developmental sense.

- Assessment must reflect the opportunity that students have had to learn.

- Test performance must be analyzed and the scores interpreted in the context of more natural and authentic assessment as well as teacher or other practitioners' descriptive narratives.

If the standardized test that is being used meets these six criteria, then it may form one piece of a student's profile. Standardized testing should never be the sole measure for any type of instructional or program decision for multilingual learners. Over-reliance on standardized, discrete measures to evaluate student learning, cognitive ability, academic achievement, and teacher effectiveness, and to diagnose learning disabilities or language disorders has reduced our capacity to see student growth, recognize divergent thinking, notice subtle changes in attitudes about learning, engage students in higher-level questioning, see progress in multilingual learners' cross-cultural competence, and recognize students' resiliency (J. S. Damico, 2019a; Herrera et al., 2012; Menken, 2008; Pacheco, 2010; van Kraayenoord, 2010). Worse yet, students have no way to see their areas of strength or growth over time. The families of these students are also bombarded with meaningless scores rather than receiving concrete evidence of their children's work and progress in school. Hence, there is a precious need for the use of authentic and more instructional classroom assessment.

Authentic performance assessment.   Many of the instructional strategies and classroom activities that teachers use can be rich sources of information for assessing multilingual learners' areas of growth or difficulty (van Kraayenoord, 2009; Washington et al., 2021). By using rubrics, checklists, and other tools that reflect the stages of language development (in the home language and English), teachers can begin to observe students across content areas, in social settings, and at home. Useful performance assessment requires that "students express their learning in direct ways that reflect real-life situations" (Gottlieb, 2006, p. 111). Interviewing the student, the parents, and teachers can give the MTSS team a more comprehensive profile of the student's oral language and literacy abilities. Gathering information about some of the less common home languages can be quite challenging. The more information we have about multilingual learners' home language, however, the easier it is to design effective learning support strategies. If a cultural liaison or an interpreter is used to obtain information about the home language, all the issues discussed in earlier chapters regarding the qualifications of such a liaison and privacy concerns must be heeded.

These evaluations entail talking to students about everyday social matters as well as observing them in content-area classes, and assessing them after they have finished a lesson or unit of study. Because they tend to be more informal and often rely on subjective judgments, these performance measures must reach some level of reliability. For example, it is important that the students be assessed using the same evaluative criteria over time and by different assessors. These measures have some significant advantages over more standardized norm-referenced tests and provide a true picture of the dynamic and complex processes of comprehending and communicating:

- They do not interrupt instruction as they are embedded in the strategies and activities used daily in class.

- They provide immediate feedback that informs and shapes instruction.

- They provide a more comprehensive profile of multilingual learners' strengths and areas that need attention.

- They are oriented to the authentic variables that are essential for effective meaning-making: a meaningful context; accomplishing the task at hand; and the availability of all the functional aspects of language structure, content, and usage when determining proficiency.

- They allow students, teachers, and parents to see growth over time.

Performance assessment can be used in two contexts to evaluate multilingual learners' language and literacy development: in classroom observations and in teacher–student conferences. Classroom observations can be completed by teachers in their own classrooms or by colleagues who sit in for short periods of time. Use of task-specific or skill-specific checklists, anecdotal note taking, and videotaping with subsequent analysis can all supply important information about what students are doing with language and literacy. A list of classroom observation strategies is provided in Box 7.2.

Teacher–student conferences provide another opportunity to assess multilingual learners' language and literacy development. When students discuss, read, and write about a wide range of topics in a variety of genres, it is useful for teachers to set aside time each week to discuss students' work with them and to talk about texts that students have read. Students of all ages and grade levels not only benefit from these conferences, they look forward to these times that have been set aside especially for them. The conference provides an opportunity for students to ask specific questions and seek clarification or guidance about their work. From the teacher's perspective, it provides insight into how students are processing instruction and how they are progressing both in content-area acquisition and language proficiency development.

Box 7.2

Strategies for Assessing Oral Language and Literacy through Classroom Observation

Sources of Language (English and home language)

- Oral language samples across content areas
- Writing samples
- Oral reports
- Audio and video recordings
- Student-selected products
- Multilingual projects
- Artifacts from portfolio created over time and across content areas
- Small-group projects
- Dialogue journals
- Interviews
- Storytelling
- Podcasts
- Blog postings, articles, essays, assignments
- Diagrams, illustrations (labeled and used to support presentations or reports)
- Language experience texts (whole group, small group, or individual)

Strategies for Assessment

- Rubrics for listening, speaking, reading, and writing
- Checklist of types of utterances
- Academic language checklist
- Rubrics for group interactions
- Rubrics for pair work
- Skill-specific checklist
- Anecdotal records
- Instructionally embedded running records
- Narratives
- Self-assessment (with clear criteria in rubrics for students to assess their own growth)

When teachers meet with students, they can keep anecdotal notes about specific issues they have discussed. Students can provide bilingual oral retellings or explanations about texts or stories they have read that teachers can record (Geva & Wiener, 2014). Teachers can jot down questions the students have and take notes on each student's reading, writing, and personal interests. Teachers can also keep informal running records and take notes on what strategies the students are using and areas that show progress (Meisuri et al., 2018; Taberski, 2000). Teachers can use information gathered in these weekly conferences to adjust their whole-class instruction and to determine the content of mini-lessons. This information can be used diagnostically to work strategically with various groups of students, thus differentiating literacy instruction appropriately. Another benefit is that teachers learn about students' interests and can find individualized reading and writing materials and projects for them. The strategies listed in Box 7.2 for classroom observation can also be used to evaluate students' oral language and literacy during conferences.

MTSS Team Activity

Have team members look at the strategies listed in Box 7.2. Determine which strategies individual teachers, bilingual reading specialists, interventionists, and other practitioners are already using. Which are being used for special support strategy considerations? Which strategies need to be implemented on a larger scale and should be given a higher level of importance? What would teachers, students, administrators, and other staff members need to begin to shift their perspective on the use of these strategies as sources of assessment information?

Comparisons with Peers

Once the school has adopted the practice of collecting authentic language and literacy information from multilingual learners, it is easier to put students' development of oral language and literacy into context. It is important that teachers begin to see what reading, writing, speaking, and listening look and sound like for typically developing multilingual learners are at various levels of proficiency in English. Teachers have a sense of what monolingual English speakers are expected to do at different ages; they need to develop that same sense for multilingual learners. This sense can be developed by looking at the performance of multilingual learners within and across grades and proficiency levels, and by looking at individual and group growth in language and literacy longitudinally over time (Ascenzi-Moreno, 2018; C. J. Flores & Delgado, 2012; N. Flores et al., 2015).

This type of "action research" provides a context in which to interpret the difficulties that some multilingual learners are having in school. It also allows staff to compare these students' performance with other multilingual learners from the same and different language backgrounds who are doing well in school, with monolingual English-speaking students who are also having difficulty in school, and with monolingual English-speaking students who are doing well academically. Only then is it possible to know what is typical, so that as a team we can recognize the unusual.

Systemic Learning Support Strategies

Making school-wide changes in order to provide multilingual learners with a better opportunity to develop oral language and literacy is a worthwhile investment for the entire student population. A list of systemic support strategies used to help oral language development and literacy in multilingual learners having academic difficulties is presented in Box 7.3.

Box 7.3

Systemic Learning Support Strategies for Oral Language and Literacy Development

Social and Academic Oral Language Development in Home Language and English

- Place a school-wide emphasis on having multilingual learners (MLs) talk with their families at home about what they learn at school.
- Help parents hold conversations about schoolwork with their children by providing them with "conversation starters."
- Have teachers post sentence frames in their rooms as resources for students to use in their exchanges with one another or in their written work.
- Have teachers set aside time (5–10 minutes) during each lesson for cross-linguistic transfer activities.
- Have teachers include language objectives when designing units and lessons.
- Highlight different collaborative learning structures each month for teachers to try.
- Increase the amount of small-group work.
- Have teachers engage in peer coaching and tally each other's exchanges with students to gather information on who is or isn't talking; what languages are being used; and how often girls, boys, or the teacher are talking.
- Have all teachers collaborate with speech–language pathologists for strategies that help students with their expressive oral language.
- During curriculum planning, engage groups of teachers to incorporate oral language into the literacy program.

Academic and Social Literacy Development in Home Language and English

- Provide professional learning opportunities on literacy strategies to use across the curriculum.
- Emphasize the importance of academic language and literacy along with academic content.
- Provide professional learning opportunities on how initial literacy development in a second language differs from initial literacy development in the home language.
- Provide teachers time to adapt literacy strategies for use with MLs in both home language and English.
- Give teachers the opportunity to coordinate the use of graphic organizers that support a variety of text structures (e.g., sequence, cause and effect, and compare-and-contrast charts) across grade levels.
- Provide initial literacy instruction in the home language at least through grade 3.

- Display student-created dual-language writing projects across grade levels and content areas on school website and in library.
- Connect with partner classroom in another country, preferably one that some MLs or their families come from.
- Ensure that the language arts classrooms support reading and writing in mathematics, science, and social studies.
- Establish a greater focus on nonfiction reading and writing beginning in the very early grades and continuing through all grade levels.
- Use multicultural, anti-bias literature throughout the school for all students.
- Provide the support of reading specialists throughout grade levels, not just in the early grades, and help them use authentic language and literacy tasks.
- Provide professional learning opportunities and co-teaching for classroom teachers on strategies that work for MLs.
- Have students create a classroom newsletter using teams of students as reporters in different content areas; make multilingual versions (digital) so that students can show their parents.
- Encourage parents and family members to read to the student in their home language (using dialogic reading strategies).
- Create a home–school reading program that includes books in all the students' languages.
- Implement a reading program with the support of bilingual high school and university students.
- Have students read and write every day in as many subjects as possible.
- Have teachers model reading and writing in every classroom in every lesson.
- Order multilingual books every school year for the classroom and school libraries and display them prominently.
- Order multiple levels of books on nonfiction topics to support content-area texts.
- Develop an extensive multilingual virtual library for all grade levels.
- Have students work collaboratively with peers to create texts and publish the stories on the school/class website.
- Initiate school-wide free-choice reading time for all students (see the *Book Whisperer* by Donalyn Miller, 2009, for guidance on developing such a program).

Box 7.4

Specific Learning Support Strategies for Oral Language and Literacy Development

Social and Academic Oral Language Development in Home Language and English

- Provide students with word banks to use across the curriculum.
- Provide students with sentence starters specific to underlying language focus (e.g., sequential, compare-contrast, cause and effect).
- Encourage students to talk at home with parents about school by ending each day with a reflection on what they learned.
- Make certain that classroom instruction is engaging and characterized by comprehensible project-, problem-, and inquiry-based learning.
- Allow students to take time to prepare and process in their home language before participating in English.
- Organize lunchtime conversation clubs.
- Have parents and community volunteers help out in small-group work to increase conversations.

Academic and Social Literacy Development in Home Language and English

- Ask teachers to capitalize on students' home language and English oral language as a bridge to literacy (e.g., creating language experience texts).

- Help students make cross-linguistic connections.
- Engage in frequent student–teacher conferencing about the student's reading and writing.
- Encourage all adults to take anecdotal notes about students' interests, strengths, and difficulties during conferences.
- Use teacher–student dialogue journals in both the home language and English.
- Have teachers use visuals to preview vocabulary in books and to assess comprehension.
- Use texts created by students to teach skills.
- Use learning logs (with dated entries) with all students as a way to assess understanding of content material and to encourage academic writing.
- Using a diary, ask parents to take their child's oral dictation of the day's or week's events.
- Implement a reading and writing workshop approach to literacy instruction.
- Ask parents, grandparents, and community members to come into the library or classroom to read in the students' home languages.

Establishing a closer tie between home and school is beneficial for all students, not just multilingual learners. Focusing on language objectives in content-area lessons will help all students process new concepts. Even strategies that bring up or involve a language other than English during a lesson or unit is sure to expand the experiences and knowledge of students who come from monolingual backgrounds.

Specific Learning Support Strategies

Many of the systemic strategies listed in Box 7.3 can be applied at a specific level with individual multilingual learners whose oral language and literacy development needs to be supported. For example, cross-linguistic transfer activities can be done at a student's desk rather than as a whole-group activity, and when an interesting linguistic feature emerges it can be presented to the rest of the class. When language objectives are set for the whole class, additional objectives can be planned specifically for individual multilingual learners. In addition to adapting systemic support strategies for individual students, a list of specific support strategies appears in Box 7.4.

Questions for Reflection and Action

1. Do we know enough about the oral language and literacy development in the home language and English of the multilingual learners we serve as well as those who are having academic difficulties?

2. If we need more information, how would we get it?
3. How can we keep track of how students' oral language and literacy are evolving?
4. How do teachers apply their understanding of the relationship between students' home language and English to their instructional planning and their selection of instructional approaches and strategies?
5. The principles of literacy instruction listed in the section "Academic and Social Literacy Development in Home Language and English" may be challenging to apply because of the popular use of packaged literacy programs. How can this challenge be overcome?
6. What are some implications of using authentic content-based assessment instead of (or in addition to) standardized tests for the multilingual learner population in the school?

Academic Performance

Key Concepts. *The fifth integral factor focuses on the quality of the academic instruction that multilingual learners receive in all content areas and how academic performance is assessed for these students. Challenges arise when new concepts are taught through a language that students are not fully proficient in. Because of the close relationship between academic concepts and the language used to process those concepts, instruction and learning support strategies must be closely tied to what the student is learning in the classroom and must support content learning by making language accessible to the student.*

The fifth integral element to consider when multilingual learners experience difficulty in school is the academic instruction that they receive and the processes used to assess academic performance. We must make sure that students are being taught new concepts, many of which are quite abstract, in a way that makes the content comprehensible without depending too heavily on having to understand the language that is used to explain and describe those concepts. Simultaneously, students need to be taught the oral language and literacy necessary to access grade level content material. Similarly, in evaluating multilingual learners' academic performance, educators must distinguish between understanding academic content and developing sufficient proficiency to express that understanding through language. This chapter introduces strategies to make this distinction. It is also important to look comprehensively at all content areas to understand what the student is expected to learn. We present some suggestions for gathering and interpreting information about multilingual learners' academic performance and the components of lesson and unit design that should enable them to learn content and concepts while developing academic language in English and their home language. We conclude with suggestions for systemic and specific strategies to help support multilingual learners' academic performance.

Key Factors in Academic Performance

Multilingual learners' academic success is influenced by all the integral elements discussed in this guide, but the crux of the matter is how academic instruction is delivered and how accessible the curriculum is to these students. Perhaps because of the emphasis on high-stakes testing in the recent past, much of the concern with academic achievement has centered on the content areas specifically tested (Antón et al., 2016; Menken, 2008; Pacheco, 2010). However, in considering the unique needs of multilingual learners, it is imperative to examine all the areas in which any learning occurs (Abedi et al., 2004; J. Brown & Doolittle, 2008; Cho, 2016; Herrera et al., 2012; Kohn, 2000; Miramontes et al., 2011).

Taking into Account All Content Areas

To develop a good profile of how a student or a group of students is doing, we must look at performance across all curricular areas (Gottlieb, 2021): the core curriculum and the fine arts, industrial technology, drama, as well as physical education programs. There are two principal reasons for looking at performance in all content areas. The first reason is that students who are facing significant challenges in one or two subject areas may be excelling in other areas. For example, a multilingual learner who is having significant challenges in language arts, social studies, and science may be advancing quite rapidly in English as a second language (ESL) and math, as well as being musically talented. This student's strengths provide us with valuable information on which to build other areas of the curriculum (Lesaux & Harris, 2015).

By looking for "bright spots" (C. Heath & Heath, 2010) in the performance and talents of multilingual learners (rather than only weakness or deficits), the team forms a more complete view of the student, making it easier to come up with specific learning support strategies that take into account many aspects of learning and performance (Kelly & Gates, 2017). Thus, it is important to see whether the challenges that particular students experience manifest equally across contexts or are limited to particular areas. This information helps the multi-tiered system of supports (MTSS) team identify and use students' strengths to improve performance in areas of academic difficulty (Wilding & Griffey, 2015). In effect, students' individual, social, and cultural resources can be used in designing future programs and assistance strategies (e.g., Carhill et al., 2008; Garmezy, 1991; Klingner et al., 2007; Milner, 2010; Pietarinen et al., 2014; Stanton-Salazar, 1997).

The second reason to monitor multilingual learners' progress in a variety of content areas is to discern trends across content areas and grade levels (Cloud et al., 2010; Janzen, 2008; Nguyen, 2012b; Yturriago, 2012b). For example, the team may find that as a group, multilingual learners perform very well in certain content areas and underperform in others. Students may do well in kindergarten through grade 2 in all areas but begin to show dramatic challenges in grades 3 and 4. Longitudinal data may show that multilingual learners who receive support in their home language while learning English reach higher levels of achievement than students whose home language or ESL support is removed after a couple of years. Teachers may notice that multilingual learners who maintain their home language and culture while learning English remain in school longer than those who do not. Examining trends across content areas and grade levels helps the MTSS team and other school personnel plan strategically when trying to address and improve academic performance across the curriculum at all grade levels. This type of longitudinal and cross-sectional information yields more effective systemic support strategies (Schall-Leckrone, 2018).

When the MTSS team looks at multilingual learners' academic performance across curricular contexts, it may also learn something from those areas in which multilingual learners perform well consistently. When identifying the areas in which these students excel, it would be of interest to know what those subject-area teachers are doing. Are they using particular strategies that are especially useful to multilingual learners? What do multilingual learners say about those classes? Why do multilingual learners say they are successful in those subjects or with those particular teachers? We can capitalize on areas of strength so that successes can be shared with the rest of the school staff. Although it is important to capitalize on student strengths, likewise, it is important to identify particular teachers who are especially successful communicating and engaging with multilingual learners in different content areas. Finding these "bright spots" in how teachers deliver instruction is also very helpful in planning professional learning opportunities around these mentor teachers (Allington, 2002a; C. Heath & Heath, 2010).

> **MTSS Team Activity**
>
> Invite one or two of the non–core-curriculum area teachers (such as an art, physical education, or music teacher) to an MTSS team meeting. Ask them how in their view their subject matter is related to the rest of the curriculum (note that this is about the subject matter, not about the teachers). How integrated is the teaching of those subjects with the rest of the curriculum? To what extent is information from these non–core-curriculum areas used in the discussions about multilingual learners who are facing significant academic challenges? How can information about multilingual learners' performance in these special subject areas be incorporated into designing learning support strategies?

Language Proficiency and Knowledge of Concepts

A major concern of general education teachers is ensuring that multilingual learners are acquiring academic concepts while developing the ability to communicate about those concepts in English (Gottlieb, 2012, 2021; Watson-Gegeo, 2004). Teachers need to be sure that multilingual learners understand the content material independent of their language proficiency in English. Teachers often ask, "How do I know they get the math that I'm teaching?" "How do I assess what they have learned if they don't speak English and I don't know their language?" How can teachers know that what they are assessing in their content-area classes is not English language proficiency? This is a difficult task in the early grades because all students are developing language and learning concepts for the first time. However, at least in the early grades the concepts being taught, typically more concrete in nature, are usually commensurate with the language that is used to talk about those concepts. The task becomes even more difficult in the intermediate, middle, and secondary grades, when the content material becomes more complex and abstract and the language needed to communicate and understand becomes more specialized. The concepts taught at these higher grade levels usually require a level of language proficiency that multilingual learners may not have attained yet. These questions indicate the complexity of what these students face in school and the specialized knowledge teachers need to have, or to get support in, to be able to meet both the academic content learning and the language development needs of multilingual learners (Gibbons, 2015; Janzen, 2007, 2008; Scheppegrell, 2004; van Kraayenoord, 2009).

One way to address this complex issue is to make an explicit distinction between when we are assessing students' academic performance and when we are assessing students' language proficiency (Gottlieb, 2012, 2021). Having an awareness of the process that students go through when acquiring a second or new language helps teachers understand why multilingual learners read, write, understand, and speak the way they do in English (Dufva & Alanen, 2005; Geva & Weiner, 2014; Schussler, 2009). It is also helpful for teachers and members of the MTSS team to understand the developmental nature and predictable stages of the process of acquiring a new language (as described in Chapter 7). With monolingual English speakers, we assume that what students are able to speak, read, or write reflects to a great extent what they are thinking. However, multilingual learners, who are in the process of learning academic content in a second language, speak, read, and write what their developing English language proficiency allows them to express in this new language, not necessarily what they know and understand about the content. The speech emergence simulations suggested as one of the MTSS team activities in Chapter 7 can help clarify this phenomenon. The more proficient multilingual learners become as readers, writers, and speakers of English in social and academic settings, the closer the match is between their ability to process concepts and their ability to express understanding and representation of those concepts in the second language (DaSilva Iddings et al., 2005; Morita, 2004; Vitanova, 2005).

The distinction between processing academic concepts and possessing the linguistic means to express those concepts is important for two reasons. The first reason is its relevance to evaluation. One of the biggest challenges with multilingual learners whose performance is not what would be expected is to know whether this academic performance indicates that the students did not have access to the curriculum or the concepts because of the way these were assessed, or if the students did not yet have sufficient proficiency in the language of instruction to comprehend what was presented in class. The second reason is its relevance to instruction. All teachers who are responsible for instructing multilingual learners need to know how to convey content concepts while integrating instruction of academic language. We examine the issue of assessment first, followed by a discussion of the best approaches to use for instruction.

Gathering Information about Academic Performance

As with literacy and oral language proficiency, the easy way to gather information on multilingual learners' academic performance is to administer one of the numerous achievement tests available on the market or, more realistically, to use the scores from the several tests that students must take under the guise of accountability of state and federal requirements. However, results from traditional paper-and-pencil (or online) academic achievement tests administered in English rarely tell us what multilingual learners who are not yet fully proficient have learned about the specific content material. Rather, these tests tell us about students' English reading comprehension or language proficiency. When these traditional approaches to assessment of academic performance are used, students with greater proficiency in academic English and those with good memory skills will do well. Others will find it difficult to show what they know. Thus, there is a need to add to the information that standardized tests provide by gathering data through more authentic measures that assess performance more directly.

Standardized Norm-Referenced Testing and Performance Assessment

In gathering information about multilingual learners' academic achievement, the MTSS team must first determine what it is that they want to know about these students' academic performance. Does the team want to find out what students know and understand about the content-area material (academic knowledge) or do they want to know how students are progressing in content-area reading, writing, speaking, and listening in either or both of their languages (language proficiency)? Or does the team want information about both of these areas? Information must be gathered from a variety of assessments, both norm referenced and performance based, to develop a good profile of multilingual learners' academic achievement (Gottlieb, 2012, 2021). Let us examine what we can find out from both types of measures.

If standardized academic achievement assessments are used, they must be based on multilingual learner populations in order to be valid and reliable measures of students' knowledge of the content area being tested. Traditionally, these tests rarely do that; rather, they are based on monolingual English speakers, not multilingual learners. Thus, especially for those at beginning levels of English proficiency, the results may be misleading, may have questionable validity and reliability, and may only show what multilingual learners can or cannot do compared with their monolingual English-speaking peers. Another important concern with standardized measures of academic achievement is the effect of cultural bias. Although test designers review their tests for such bias, it is impossible to find every instance of bias for every culture represented in a diverse school. Indeed, the whole process of assessment includes culturally specific elements. Thus, it is not really possible to eliminate all cultural, gender, socioeconomic, or other biases from any test procedure or format. It therefore becomes important to analyze carefully the test performance and account for limited validity and reliability and the impact of cultural bias when interpreting the results of such tests.

Any standardized norm-referenced measure is likely to include certain contexts, visual aids, and language that are unfamiliar to multilingual learners and interfere with their ability to demonstrate what they know about the academic content presented on the test. If norm-referenced measures in English or the home language are included as part of the data collection, they represent only one piece of the academic achievement puzzle for multilingual learners. As a consequence, that standardized test piece cannot be the biggest or the most important part of the puzzle (Artiles, 2015; Gottlieb, 2021; D. Taylor, 1993; Troia, 2005).

If the team's purpose is to gather information about what students have learned in academic content areas, then the learning tasks and activities that occur every day in classrooms are a rich source of information (J. S. Damico, 2019d). Assessment based on such activities is known as *performance assessment* (Afflerbach, 2007; Artiles & Ortiz, 2002; Chappuis et al., 2012; Dirksen, 2011; Heritage, 2010; Heritage & Wylie, 2020; Shea et al., 2005). Effective schools and educators observe their students as they process information in both of their languages, collect student work in portfolios in both languages (Escamilla et al., 2014), have students reflect on their work, and create interesting learning activities in which students can show what they understand and what they need to work on (Opitz et al., 2011). These teachers ask their students to write and read every day in all of their languages, observe the students as they work with graphic organizers, look at their progress over time, and provide feedback that helps students know where they need to improve and how. All of these activities provide excellent opportunities to assess learning while serving an instructional purpose.

When school administrators provide time and opportunity for teachers to set up an assessment system in which they formalize the information acquired in class, teachers are able to not only use the data for their own instructional purposes, but also to defend their decisions regarding the support that students need (DuFour, 2004). Several publications have practical suggestions on how to collect and report authentic information about multilingual learners (see e.g., Gottlieb, 2021).

These performance assessment procedures not only yield valuable information about multilingual learners' academic achievement, they are also effective for instruction. This dual use of materials and procedures for both assessment and instruction is exemplified by the widespread use of student portfolios for both assessment and pedagogical purposes (Cambourne & Turbill, 1994; Howard, 2012; Opitz et al., 2011; Spandel & Stiggins, 1997). This kind of assessment does not take away from valuable instruction time because it is embedded in the learning cycle itself. Performance assessment measures provide a variety of ways to see students' growth over time and yield information about academic achievement that is comprehensible to students, teachers, parents, and the community.

Obtaining Information in Students' Home Language and English

Because it is typical for bilingual learners to use their knowledge and skills in both (or all) of their languages in flexible ways and to process information and concepts in one or both languages concurrently (Ascenzi-Moreno, 2018; O. Garcia et al., 2016) it follows that information on academic achievement, both oral and written, should be gathered in all of the students' languages and in as many content areas as possible (Gottlieb, 2021). For multilingual learners who have had any amount of schooling in their home language, this is absolutely essential. Chronicle 8.1 illustrates what happens when a teacher takes into account a multilingual learner's home language.

Even for multilingual learners who have not had much instruction in their home language, the insight that can be gained about students' understanding and processing of concepts when we let them perform in both of their languages is invaluable. However, if bilingual instruction has not been provided, academic language development in the home language is not likely to be at grade level. In a school where students' home languages play a prominent role (even if no formal instruction is given through those languages), looking at information and work samples that include those languages becomes routine.

When trying to explain a specific academic challenge that the student seems to be facing, it is important to determine whether the challenge manifests in productive or receptive language domains (or both), and in all of the multilingual learner's languages. This information helps the team narrow the range of support strategies that are most likely to help the student overcome that challenge. Because a true intrinsic impairment is located at a deeper level of proficiency than the superficial manifestation of home language or English, the assessment team should expect a true impairment to manifest in similar ways in both languages (Cummins, 1984; J. S. Damico et al., 1996). Teachers who invite and incorporate multilingual learners' home language into instruction are able to assess comprehension, for example, even if the students are at early stages of acquiring English. If the teacher reads a story aloud to her students in English, the teacher is able to assess how much they understood through their sequencing of visual manipulatives while retelling the story in their home language (Howard, 2012). When teachers give multilingual learners opportunities to talk, research, and plan in the home language before writing in English, they begin to see improvement in English writing over time. When educators view students' languages as resources and apply what they have learned about bilingualism, examples like these become commonplace (Antón et al., 2016).

Comparisons with Like Peers

Once the practice of using authentic assessments and collecting students' work across content areas in all of the language domains is established, a rich bank of comparative samples becomes available. The school in general, and

Accessing Academic Knowledge Across All Languages

By a Mathematics Teacher

In my grade 5 mathematics class which I teach in English, students were furiously writing the answers in English to five math reflections. I noticed that Josue was not producing much and appeared to be struggling a great deal. He paused between each word he wrote and placed his left hand on his forehead as he wrote. This struggle continued for 35 minutes, at which point he had reached the end of the first page. He looked up at the clock and muttered something under his breath as he realized he had only 15 minutes left of class. He flipped his paper over and seemed to be writing with ease and quickly filled the second side of his page. It was astonishing to see the change.

When class was over students handed in their work, and since my curiosity had been piqued, I couldn't wait to look over this particular student's paper. On the front side of the paper (Figure 8.1) he had written two answers in English to the first reflection question. It was difficult to understand his written English, but he had added some diagrams to illustrate his written responses that helped me to see that the math was correct. Josue had summarized the main points of the lesson as I had done when I had summed up the lesson for the entire class. Something else I noticed about this side of the paper was that there were marks left from the sweat on his hands. I was amazed that this very good student took 35 minutes to write the answer to the first question.

As I turned the paper over, I was surprised to see that Josue had easily finished writing his answers to the last four questions, and there were no sweat marks on this side of the page (Figure 8.2). However, he had finished writing the assessment in

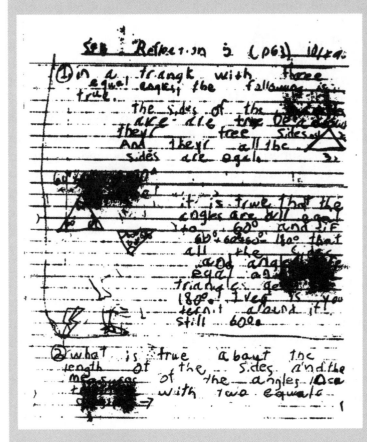

Figure 8.1 Josue's work on questions 1 and 2. The following is a transcription of the front side of Josue's paper:

1. (Question 1 copied onto page from book) In a triangle with three equal angles, the following is true. *Answer:* the sides of the triangles are are tree becasw theyr tree side And theyr all the sides are egal. / it is true that the angles are all egal to 60° and if 60° + 60° + 60° = 180° that all the sides and angles are egal and triangle gets to 180°. Iven if you ternit around it still 60°.
2. (Question 2 copied onto page from book) What is true about the length of the sides and the measures of the angle. Draw triangles with two equal angles. *Answer:* on side 2 of paper.

Chronicle 8.1

continued

By a Mathematics Teacher

Spanish! I do not know much Spanish, so I asked a colleague to tell me what he wrote. I was thrilled to see quite profound mathematical observations in Spanish! It was clear that those ideas flowed in the last 15 minutes of class. I was glad he had felt comfortable enough in my class to use Spanish. If he had not, I would have missed out on his creative mathematical thinking. When we work in class, he can answer very well orally in English, but needs more time to write.

It dawned on me that there may be other students who, like Josue, are not able to show what they know in math because everything is in English and they have to complete tasks under time constraints. From that moment on, I encouraged all my multilingual learners to take time to plan and think through problems in their home language before writing in English, and they do so much better since I started this practice. It's so fortunate that these students have continued to develop their home languages so that I can make them feel comfortable using it in my class and see more accurately what they have learned.

Questions for Discussion

1. What needs to happen for the practice of encouraging multilingual learners to respond in their home language to become part of the school routine?
2. How would responses in the home language be used for student evaluation, even for languages with few resources?

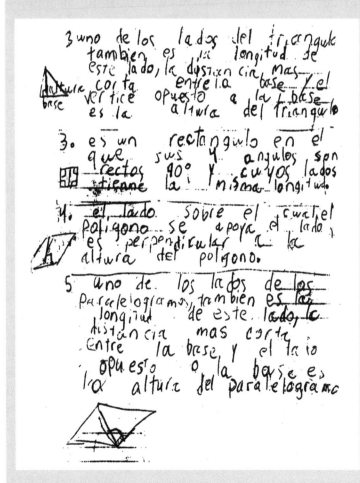

Figure 8.2 Josue's work on questions 2 through 5. The following is a translation of Josue's work on the back side of the paper.
(Answer for 2 from front side of this paper)
   One of the sides of the triangle is also the length of that side, the shortest distance between the base and the vertex opposite the base is the height of the triangle.
3. it's a rectangle in which its 4 angles are right 90° and whose sides have the same length.
4. the side on which the polygon rests, is perpendicular to the height of the polygon.
5. one of the sides of parallelograms, also is the length of that side, the shortest distance between the base and the side opposite to the base is the height of the parallelogram.

the MTSS team specifically, would have collected digital oral retellings, writing samples, learning logs, anecdotal notes, dialogue journals, dual language projects, electronic portfolios with digital photographs, audio recordings, and samples of student writing, among other artifacts. This bank allows the work of multilingual learners who are experiencing difficulties to be compared with the work of multilingual learners who are developing typically. It is useful to compare multilingual learners' work with the work of students from similar linguistic and socioeconomic backgrounds and with similar past educational experiences. Looking at academic work from dissimilar multilingual learners is also useful. Such an evaluation could show, for example, the impact that formal schooling or the level of language development in students' home language (or socioeconomic status) might have on students' academic achievement. Comparing multilingual learners' work with the work of multilingual learners with diagnosed learning disabilities may also provide useful insights, assuming that the diagnosis was accurate. When multilingual learners' work samples are compared with those of typically developing monolingual English students as well as students with learning disabilities, patterns of the way disabilities manifest themselves regardless of language background may emerge.

In keeping with the recommendation to compare multilingual learners' work samples with that of other multilingual learners, their true peers, the same should be done with standardized test data. Disaggregating standardized test data into subgroups (multilingual learners who have not reached advanced levels of English proficiency, those who are English proficient, and those at varying levels of English proficiency) can help make data from standardized tests more informative. Also, by delving into intersectionality within the data (multilingual learners who excel, those with Individualized Education Programs [IEPs], those with behavior reports) can reveal trends and patterns.

Current and Past Academic Performance Data

Examining past as well as recent information on academic performance is useful during the data gathering period. This type of longitudinal information provides a sense of how multilingual learners have progressed over time. If students come from within the school system, it is easier to look at their electronic portfolios and other documents. If students come from outside the system, all effort must be put into retrieving previous work samples and school records. If students come from outside the country, then staff often must rely on accounts provided by parents, students, and other family members regarding previous academic performance. Although this source of data is not always ideal and the data cannot be easily verified, it may be all there is. In such instances, care must be taken in interpreting the unverifiable data. If general information can be obtained about previous schooling experiences, it provides an important context for students' current performance. It is useful to compare past and present academic performance. Has there been dramatic growth in a short time? Has the student stopped progressing? Is there slow and steady progress? Are there identifiable gaps?

We must also look at the type of services and instruction the students received prior to entering the school, as well as the approach to instruction that was used. If multilingual learners received inappropriate instruction with little or no support, then the team can assume that a poor learning environment was a major contributor to these students' current academic challenges. The opposite can also be true. If students come from an enriched multilingual learner learning environment and then enroll in a school that provides little or no support for multilingual learners, their academic performance is likely to falter.

Evidence of Effective Instruction

In any discussion about a student or group of students whose performance in school is not progressing as expected, it is essential to focus on the quality of instruction these students have received or are receiving currently (Bassok & Galdo, 2016; Chiang, 2016; N. Flores et al., 2015; Y. Freeman & Freeman, 2002). First, ascertain whether these multilingual learners have had continuous and full access to the academic curriculum. Opportunity to learn is a key factor in any student's academic achievement, and multilingual learners are often pulled out of content classes to receive additional support and intervention. Although well intentioned, if these additional supports are not coordinated and connected to the content area instructional theme, students may end up with an education that has significant holes in it (the Swiss cheese effect of pull-out models). Likewise, in response to intervention (RtI) approaches that take a standard protocol approach, multilingual learners often receive instruction that is not cohesive as students are pulled out to work on different skills with different materials that are disconnected from classroom instruction (Allington, 2009). In other RtI approaches, the focus of instruction in the early grades has been on reading instruction that at times has neglected instruction in the areas of science, social studies, and mathematics. When students reach grades 3 and above, teachers find that these students have gaps in academic content and vocabulary knowledge because of lack of opportunity to learn.

Even if multilingual learners have had continuous and full exposure to the curriculum, we need to make sure that the instruction has made the learning of new, and usually abstract concepts accessible. One way to ensure accessibility of content-area instruction throughout the school is to make certain everyone who works with multilingual learners knows specifically what language and content are to be taught at different grade levels. The grade-level expectations and academic curriculum map, or at least locally created standards exist in practically every school district. In addition, academic English language development standards and principles documents (TESOL International Association, 2006; 2020) can provide guidance as to which language skills are expected in different content areas at different grade levels.

The WIDA consortium organizes language development and growth within grade-level clusters (see Can Do Descriptors, Key Uses Edition at wida.wisc. edu). The Can Do Descriptors may serve as another way to collect classroom language data; they should also be shared with colleagues as they indicate expected and typical milestones for English language development. So the next logical step is to identify the specific procedural language and vocabulary needed for every content area. It is essential for all teachers to realize the necessity of having language objectives for multilingual learners in every content lesson they teach (see, for example, the Sheltered Instruction Observation Protocol, http://www.cal.org/siop/about/).

When developing these academic language maps, it helps to look at the language requirements of professionals in different fields. What language do scientists use to communicate their subject matter? What language do historians or mathematicians use in their fields? What kind of reading and writing is required in these fields? The WIDA Consortium has reviewed content standards used in the United States and developed descriptions of the ability to produce and understand the following Key Language Uses in the classroom: Narrate, Argue, Inform and Explain. Staff need to be able to articulate what the academic language instruction looks like at different grade levels and language proficiency levels. The standards developed for multilingual learners at the national, regional (see, for example, the performance descriptors at wida.wisc.edu), and district levels can be helpful in creating this academic language map (see also pp. 126–131 in Cloud et al., 2009). Taking a long-term view of language planning helps ensure that students build their academic language over time from grade to grade (B. A. Collins et al., 2014; Commins & Miramontes, 2005).

MTSS Team Activity

As a preliminary step in suggesting learning support strategies, the MTSS team can develop some examples of specific language functions they believe students need in various content areas. As a group, team members can brainstorm examples of academic genres or discourse and process language that scientists use in their fields, and examples of the kind of reading, writing, speaking, and listening scientists do. After that, small groups or pairs could do the same work for other content areas. This exercise could be used as a springboard for cross-grade academic language articulation. These language functions could also become the focus of support strategies that teachers try out to help students in need of assistance.

Home Factors

The formal educational levels and socioeconomic background of the parents are important predictors of academic achievement for all students, regardless of their linguistic or cultural background (Cho, 2016; Hart & Risley, 2003; Ladd, 2012; Miech et al., 2001; D. Taylor, 1983). Parents who have had years of formal education have access to the academic content that their children are studying. Those at a higher socioeconomic level have the means to use books, computers, and transportation to access even more resources. Regardless of the parents' economic status or education level, however, all families have personal, cultural, cognitive, and professional funds of knowledge that relate to academic content areas that benefit their children (Arnold & Doctoroff, 2003; Bettini & Park, 2021; Evans & Kim, 2013; Moll et al., 1992). Schools must make the effort to access these funds of knowledge. The experiences and historical knowledge of multilingual learners' families as they relate to various content areas must be brought into the classroom and integrated with instruction (P. Smith, 2012), thus making lessons more culturally relevant and responsive to these students while enriching the learning experience for all students (Ladson-Billings, 2014).

Whenever we ask parents to reflect on experiences they share with their children that could support their learning in school, we get a wealth of ideas. One parent talked about the castle he built for his 4-year-old daughter out of an old cardboard box and how she played with it all the time. They went to the library and checked out many books about castles. The books were in English, and neither parent nor daughter could read them, but they looked at the pictures and discussed what they saw. Later, when she entered grade 6, those experiences helped her when the class studied medieval history. The child's father noted that it was not an expensive activity and it helped her learn. Another parent described hanging her young son's drawings (scribbles, actually) on the side of the cabinets in their apartment and how the boy would take visitors by the hand and begin talking about his works of art in his home language. The mother realized how this helped the child become confident about speaking to others about what he was thinking. Teachers commented on how eager this child was to share in class and how he was sufficiently confident to ask for help when he did not understand something. The mother was very proud that she had helped her son develop those skills. It is important to find out what sorts of informal learning experiences students have had, and continually encourage parents to see the value of these experiences for their children.

One way to capitalize on multilingual learner families' funds of knowledge is by creating identity texts, as discussed earlier with regard to the advantages of using dual language identity texts (Chow & Cummins, 2005; Neokleous et al., 2020; Schecter & Cummins, 2003), to help multilingual learners develop literacy in both their home language and English and as a way to bring their experiences and lives as bilingual bicultural individuals into the classroom. Oral and written dual language projects can be used across the curriculum and are a wonderful way to engage multilingual learners' parents, families, and community members in their academic learning.

Another way to continue students' learning is by asking multilingual learners to talk at home about what they are learning in school. This requires few resources and is immensely helpful for students and parents alike (Marshall & Toohey, 2010; Taberski, 2000). It is an easy way to maintain a constant flow of communication between home and school. Although some families may not have many material resources, they have other types of linguistic, cultural, and experiential resources that need to be used to full advantage.

Schools can do a lot to help multilingual learners be proud of their cultural backgrounds and of the great resource their parents and extended families provide to help them succeed.

Systemic and Specific Learning Support Strategies

For most students, the main venue for learning academic content is school. Therefore, if improvement is needed, the curriculum and the way it is taught are the prime candidates to increase the likelihood that multilingual learners learn what they need to know about the world they live in. The elements described in the following sections are crucial characteristics of the curriculum and instruction that are most effective for multilingual learners. Box 8.1 includes suggestions for systemic and specific learning support strategies.

Coordination

Effective content-area instruction is characterized by strong cross-grade coordination. This was discussed briefly earlier in the "Evidence of Effective Instruction" section of this chapter. To summarize, the school must have a curricular map that addresses the language that multilingual learners need to advance within and across grades for all the content areas. Monolingual English-speaking teachers must realize that they are language teachers as much as content-area teachers as far as multilingual learners are concerned. They need to be aware of these students' crucial need to learn the language of each content area as they learn the new concepts (Hadjioannou, 2007; Janzen, 2008; Snow et al., 1989). Preferably, students should have a chance to learn the language of the new concepts in a meaningful way throughout the lesson (National Academies of Sciences, Engineering, and Medicine, 2017).

Time and Resources

To complete this coordination, time and resources must be reserved for content-area experts from all grade levels, bilingual/ESL teachers, and administrators to come together to plan what is to be taught and how. When teachers use the curricular expectations and the academic language map to plan instruction, all students benefit—not just multilingual learners and those who are having academic difficulties. This improvement occurs because there is a conscious effort by all instructors to focus on content comprehension and mastery and language development (Janzen, 2007). Having this school-wide (or district-wide) academic language map encourages all teachers to write language objectives to accompany content objectives for every unit or lesson they teach.

Coherent Learning

Another way to ensure that multilingual learners have access to academic content as well as academic language is to organize learning tasks to promote coherent learning. Even the order in which activities are presented to

Box 8.1

Systemic and Specific Learning Support Strategies for Teaching Academic Content

Systemic Support Strategies

Instruction

- Implement an instructional learning cycle to organize instruction for all learners.
- Incorporate essential understandings and big ideas into unit/lesson planning rather than teaching topics.
- Present academic concepts visually and experientially.
- Engage students' home language actively as a resource to build background, to ensure access to academic concepts, and to facilitate transfer of knowledge between students' languages.
- Incorporate reading and writing in students' home language into instruction.
- Use multiple-level reading materials across the curriculum for every study unit.
- Use graphic organizers that match text structures in home language and English.
- Articulate content objectives clearly.
- Articulate language objectives clearly for academic listening, speaking, reading, and writing.
- Incorporate multilingual learners' (MLs') linguistic and cultural background and experiences into curriculum and materials.
- Assign teachers with expertise in content areas and ESL/bilingual methods to provide instruction to MLs.
- Develop curriculum maps for all grades.
- Develop academic language maps for all content areas and for all grades.
- Increase and expand use of MLs' home language (speaking, listening, reading, and writing) to enable students to process concepts.
- Invite parents and community members to come in on a regular basis to assist students, their home languages.
- Recruit secondary or university students to tutor MLs in their home languages and English.
- Create dual-language projects across the curriculum at all grade levels.
- Conduct meetings with ML parents to encourage them to use their home language at home and to talk with their children about school in their home language (for example, see brochures about the benefits of bilingualism for parents at http://www.mylanguage.ca/resources.html).
- Reserve professional learning money for teacher stipends to allow teachers to work collaboratively on curriculum development and lesson planning during the summer.
- Create common plan time for teachers to use to coordinate instruction during the week.
- Begin each lesson with a shared experience to develop schemas on which to build the rest of the lesson.

Assessment

- Collect and organize work samples in digital and paper portfolios across content areas in home language and English.

- Emphasize product, projects, performance, and process in assessment.
- Capture listening, speaking, reading, and writing in students' home language and English.
- Use teacher observation checklists across the curriculum.
- Use anecdotal notes from teacher–student conferencing.
- Include student self-assessments in the data-gathering process.
- Demonstrate progress over time through students' work samples, writing, oral language retellings, and so on.
- Present rubrics with clear criteria for work samples.
- Provide students with multiple methods they can use to show what they know.
- Design clear criteria for all academic projects so that students understand what they are assessed on; provide examples of excellent work so students have an idea of what they are to do for each assignment.

Specific Support Strategies

Many of the systemic support strategies can also be used with specific students in specific contexts; the following list of specific support strategies may be helpful.

Instruction

- Conduct student-directed portfolio conferences during which the student talks to the parents in their home language about schoolwork in lieu of traditional parent conferences.
- Help the student to talk with his or her parents/guardians at home about what the student has learned in school by giving the student discussion starter phrases to use, preferably in the home language.
- Find out what life experiences the student and family have had with the content-area material.
- Get to know the student and incorporate strengths, talents, interests, cultural and linguistic resources, and background and life experiences into instructional units of study.
- Use free online multilingual resources with students on a regular basis.
- Display work in students' languages in the school and on the school websites.
- Make certain that classroom instruction is engaging and interesting through the use of project-based or inquiry-based projects, integrated cross-curricular units of study, and service-learning projects (this guarantees that students continue to discuss what happened in school outside of class).

Assessment

- Use materials (e.g., manipulatives, visuals, charts, maps, graphic organizers, video clips) from the preparation phase of the instructional learning cycle to assess students.
- Interview students about times they have understood content-area material very well. What made those experiences so positive? Use the information

(continued)

Box 8.1 (continued)

to improve academic opportunities for multilingual learners.

- Ask students to practice talking about their academic portfolios on a regular basis, and fill out self-assessment forms.
- Review completed standardized tests with the student using something like a "think aloud," during

which the student explains how he or she got to answers to certain items; this can be done in the home language and/or bilingually.

- Assess students in ways that capture the process of learning and the thinking behind the learning, not just the end result.

multilingual learners can have a huge impact on how well the learners will understand what is being taught (Hadjioannou, 2007; Schussler, 2009). In most prekindergarten through grade 12 classrooms, instruction typically begins with reading a text in English. In the very early grades, a teacher reads a big book multiple times before continuing on to the rest of the lesson. In the intermediate grades, instruction begins with the text. Once students have learned the material, activities are introduced, such as experiments, video clips, field trips, or simulations. Many teachers think of these activities as "fluff" or even as "rewards," when in fact they are essential elements on which multilingual learners base the textual learning. In the later grades, access to the academic content relies almost exclusively on students' ability to independently read and interpret the text. The problem for multilingual learners is that if instruction is in English, their developing proficiency in the language of the text keeps them from fully understanding what the study unit is about. They might finally understand what was being studied once the experiment, video clip, manipulatives, or other aids have been used to illustrate the main concepts. Engaging in these shared experiences earlier in the unit or lesson can help engage multilingual learners at all levels of proficiency and prepare them to understand the content and accompanying texts. When the order of instruction is rearranged, some of these difficulties are alleviated. Chronicle 8.2 provides an example of what a student can do with content when writing in his home language.

Common Framework

When teachers use a common instructional framework, the steps that students need to take in order to learn become more predictable. We have used the *instructional learning cycle* framework presented in Box 8.2 with whole schools and individual teams of teachers to help them organize instruction in a way that optimizes comprehension and participation for multilingual learners. A framework such as this can be used in the content-area classroom but also should be used when implementing any sort of specific support strategy. Unless they occur within a shared framework, strategies used to support reading, writing, listening, and speaking are ineffective for multilingual learners.

This cycle of learning is meant to give school staff a long-term approach to planning instruction. It also allows teachers to make certain that they address

Chronicle 8.2

Going from Remediation to Preparation

By an ESL Teacher

I used to see my students whenever their homeroom teacher felt they could spare a half hour away from the "real" instruction going on in the monolingual English classroom. They would bring a homework assignment or a project they were struggling with, and in half an hour I would attempt to bring them to an understanding of the content that their mainstream teacher was unable to achieve in 1 hour. I was frustrated because the assignments were often not developmentally appropriate (spelling words at a fifth-grade level when they were at beginning levels of English proficiency) or were difficult to identify with culturally (write about what you would do if we had a snow day). I never felt like we were getting ahead—we were always playing catch-up. It was frustrating for me and for the students. I felt as though I was an overpaid tutor, and the students started to feel as though they never had any successes.

This year we changed the arrangement. The multilingual learners are targeted or clustered into specific homerooms and scheduled for protected instructional time with me. Our administrator has set aside professional learning time so that ESL teachers and content-area teachers can work together to plan instructional units of study. During that time, I am able to incorporate language objectives as well as strategies and resources that allow the multilingual students to access the material. Because the staff plan together, we all use the same strategies and resources across the different learning environments, and we understand when we are assessing language and literacy and when we are

assessing content. Instruction for multilingual learners is more cohesive and coordinated throughout the unit of study. Because of this arrangement, students are able to draw on the prior experiences they have had with me, such as the vocabulary I have already introduced and they have practiced. After instruction in the monolingual English classroom, the multilingual learners return to me for a review lesson. I use this time to fill in any gaps in their understanding, clarify concepts, extend concepts, and so on. Sometimes we, two teachers, co-instruct and I take the lead occasionally.

This arrangement is working much better than the one we had before did. The students now experience success and are more confident in the monolingual English classroom. The teachers report that motivation has improved and the students are much more willing to participate in small-group activities. Multilingual learners say they feel better about coming to school and that learning in both classrooms makes more sense. I no longer feel as if I am spinning my wheels. The students are making great gains in achievement, and my principal marvels at how far they have come!

Questions for Discussion

1. How does the infrastructure of the program affect students? Teachers? Students' academic performance?

2. What does the research say about the resource, or pullout, configuration for multilingual learners? For special education students?

academic listening, speaking, reading, and writing as well as academic content with all students. Planning in this way gives multilingual learners access to the content from the beginning of the unit and allows them more opportunities to gain mastery and a deeper understanding of the subject matter. Table 8.1 provides a sample science unit for early elementary grades that uses this instructional learning cycle. A similar unit for intermediate grades can be found in the online resources (see "Sample Health Education Lesson (intermediate level)").

Another advantage to using this type of planning framework is that it allows ESL, bilingual, general education, and special education teachers and others involved in supporting multilingual learners a way to coordinate their efforts. Perhaps the bilingual teacher presents the information in the preparation phase in the students' home language to ensure understanding of the main idea and to build conceptual understanding. In the instructional phase,

Box 8.2

An Instructional Learning Cycle

Preparation Phase

- Present key concepts experientially, concretely, and visually.
- Discuss and preview concepts, content, and stories in students' home languages.
- Engage students in conversations about the content and establish collaborative tasks.
- Use shared academic experiences (e.g., experiments, simulations, video clips, viewing diagrams) to pique students' interest in the unit/lesson topic.
- Build on students' linguistic and cultural experiences.
- Expose students to conceptual vocabulary through experiences and visuals, thereby forming a dual code: verbal and experience/imagery.

Instructional Phase

- Build a language experience approach text with students based on the shared experiences used during the preparation phase of the learning cycle.
- Introduce text using a variety of reading materials (in home language and English) about the topic.
- Use graphic organizers that reflect the structure of the text and allow students to organize important information from readings

- Use during-reading comprehension strategies
- Begin an in-class research project: Engage in questioning, inquiry, problem-based learning, and interviews.

Application Phase

- Use notes and graphics from the comprehension reading strategies as a springboard for writing.
- Have students prepare small-group presentations, museum displays, expert groups, and performances/debates.
- Engage in discussions and debates about the concepts just learned.
- Complete work on the product, project, or performance suggested in the lesson (Gottlieb, 2021).
- Investigate or identify how the concepts apply to our or our communities' daily lives.

Adapted from Karen Beeman and John Hilliard, based on the work of Jeanette Gordon, Illinois Resource Center, Arlington Heights, IL.

the ESL teacher may present a prereading activity in English followed by creating a language experience text using appropriate reading strategies such as Collaborative Strategic Reading (Beeman & Urow, 2013; Klingner & Vaughn, 2000; Klingner et al., 2004; van Kraayenoord, 2009). Students may then return to the bilingual teacher, who checks for understanding and begins the application phase of the lesson cycle with a writing activity using the graphic organizers that students prepared in the previous phases. This is just one example of how educators can share responsibility for multilingual learners' instruction.

MTSS Team Activity

Examine the lesson plan provided in Table 8.1. To what extent is this plan similar to how monolingual English-speaking classroom teachers teach their content-area lessons? If there are significant differences, what are they? Is there a need to have general education teachers change their approaches? If so, what would be a good professional learning plan?

Wide Scope

What is taught is as important as how it is taught. Even if a framework, such as the instructional learning cycle, is followed, a narrowly designed lesson is not as effective as one that gives students a wider scope of the concepts being introduced. If multilingual learners' instruction has been narrowly

Table 8.1 Sample Science Unit (early elementary level)

Underlying Principle/Essential Understanding: All living things pass through life stages and have basic needs for water, nutrients, protection, and energy in order to survive and grow.

Preparation Phase

Content Objectives

Students will

- Sequence pictures of the different stages of the plant cycle.
- View a 4-minute live-action video clip of a plant's life cycle from seed to maturity.
- Practice key vocabulary from sequencing and from video to place correctly on plant life-cycle diagram.

Language Objectives

Students will

- Use descriptive (adjectives, comparison words) and sequential sentence structures (*first, second, next, finally,* or *last*) to explain the stages of a plant's life and what it might need to grow.

Strategies

- Predicting/sequencing: Do this prior to viewing video.
- Visuals: Use 4-minute video clip of life cycle, sequencing cards, plant diagram with key vocabulary.
- Collaborative learning: Done after taking time to think and conjecture individually.

Differentiation

- Provide visual support through use of video and cards.
- Provide sequencing vocabulary and a range of sentence frames to encourage oral language practice.
- Preview vocabulary and process in students' home language.

Cross-Cultural Connections

- Students are asked to find out what and how things are planted at home or in the neighborhood and make a collective inventory.

Flexible Grouping

- Individual: Predictions are prompted by visuals and realia.
- Partners: Pair students to sequence the picture cards and to plant beans.
- Whole class: View video.

Instructional Assessment

- Use observation of picture sequencing (before and after video); checklist.
- Assess students' use of academic language (sequential and descriptive) through observation and by collecting sequence graphic organizer and sentence frames.
- Students enter their completed plant life cycle artifacts into their learning logs.

Instructional Phase

Content Objectives

Students will

- Predict basic needs that plants require, based on what humans need.
- Conduct an experiment (plant two beans, one without basic needs met and the other with needs met, to collect data on their life cycle).

Language Objectives

Students will

- Use language needed to predict and confirm or refute predictions.
- Use language of the scientific method.

Strategies

- Use wall chart for LEA approach: Record student predictions (shared writing).
- Teacher demonstrates experiment.
- Visual: The experiment setup is put on chart paper.
- Questioning: Use partner sharing; ask which bean will grow better? Why?

Differentiation

- Common shared experiences are used to build content schemas (experiment).
- Use speaking/writing frames (bilingual): "I predict . . . because . . ."
- Provide multiple-level reading resources in home languages and English.
- Provide teacher modeling.
- Provide visual support throughout lesson.

Cross-Cultural Connections

- Ask students to predict and then dictate their predictions bilingually.
- Use a variety of plant/seed examples from across the world.

Flexible Grouping

- Individual: Use vocabulary chart with illustration/learning log entries.
- Partners/small groups are used during predictions and experiment.
- Whole class: Students view teacher demonstration and use LEA.

Instructional Assessment

- Consider LEA text of students' predictions.
- Note anecdotal reading remarks.
- Use student checklist of experiment setup procedure.
- Assess illustrated plant life-cycle vocabulary chart.

Application Phase

Content Objectives

Students will

- Graph height vs. time of their two bean plants.
- Record their plant observations in learning logs.
- Research other living things and prepare a dual-language poster to display results.

Strategies

- Illustrated learning log: Complete dated entries.
- Data reporting: Graph height and growth time in days.
- Poster: Display the life cycle related to new living thing with plant's particular needs highlighted (results of initial exploration of plants grown at home or neighborhood, research through interviews with parents and older students and through Internet viewing and resources in home language).

Flexible Grouping

- Individual: Write learning log entries.
- Partners/small groups: Use research teams to create posters.
- Whole class/individual: Graph results.

(continued)

Table 8.1   *(continued)*

Underlying Principle/Essential Understanding: All living things pass through life stages and have basic needs for water, nutrients, protection, and energy in order to survive and grow.

Language Objectives	Differentiation	Instructional Assessment
Students will	• Provide a variety of reading-level resources.	• Learning log entries about the growth of two plants over time and how their basic needs affect life stages
• Use descriptive scientific language and the language of comparing and contrasting when observing how the plants have changed over time.	• Rehearse.	
	• Use collaborative research teams.	• Graphs
	• Visual supports provide scaffold for oral language, writing, and reading.	• New lifecycle poster rubric
	• Teacher models use of language and writing.	• Oral presentation rubric
• Write using the language of the scientific method in a lab report or shared experiment summary.	**Cross-Cultural Connections**	• Reflections (oral/written/illustrated): Description of the use of plants in various settings (community, their experiment, farms, gardens) and what is needed for these plants to grow and thrive and why plants are important
	• Ask students to compare how the home/neighborhood plants grow compared to their experimental plants.	
	• Have students describe who tends to the plants and how the plants receive everything they need to grow.	

LEA, language experience approach.

designed around a single topic and the students have had to memorize many facts related to this topic, then performance on a test could be misleading, as it may reflect memory more than actual understanding of concepts. For example, in a unit developed around plants, is what is important about the topic clear? What should students focus on? If these questions are not clarified, multilingual learners (and other students) inevitably focus on memorizing everything about plants that is presented to them to the best of their ability and as their language proficiency allows. In this type of study unit, assessments usually focus on how well students can recall the facts. They take the form of multiple-choice, fill-in, true–false, or short-answer tests. These sorts of assessments are troublesome for multilingual learners because they must rely on their developing English language proficiency to memorize concepts that they are still learning.

In the example unit about plants, the lesson can shift from studying the topic of plants to studying the principle that *all living things pass through life stages and have basic needs for water, nutrients, protection, and energy in order to survive and grow*. Plants then become an example illustrating this principle, which also applies to the animal kingdom. In addition to giving students more substantial knowledge by giving them the principle rather than just the facts, this approach allows students to demonstrate the understanding of an organizing idea or enduring principle rather than merely the ability to recall facts. This is why many educators advocate making a *big idea* or an *essential understanding* the focus of study units and making the statement: *"I want my students to understand that . . ."* the guide for developing lessons (Wiggins & McTighe, 2004). Students can be assessed for their understanding of a principle through more authentic assessments (performance, projects, and products) independent of their proficiency in English. Even the facts that are presented during these lessons are more comprehensible because students have a structure on which to map these facts.

MTSS Team Activity

Examine the lesson plans offered in Table 8.1. Create a list of the kind of student work that would be generated throughout the unit. Discuss the quality, amount, and variety of student work that emerges from this approach to instruction and assessment. How does this assist the team in trying to support multilingual learners who seem to be facing significant academic challenges? How does this affect the sort of systemic and specific support strategies that are suggested in Box 8.1? What can this kind of student work tell you about multilingual learners' academic performance?

Questions for Reflection and Action

1. What do we know about academic content learning in the home and additional languages of multilingual learners who are experiencing academic challenges?
2. What are some examples of instruction in our school that uses the content-area instruction strategies described in this chapter?
3. What are some unique features of the sample unit of study shown in Table 8.1? How are assessment and instruction connected in the study unit?
4. How are teachers addressing language objectives and content-area objectives in the course of their instruction? Share this information with teachers, then solicit their ideas for improvement and weave those ideas into a professional learning plan.
5. Analyze the instructional framework currently used in your school/district in terms of effectiveness and cultural and linguistic responsiveness. Does it meet the academic and linguistic needs of the multilingual learners you serve? What are some ways that educators have embedded students' cultures meaningfully into unit/lesson planning?
6. How are students' home languages incorporated into lessons? What suggestions can you offer for improvement?

Cross-Cultural Factors

Key Concepts. *The sixth integral factor involves the role of culture in learning. As a complex social phenomenon, learning is always situated within one's experiential context and this context is influenced by the values, expectations, and practices that are preferred by students' communities; that is, their cultural context. When multilingual learners find themselves in an unfamiliar cultural environment, any academic challenges that these students experience must be interpreted in light of that unknown cultural context. Similarly, learning support strategies must be culturally responsive and relevant to the student.*

The sixth integral factor to consider when a multilingual learner experiences linguistic or academic challenges in school is the influence of culture on learning. Because schools often do not reflect the cultures and languages of many students they serve, the multi-tiered system of supports (MTSS) team should try to determine whether the challenges that the student experiences can be explained by this mismatch. There may be disconnects among the students' home culture, the culture of the immigration process, and the culture of the new school and community (Brown-Jeffy & Cooper, 2012). Such disconnects can contribute to misunderstandings, miscommunication, and differences in performance expectations (F. Bailey & Pransky, 2005; Chappell & Faltis, 2013; E. Lee et al., 2008; McDermott & Varenne, 1995; G. Noble, 2017; Philips, 1983). In some situations, rather than being a resource for learning and understanding, culture can be seen by school personnel as yet another hurdle that must be overcome on the way to achieving optimal academic performance. Far from just tolerating or even acknowledging students' cultural backgrounds, schools must seek to develop culturally sustaining practices that integrate and center on students' cultural way of being and communicating (D. Paris & Alim, 2014; Sleeter, 2012).

Culture is a complex construct that is ever changing, emerging, and dynamic as are the young people, children, families, and communities that schools serve. School administrators, educators, and all practitioners should therefore examine closely the cultural values and positions represented by the school. Do the policies, curricula, and pedagogies used by schools highlight and include all voices? Do schools seek to bring multiple perspectives into the curriculum, valuing the experiences of historically marginalized people? Or do schools maintain the status quo, which excludes some students and represents only a narrow set of experiences of ways of being and knowing? Do our schools ask students to leave part or all of who they are at the school entrance? These are critical questions to ask when we see that some students are not flourishing, are silenced, or feel invisible or oppressed. Seeking to understand the cultural values of our school leads us to examine our own personal cultural perspectives, biases, and experiences. We must do this reflective work ourselves before we can begin to understand the norms and values of anyone who has experiences and behaviors that are different from our own (Kalyanpur, 2019). All educators and practitioners working with multilingual learners must learn how to create learning environments that take into account a wide range of cultural experiences so that multilingual learners in these contexts begin to see themselves in the curriculum and affirm their personal and intellectual identities in supportive environments (Artiles, 2015; Asher, 2007; Cabrera et al., 2014; Dee & Penner, 2016; Hammond, 2014; Pransky & Bailey, 2002; Rodgers, 2002).

In this chapter we discuss some characteristics of culture and some of the ways culture affects learning, engagement, and identity. We then suggest ways to gather information about these cultural aspects to better describe students' cultural backgrounds. We also suggest procedures for assessing the school staffs' cultural competence (Kalyanpur & Harry, 2012) and how well students are functioning in the current learning environment. The chapter ends with recommendations for drawing the best out of a culturally and linguistically rich learning environment. Here we present strategies to create and implement culturally sustaining learning environments (D. Paris, 2012; D. Paris & Alim, 2017) systemically and for individual students.

Key Characteristics of Culture

What Is Culture?

Schools often look at visible surface manifestations of cultures, such as food, festivals, fashion, and the fine arts, to represent a group of people when asked what constitutes *culture*. Those surface aspects of a culture are what teachers may look to (and sometimes purchase) when wanting to make their lessons more reflective of their students' backgrounds. Unfortunately, these very familiar and visible elements alone can lead to stereotypes, and even worse, to negative consequences that are demeaning and damaging. Culture is far more complex and deeply penetrating than its superficial manifestations (Agar, 2013; Hoffman, 1999; Milner, 2007; Sahlins, 1999). We use the metaphor of an iceberg to illustrate this complexity. As represented in Figure 9.1, the most visible forms of culture are seen at the tip of the iceberg and the less visible more abstract aspects of culture are shown beneath the surface (Hamayan, 2012). Limiting our view of another person to just the visible aspects of culture can lead to tokenism and stereotyping (Grosjean, 2015b; Kibler, 2005; Ladson-Billings, 2006; Milner, 2007). We are all multifaceted and complex, with identities formed by life experiences, family customs

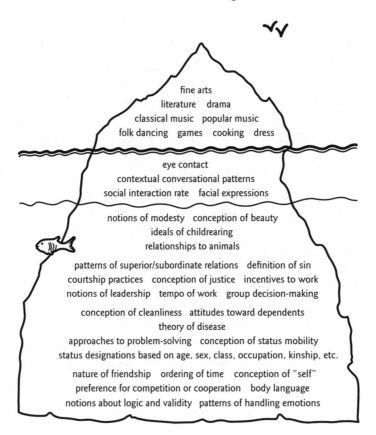

Figure 9.1. The iceberg model of culture. (Illinois Resource Center, Arlington Heights, Illinois, 1997)

and experiences, the use of all our means of communication, physical and psychological realities, and the influence of people in our lives. As educators we must acknowledge our own biases, which may be based on a superficial understanding of others, and decide to do better. We must get to know our students and their families and communities in real and meaningful ways or our students will suffer negative consequences in their learning (F. Bailey & Pransky, 2005; S. Brown & Souto-Manning, 2008; Freire, 2014; Mattingly, 2008; McDermott & Varenne, 1995; Ozfidan & Toprak, 2020; Trueba, 1988).

Heeding this warning about the visible and superficial aspects of culture, there is something to be said for schools meaningfully integrating the visible aspects of multilingual learners' home and community lives into the everyday functioning of the school (C. J. Flores & Delgado, 2012; Marshall & Toohey, 2010). These familiar elements can make the learning environment more welcoming to students from all backgrounds. When the cafeteria offers halal food, rice noodles, and vegetarian dishes, for example, it exposes all students to a broader diet and affirms the value and heritage of food from all the communities represented among the student population. When the art teacher addresses the academic standards integrating artists, artifacts, and techniques from Indigenous societies, Latin America, Asia, Africa, other than Western Europe, it shows the students that the school values global contributions, not just those from Western cultures. When teachers regularly engage students in multilingual projects and when the school posts important signs in the various students' languages, it creates an environment in which all languages are valued equally. Although these may be the more visible aspects of culture, their integration into school life helps all students grow to see them as a normal and expected part of their own lives.

Understanding that surroundings affect students' development of self makes schools take very seriously the need to create safe and culturally and linguistically supportive and sustaining learning environments in classrooms, school hallways, cafeterias, clubs, sports, the arts, and every other aspect of school so that students' identities continue to develop in positive and healthy ways. Purposefully planning ways for all students to see themselves positively reflected and supported in the curriculum, during school events, and in conversations with peers and school staff must be a priority in school improvement initiatives.

Just beyond the visible aspects of culture seen in Figure 9.1 are those aspects that overtly influence and govern how we interact with one another. They may become visible as we take the time to look and develop interpersonal sensitivity. These aspects of culture are often sources of misunderstandings resulting from miscommunication (Artiles, 2015; S. B. Heath & McLaughlin, 1993; Meisuri et al., 2018; Ngo, 2008; Philips, 1983; Weisner, 2009). Responding to a signal from someone with whom we are interacting without understanding the attitudes and values that motivate and support the other person's behavior can lead to erroneous interpretations of the behavior and false conclusions (Bak, 2016; Mattingly, 2008; Wax, 1993). The most common example of this involves the different patterns of eye contact considered appropriate in different cultures. In many Anglo-American families, eye contact is used to convey interest, honesty, and respect, but in many other cultures it is considered impolite or even challenging to make direct or prolonged eye contact with someone. In the case of children, such a violation of cultural behavior would be even more egregious. Yet, when reprimanding a student, many monolingual English-speaking teachers may say, "Look at me when I am talking to you!" They do not realize the misunderstanding to which they are a party if they conclude, based on the student's lack of eye contact, that the student is dishonest, disrespectful, or inattentive. Understanding the role of eye gaze patterns in their own culture and the student's culture helps teachers better evaluate the student's behavior and contributes to a more culturally responsive pedagogy.

Other aspects of culture are found far below the surface, and although they are often seemingly invisible to those inexperienced with the culture, these less visible aspects of culture are actually the most important. They provide the context and mechanisms from which culture as an intra-personal and inter-personal entity operates (Hoffman, 1998; McDermott, 1999), and they provide a route to the explanation of observable behaviors. These aspects of culture represent beliefs, attitudes, and values and can help provide insight into students' motivation, expectations, goals, dreams, and their identities.

Over the past 30 years, as anthropologists and educators applied increasingly complex models to the study of culture in educational settings, there was a realization that our social and cultural lives and identities in any context, but especially in the context of education, are not static and fixed. Rather our cultural identities—how we are defined by others and how we define ourselves—change as the expectations, interactions, behaviors, and relationships around us change (Baltaci, 2017; Davidson, 1996; Hammond, 2015; McDermott, 1999; Ngo, 2008). That is, our perceived identity within any given sociocultural context at any given time is a construction based on the input and expectations received and the reactions that we had to this input. As an interpretive lens for viewing the continual changes in student behaviors and the numerous reactions and interactions that occurred in classrooms, the sociocultural account of identity makes a great deal of sense (Charles, 2008). For example, the concept that one's operational identity is not static but is influenced by contextual variables has enabled the creation of workable models and explanations for a host of observed behaviors and practices in the classroom (Bower et al., 2015; Carter, 2006; Hammond, 2015; S. Lee, 1996; Li, 2006; McDermott, 1997; Nasir, 2002; Phelan et al., 1993; Spindler & Spindler, 1994). In authentic settings, the concept of fluidity and an emerging identity is consistent with what has been observed (N. Flores et al., 2015; D. Paris & Alim, 2014).

We can say that identity is not merely a manifestation of culture but is partially constructed by a deeper aspect of culture—the "self." As a deep aspect of culture, self is an amalgam of some inherent psychological construct within the person and various social, cultural, and interactive variables that act on that person from outside. In effect, self is a psychosocial construct that is manifested according to various sociocultural variables and can be recognized as identity and in several affective reactions to different cultural variables (Bruner, 2008; Mattingly, 2008; Whiting, 1990). As stated by Jen, this makes the self "more than the sum of her social facts" (1997, p. 19). That is, although there is much variability in the manifestation of cultural identity, depending on context, there is still some cultural stability, owing to the deeper aspect of self that is a component of the emergent behavior recognized as one's cultural identity.

This example illustrates two important concepts. First, there are deeper aspects of culture that, although not immediately observable, are important to cultural explanation and understanding. Second, this knowledge and understanding have practical implications. For example, if we are to be effective interpreters of culture as an operational variable in education, we cannot adopt a static view of a student's identity in the classroom. Neither can we assign a fixed social identity or cultural role to the student. We have to recognize that multiple explainable aspects of their identities may emerge in our students, depending on context (Hammond, 2015; Ngo, 2008; Steele, 2004). Therefore, rather than creating oppositional frames such as "us versus them" regarding cultural considerations, we should strive to focus on the characteristics of culture that help establish the fluid, situated, and negotiated character of each individual's identity in a given cultural context (Hammond, 2015; Hoffman, 1999; Whiting, 1990).

The deeper aspects of culture are less prone to stereotyping. Educators who seek first to understand their own culture, then the culture of the school, and only then the culture of their students and their students' families according to these invisible and fluid aspects of culture can expect to move toward more accurate insights (Hammond, 2015; Kibler 2005; Milner, 2007; Varenne, 2008). They are more likely to pinpoint cultural mismatches and conflicts, as well as commonalities and similarities, especially if they remember that culture is not limited to race, ethnicity, or language group.

The Multiple Facets of Culture

Many educators who work with multilingual learners tend to think of cultural diversity in terms of ethnicity, race, country of origin, and language. Although these are very important aspects of one's identity, culture goes far beyond those components (Skrentny, 2008; Sternberg, 2007a). This understanding of culture should be expanded to include socioeconomic and education levels, gender, sexual orientation, geographic location, and occupation (Banks, 2001; Lesaux & Harris, 2015; Ngo & Lee, 2007). All these aspects of culture provide members of the cultural group with unique experiences, which in turn help to shape and influence members' perspectives and interpretation of events (Kao & Thompson, 2003). For this reason, educators should keep in mind that large groups of individuals seldom, if ever, conform to the same cultural values, attitudes, and behaviors. Imagine, for example, 100 women at a supermarket near your house. Within that homogeneous group of 100 individuals (the group under discussion being defined by gender) is a tremendous amount of diversity. No one would argue that all the members of such a group subscribe to the same political beliefs, concepts of beauty, work ethic, or child-rearing practices.

Educators must guard against the tendency to make similar statements about students who come from the same country or the same home-language background (Kibler, 2005). Indeed, one should not expect the student to take the same cultural role or engage in the same behaviors when various aspects of the context change. Culture is more complex and more emergent than that. The unit that we must focus on consists of the students and their immediate families.

Culture as a Dynamic Process

Not only must we avoid making generalizations across individuals when dealing with culture, we must also view culture as a dynamic process, not a static concept (Agar, 2013; Hall, 2001; McDermott, 1999; Paradise & Rogoff, 2009; Wax, 1993). Culture is always changing, subject to the experiences of individuals and their interpretation of such experiences. For example, with the common use of cellular telephones family members are able to communicate with one another at any time and many parents allow their children to go places that in the recent past they were not allowed to go unaccompanied by adults. Parents now feel they can monitor their children from a distance, through their cell phones. This has led to a change in the degree of responsibility expected of children, the age of independence from parents, the understanding of parents' authority, and a host of other cultural values and beliefs.

Every new experience we have and every new context we encounter may change our perspective slightly, and may alter the way we interact with our environment subsequent to that experience. This is especially true of multilingual learners, who are in the process of discovering novel customs. More than any other students, multilingual learners experience the dynamism of culture (Carneiro, 2007; Carter, 2006). We must keep that changing nature of students' culture in mind when we are gathering information, and we must try to understand multilingual learners as they are adapting to the new culture.

Adapting to a New Culture

When students and their families settle in a new community from a different country with different customs, the process of adapting to a new culture will be long and complex. According to one analysis, people go through seven stages until they reach the highest level of acculturation (Berry et al., 2002). This depiction of acculturation is simply a semblance of what many people go through but can be useful in understanding what it takes to adapt to a new culture. Table 9.1 summarizes these stages.

In the preliminary stage, the recently arrived immigrant is fascinated by the novelty and is excited to learn about the new things in this environment. In the second stage, the immigrant becomes more aware of the differences between the new home and the old, and this is followed by the third stage of increased participation, with the clash of the two cultures becoming more apparent. The fourth stage, culture shock, is a stage of emotional overload resulting from the loss of all familiar aspects of the home culture. In the fifth stage, instrumental adaptation, the individual feels a need to choose a path: Retreat into the home culture, give up the home culture altogether in favor of the new one, or adopt parts of the new culture while maintaining some of the home culture. The sixth stage, integrative adaptation, depends on the choice that was made in the previous stage: The individual either experiences a culture split (for the first two choices) or successful acculturation (for the third choice). In the last stage, structural adaptation, the individual reaches the highest level of adaptation and is able to maintain a comfortable balance between the two cultures most of the time.

This stage model suggests that it is possible to reach a level of acculturation that integrates some aspects of both cultures and to feel somewhat comfortable in both contexts. Some multilingual learners may be able to reach the stage of structural adaptation by creating their own mixed culture; they maintain their home culture while having acculturated into the new environment. This is not an easy task because many norms and values from the home

Table 9.1   Stages of Acculturation

Stage	Characteristics	Typical States
Preliminary	Preparation/Anticipation/Migration—Sometimes referred to as the *honeymoon stage* or *initial stage*, including a time of euphoria—if considered a "good" move, a child may be fascinated with everything and excited to learn.	Cooperative, displays a desire to please
Spectator	Occurs when the concept of "change" overcomes the concept of newness and the reality of the situation sinks in.	Fearful, anxious, lonely
Increasing participation	Sometimes referred to as the *uprooting stage*; survival instincts are awakened and the clash of the two cultures becomes apparent in all its complexity.	Mixture of emotions in combination
Culture shock	Emotional overload; change in its most profound context resulting from a loss of many familiar signs, symbols, and cues of the original culture, creating a mistrust and fear of the new situation that may not have existed previously; a most difficult time, when patience and tolerance are very important and affect all future decision-making.	Depressed, frustrated, insecure, withdrawn, and hostile; criticizes everything
Instrumental adaptation	Sometimes referred to as the *adaptation period*; based on a variety of factors, students choose ways of dealing with the emotional, educational, and social issues in their lives: • *Encapsulation:* Retreats into the first culture • *Assimilation:* Belief that one must give up the original culture in order to fit into the mainstream culture • *Acculturation:* One becomes part of the new culture while still holding onto the customs and values of the original culture	Flight/Fight/Integration
Integrative adaptation	Sometimes referred to as the *mainstream phase*; based on their decisions in the previous phase, students experience either a *culture split*: split between home life (first culture) and school (all out-of-home aspects) life or *successful acculturation*: acceptance and integration of parts of both cultures into their lives and school experiences	Fear of embarrassment and lack of acceptance of first culture in mainstream culture
Structured adaptation	The deepest level of the adaptation experience during which an individual grows truly comfortable in the second culture while maintaining a deep and integrated connection with the first culture; typically doesn't happen in the first generation	

Adapted from Kibler, J. (2005). How does one develop an intercultural perspective? *International Forum of Teaching and Studies*, *1*(1), 9–12.

culture may clash with those of the school, especially when those norms are from the deeper part of the iceberg (see Figure 9.1). For example, if the home culture views modesty for adolescent girls as important and the corresponding dress code is one that requires covering shoulders and arms, but the school culture is more permissive, a young girl may find it difficult to juggle those two norms. Naturally, not everyone reaches the stage of structured adaptation. In fact, many immigrants who left their home country by choice return to it, at least partly because they could not get over the culture shock (Aldana & Martinez, 2018; Berry et al., 2002; S. Brown & Souto-Manning, 2008). Multilingual learners who are going through stages two to four and those who have chosen a nonadaptive path in stages five and six are likely to be in a state of anxiety or discomfort that may stand in the way of optimal learning. Chronicle 9.1 provides an example of culture shock.

Educators should also consider the resources multilingual learners have at their disposal when they are in the midst of the process of acculturation. Many immigrants may not have the financial, physical, and emotional support that one needs to lead a comfortable life (Evans & Kim, 2013; Weisner, 2009). The presence or absence of these resources influences the quality of experiences the multilingual learner may have in the face of acculturation. Information regarding these resources in students' lives can also offer insight as to culturally responsive pedagogy and appropriate strategies to help students navigate the culture in their new country (Aldana & Martinez, 2018; Asher, 2007; Carter, 2003). The extent to which school personnel get to know their students and families and deliberately integrate these students'

Chronicle 9.1

Nightmares in Saltillo

By a Bilingual Special Education Teacher

At age 20, I decided to travel to Saltillo, Mexico, to live there and take college classes. I had been studying Spanish since I was in fifth grade; I was a member of the National Spanish Honor Society and had taken graduate-level Spanish classes as a college freshman. Sadly, all that language instruction failed to prepare me for culture shock I experienced. It started innocently enough: One night I had a nightmare and woke up screaming. The next morning my housemates and the members of the family I was living with gave me sidelong glances and good-natured kidding.

To my surprise the same thing happened the very next night. The following morning, the good-natured ribbing was replaced with genuine concern. "Are you okay? Is something wrong?" my housemates asked. My housemother made me an extra-special breakfast. To my horror, it happened repeatedly, night after night. Each night the dream was the same—I dreamt that I was covered in bugs and I would be screaming as I tried to brush the bugs off my body. Now the neighbors, who heard the screams, were asking about me.

Word spread throughout my classes that I was having nightmares. My tutor asked me if I was okay. I was perplexed, as I had never had dreams like this before. I was exhausted and feeling as though my behavior was beyond my control. After a week, my housemother sent me to a doctor. The doctor asked me whether I was taking any drugs. I wasn't. When he found nothing physically wrong with me, he sent me home, back to the United States. Just as quickly as the nightmares came, they disappeared and never returned.

Since then, I have visited Mexico several times. Those trips have been the highlight of my life and career. I became a bilingual special education teacher and have worked with Spanish-speaking students. I have gotten to know their families and have established close relationships with some of them. I guess at the age of 20, being immersed in another culture was more than I could handle.

As I reflect on this experience, I cannot help thinking about some of the families of my students. I realize that they do not have the choice to get on an airplane and go home to assist them with their culture shock. How difficult it must be for a child who is going through this stage to put on a happy face and come to school, to be bombarded day after day with the strange and foreign culture.

Questions for Discussion

1. People experience culture shock in all sorts of ways. Discuss different ways culture shock may be experienced.
2. How can people help those with culture shock, short of sending them home?

languages and cultural ways of being and knowing into the learning environment will impact directly how anchored students' identities will be as they navigate schooling in their new country. They may learn new ways of being but may never feel compelled to lose any part of themselves in the process.

MTSS Team Activity

For this activity, MTSS team members should think of a way to place themselves in situations that are unfamiliar to them and then report back to the group on their emotional reactions, coping strategies, and successes or failures. Examples of possible situations could be attending an art gallery for someone who has no interest in art; attending a National Association for Stock Car Auto Racing event for someone who doesn't drive much; for someone who has never tried food from Africa, it could be eating at a Nigerian restaurant. It could also mean reading books about immigrant and refugee experiences as a book study. The important part of this activity is to encourage team members to practice getting outside their comfort zone to better understand how it feels to be in a stressful or unfamiliar situation. This activity should be repeated more than once throughout the school year to promote the desirability of voluntarily participating in activities outside one's comfort zone. Perhaps each meeting could begin with one team member recounting how they voluntarily stepped outside their comfort zone and what was learned as a result.

The Role of Culture in Learning

The norms and values that make us who we are influence how we learn (Hamayan, 2012; Rapley, 2004; Rogoff, 2003; Steele, 2004; Sternberg, 2007b). First, they provide us with a context for making sense of the world around us. Thus, when we are presented with a new concept, we internalize it in a way that fits our worldview. When children who have been taught that animals belong outside of the house and under no circumstance should they be let inside reads a story about pets, they may get very confused and misunderstand the story altogether. Thus, multilingual learners are faced with learning new, often quite abstract concepts through a language they are not yet proficient in. When the lesson to be learned assumes a certain set of norms and values that are divergent from the learner's norms and values, additional hurdles materialize. When there is a mismatch between the student's own cultural context and that of the curriculum, those differences make it more challenging for the student to learn the concepts presented in the curriculum (F. Bailey & Pransky, 2005).

The second way in which cultural differences affect learning involves the general level of discomfort that students may feel when they cannot see themselves reflected in the school environment (Kibler, 2005). Students whose ways of doing things are markedly different from the way things are done in school are likely to be on edge and to experience anxiety. Learning takes more effort in a state of agitation and may seem to students to be impossible at times (J. S. Damico & Damico, 1993a; Fan & Wolters, 2014). A student whose notion of a classroom setting is one in which the teacher directs everything and students have no choices may feel completely at a loss in a classroom where students determine tasks, activities, and timing (Garmezy, 1991). A female student who is discouraged or even prohibited from socializing with males who are not immediate family members may feel so uncomfortable with a male teacher that learning is significantly hampered.

The beliefs, attitudes, and values that each of us holds not only shape our perceptions of the world around us, they also make it easier, or more challenging, for us to build new knowledge (Corsaro & Nelson, 2003; Gutierrez & Rogoff, 2003; Hammond, 2015; Nieto, 2002; Vadeboncoeur, 2006). The first step for a school to take is to find out as much as possible about the various cultures it represents, starting with one's own culture, and the norms and values that families who come from that cultural background are likely to have. The next section presents suggestions for gathering information about the cultures represented in the school, evaluating students' ability to function in the culture of the school, and assessing how well school staff have embraced an attitude of cultural reciprocity with students and their families.

Information Gathering and Evaluating Cultural Difference Factors

It is neither expected nor feasible for teachers to know everything about the cultural aspects of every student in their classrooms. However, educators should attempt to find out as much as they can about the cultures in their classrooms, despite being outsiders to those cultures (Isaacs, 2012). They can do this by engaging firsthand with the best resources available to them: students and the students' families. The topic of culture is frequently overwhelming. Where does one begin to understand the identity of students and their families? How does one organize the information that is obtained, typically in bits and pieces and over a period of time? Figure 9.2 provides

Family Life
Temporary $\Leftarrow \Rightarrow$ Permanent
Extended $\Leftarrow$ Nuclear $\Rightarrow$ Linear
Emotionally close $\Leftarrow \Rightarrow$ Emotionally distant
Matriarchal $\Leftarrow \Rightarrow$ Patriarchal

Social Interactions
Physically close $\Leftarrow \Rightarrow$ Physically distant
Much eye contact $\Leftarrow \Rightarrow$ Little eye contact
Formal $\Leftarrow \Rightarrow$ Informal
Symmetrical $\Leftarrow \Rightarrow$ Complementary
Demonstrative $\Leftarrow \Rightarrow$ Undemonstrative

Formal Education
Highly valued $\Leftarrow \Rightarrow$ Not so highly valued
Teaching as prestige $\Leftarrow \Rightarrow$ Teaching not prestigious
One teaching style $\Leftarrow \Rightarrow$ Varied teaching styles

Work and Achievement
Competition $\Leftarrow \Rightarrow$ Cooperation
Work defines person $\Leftarrow \Rightarrow$ Work does not define person
Survival $\Leftarrow \Rightarrow$ Self-actualization

Individuality
Rigid roles $\Leftarrow \Rightarrow$ Flexible roles
Independence $\Leftarrow$ Interdependence $\Rightarrow$ Dependence
Confrontation $\Leftarrow \Rightarrow$ Harmonization
Rebellion $\Leftarrow \Rightarrow$ Conformity

Wealth and Materialism
Importance of tangibles $\Leftarrow \Rightarrow$ Importance of intangibles
Immediate goals $\Leftarrow \Rightarrow$ Lifelong goals

Time
Rigid adherence $\Leftarrow \Rightarrow$ Flexible adherence
Past orientation $\Leftarrow$ Present orientation $\Rightarrow$ Future orientation
Time walks $\Leftarrow \Rightarrow$ Time runs
Monochronic $\Leftarrow \Rightarrow$ Polychronic

Age
Ages highly segregated $\Leftarrow \Rightarrow$ Ages mixed together
Children given choice $\Leftarrow \Rightarrow$ Children not given choice
Elderly have vital role $\Leftarrow \Rightarrow$ Elderly do not have vital role
Children have critical responsibilities $\Leftarrow \Rightarrow$ Children do not have many responsibilities

Space
Individual space clearly defined $\Leftarrow \Rightarrow$ Individual space not defined
Generous $\Leftarrow \Rightarrow$ Restricted use
Dense cohabitation $\Leftarrow \Rightarrow$ Sparse cohabitation
Closed individual space $\Leftarrow \Rightarrow$ Open individual space

Communication and Language
Heavy dependence on technology $\Leftarrow \Rightarrow$ Minimal dependence on technology
Verbal $\Leftarrow \Rightarrow$ Nonverbal
Dependent on literacy $\Leftarrow \Rightarrow$ Oral

Religious Tenets
Monotheistic $\Leftarrow \Rightarrow$ Polytheistic
Spiritual $\Leftarrow \Rightarrow$ Humanistic
Part of daily life $\Leftarrow \Rightarrow$ Distant from daily life

Nature
Industrial $\Leftarrow \Rightarrow$ Agricultural
Dominance over $\Leftarrow \Rightarrow$ In harmony with
Technologically developed $\Leftarrow \Rightarrow$ Technologically simple

Figure 9.2. Cultural dimensions continua. (Adapted from the work of Barbara Marler, Illinois Resource Center, Arlington Heights, Illinois.)

a categorized list of cultural dimensions that can provide structure to the information obtained. It can also be useful for exploring one's own culture and that of the school.

There are two stipulations in gathering information about others' ways of doing things and their values and beliefs. First, information gathering must be totally free from prejudice and judgment (Harry & Klingner, 2014; Milner, 2007). Norms and values that are different from what we may be used to are just that—different—neither worse nor better. Second, information about beliefs and ways of being applies to the particular family under study and cannot be generalized to the whole group of families within that community.

Some of the knowledge about students' cultures can be built as other information is being gathered, for example, details about the student's current and past learning environment and physical, psychological, personal, and family factors. However, it is best for this information to emerge from informal discussions with students and their families, from mini research projects that the students themselves undertake, or through dialogue journals that some students keep with their teachers (C. J. Flores & Delgado, 2012; Peyton & Stanton, 1993). As with other information that comes from a context that we are unfamiliar with, a cultural insider or liaison is needed to provide the appropriate context for interpreting cultural information the student or family offers (Ladson-Billings, 2006; Westernoff, 2019). Someone who has deep, firsthand knowledge about the home culture as well as an understanding of the student's new culture (typically that of the school) can explain the family's beliefs, attitudes, and values in terms that are comprehensible to others. The cultural liaison can also help initiate meaningful interaction and rapport among the school, home, and community.

Information about the cultures represented in a classroom can also be obtained in ways that are integrated into instruction and that are connected to curriculum objectives. The following activity suggested by a middle school teacher not only provided a rich source of information about norms and customs that were part of students' lives, but did so in a way that did not single out multilingual learners as being the "other" about whom we need to learn. This teacher designed the first literature unit of the year around the following idea: "I want my students to understand that we are connected to other generations and we can learn from our elders and ancestors who came before us and lived history." She was able to connect all the stories in the unit of study to that organizing idea, and had students read memoirs and then interview their own grandparents and parents about what they liked to do when they were young and what aspirations they have and what they learned about life from their parents and from their upbringing. Students created their own storyboards and chose photos and music, and then wrote their scripts to narrate digital biographies of their grandparents and parents. This teacher reported that her students were engaged from the first day of the study unit, and they created beautifully written and narrated stories.

MTSS Team Activity

Using Figure 9.2 as a guide for various topics to explore, have team members first think about their own norms and values. Divide the list so that each member has two to four dimensions to think about. Then let team members share their thoughts with a partner and end with a group discussion. Either concurrently or on another occasion, have team members also think about the culture that is reflected in the curriculum, in the way the school is run, and the way that their classrooms are organized and managed. Discuss how similar the individuals' and the school's cultures are and where they diverge from one another.

Assessing Educators' Attitudes toward Cultural Reciprocity

In addition to becoming aware of the norms and values that different students bring with them to the classroom, it is important for teachers to assess how accessible and malleable the school culture is in order to recommend appropriate support strategies or changes in practice for the student(s) experiencing significant challenges in school. Educators should have a clear sense of how the school is supporting the acculturation process for different groups of students. The descriptions provided in Table 9.1 may be useful in giving teachers and counselors a sense of which adaptation stage the student is passing through. This is not something that can be measured by numbers or ratings and the stages may very well blend into each other for many students; these descriptions can guide educators generally in exploring students' comfort levels and evaluate how welcoming the school is to various groups of students. A student survey can be developed in various languages to give school personnel a sense of how comfortable students and their families feel with the school and its procedures.

It is equally essential for schools to consider how well their staff members are embracing an attitude of cultural reciprocity. Do school staff seek to learn about and listen to what students and their families' perspectives are on a whole host of ideas, topics, events, and ways of being? Does everyone who works closely with multilingual learners and their families value their perspectives and take these perspectives into account during the solution-seeking process? The idea of cultural reciprocity represents a process in which learning occurs in both directions: from schools toward students and their families, and from students and their families toward schools.

Systemic Support Strategies

All schools with diverse populations should put into practice systemic support strategies that better reflect the school's cultural diversity because this step would enrich every student's learning regardless of the student's ethnicity, immigration status, or socioeconomic level. The following improvements in school climate are particularly helpful for making multilingual learners' learning environment optimal.

Capitalizing on Diversity

When a school has students from different cultural backgrounds, be they ethnic, racial, socioeconomic, or other dimensions, it is essential that teachers and administrators celebrate the diversity within the school community and focus on it as a way to enrich the lives of all their students. Multicultural education with a focus on social justice is fundamentally a perspective that centers on the histories and experiences of people who have been marginalized and either left out of or misrepresented in textbooks and the curriculum in most U.S. schools (Freire, 2014; Jurado & Garcia, 2018; C. D. Lee, 2008; Ngo, 2008). Taking this multiple-perspective approach will ultimately benefit all those within that school system (Milner, 2007; Ozfidan & Toprak, 2020). All students need to learn about each other's cultures, and they need to become skilled in dealing with others whose perspective differs from their own. In addition, all students need to see the value in diversity and to honor and respect other cultures' perspectives. Another goal of multicultural education that is beneficial for all students is to equip students, parents, and teachers with the tools needed to combat discrimination. Failure to implement multicultural education is seen by many as promoting monocultural, discriminatory education (F. Bailey & Pransky, 2005; C. D. Lee, 2008; Marshall & Tooney, 2010; Rodríguez-Mojica et al., 2019).

Contextualizing Instruction

Research points consistently to the need for contextualizing instruction and relating newly acquired concepts to real-life purposes and settings (Cloud et al., 2009; Milner, 2010; Nieto, 1999; Purcell-Gates et al., 2007). Teachers must show students how abstract concepts are drawn from and applied to the world in general and their world in particular. Relating instruction back to the cultural background and environment that the multilingual learner is most familiar with can make a lesson come alive (Kibler, 2005). Assisting students in making those connections strengthens previously learned material, paves the way for acquiring new knowledge, and encourages the multilingual learner to take responsibility for learning. Box 9.1 lists some suggestions for making instruction more relevant to students' home and community contexts and for introducing new concepts in a way that relates to students' perspectives.

Building Staff Knowledge and Understanding

Engaging multilingual learners requires a staff that has knowledge and understanding of cross-cultural differences and ways of making the curriculum more culturally and linguistically sustaining for the wide range of diversity among the student population. Thus, another systemic strategy that can be implemented involves the assessment of how culturally responsive staff is and then offering professional learning opportunities to support staff's movement to more culturally and linguistically sustaining teaching and learning.

Box 9.1

Connecting School to Students' Cultural Resources

- Instructional activities begin with what students already know from home, community, previous learning experiences, and school.
- Instructional activities are designed to be meaningful to students in terms of local community norms and knowledge.
- Teacher begins by eliciting students' perspectives on an issue or particular content, and then integrates these ideas into the study unit.
- Understanding of local norms and knowledge is attained by talking to students, parents and family members, community members, and by reading pertinent material.
- The teacher assists students in connecting and applying their learning to the home, community, and the world.
- The teacher and students plan jointly to design community-based learning activities, service-learning projects, or student-directed study units.
- Opportunities are provided for parents or families to participate in classroom instructional activities.

- Instruction is varied to include students' preferences, from collective and cooperative to individual and competitive activities.
- Styles of conversation and participation are varied to include students' cultural preferences, such as co-narration, call-and-response, and choral reading, among others.
- Administrators provide opportunities for teachers to plan units and lessons that integrate multiple perspectives and encourage divergent thinking and problem-solving: from mathematics to history and from literary analysis to scientific inquiry.
- Schools focus on social justice and equity in their organization and throughout their curricula.
- Students are encouraged to put forth their solutions to school, community, and world problems and focus a portion of the week on implementing these ideas (e.g., school-wide reduction of waste or purchasing fair trade products for the school).

One involves the use of "cultural therapy" (Spindler & Spindler, 1994). This approach examines the complexity of culture as it affects the individual. That is, the deeper aspects of culture—the implicit, tacit, and even unconscious aspects of culture—are brought to awareness and scrutinized for their impact on the individual (teacher or student). For example, a person's attitudes toward authority can have a significant impact on student–teacher relationships from both the teacher's and the student's perspectives. In addition, these aspects of culture are not seen as static and deterministic. Instead they can be identified and understood from a practical perspective, they can be modified; the individual need not be a victim of cultural "constraints." Cultural therapy is proactive and empowering and has been employed effectively over a number of years as an alternative to some less efficacious multicultural practices (e.g., Phelan & Davidson, 1993; Trueba, 1993). Another program that can be helpful is the social–emotional learning (SEL) curriculum. This research-based program teaches critical social competencies such as resiliency, self-management, and responsible decision-making skills (Collaborative for Academic, Social, and Emotional Learning [CASEL], 2017). When placed within the context of diversity, it can be a valuable tool for educators of multilingual learners. Table 9.2 provides a tool that staff can use to identify their own cultural strengths as well as areas that need support.

Home–School Communication

Finally, educators must create opportunities for connections between home and school in ways that communicate value and respect for the families' home culture, as well as providing avenues for parent involvement that are

Table 9.2   Essential Elements of Cultural Proficiency Self-Assessment

Reflect on your cultural strengths and areas that need support by selecting a number 1 through 4 where:
1 = not at all, 2 = very little, 3 = somewhat, 4 = a lot

Knowing about Culture

Naming the Differences

How well do you

• Describe your own culture and your school's cultural norms?	1	2	3	4
• Recognize how your culture affects others in the environment?	1	2	3	4
• Understand how the school's culture affects those whose culture is different?	1	2	3	4

Valuing Diversity

Claiming the Differences

How well do you

• Recognize differences as diversity, rather than as inappropriate responses to the environment?	1	2	3	4
• Accept that each culture considers some values and behaviors more important than others?	1	2	3	4
• Seek opportunities to work with and learn from people whose culture and values may be different from yours?	1	2	3	4

Managing the Dynamics of Diversity

Reframing the Differences

How well do you

• Understand the effect of historic distrust of difference on present-day interactions?	1	2	3	4
• Realize that you may have misjudged another's actions based on your own learned expectations?	1	2	3	4
• Learn effective ways to resolve conflicts among people whose culture and values differ from yours?	1	2	3	4

Adapting to Diversity

Extending Knowledge about Differences

How well do you

• Change the way you do things to acknowledge the differences present among staff members, students, parents, and other community members?	1	2	3	4
• Align programs and practices with guiding principles of cultural proficiency?	1	2	3	4
• Institutionalize appropriate strategies for conflicts and confusion caused by the dynamics of difference?	1	2	3	4

Institutionalizing Cultural Knowledge

Changing the Role of Differences

How well do you

• Incorporate cultural knowledge into the mainstream of the school?	1	2	3	4
• Develop skills for cross-cultural communication among staff?	1	2	3	4
• Integrate information and skills into the school's systems that enable all to interact effectively in a variety of cultural situations?	1	2	3	4

Adapted by John Kibler from Nuri Robins, K., Lindsey, R., Lindsey, D. & Terrell, R. (2002). *Culturally proficient instruction: A guide for people who teach.* Thousand Oaks, CA: Corwin Press.

congruent with the parents' culture. Chronicle 9.2 describes how a mismatch between parents' and school's norms was resolved.

Specific Support Strategies

For individual multilingual learners whose challenges in school are thought to have a cultural base, it is essential that a counselor or social worker who is sensitive to cross-cultural issues explore the student's comfort level moving between home and school. An older student who is comfortable navigating home and school and has developed an understanding of some of the invisible norms of both may be recruited to be a buddy to that multilingual learner. With the guidance of a counselor, the pair can share their experiences, and the older student can help the multilingual learner by answering questions, clarifying misconceptions, and providing insights. It is also essential that a teacher get feedback from the student regarding the aspects of school life that seem most foreign or most stressful. On that basis, that

Chronicle 9.2

I Would Never Let My Child Do That!

By an ESL Teacher

In our school, every year the sixth-grade class went to either White Pines or Lorado Taft Field Campus for 3 days and 2 nights for outdoor education. Historically, the multilingual learners had not participated in this fantastic learning experience. Everyone thought that the parents simply did not want their children to go. My colleague Bonnie and I hypothesized that the reason parents did not send their children on the outdoor education trip was because they did not know or trust the teachers who were chaperoning the trips. We also figured that this type of educational activity was foreign to them.

As English-as-a-second-language (ESL) teachers, Bonnie and I had not been relieved of our duties teaching other grade levels to enable us to go on these trips. We approached our principal and asked him to allow us to go as chaperones and to secure substitutes for our classes while we were gone. As the translated paperwork was sent home, we announced that this year, we would be accompanying the multilingual students on the trip. Surprise! All of the multilingual students signed up. It was a positive experience for them. For many, it was their first overnight stay away from home. They were able to go horseback riding, take night hikes, identify leaves found in the forest, study the stars at night, and sit around the campfire with the entire sixth grade, singing songs and telling ghost stories.

During parent–teacher conferences later in the year, the parents told Bonnie and me that since their children were not that comfortable with the monolingual English-speaking teachers and since they had never heard of such school outings before, they had previously felt it was not suitable for their children to go on the trip. With trusted teachers staying with their children and endorsing the activity as worthwhile, they felt their children could participate.

Questions for Discussion

1. If multilingual learners do not participate in activities that are a part of the curriculum, how can you determine the reason why?
2. What can you do to ensure that multilingual learners are able to participate in all curriculum activities?
3. What would you add to the current plan for the 3-day activity now that multilingual learners are participating?

particular student's school environment can be modified to make it more congruent with his or her cultural norms and expectations. The multilingual learner may also be asked to suggest ways to make the classroom or school more culturally welcoming and familiar by adding aspects of the family's and community's culture to the curriculum and the physical surroundings. This confirms the value of the multilingual learner's home culture and helps raise the student's self-confidence, which helps him or her form a strong multicultural identity.

Questions for Reflection and Action

1. What do we know about our own individual and school cultures?
2. What do we know about the culture of the multilingual learners we serve?
3. How has the school transformed its culture to be more inclusive and responsive for all students?
4. How can teachers, counselors, social workers, therapists, and psychologists be assisted to make their support more culturally and linguistically relevant for diverse students?
5. What could be included in a professional learning plan to help teachers gain more awareness about their own cultural identities and how their cultural identity influences their teaching style and the expectations they hold in the classroom?

6. Using the iceberg metaphor, what are the matches and mismatches that occur when the school's cultural iceberg is compared to that of the students and their families?

7. Select a study unit or a curricular area and analyze it in terms of cultural perspective.
   - Do the concepts studied consider the cultural vantage points of multilingual learners?
   - Do the instructional activities reflect and build on the cultural experiences of the students?
   - Are the instructional materials culturally sustaining?
   - To what degree are the assessment measures authentic and free from linguistic and cultural bias?

10

Describing before Identifying: When Specific Challenges Persist

Key Concepts. *For multilingual learners who continue to face academic challenges, a focus on specific behaviors becomes necessary. However, we must ensure that any intervention that is suggested must fit into a continuum of support for those students. The first step in providing a continuum of services is to gather information about the specific observable challenges that a student exhibits by describing those behaviors as specifically as possible.*

In the preceding chapters we described a process focused on the core learning environment, or Tier 1, in the multi-tiered system of supports (MTSS), which includes (1) examining and evaluating the learning environment created for multilingual learners, (2) gathering information about six integral factors that may lead to academic challenges for these students, (3) providing multilingual learners with various learning support strategies, and (4) monitoring students' academic performance as these strategies are applied. When implementing these changes in the learning environment, the instructional approach and the everyday workings of a school will make it possible for many multilingual learners to overcome the hurdles that led to their academic challenges. For some multilingual learners, however, challenges with academic, language, and literacy development as well as social–emotional well-being may persist. These are the students who may need additional specialized interventions (Tier 2) to help them overcome any specific difficulties they may be experiencing.

To provide the most effective support for these students, it is necessary to describe in detail their actual observable behaviors as specifically as possible (J. S. Damico 2019d). That is, it is essential that we focus on behaviors that allow us to get to know the strengths and challenges of the students within the context of the classroom or other learning and social environments before we discuss what the underlying causes might be for differences in the students' performance. The primary reason is that identification, no matter how seemingly straightforward, is a complicated process, fraught with many potential missteps that may lead to inaccurate conclusions.

To avoid such inaccuracies it is necessary to be maximally descriptive when collecting data on the students, their contexts, and the teaching and learning interactions they have with others. Personal experience has demonstrated the power of rich description during the diagnostic process. Further, a number of recent studies have shown that quantitative data based on standardized tests, high-stakes testing, and the kinds of quantitative measures employed in many assessment activities—including most response to intervention (RtI)—are insufficient to understand and accurately explain multilingual learners' classroom performance and how any difficulties they are exhibiting may be overcome (Afflerbach, 2007; Artiles, 2015; Sloan, 2007; Valenzuela et al., 2007). It is for this reason that a number of researchers in RtI/MTSS are suggesting that we must be very cautious in employing this system with multilingual learners as it has been advocated in many texts and workshops (Herrera et al., 2012; Klingner et al., 2007; Speece & Walker, 2007). Relying solely on a protocol approach to RtI as a solution to the academic problems that multilingual learners face daily often leads to a "diagnosis" of sorts with the motive of moving these students quickly through Tier 2 and then Tier 3.

In some cases the opposite is true. Some school teams keep multilingual learners in the RtI/MTSS process for various years without any attempt to address more significant needs through a special education referral. Implementing RtI/MTSS in a one-size-fits-all way aggravates the situation and increases the anxiety that students and their teachers already feel. The continuum of services framework described in this guide offers a procedural solution that stresses obtaining a sufficient description of the student and the various contextual variables involved before assigning causes. In this framework the learning environment is seen as a fundamental determinant of academic performance, and the six integral factors described in this guide are seen as requisite for interpreting students' performance in an academic setting.

In this chapter, we lay out a process that focuses on specific challenges that multilingual learners face and a method by which possible explanations can be considered and accurately assigned to address each of these difficulties. Such explanations form the basis for the interventions designed for a particular student or a group of students exhibiting similar behaviors. We also present a list of typical difficulties that multilingual learners often demonstrate and suggest that the MTSS team, in collaboration with others in the school, generate such an inventory of behaviors for individual students or groups of like students.

The Importance of Describing before Identifying

When a red flag is raised about a student or a group of students who are having significant challenges at school, typically after a review of screening data, or observations by a classroom teacher, there is a tendency to focus on the students' general performance. We hear statements like, "They are having trouble learning." "They can't read." "I have concerns about this student." "They are not fluent readers." or "They can't remember things." Although these statements may describe generally what these students are experiencing, at least two problems are associated with such general evaluations. First, because they are general ratings of performance, such statements do not help us understand specifically what challenges the student is experiencing, which makes designing appropriate interventions quite difficult. Second, these general ratings influence teachers' perceptions of the student's performance in other academic areas as well, even if there are no problems or the problems are less severe, and this further complicates the issue. This tendency, known as the *halo effect* or the *devil effect*, has long been recognized by social scientists as a cognitive bias whereby a general evaluation of one attribute, skill, or trait influences the evaluation of other attributes, skills, or traits (such as academic skills; G. Cook et al., 2003; Thorndike, 1920; Willingham & Jones, 1958). As a consequence, these more broad-brush evaluative statements may inappropriately influence both the evaluations of and expectations for the identified students in areas that may not be as problematic, resulting in undesirable inaccuracy across various dimensions of performance (J. S. Damico et al., 2021; Feeley, 2002; Palmer & Martínez, 2013).

In addition, we often find that when a multilingual learner (or group of multilingual learners) is identified as experiencing challenges in school, there is a tendency to assume something is intrinsically wrong with the student. We hear statements like, "Jorge has problems with math" or "They can't process information fast enough" rather than "Jorge can do computation but has difficulty completing math word problems in English" or "Samir has difficulty with his nines multiplication facts in English." The first step that needs to be taken, therefore, is to describe students' observable behavior as specifically as possible without attributing the behavior to a specific cause. This requires that the MTSS team get to know the students in terms of the behaviors presented and how they indicate the students' strengths and weaknesses from what can be observed, such as work samples, rather than draw unwarranted conclusions from generalized statements, assumptions, and perceptions. No placement decisions or intervention efforts will be sufficient if the data on which they are based are inaccurate, invalid, or insufficient.

The MTSS team must urge teachers and everyone who works with a particular student or group of students to answer the question "what?" before attempting to answer the question "why?" Refraining from asking "why" first is challenging for many teachers, because in an effort to meet the needs of multilingual learners who experience difficulties, the first question that is often posed is, "Is it a learning disability or is it related to second language acquisition?" That is, there is a strong tendency to try to determine whether the cause of a student's difficulties is a special education need or a result of typical second language learning processes as soon as a problem is identified. Teams traditionally choose one or the other of these options too early in the process.

There are several compelling reasons to reframe the approach to causal attribution and to avoid making a diagnostic decision so early in the process.

Similarity of Surface Behaviors

When observing typically developing multilingual learners in English, the difficulties they demonstrate often appear similar, if not identical, to the observable difficulties demonstrated by students with diagnosed learning disabilities (LD) and developmental language disorders (e.g., J. S. Damico & Damico, 1993a; Jacobson & Schwartz, 2005; Jia & Fuse, 2007; D. Martin, 2009; Paradis, 2005; Salameh et al., 2004). Because there are only so many ways that difficulties may manifest behaviorally, the mere presence of these behavioral markers is not sufficient for accurate or adequate causal interpretation (Damico, 2003; 2019a; Damico & Nelson, 2005; Paradis et al., 2021; Perkins, 2005). The behaviors don't point directly to the cause or reason. Thus, when viewed superficially, multilingual learners in the normal process of learning English and students with a diagnosed special education need may appear to be experiencing the same difficulty. For example, although multilingual learners often exhibit what look like language disfluencies associated with disability, disfluencies are a natural part of second language development (Cloud, 1994). Even the ability to perceive and organize information can be distorted when students are learning a second language. However, the causes of these observable behaviors may be quite different for multilingual learners who are still developing proficiency in their second language and for multilingual learners or other students with disabilities.

Some further examples of challenges that multilingual learners might experience in English that could be misinterpreted as attributable to a special education need include forgetting words that are taught in class from one day to the next, needing extensive wait time to prepare for oral production, understanding more than they can express either orally or in writing, difficulty following spoken directions, experiencing anxiety during the school day, and "freezing" when asked to answer questions in English in a classroom setting. Students with the kinds of intrinsic meaning-making difficulties that appropriately identify them as exceptional may demonstrate the same behaviors, but for different reasons. Multilingual learners' performance during English instruction time may be explained by the fact that they are in the process of developing proficiency in English, whereas students with a diagnosed special education need may have underlying difficulties with comprehension that are present across most or all contexts. Multilingual learners may appear distracted at different times throughout the day and sometimes seem to shut down, especially when they are in academic English settings when the level of English input is beyond their level of proficiency in that language. Students with learning challenges may perform similarly, given the intrinsic nature of the challenges they experience across learning contexts throughout the school day.

These are just a few of the many possible observable behaviors that multilingual learners may exhibit to a greater or lesser degree when the extrinsic learning environment is not meeting their learning needs. Students with special education needs may exhibit some or all of the same behaviors; however, if they are also multilingual learners, these difficulties will be evident in both languages and across many learning contexts (Crago & Paradis, 2003; Cummins, 1984, 2000; J. S. Damico et al., 1983; Kay-Raining Bird et al., 2016; Martin, 2009).

The Tendency to Choose Disability Explanations

When learning challenges are initially identified, there is a tendency to locate them in the student rather than in the practices and biases of the schools or school personnel (Carroll, 1997; Cummins, 2000; Gutkin & Nemeth, 1997; Samson & Lesaux, 2009; Ullucci & Howard, 2015). This is likely a primary reason for the overrepresentation of multilingual learners in some categories of special education (Artiles & Ortiz, 2002) because a team of teachers is more likely to come up with a special education explanation before they look to a second language learning process explanation. The professional schemas of the team members are more likely to be rooted in special education than core instruction for multilingual learners. This is why we suggest a thorough assessment of the learning environment created for multilingual learners as a starting point in our framework. This trend is exacerbated when monolingual English-speaking teachers have not received sufficient information on the principles of linguistic and cultural diversity and their impact on academic contexts. The MTSS team's exploration into the six integral factors is invaluable. School staff may not be as familiar with typical behaviors of multilingual learners who are in the expected developmental process of learning in a second language and how these difficulties can look like characteristics demonstrated by students with a special education need. Chronicle 10.1 provides an account of one such situation.

Because most assessments of multilingual learners are done primarily, if not exclusively, in English (Caesar & Kohler, 2007; Cummins, 2008; N. Flores & Schissel, 2014; Gunderson & Siegel, 2001; Roseberry-McKibbin et al., 2005), educators may initially misinterpret the multilingual learners' behaviors as reflecting a special education need. School staff may be more accustomed to associating the behaviors they observe in multilingual learners with students who are in special education programs, especially because the difficulties exhibited by the two groups of students appear very much alike on the surface.

The Nature of Second Language Acquisition

Because multilingual learners are in the process of developing proficiency in English, their new language, they usually experience difficulty learning academic content-area material that is presented exclusively in English. This is part of the expected developmental process of learning a new or additional language (Bialystok, 2001; B. A. Collins et al., 2014; Hamayan & Freeman Field, 2012; Janzen, 2008; Paradis et al., 2021). Interpretation of multilingual learners' academic performance is further complicated by the fact that students may sound proficient in English in some contexts, leading teachers to believe that because they hear students use English in daily

Chronicle 10.1

The Tendency to Choose Intrinsic Explanations

By a Bilingual Coordinator

A kindergarten teacher asked me to observe a student in her class. She was concerned that this child was unable to discriminate initial consonant sounds in words. When I arrived, I was impressed with her class. All the students were very engaged in learning, and she made instruction comprehensible through the use of visuals, manipulatives, pictures, and the use of many gestures and facial expressions to accompany what she said. I noticed that the children had dictated a language experience story about their school routines, and the teacher had written out the entire story on large chart paper. The dictated story was being used as a meaningful context to teach some skills to the students. The day I visited the class, the teacher concentrated on initial consonant sounds so that I could observe the particular multilingual student about whom she had concerns. She asked the students to think of words from the story that started with the /t/ sound. The students "read" aloud the story they had dictated and stopped when they heard words that started with the /t/ sound. She asked what that word meant, and the students took turns answering orally or with gestures, then they moved on to the next example. It was great to hear the students read their story. The multilingual student I was observing seemed very attentive and paid close attention to everything in the lesson.

Afterward, the teacher asked different students to tell the class a word that started with the /t/ sound. The monolingual English-speaking students gave examples: "tooth, treat, tower," they yelled. Finally the multilingual child raised his hand. The teacher asked whether he had a word that started with the /t/ sound, and he nodded yes. "*Maestra*" he blurted out confidently. The teacher looked at me with a great deal of concern. She asked him whether he was sure, and he said yes. She gently pointed out that the word he had mentioned started with the /m/ sound. The multilingual student seemed confused, and looked down at the carpet. After the lesson, the teacher and I had an opportunity to talk about what happened. She was glad that I had witnessed the student's difficulty. When I told her that *maestra* was Spanish for "teacher," her eyes opened wide and she shook her head. We realized that the student had understood exactly what the teacher was asking of him, but he didn't speak enough English yet to say all the words he understood. I assured her that it is common for second language learners to have a larger receptive vocabulary than an expressive one. The teacher's face lit up with this realization. She had thought that she was not getting through to the student and didn't know what else to do. She was beginning to doubt herself and started to think that his difficulties must be due to something intrinsic. I told her it is always a good idea to get support from English-as-a-second-language (ESL) bilingual staff when she had concerns about any multilingual student. I suggested that she continue to find ways to assess what her students knew separate from their ability to tell her in English. She immediately thought of an example. "What if during that exercise I had given the students visuals to use in supporting their oral answers? Also, I could have encouraged them to share their answers through gestures." Even if her multilingual learner had answered in his home language, she would have known that he understood because he would have shown her a picture of a teacher or pointed at her when he said *maestra*.

Questions for Discussion

1. In this example, how could knowledge of the second language acquisition process inform instruction?
2. How would knowledge of reading in a second language inform instruction?
3. What else could the teacher do to assess the student's knowledge of concepts and skills?
4. How could the home language be used to validate the difficulty that the student was having?

interactions with peers, the students should be able to access the language of textbooks and lectures in all academic content areas without any support or instruction (Antón et al, 2016; Carhill et al., 2008; Cummins, 2012; Genesee et al., 2006; Monz & Rueda, 2009).

Because of this confusion, we need to pay attention to the issues regarding oral language, literacy, and academic performance. It is also essential that the diagnostic decision be made after some information regarding the specific behaviors that multilingual learners are exhibiting is collected. That is, it is essential to answer the "what" question before we drift into the vicinity of the "why" question. The process of data collection and explanation discussed in the next section will assist the MTSS team in meeting these responsibilities.

The Process of Data Collection and Explanation

Assessing multilingual learners requires the use of a framework based on equity that allows for a broad range of performance in the assessment process. Among many considerations, we must understand the dynamic nature of bilingualism (O. Garcia et al., 2016) as well as apply our knowledge of the stages of second language acquisition. We must also understand the fluid nature of students' cultural identities as multilingual learners navigate home, school, and community expectations. The MTSS team must be able to do their work in a context where this possibility is institutionalized. The framework presented in this book can be achieved by employing a **bi-level analysis paradigm** (Damico et al., 1996). This requires that an initial **descriptive analysis** of multilingual learners' classroom performance be completed before an **explanatory analysis** is attempted. That is, we must first focus on *what* the students are specifically able or unable to do and interpret this information based on information gathered about these students. Only then can we begin to speculate on the explanations for those difficulties and how to support those students.

In the first stage of description, the MTSS team collects information on the specific observable behaviors exhibited by a particular multilingual learner or a small group of multilingual learners. The purpose is to ask and answer the "what" question: "What challenges is the multilingual learner experiencing and what behaviors does the teacher observe as evidence of these challenges?" Among the many ways of accomplishing this task three stand out: (1) generating a list of specific observable behaviors unique to this particular student that reflects challenges in an academic setting, (2) referring to an inventory of typically observed challenges that students with academic difficulties exhibit, or (3) comparing the student's classroom performance against evidence-based descriptions of levels of language proficiency, such as the WIDA Can Do descriptors (wida.wisc.edu). Thus, the MTSS team acquires data that document the multilingual learner's significant challenges, the student's strengths and resources and overall success or difficulties in the classroom, and even the multilingual learner's progress over time (when pre- or post-analyses are conducted). If more data are needed, the teacher can ask another educator to come into the classroom to observe how the students respond to instruction in the most authentic learning environment possible. At this level of analysis, the MTSS team functions primarily as an agent of the school to determine what types of challenges the multilingual learner exhibits.

The second stage of this MTSS framework involves an explanatory analysis and directly addresses the "why" question. This process seeks to determine explanations for the difficulties noted in the descriptive analysis. At this analytic level, the team endeavors to determine possible explanations for these challenges, and at this time, the MTSS team views the observable behaviors through the lenses of linguistic and cultural diversity and functions more as an advocate for the multilingual learner. Some MTSS team members have described this process as "seeing school from the perspective of the multilingual learner."

The explanatory stage of our framework involves a deeper interpretation of the data collected in the descriptive stage. The MTSS team attempts to explain how variables, such as aspects of the context, the student's sociocultural experience, or the student's linguistic proficiency, can account for the described challenges. Thus, this attempt at explanation is based on informed speculation and hypothesis formation. At this point the information that is being (or has been) gathered about essential characteristics of the students is crucial.

Step 1: Producing an Inventory of Specific Observable Behaviors

The MTSS team must begin to elicit from all staff a list of specific observable behaviors that multilingual learners with continued difficulties seem to exhibit at school. There is both a generality and specificity in this approach. The generality comes from looking at groups of students rather than a single student. This step would be carried out in the first part of this framework when staff examines the school's learning environment and begins to gather information about the six integral factors. Specificity comes from honing in on explicitly observed behaviors of students who are continuing to face challenges at school rather than making broad statements. For example, a specific observation, such as "When I read a story aloud to the class, these students have difficulty retelling the events of the story back to me in English," offers more useful information than a general statement, such as "Students have difficulty comprehending." By taking the broad systemic approach in our framework, which gives us specific information on students' performance, we ensure that all students are taken into account early on, rather than in an RtI system, for example, where one waits until individual students have reached Tier 3 or Tier 4 to look at particular difficulties (J. E. Brown & Doolittle, 2008; Klinger & Edwards, 2006; Rinaldi & Sampson, 2008). Rather than depending on large-scale screening or other standardized assessment data, we suggest that teachers focus more explicitly on actual behaviors that can be observed in the classroom. Then, an **inventory of specific observable behaviors (ISOB)** is compiled by putting all the observations together.

Generating an independent inventory of observable behaviors.   MTSS team members ask their colleagues to observe multilingual learners closely and to submit brief descriptions of behaviors or examples of tasks that students have difficulty with, or they may collect such data themselves. Generating an original ISOB from scratch is the more valid way to identify challenges observed in multilingual learners. The observations are not tainted by someone else's suggestions or their frame of mind, and the observers must pay close attention

to what the students are doing and then construct the behaviors themselves. The key to this process is to ensure that the focus is on actual behavior, not on generalized statements or inferences about behaviors. Such generalizations or inferences about behavior typically result in inappropriate or inaccurate data. Although generating an original ISOB is the more recommended way of proceeding, very few schools or districts have the resources to embark on such a complex project. If that is the case, then the MTSS team must take all the precautions and work with the second option, that of starting with a pregenerated list of behaviors that may need what in RtI/MTSS would be referred to as Tier 2 or 3 interventions.

Working with a predetermined inventory of observable behaviors.   Another way of obtaining a list of specific observable challenges is to start with a previously constructed list, for example, one obtained from a textbook or an observation or assessment tool or rubric. Specific applications and observable behaviors may be found within the disciplines of speech–language pathology and special education (e.g., Babatsouli et al., 2017; J. S. Damico, 2019f; J. S. Damico & Oller, 1985; Dunaway, 2021; Pieretti & Roseberry-McKibbin, 2016; Roseberry-McKibbin, 2014). MTSS team members then ask staff to check off those behaviors that they observe in their contact with multilingual learners. Although working from a predetermined ISOB may predispose staff to inaccurate observation of a given behavior in a student, this approach may sometimes be necessary. Opportunities for direct observation in classrooms may be limited, and it is more time-consuming to generate an original list than to work from an existing list. Moreover, our experience suggests that many teams resist generating the ISOB themselves. Thus, we offer the option of a preconstituted list that can serve as a starting point for generating a school-specific or even student-specific ISOB. Care must be taken to record only those behaviors that have empirical/actual evidence showing their utility as a potential diagnostic index. Further, a predetermined list should not negate the need to view the challenges of any referred multilingual learner directly and with "fresh eyes," so that behaviors not on the previously constructed list can still be considered.

The easiest way to determine whether the data collected are behaviorally specific enough is to employ the following strategy. Once a statement is provided, read that statement and ask yourself, "As evidenced by what?" If the answer to this question seems circular, then the statement refers to an actual behavior. For example, if the teacher states, "She does not participate in classroom discussions," and you ask, "As evidenced by what?" and the teacher answers, "Well, when we have classroom discussions in English, she doesn't raise her hand to join in the conversation" or "She does not talk in class," then the difficulty that has been identified is an actual behavior. However, if the answer to the question is not circular but provides another behavior, then it is likely that the original difficulty as stated was an inference. For example, if the teacher states, "She refuses to participate in classroom discussions," and you ask, "As evidenced by what?" and the teacher answers, "Well, she doesn't talk in class," then all we know and can observe is that she is not talking in class, but we cannot infer that it is because she is "refusing" to do so. The team can only address the behavior of "not talking in class." There may be many explanations for why a multilingual learner may not be speaking English in class. If the team proceeds to address the "refusal" part (which is an inference), then the interventions and supports will focus on the assumption that this challenge is the result of problematic intrinsic issues.

Lists of typical academic challenges can be found in many introductory special education and language arts textbooks (Allington, 2002b; Cunningham & Allington, 2011; Frank & Richards, 2020; Howard, 2012; Kauffman et al., 2018; Kuder, 2013). We have compiled a list of the most common behaviors that are brought up when we work in schools and during our workshops with teachers and special education specialists. A partial list of these behaviors is given in Box 10.1. This list consists of the academic difficulties most commonly identified for multilingual learners who are having a particularly challenging time in school. A more comprehensive list is provided in the Online Resources (see "Observable Behaviors that Multilingual Learners May Exhibit in English"). If educators decide to use a preconstituted list like the one in Box 10.1, we recommend starting with that list and adding personal observations to it rather than starting with a more comprehensive list that someone else has generated. It is too easy to imagine problems where none exist.

As mentioned previously, the key to good data collection, whether it is obtained through a preconstituted list or generated by staff, is to triangulate the data obtained. Once a teacher has provided a set of behaviors that serve as indices of difficulty for the multilingual learner, that set should be crosschecked against a second person's set of observations, and, if possible, a third set of observations before returning to the original observer for confirmation. Employing triangulation as a verification strategy helps ensure the accuracy and appropriateness of the data (e.g., J. S. Damico & Simmons-Mackie, 2003; Fielding & Fielding, 1986; Flick, 1992).

Box 10.1

Partial List of Potential Challenges That Multilingual Learners May Demonstrate in English in an Academic Setting

- Omits words or adds words to a sentence either orally or in writing; forgets names of familiar things—has to describe them.
- Becomes distracted easily.
- Has trouble following directions.
- Can do rote arithmetic on paper, but has difficulty with math word problems.
- Avoids writing.
- Does not seem to transfer learning from one lesson to another; has to be retaught each concept.
- Very literal—misses inferences, subtleties, nuances, and innuendoes.

- Often understands concepts, but has difficulty showing understanding in written symbolic form with paper and pencil or through multiple-choice tests.
- Learns from watching more than from listening.
- Has difficulty categorizing, classifying, or summarizing information.
- Has difficulty providing an oral narrative of a story that was just read.
- Has low frustration tolerance; gives up easily or explodes.

To assist in focusing on actual behavioral statements of difficulty, the following processes can be applied:

- Explain to all who will collect data or contribute to the ISOB the importance of observing and describing specific challenges manifested by multilingual learners.

- Provide the data team with instructions to observe and code: "Over the next several days, observe the students in a range of contexts and note the kinds of specific challenges they seem to have. Notice especially their attempts to work on academic subjects, their reactions, and any attempts to problem solve. It is important to jot down descriptions of behaviors so we can get a sense of the kinds of challenges these multilingual learners exhibit."

- After observable behaviors have been listed, determine whether the data are sufficient.

- Contextualize the behaviors by asking follow-up questions if the data provided are not sufficient. Two types of questions enable contextualization: experience questions ("Can you think of an instance when you saw this behavior in Peter?") and example questions ("Can you give me an example of what he actually does when he is doing x?").

- If at all possible, verify the accuracy of the observed behaviors by triangulation. That is, collect these data across different times, locations, or by different methods or from different observers so that the various data can be compared, contrasted, and verified.

Another way of ensuring data quality is by using different data-collection and analysis methods over different sampling periods and then comparing data from different sources. By requiring staff to collect qualitative descriptive data, we avoid depending inappropriately on quantitative information only, a tendency that we see too often in too many districts. We have seen many examples of what happens with faulty or culturally and linguistically inappropriate initial screenings. A group of multilingual learners is identified as "nonreaders" in a school where RtI/MTSS is in place. They get moved up to Tier 2 almost immediately. When we ask, "As evidenced by what?" in problem-solving meetings, the RtI team, teachers, principals would say, "As evidenced by their AIMSWEB, FastBridge or NWEA-MAP assessment results." This is simply unacceptable. We are cognizant of the fact that many educators, especially administrators, who are under pressure to show scores and work with numbers, are dubious of the value of teacher observations. However, evidence shows that teacher observations are invaluable in making placement, programming, and instructional decisions (Allington, 2009; J. S. Damico, 2019f; Howard, 2009; van Kraayenoord, 2010; Valenzuela et al., 2007). By examining, comparing, and contrasting the information obtained by different methods and by a variety of people, the MTSS team can estimate how similar the data are and whether or not a particular collection procedure or contextual variable affected the representativeness of the data. Another effective way to counter the inappropriate use of universal screeners is to embed data from screeners in second language acquisition data, such as the WIDA Can Do descriptors. If language proficiency data are left out or considered later, the opportunity to calibrate to a student's language level is lost.

Once the list like the one in Box 10.1 has been turned into an ISOB by culling items and removing repetitions, the next phase begins. In fact, this next phase, coming up with possible explanations for these behaviors, can begin as soon as any challenges have been identified.

Step 2: Explaining the Observed Behaviors

As mentioned previously, although on the surface the performances of multilingual learners in the process of learning academic English and students with diagnosed disabilities may look very similar, the explanations of these surface behaviors differ (Jacobson & Schwartz, 2005; Jia & Fuse, 2007; Martin, 2009; Paradis et al., 2021; Perkins, 2005). Different explanations require different educational programming and learning support strategies and interventions, depending on whether the difficulty arises from typical second language learning needs or from an intrinsic learning or processing difficulty. Exploring the possible extrinsic and/or intrinsic explanations is critical to providing the additional and more intensive programming these students require to make progress and be successful.

There are always underlying influences that are extrinsic to multilingual learners that could lead to academic challenges, such as aspects of the school environment that may not be conducive to learning or the effects of any of the six integral factors. If a group of multilingual learners (or an individual multilingual learner) is encountering academic challenges, these extrinsic factors must be addressed, regardless of whether or not the student has a disability, which is why the MTSS team must address the learning environment and the six integral factors early in the process. Even though the challenges that multilingual learners experience may be typical manifestations of learning another language, they might be intensive enough that the students are still very much in need of programming to address their unique needs and circumstances. It is also possible that the difficulties that some multilingual learners experience are indicative of an underlying intrinsic disability in addition to being a manifestation of learning another language. These students are challenged through both extrinsic (second language) and intrinsic (disability) factors.

Finding explanations for these students' challenges in school begins by considering, during the explanatory phase of the process, the learning environment created for multilingual learners as well as the six extrinsic factors before assuming the existence of intrinsic causes resulting from a disability. As the MTSS team becomes more familiar with the characteristics of these students as portrayed in the six integral factors, better explanations for multilingual learners' difficulties can be considered.

To illustrate the different explanations that may underlie the same apparent observable behavior, Table 10.1 contrasts possible explanations for a specific behavior, difficulty retelling a story in sequence. The left column lists possible language and literacy learning explanations for this behavior; the right column lists possible special education explanations for the same surface behavior. The more specific the behavior, the easier it will be to generate explanations for it. It also helps to discuss the circumstances and the various contexts in which the observed behavior occurs.

The example in Table 10.1 was used to explore a teacher's concern about a particular student. The teacher initially said that the student had "no comprehension." A few probing questions were asked:

- Can you tell us when you observed the student having difficulty with comprehension?

- Can you give us some specific examples of when you noticed that he "had no comprehension"?

- Is the behavior observable in the home language or only in the second language?

- What is the student's academic English proficiency level?

- Can you observe the behavior in oral language, written language, or both?

- When does the student exhibit this behavior?

- Is the challenge apparent with fiction only or with nonfiction texts as well?

- Has there been (or is there) a tradition of storytelling at home?

- What happens to the student's performance when sensory supports, graphic organizers, or interactive support is provided?

Only after such questions were asked did a specific description of the observable behavior emerge. It turned out that when the student heard a story in English, he could not retell it in English. It was critical to get that very specific information before proceeding to the next steps of generating possible explanations and then creating interventions in all of the student's languages.

The teacher's first comment was a diagnosis: "He has no comprehension." The subsequent description uncovered precise observable behaviors and the context in which they occurred. The latter approach is much more useful because it provides specific information to guide the problem-solving process.

Benefits of discussing possible explanations.   The MTSS team benefits from doing this exercise together as a team because the members learn from each other about their differing perspectives and areas of experience and expertise. Team members can clarify what different professionals mean when using certain terms, thus generating a shared vocabulary. Although there are

Table 10.1 Possible Explanations Based on Different Perspectives for a Student Who Has Difficulty Retelling Events of a Story in Sequence

Possible ML Explanations (Observed in English)	Possible Special Education Explanations (Observed in English and the Home Language in Several Contexts)
General • It may take the student more time than expected to comprehend information that requires a proficiency level that is higher than the student's.	**Listening** • The student may have difficulty understanding more abstract vocabulary (i.e., content, temporal, causal and/or organizational words such as *subsequent, first, next, last, consequently*), story events, inferred information, or narrative structure in the home language and English. • The student may have difficulty with working memory, making it difficult to retain lengthy information.
Listening • The student may not understand many stories because they are in English or because the cultural context of the stories or events was irrelevant or unfamiliar.	
Speaking • The student understands stories told in English, but does not feel comfortable enough in English-speaking abilities to retell stories. • The student may have developed social English skills, but may not have been taught the academic language needed to deal with the temporal, causal, or sequential dynamics of narratives (e.g., *before, first, then, next, later*) to be able to retell stories smoothly. • The student may be able to retell events or stories in the home language after hearing a narrative in English. • The student's home language has a different structure for telling stories and so retelling in English sounds "out of order/out of sequence."	**Speaking** The student may have oral expressive difficulties in both languages, making it difficult to: • Formulate ideas into sentences that clearly relay the meaning of the story. • Gain control of the primary topic of the story. • Organize information into story structure, employing complex grammar of deixis (utterances requiring contextual information for comprehension). • Incorporate changes in time and space; this must be done during the narrative use of cohesive devices (e.g., using conjunctions and pronoun references) to connect the story.
Reading Comprehension • Stories do not match the student's stage of proficiency in English reading and so he or she does not understand enough of the story to retell it. The student could recount some details that correspond to pictures if the necessary English vocabulary has been acquired. • The reading material provided is beyond the student's English proficiency level, and may contain unfamiliar words. • Reading instruction in English was focused on skill-building out of context and so the student is too oriented toward the graphophonemic code (sounds, individual words) rather than the actual meaning of the text.	**Reading Comprehension** • The student may not be able to employ crucial strategies for constructing meaning when text is unfamiliar. • The student may not understand the vocabulary (i.e., content and/or organizational words, such as *first, next, last*), story events, inferred information, or narrative structure in the home language and English.

Writing
• The student may be in the early stages of English language acquisition and is still developing writing.
• The student may be using home language structures to negotiate writing in the second language; this may make the written text sound "out of sequence" in English.
• The student has not had sufficient opportunity to engage in authentic writing that focuses on meaning construction rather than splinter skills like spelling or punctuation.
• The student has not been provided writing instruction in the home language.
	Writing
	• The student may have difficulty in formulating and/or controlling ideas or topics in both languages.
	• The student can have difficulties in
	  • Sentence formulation
	  • Use of cohesive devices in both languages (e.g., conjunctions, pronoun references)
	  • Organizing the information into story structure

Cultural Influences • The cultural context of the story may be wholly unknown to the student, who may be appalled and distracted by a story that doesn't make cultural sense. This makes it difficult for the student to concentrate on comprehension and on the sequence of the story. • The student's home language may have storytelling structures that differ from English.	**Social–Emotional Domain** • The student may be nervous performing in a large group due to past difficulties with a similar task. • Being well aware of areas of difficulty, the student will find ways to avoid answering and wait for others to do so. • Reading instruction for this student may only include decodable texts that are not interesting enough to merit retelling. The students may feel bad about having to read low-quality material.

ML, multilingual learner.

tremendous long-term benefits to having this discussion and engaging in the negotiations that ultimately result when a diverse group of professionals tries to find a solution to a puzzle, many teams are reluctant to explore diverse explanations of challenges completely on their own and request guidance, a facilitator, or an example they can follow. Table 10.2 provides an example of the results of a discussion about the 12 sample behaviors listed in Box 10.1 that multilingual learners may display.

The examples given in Table 10.2 are merely examples. They are by no means definitive or final answers to the question, "What could be the explanations for each challenge?" MTSS teams can use the examples in Table 10.2 as a springboard for developing their own explanations for various challenges observed in their students, and remember that this exercise is just an exercise. Chronicle 10.2 recounts the experience of one teacher who used the list in Table 10.2 in a way that limited her analysis of a student's performance rather than helping her explore possible reasons for the student's difficulties.

MTSS TEAM ACTIVITY

Use the list of observable behaviors given in Table 10.2 to generate additional or other observable difficulties that students may exhibit in the school setting. Next, practice generating possible explanations for each behavior using contrasting perspectives.

Working in a timely fashion. The process of exploring reasons for the specific challenges encountered by students must begin as soon as a specific challenge is identified. In the interest of providing students with the most effective interventions as quickly as possible, the team must formulate hypotheses regarding the sources of difficulties in order to determine the specific and the more general systemic learning support strategies they want to see in place. Information about the learning environment and the six integral factors will serve as a foundational context for these hypotheses and the support strategies that emerge. Interventions can be put in place to support multilingual learners across these integral factors as well as in the general school environment while the team analyzes the challenges to see whether they cut across contexts and languages. If the team finds that to be the case, then the difficulties may be caused by factors that are more intrinsic in nature.

Remembering the myths. During this process, it is critical to keep in mind the various myths about multilingual learners introduced in the beginning of the book:

Myth 1: If we label multilingual learners as learning disabled, at least they get some help.

Myth 2: We have to wait 5 to 7 years for multilingual learners to develop their English language skills before we can rule out language as a cause for the student's difficulty.

Myth 3: When a multilingual learner is identified as having a disability, we need to shift to English-only instruction so as not to confuse the student.

This reminder keeps the MTSS team from falling prey to misconceptions at this critical moment of the team's work and ensures that effective interventions are crafted for multilingual learners according to whether or not they also have a disability. Whether or not a disability is present, there is no need to withhold support services that a multilingual learner might need while

Table 10.2 Possible Explanations for Typical Academic Difficulties Encountered by MLs

Observable Behavior	Possible ML Explanations	Possible Disability Explanations
Omits words or adds words to a sentence; forgets names of things that he or she knows—has to describe them.	• Word is not in English vocabulary yet. • Word/concept not learned in home language yet.	• Limited vocabulary due to poor oral comprehension and lack of opportunity to use vocabulary • Memory limitations • Word-retrieval problems
Becomes distracted easily.	• Is not getting comprehensible input in English. • Is not getting visual/concrete support for material in English. • Student may be exhausted from having to function in English all day.	• Poor oral comprehension due to lack of lexical development or grammatical mastery • Difficulties maintaining attention
Has trouble following directions.	• At early stages of English proficiency and therefore unable to understand what is being said. • No demonstrations or context provided for directions/procedure.	• Difficulties with processing the entire set of directions with sufficient speed • Distractibility • Memory limitations • Not able to understand the temporal or spatial concepts
Can do rote arithmetic on paper, but has difficulty with math word problems.	• In word problems the computation is embedded in language that the ML may not have acquired yet. • Numerals may be unfamiliar to MLs across linguistic and cultural contexts.	• Comprehension deficits • Abstract reasoning difficulties • Difficulty with generalizing learning across contexts • Difficulty retaining abstract concepts while performing the processes
Avoids writing.	• Writing proficiency in English often takes longer to develop than reading. • Student is afraid of making mistakes on paper.	• Fine motor difficulties • Grammatical and lexical limitations that negatively affect clarity, topic expansion, and/or voice • Has difficulty expanding and/or controlling ideas • Frustration from over-correction • Expressive language difficulties
Does not seem to transfer learning from one lesson to another; has to relearn each concept.	• May be in the early stages of learning English. • English content was taught through lectures with no context to make languages meaningful.	• Difficulties with memory (visual, auditory, short or long term) • Difficulties with comprehension • Poor ability to create inclusive conceptual categories to generalize learning
Very literal—misses inferences, subtleties, nuances, and innuendoes.	• Has yet to acquire enough English to express/represent abstract concepts.	• Abstract reasoning difficulties • Comprehension difficulties
Learns from watching, not listening.	• Student is in early stages of English development and depends on visual contexts to understand input.	• Oral comprehension difficulties • Distractibility
Has difficulty categorizing, classifying, or summarizing information.	• Student is in the early stages of English development and does not have the language to understand topic of study. • The directions in English are presented orally with no referent or model to make the language comprehensible.	• Difficulties with organizational skills • Executive functioning difficulties
Difficulty retelling a story in sequence or in summary.	• May understand story but may not have enough expressive language to be able to retell it.	• Organizational issues • Poor lexical cohesion • Experiential coherence problems • Comprehension difficulties
Has low frustration tolerance; gives up easily or explodes.	• Student is in the early stages of English development and repeatedly cannot understand. • Student is exhausted from having to function in English all day. • Student is conscious of constantly making mistakes in English and doesn't feel successful.	• Stigmatized • Poor affective/emotional control • Doesn't understand message • Student conscious of falling behind

MLs, multilingual learners.

Digging Deeper for the Cause: The Dangers of the List

By an MTSS Team Leader

An ESL teacher approached me about a student who was having significant difficulty in her class. She pulled out a chart we had used for discussion at a recent MTSS team meeting. The chart listed possible explanations for typical academic difficulties encountered by multilingual learners (MLs) (see Table 10.2). I was surprised to see the list in her hands because it had not been intended for distribution to staff. At first I was glad to see something that we had found quite useful in our team meeting being used by one of the teachers, but later I regretted not having made it clear to everyone that this list was not to be distributed and used by others until we had had a chance to discuss it with the staff and to offer some professional learning opportunities on the topic.

As soon as the teacher started telling me about the student, she pointed to two items on the list. She said, "We think that Andreas has either memory processing or word-retrieval problems. Or it could be some kind of language processing issue," pointing to numbers 1 and 6 on the list. She was certain he had some sort of disability and she had already begun the process to have him evaluated. She felt that he could not retain concepts once he learned them and had difficulty acquiring them in the first place. He was quite proficient in academic English even though he had been in the United States only since the summer. I asked her for an example of what he was having difficulty with. She told me about the first social studies unit they were studying. It was focused on the Colonial period in U.S. history. This is when she began to suspect his difficulties were due to intrinsic causes. She noticed a few times during this unit that this student was not able to grasp concepts. One example came with the concept of *antique*.

I asked her to describe the strategies she had used in teaching the student this concept. It seemed to me that she had done everything right. She had brought in real objects. She showed the student antiques that would have been used in Colonial times in the United States, such as a stovetop iron for clothes and a bed warmer. She had shown the student pictures and discussed each item and compared them with items in his home today. She even asked the child to find out what each of these items was called in his home language. I was stumped. She seemed to have done everything right, and the child seemed to follow her, but he just couldn't explain to her what an *antique* was. I asked her what the special education teachers had suggested, and she said they could help him with memory and word-retrieval strategies and some expressive language exercises, but he would first need to have a full case study done to see whether he qualified for their services.

I was not convinced. Very little information had been collected. We were still in the early stages of trying to change the school so that our MTSS team could process requests for intervention from teachers, and we did not have a system in place yet. Before we ended our conversation, I asked her to keep in touch with me about what happened with this student. As an afterthought, I asked her where the student had come from. She told me he had moved from Greece the past summer. I couldn't believe I hadn't thought to ask that question before! That changed everything! I told her that his background gave him a much different notion of what is *old* or *antique* than what we have here in the United States. He came from the land of the Acropolis and the Parthenon. It was quite possible that the objects the teacher brought in to illustrate the concept of *antique* were still being used in homes in Greece today. I told her that perhaps a referral to special education was not yet called for. The teacher could try some other interventions first. One example I suggested was that they build a timeline comparing the history of his country and the history of the United States, and then study the influences of Greece on other civilizations around the world. This might be more relevant to him and even quite interesting to the other students in the class.

I realized that we needed to use tools, such as the list of difficulties, very carefully to avoid a situation like this one. This very good teacher and her caring special education colleagues had made the mistake of using the multilingual learner/disability possible causes chart as if it were an exhaustive list. Because the child did not respond to the interventions for the multilingual learner causes provided in the chart, they assumed that they should jump over to the disability explanations. This is the danger of assuming that any student will fall neatly into a particular category or will exhibit the traits on a predetermined checklist of characteristics. We must dig below the surface to find out what might be causing a student's difficulty. Finally, we must collect as much information as possible as quickly as possible.

Questions for Discussion

1. What are some procedural errors that might exist in this school's process for referring students for a special education evaluation?
2. What could have been done to prevent this situation from going as far as it did?
3. What other pieces of information about this student need to be gathered?
4. What is the specific difficulty that this multilingual learner is exhibiting? List other support strategies that the school could implement to support this student and to capitalize on his linguistic and cultural resources.

developing proficiency in English. When multilingual learners are progressing in a normal manner without disabilities, it is imperative that they not be directed into special education, as these programs are unlikely to meet their language learning needs or help them achieve their academic potential. The perspective that "at least they will get some help in special education" is dangerously misinformed. Often special education employs methods of intervention that are not favored for authentic learning (Brinton & Fujiki, 2021; Commeyras, 2007; J. S. Damico et al., 2021; S. G. Paris, 2005; van Kraayenoord, 2010; Vaughn & Klingner, 2007) and it is generally oriented to working in the dominant language of the school rather than both of the multilingual learner's languages. Limiting the student to one language is a common approach that is misinformed and straitjackets multilingual learners by limiting them to using only some of their language and processing skills during the school day. As Paradis et al. (2021) have observed, children are capable of learning through two languages, even under conditions of impairment.

MTSS TEAM ACTIVITY

Using Table 10.2, generate discussion among team members regarding the validity of the explanations attributed to each of the 12 observable activities. Assign one of four roles to team members: (1) *critic:* examines the explanation(s) critically, (2) *supporter:* comes up with ideas to support the explanation(s), (3) *multilingual learner detective:* finds additional possible multilingual learner explanations; (4) *special education detective:* finds additional possible special education explanations. The four groups develop their ideas and arguments and the whole group reassembles to discuss them.

Reframing the Issue: Describe, Explain, and Support

The question of whether a multilingual learner's academic challenges are caused by the second language learning process, or due to a disability, is no longer a useful formulation. The answer is rarely neat enough to be of any use. The source of some difficulties in English will, for a great part of multilingual learners' school careers, be due to the normal process of learning academic content in a nonproficient language. It is difficult to attend to both language and academic content when one is not yet proficient in the language of instruction, or when one knows the language of instruction conversationally but not in the academic realm. A more useful approach to take in this problem-solving process is to reframe the question thus: If the challenges that multilingual learners are encountering are looked at through a lens of linguistic and cultural diversity at their source, what would be a possible explanation for those specific behaviors? In addition, if the challenges that multilingual learners are encountering have a language or processing impairment or cognitive learning disability at their source, what would be a possible explanation for those specific difficulties? Once explanations have been laid out, the next step is to identify interventions from the bilingual/bicultural/English as a second language (ESL) perspective first, and then from the special education field if needed.

We have proposed a process whereby the MTSS team begins its work by suggesting learning support strategies for multilingual learners in general based on an assessment of the learning environment at school and the six integral factors presented in preceding chapters. Addressing these learning support strategies can enrich the experiences of all students at that school. For multilingual learners whose challenges persist even with an enhanced general learning environment, it would be beneficial for MTSS teams, teachers, and other staff to describe students' observable behaviors specifically, rather than broadly diagnosing them from the outset. In the next chapter, we look at a process for verifying whether the observed challenges are occurring in just the academic English setting or in both of the student's languages, and across social as well as academic settings. If the student's difficulties are observed only during English instruction contexts that do not include appropriate supports for multilingual learners, and the difficulties are not seen in the home language and do not occur in all settings, it is more likely that the student is experiencing the typical challenges that arise in learning academic content through a second language. However, the student may need more support and intervention than other multilingual learners who are making steady progress in an ESL/bilingual program. If the difficulty manifests in all settings and across languages, then the team begins to explore possible special education needs as an explanation for the observed behaviors. We continue this solution-seeking process by showing how teams can create instructional supports and interventions that address both the extrinsic and intrinsic explanations for the challenges that multilingual learners exhibit. We also show how to document students' progress and assess their response to these interventions.

Questions for Reflection and Action

1. Make the case for the use of a generated inventory of difficulties and/or a predetermined inventory of difficulties. Support your argument with rationales and details about advantages and disadvantages.
2. What needs to happen so that educators guard against the tendency to choose intrinsic explanations first?
3. Have you found any myths in operation, in addition to those listed in the guide, in your current situation? What are they?
4. Articulate your response to the reframing of the issue away from second language versus disability to a process of description, explanation, and support.

Delivering a Continuum of Services

Key Concepts. *When multilingual learners in your school continue to progress at a rate that is less than expected or to show specific difficulties after systemic learning support strategies have been put into place, then it is important to add effective meaning-based interventions drawn first from the fields of bilingualism, multiculturalism, **dual language education**, and teaching English as a second language. As the intensity of intervention increases (with smaller groups and more frequent implementation) and multilingual learners do not make the progress that is expected, then interventions from the field of bilingual special education can be offered at an individual (specific) or small-group level.*

Creating an effective program for students who are experiencing significant academic challenges means providing support in a timely manner as soon as specific needs are identified. Although the natural acquisition of skills and knowledge is never truly sequential and time-linked (Kagan, 2013; Nelson, 2007; Wells, 1986), learning as dictated by a curricular approach, is linked to places, schedules, timetables, and calendars. Thus, students who, for whatever reason, cannot benefit according to the designated sequences, timetables, and placement are at a disadvantage. Consequently, rapid response in terms of identification, planning, and implementation should be a priority if the multi-tiered system of supports (MTSS) team is to have a real impact.

In light of the information presented in this book, two facts should be clear. First, the approaches historically used to identify and serve multilingual learners who may have special education needs—particularly when they hinge on traditional components and phases of special education—are not sufficient to meet the needs of these children. In the traditional service delivery system, the time between the appearance of specific observable behaviors and the implementation of an intervention can be quite long, and additional problems arise for multilingual learners in this traditional system (such as the inappropriate use of standardized tests, resulting in over- or under-identification). Second, with the push for multi-tiered interventions like those used within response to interventions (RtI) and MTSS, the emphasis on a timely response to difficulties has improved the setup for multilingual learners. However, many of the approaches currently being used under the guise of RtI are inappropriate for multilingual learners (Allington, 2009; Klingner et al., 2007; van Kraayenoord, 2010). The MTSS team approach suggested in this book helps ensure that attention is first paid to the general learning environment that has been created for multilingual learners. At the same time, for those multilingual learners whose challenges persist, we ensure that whatever is being done in these early interventions (e.g., in an RtI/MTSS system) is, in fact, appropriate for multilingual learners as it provides a viable alternative to ineffective traditional approaches. If employed appropriately, the framework described in this guide meets the needs of multilingual learners who are believed to be progressing at a lower than optimal rate in school.

This chapter presents a collaborative solution-seeking approach to providing a continuum of services to meet the range of challenges that some students continue to experience in the classroom, and one that can be implemented in a timely manner. The approach described is an alternative to traditional practices still employed in many special education programs, which typically require referrals and standardized assessment to determine eligibility for service before interventions can be put into place. This collaborative approach also provides support for anyone in an established RtI/MTSS system, and it helps to avoid some of the potentially problematic practices currently suggested by some RtI/MTSS advocates (e.g., D. Fuchs et al., 2003; Haager et al., 2007; Justice, 2006; Wright, 2005). Much of our framework depends on the creation of a forum within schools to allow English as a second language (ESL)/bilingual, monolingual English-speaking teachers, and special education teachers the opportunity to consult one another and provide support across their professions. We discuss the challenges involved in shifting from current models to this more responsive one, along with related legal and fiscal issues. We argue that by intervening across languages and contexts, the MTSS team can better decide what type of support is most effective for the students. We also show how important it is for the home language and culture to be engaged as resources in the multilingual learner's school environment.

The collaborative solution-seeking approach we describe may be viewed as a hybrid of several previously described approaches used to address the needs of learners who show significant challenges in school (e.g., Chalfant et al., 1979; Chandler et al., 2005; Clay & Tuck, 1991; York-Barr & Rainforth, 1997), but it is uniquely linked to multilingual learners.

Providing Support in a Timely Manner

Once the MTSS team begins to discuss possible explanations for the variety of multilingual learner difficulties that are observed on the inventory of specific observable behaviors (ISOB), a logical next step is for the team to continue supporting these students with instructional strategies and to generate a variety of more specialized interventions for the multilingual learners. A solution-seeking mindset can be used to determine the best possible interventions for specific observed behaviors. It is important that support be provided without delay. Rather than waiting for problems to occur, we suggest taking a proactive stance. MTSS teams strive to anticipate and prevent difficulties rather than intervening only after difficulties have become manifest. The suggested systemic changes to the learning environment and the learning support strategies based on the six integral factors are designed to do just that. In this way the MTSS team (1) builds capacity for addressing the needs of multilingual learners who are currently at school and those who are going to be coming in subsequent years, (2) improves and enriches the learning environment for the whole student population (and staff), and (3) establishes an effective collaborative relationship among teachers and other staff at the school. Taking a proactive stance to address the needs of multilingual learners is necessary, especially in environments where professionals may have little or no information or experience with second language acquisition, bilingualism, and bilingual education (e.g., Calderón et al., 2011; Carhill et al., 2008; Janzen, 2008; Roseberry-McKibbin et al., 2005; N. Flores & Schissel, 2014; Harry & Klingner, 2014; Wiley & Wright, 2004).

Benefits of RtI/MTSS for Multilingual Learners

RtI/MTSS approaches can benefit all students by providing timely support in the classroom as needs are identified. If employed appropriately and carefully in a culturally and linguistically responsive manner, RtI/MTSS can also introduce high-quality instruction into general education, ESL, and bilingual classrooms across the grades (Sánchez-López & Young, 2018). Ideally, a student with academic delays can be provided with one or more effective interventions, and because the response to the intervention is monitored, appropriate changes and additional support or placements (if needed) may be provided. Using the RtI/MTSS process, then, educators can avoid placement decisions on the basis of standardized tests in English, which are often problematic in relation to accurate prediction, and the more authentic instructional information gathered as a result of RtI/MTSS can be used to document those specific instructional strategies found to be effective for a particular student (Cloud, 1994; Echevarria et al., 2017; Reutebuch, 2008). In such cases the students, teachers, and parents all benefit.

This approach can be especially beneficial for multilingual learners who experience typical challenges, as they often need enhanced instructional support to make progress in dual language, bilingual, ESL, or monolingual English classrooms (Collier & Thomas, 2017a, b; Escamilla et al., 2014; Gibbons, 2015; Hadjioannou, 2007; Janzen, 2008; Lucas et al., 1990; Saenz et al., 2005; Ukrainetz, 2006). The flexibility that RtI/MTSS provides is important in that multilingual learner difficulties may arise at any grade level and can be as varied as the number of multilingual learner students enrolled in the school. We cannot stress enough the fact that there is no single intervention, program, strategy, or resource that will address all multilingual learners' needs.

As an operating approach RtI/MTSS may provide the context for the sort of creative problem-solving that addresses students' needs in our schools. As discussed in earlier chapters, although multilingual learners with academic difficulties may appear on the surface to be similar to students with intrinsic disabilities and are often referred to special education when difficulties arise, typical multilingual learners do not require special education interventions to learn effectively. In fact, more traditional reductionist special education approaches can place them at a disadvantage (Babatsouli, 2021; Cloud, 2012; Herrera et al., 2012; McMaster et al., 2006; van Kraayenoord, 2010). Conversely, these similar surface behaviors may cause a team to avoid seeking special education services for multilingual learners who may need them because team members do not want to mistakenly place a student in special education who is simply in the process of developing English.

An RtI/MTSS approach can be employed proactively to address the needs of multilingual learner students across grade levels throughout the school, without students having to wait for referrals for assistance. If properly implemented, RtI/MTSS can promote high-quality, consistent, and effective instruction in general education, ESL, and bilingual settings for multilingual learners. This, in turn, can prevent failure and frustration. Another potential benefit of this approach is that it includes assessment that can be designed to be closely linked to instruction, so that assessment provides diagnostic information and also functions to guide instruction. As well, assessment can be embedded in instruction, making it less disruptive to the learning process. Appropriately employed, RtI/MTSS approaches shift the focus to more authentic assessment and away from over-reliance on standardized measures, which are often administered with no meaningful context (Allington, 2009; Gottlieb, 2006, 2021). In this way, intervention that can improve students' academic performance from the outset can be introduced without waiting for students to experience significant failure first. An RtI/MTSS approach also provides opportunities for collaboration across disciplines to plan, coordinate, and implement classroom interventions. An increased focus on intervention can provide expanded or new roles for problem-solving team members to co-instruct with colleagues, demonstrate strategies, or model lessons in the classroom.

It is important that innovations like RtI/MTSS are, in fact, innovative. There is a tendency to use the RtI/MTSS tiered system, but to do so with interventions that are inappropriate for any student, let alone multilingual learners. For example, as numerous authors have stated (e.g., Allington, 2009; J. S. Damico & Nelson, 2012; Howard, 2009; Jaeger, 2019; Troia, 2005; van Kraayenoord, 2010), tasks that are not rich in context, are fragmented, or artificial, and that have invalid monitoring and assessment tools (e.g., L. S. Fuchs, 2003; Justice, 2006; Vaughn & Fuchs, 2003) can easily subvert the process. The great advantage of RtI/MTSS hinges on the application of authentic innovative teaching and strategies; also, descriptive and authentic monitoring and assessment are essential elements in this process. Taking a protocol approach rather than a problem-solving approach and using decontextualized phonemic awareness activities, tests of isolated skills with no meaningful context, or highly suspect tools, such as the DIBELS (Dynamic Indicators of Basic

Early Literacy Skills) or Aimsweb, does not benefit multilingual learners (e.g., Goodman, 2006; Lesaux & Harris, 2015; Milner, 2010; Wells, 1998). Meaning and relevance to the students' context must be key elements in the types of interventions and assessment that we give to multilingual learners. The knowledge that is developed from exploring the six integral factors is invaluable in ensuring that interventions and support strategies are linguistically and culturally meaningful to the student.

A Solution-Seeking Approach Based on Meaning

In our continuum of services framework, the MTSS team takes a solution-seeking approach to create the best possible interventions to address specific difficulties that some multilingual learners continue to face. The MTSS team begins by describing observable student behavior as specifically as possible. This constitutes the descriptive phase of the bi-level analysis paradigm. Then the team enters the explanatory phase of the paradigm by generating the possible explanations from both an extrinsic (multilingual learner) and intrinsic (disability) perspective. As soon as this is accomplished, it is time to craft interventions based on the explanations that have been identified. Throughout this process, the information that is being gathered about the learning environment at school and the six integral factors serve as a pivotal context for both interpreting student performance and crafting learning support strategies and more specialized interventions.

There are several criteria for developing effective interventions, which we discuss in a later section of this chapter. However, one criterion is fundamental: All interventions must have meaning for the students. Regardless of whether multilingual learners with academic difficulties are simply in the process of second language learning, or they have an intrinsic disability, they are constantly trying to make meaning out of an unclear linguistic, and possibly cultural, environment. The focus on meaningfulness is based on the fact that all learners are oriented toward finding systematic patterns in their academic, cognitive, and social contexts that allow them to make that context and its events comprehensible. This constructivist orientation to constantly creating meaningfulness is based on each individual's symbolic capacity, what Vygotsky (1978) referred to as "semiotic ability," which is of primary importance to all human beings. Consequently, students who are encountering academic challenges because of their second language proficiency, as well as those who have an intrinsic disability, may appear to have particular kinds of problems. However, they are still meaning makers and adhere to the primary principles of meaning-making (Bransford et al., 2000; National Academies of Sciences, Engineering, and Medicine, 2017; F. Smith, 2004; Wells, 1986, 2003). Therefore, the best choices for any kind of intervention or instruction that students receive must have meaningfulness as their base. When a team begins to explore interventions for multilingual learners, it is essential that they begin by assuming that the student who is having difficulties is a typical multilingual learner without a disability (J. S. Damico et al., 2021). The goal is to address first all possible explanations for a typical multilingual learner experiencing significant challenges in school. These possible explanations can result from a learning environment that is not the most effective for multilingual learners or from any of the six integral factors.

There are a number of reasons for determining interventions for those students who continue to experience challenges from the multilingual learner perspective first rather than beginning with the disability perspective. By implementing special interventions from the multilingual learner context first, one can observe how these students respond when their learning environment is enriched and their challenges are specifically addressed. In keeping with the mediational and constructivist approaches to learning that have been addressed throughout this book (e.g., Bransford et al., 2000; Cloud et al., 2009; Lightbown & Spada, 2006; Nelson 2007; Vygotsky, 1978; Wells, 1998), prioritizing the multilingual learner perspective will determine whether the contextualized mediation is all that is required. If students need a meaningful learning environment that is more effective for mastering a second language and for learning through that language, their performance will improve quite quickly when learning support strategies and specialized interventions and programming address their multilingual learner needs (e.g., Cloud et al., 2010; Echevarria & Short, 2003; Y. Freeman & Freeman, 2002; Genesee et al., 2006; Gibbons, 2015; Nieto, 2010; Palmer & Martínez, 2013; Wells, 1998). When the core of the instructional day addresses multilingual learners' linguistic, academic, and cultural needs, the majority of multilingual learners will thrive and make progress (Lindholm-Leary, 2012). Knowing this will make the MTSS team's first task of assessing the learning environment a little easier.

This brings us to a second reason for creating and implementing multilingual learner interventions first. If the observed behaviors are truly related to learning English, there will be a clear contrast between what is observed in English and what is observed in the student's home language and familial context. Later in the chapter we elaborate on this process of using students' responses to these interventions to validate that the observed behaviors are expected manifestations of learning a second language for them as multilingual learners.

Seeking Language Educators' Expertise to Generate Interventions

At this point in the solution-seeking process, the language educators on the team can filter each of the suggestions made by team members through a multilingual learner perspective. They do this using what they know about the second language learning process, bilingualism, and multilingual learners. This includes their knowledge of how multilingual learners learn (Bialystock, 2001; de Jong, 2011; Hoff et al., 2012; Ryu, 2019), research on second language reading and writing (August & Shanahan, 2008; Cloud et al., 2009; Genesee et al., 2006; Neokleous et al., 2020; Niazifar & Shakibaei, 2019), cross-cultural education (Banks, 2005; Bennett, 2011), second language acquisition

(Lightbown & Spada, 2006), linguistic and literacy transfer (Cummins, 2008), use of the home language as a resource (O. Garcia et al., 2016; Licona & Kelly, 2020), and research on bilingualism and bilingual education (Babatsouli, 2021; de Jong, 2011; Genesee et al., 2006; Verdon et al., 2014). Although suggestions for interventions are welcomed from all MTSS team members, at this end of the continuum of services the team typically defers to the members with the most experience and theoretical background in teaching multilingual learners. If teams fail to listen to these professionals, they tend to jump to intrinsic, special education approaches and strategies that should begin to appear only in the second half of the continuum.

Table 11.1 lists interventions considered most effective by one of the MTSS teams that has worked with this book that were used when a multilingual learner was experiencing difficulty providing an oral narrative of a story that had just been read to her. The limited set of interventions listed in the table is provided as an example, and may not be appropriate for all multilingual learners.

The support strategies that are most likely discussed at this stage include instructional strategies and activities that address the extrinsic factors in multilingual learners' learning environment that typically account for the challenges they experience. This includes an examination of all the systemic changes that were made after the team assessed the effectiveness of the learning environment for multilingual learners. Any additional support strategies or interventions coming from a special education context must be based on a multilingual learner research base (Oxley et al., 2017; Palmer & Martínez, 2013; Sánchez-López & Young, 2018), be meaningful to the students, and introduced as soon as they are identified (for either an individual student or a group of students). There is no need to put off support until extensive information has been gathered about the more general aspects of the student's home and school life or about the six integral factors discussed earlier. Thus, the services provided to these students flow smoothly and continuously. Who is to implement the strategies, in what contexts, toward what goals, and according to what timelines are matters determined by the team.

As information continues to be collected, both about the specific behaviors exhibited by multilingual learners at school and about the integral factors affecting them, the MTSS team also considers the strategies that enhance the learning environment at the systemic level and that are most appropriate to remedy any of the more general challenges. After the MTSS team members help teachers implement specific support strategies and the accompanying ongoing, authentic assessments based on observations for a period of time, perhaps 2 to 4 weeks, the team reconvenes to examine the outcome. MTSS team members then examine the qualitative and quantitative information that was collected before and during the interventions. If the challenges that multilingual learners have been experiencing have resolved with specific and systemic support strategies, plans need to be put in place to ensure that they become part of the students' daily learning environment. Using the template titled "Generating Multilingual Learner Interventions: Listening, Speaking,

Table 11.1   Generating Interventions for Multilingual Learners in Listening, Speaking, Reading, Writing, and Cultural Influence

Possible ML Explanations	In Home Language	In English
Listening		
• The student may not understand many stories because they are in English or because the cultural context of the stories or events was irrelevant or unfamiliar.	• Have student listen to stories in the home language. • Preview the story or talk about the content of the book in home language prior to listening to the story in English. • Show and talk about objects from the story that may be unfamiliar. • Explain the cultural norms that govern the story. • Have parents tell stories to their child on a regular basis.	• Provide graphic and interactive aids during the storytelling as in dialogic reading (Whitehurst et al., 1988). • Introduce content and build schemas through visuals, video clips, and manipulatives to pique students' interest and prepare for comprehension. • Make certain the story/text is at the student's instructional and English proficiency level and that the classroom instruction is highly contextualized and comprehensible with the use of many visuals and much modeling/demonstration. • Read the English version of a story aloud to the student **after** the content has been previewed in the student's home language.
Speaking		
• The student understands stories told in English but does not feel comfortable enough with English speaking abilities to create a narrative. • The student may have developed skills using social English but may not have been taught the academic language of temporal organization (e.g., *first, then, next*) to be able to effectively narrate stories. • The student may be able to tell stories in the home language after hearing a story in English.	• Provide parents a schedule of daily school routines and request that they ask their child to retell the events of school in the home language(s) every day for a period of time. • Ask parents to tell their child stories from their culture and then have the child narrate the stories to others on different occasions, and ask parents what they observed about the narratives. • Provide the child with pictures and a sequence graphic organizer during storytelling and then have the child retell the story, event, or procedure in the home language using the visual supports. • Teach parents to use the interactive strategies of dialogic reading (Tsybina & Eriks-Brophy, 2010). • Focus more directly on organizational language using a writing workshop approach that focuses on structural organizers during writing in the student's home language; have parents, tutors, and volunteers who are proficient in the student's home language practice retellings with the student at first using speaking prompts and graphic organizers and eventually without these supports. • Have student retell interesting events from the news, past events, or movies, and then complete a story using the LEA approach, which the student can read and reread. • Preview important vocabulary from the story or content-area text in the student's home language.	• Provide a graphic organizer during the story retelling. • Use a dialogic narrative format to create a short play (Paley, 1994). • Provide opportunities for the child to orally practice this language with a peer, adult, or in a small group. • Model this language by incorporating it into an LEA activity. • Allow the child to "retell" the event, story, or procedure using visuals, pictures, or manipulatives, by pointing, sequencing the pictures, or by recreating the event. • When appropriate, conduct a mini-lesson on various story structures used for storytelling around the world. Compare and contrast different story structures with the structure the student is accustomed to. • Provide a word bank of the key terms and verbally scaffold the language needed to recount the story. • Focus on informational texts, topics, and events that the student can retell. Compare the quality of the narrative the student provides when focusing on nonfiction topics rather than solely on fiction topics.
Reading		
• The story was not at the child's proficiency level in English and so the student did not understand enough of the story to retell. The student could recount some details that correspond to pictures if the vocabulary had been acquired. • Perhaps the child's home language has a different structure for telling stories and so the retelling in English sounds "out of order/out of sequence" because it does not reflect the rhetorical structure used in the child's home language.	• Prepare sets of books with audio recordings for students to listen to and read along with at home and at school. • Provide a summary or preview in the home language of the topic or content that will be addressed later in English. • Ask students to read and reread any LEA texts they have produced about nonfiction topics, story retells, or personal events. Highlight the sequential and transitional vocabulary used in the retell narrative.	• Provide a sequence graphic organizer during the reading. • Do some prereading activities (such as previewing vocabulary with pictures and asking children to practice the words orally) to prepare the student for comprehension. • Have students read an LEA story they have produced about the content they are studying prior to reading a book about this content. • Make certain the story/text is interesting and is at the student's instructional level and that the classroom instruction is highly contextualized and comprehensible with many visuals and much modeling/demonstration.

Possible ML Explanations	In Home Language	In English

Writing

- The student may be in the early stages of English language acquisition and is still developing writing skills.
- The student may not have been explicitly taught to write in English by someone who knows ESL strategies.
- The student may be using the home language structures to negotiate writing in the second language; this may make the written text sound "out of sequence" in English.
- The student may need to develop writing skills in the home language on which to build writing in English.

In Home Language (Writing):
- Take digital photographs from real-life events (e.g., family gatherings, cultural celebrations) and use the images as prompts for oral narratives that then can be written and turned into a dual-language podcast.
- Teach the student the specific sequential vocabulary to use when writing in her own language.
- Ask family members and others who know the student's language to incorporate sequential writing into daily events at home.
- Create LEA stories in the student's home language to model the sequential nature of a story or event.
- Use a sequential writing frame template (teacher copy and student copy) when modeling (shared writing).
- Post dual-language narratives on school website, blog, or other educational forum.

In English (Writing):
- Provide a sequence graphic organizer during the writing task.
- Provide the language of sequence in English in writing.
- Model this language by incorporating it into the writing of an LEA story, always connecting students' oral language to writing.
- Allow the child to "write" the event, story, or procedure using visuals, pictures, or manipulatives by pointing, sequencing the pictures, or by recreating the event.
- Explicitly teach the story structure used in various cultural contexts and from various storytelling discourse styles both orally and in print.
- Provide a word bank of the key terms and the sequential language needed to recount the story.
- Use a sequential writing frame template (teacher copy and student copy) when modeling (shared writing).

Cultural Influences

- The cultural context of the story may be wholly unknown to the student; for example, the student may come from a culture in which people do not keep animals in their houses as pets, and may be appalled and distracted by a story about pets. This makes it difficult for the student to concentrate on reading comprehension and on the sequence of the story.
- Different languages may have storytelling structures that differ from English.

In Home Language (Cultural Influences):
- Contrast how storytelling or retelling differs in the home language and English.
- Ask the student to tell stories from the home culture and discuss similarities or differences.
- Use books and events from the family's native country to practice retelling in the home language.
- Have the student(s) bring in materials, books, and oral legends in their own language from their own culture and have them retell and become comfortable in the home language before asking them to do this in English.
- Invite family members to record oral retellings of legends from their home culture.

In English (Cultural Influences):
- Use books in English that relate to the students' home language or culture.
- Take the time to teach students about the cultural context of the story if reading fiction and preteach unfamiliar content when reading nonfiction.
- Build the classroom multicultural book library to represent as many different perspectives as are available in quality publications.
- Work with adults and children to develop oral English versions of cultural legends; capture these oral stories in written form (dual-language projects, digital-authoring projects that can be posted on school website, blog, or other educational forum).

ESL, English as a second language; LEA, language experience approach; ML, multilingual learner.

Reading, Writing, and Cultural Influences," available in the Online Resources, the MTSS team works together to generate a set of multilingual learner interventions for each possible explanation that emerged earlier.

Seeking Special Educators' Expertise to Generate Interventions

When students' difficulties do not resolve with implementation of specific and systemic learning support strategies developed using a multilingual learner perspective, the MTSS team continues to seek solutions. In addition, the team takes the next step of revisiting the specific difficulties from the perspective of any new information that has been added about the student, this time considering possible explanations from a special education perspective. That is, what could account for this specific behavior if it were related to an intrinsic condition such as a learning or reading disability, a specific language impairment, or some other special education need?

Table 11.2 provides a continuation of our example of the student who was identified as experiencing difficulty providing an oral narrative of a story that

Table 11.2   Generating Special Education Interventions in Listening, Speaking, Reading, and Writing

Possible Disability Explanations (behavior is observed in student's two languages in academic and social contexts)	Special Education Interventions in Home Language and English (interventions should be provided in individual and small groups in addition to whole class)
Listening • The student may not understand the vocabulary (i.e., content and/or organizational words such as first, next, last), story events, inferred information, or narrative structure in home language and English. • The student may exhibit distractibility.	• Ensure that each activity is contextualized and that the interactions between the student and the teacher provide the appropriate level of mediation (Crowe, 2003; Wells, 2003), so that when you present a story in the home language to practice oral retelling it will be comprehended. With effective modeling and interspersed mediation (J. S. Damico & Damico, 1993b), transfer process to orally retelling in English. • Use home language to mediate and reduce overload (Crowe, 2003; G. M. Johnson, 2004). • With appropriate mediation during shared reading activities (Dionisio, 1994), teach balanced comprehension strategies (Afflerbach et al., 2008; J. S. Damico & Damico, 1993b). • Present story with visual support (e.g., pictures, book) or dramatically (e.g., voices, demonstration, sound effects with culturally and linguistically appropriate context and references).
Speaking The student may have oral expressive difficulties in both languages: • Formulating ideas into sentences that clearly relay the meaning of the story • Using cohesive devices (e.g., conjunctions and pronoun references) to connect the story information • Organizing information into story structure	• Rehearse a well-organized scene from an informational text or story that is rich with the needed vocabulary. This can culminate in a performance in front of other students. Provide appropriate verbal support, mediation, and any necessary visual support (two–eight picture cards); transfer to English using the same events; then extend to stories of increasing length presented aurally. • Employ appropriate exposure to necessary vocabulary and utterances of different length and complexity using communicative reading strategies (Norris, 1988). • During storytelling activities provide sufficient modeling and then retelling of personal narratives employing interspersed retelling techniques (Koskinen et al., 1988) with a conversational format (Brinton & Fujiki, 1994). • Target specific grammatical and cohesive devices and provide contextualized exposure via modeling and then interactional commentary during representational play activities (Culotta, 1994). • Provide parents a schedule of daily school routines and request that they ask their child to tell them the events that occur in school in the home language every day for a period of time. • Ask parents to tell their child stories from their culture and then have the child tell the stories to them on different occasions and ask parents to add details and new events to the cultural narrative and observe as student's retellings become more complex with more details over time. • Ask the student about interesting events from the news, from her past, or about a movie she saw recently.
Reading Comprehension • Poor comprehension results from inability to employ predictions and efficiently use background information.	• Use mediational techniques like modeling, rereading, foreshadowing, characterization, and synopsis during shared reading to weave meaning into the text when fluency changes suggest the child has lost comprehension (J. S. Damico, 2006). • Provide ample practice retelling the story orally with partners with the same home language background (e.g., volunteers, parents [for homework]; Myhill & Jones, 2009). • Activate background knowledge and ensure that vocabulary and cultural references are understood with activities and online discussion, prior to and during story reading; ensure that necessary mediation strategies are used during teachable moments (Dionisio, 1994; Wells, 2003). • Check comprehension frequently to prompt explanation/demonstration of vocabulary, events, and reasoning (Keene, 2008). • Provide material that the child can read independently about the story (Allington, 2009). • Use books with visual support to aid comprehension.
Writing • The student may have difficulty spelling in all languages. • The student can have difficulties in oral language production that are also evident in written expression, including sentence formulation, use of cohesive devices in both languages orally and in writing (e.g., conjunctions, pronoun references), and organizing the information into story structure.	• Provide ample practice orally retelling stories with partners of the same home language background (e.g., volunteers, parents [for homework]) before written retelling is required (Myhill & Jones, 2009). • Develop spelling skills in context of writing story retell in home language (Weaver, 1996). • Ask student to read her writing aloud and edit together for sentences and overall organization to ensure that it clearly relays what the student has understood; practice in home language as well as in English. • Build and activate background knowledge and ensure that vocabulary and cultural references are understood with activities prior to an online discussion during story and informational text reading. • Provide frequent comprehension checks and mediated activities that prompt explanation/demonstration of vocabulary, events, and reasoning (Keene, 2008). • Use culturally and linguistically relevant texts with visual support to provide a model for writing and to aid comprehension. • Explicitly teach story structure, highlighting its parts and organization.

had just been read. In this table, we list special education interventions considered most effective by an MTSS team. The interventions listed in Table 11.2 are a limited, exemplary set. Remember that the strategies selected and the mediational level employed should always be tailored to the needs of the specific multilingual learner and their disability. These interventions or supports would be added to those already in place on the multilingual learner end of the continuum.

When an individual has an intrinsic condition such as a learning disability or a language disorder, that individual exhibits both similarities to and differences from typically developing learners (J. S. Damico, 2003; J. S. Damico & Nelson, 2005; Perkins, 2005). In terms of similarities, the basic need for meaning-making plays an essential role regardless of the differences caused by the person's intrinsic impairment (Brinton & Fujiki, 2010; H. L. Damico et al., 2017; J. S. Damico et al., 2021; Duchan et al., 1994). Effective and efficient acquisition and use of any meaning-making manifestations (e.g., oral language, literacy, cognition, memory, and intelligence) depend on immersion in a meaningful context in which the individual has an opportunity to observe and actively engage in the process of meaning construction. In the contexts of language use or learning, there is always the need to create practical or pragmatic maps of the world by combining one's semiotic capacity with the linguistic conventions of one's language community, so that meaning is constructed as an emerging phenomenon (J. S. Damico & Nelson, 2005, 2010; Perkins, 2005). This is accomplished through social interactions with more competent meaning makers who serve as models, guides, and mediators (Cambourne, 2002; Keene, 2008; Nelson, 2007; Vygotsky, 1978; Wells, 1986, 2003).

As a result of an intrinsic impairment, however, the individual with the exceptionality also exhibits some differences from the typically developing learner and language user. For example, the individual with an intrinsic disability does not acquire skills or knowledge as easily, efficiently, or quickly as the typically developing individual. Second, this individual requires more focused mediation from more competent meaning makers in order to acquire new knowledge. Thus, it is important to carefully tailor input and activities to the individual's zone of proximal development (Vygotsky, 1978). Sufficient and appropriate mediation is crucial when working with individuals with exceptionalities (Wells, 2003). Third, owing to the intrinsic impairment, individuals do not easily create independent and efficient strategies to help themselves overcome the difficulties. Rather, more competent mediators may have to provide these strategies to the individual. Finally, learners with exceptionalities often exhibit difficulty in extending what they have learned from one context to another. Consequently, it is best to work on effective and needed meaning-making strategies within the authentic contexts of usage.

In reality, the difference between general education and special education does not rely on specialized techniques and strategies. Regardless of one's intrinsic capacity, the same meaning-making principles apply (Afflerbach et al., 2008; Allington, 2002a; H. L. Damico et al., 2017; Fennacy, 1998). When working with the exceptional individual, however, the teacher or interventionist must have more patience, must plan more carefully and implement appropriately targeted mediation, and must directly model and teach effective strategies to help the learner overcome the difficulties; and these activities should be accomplished in the contexts of need.

Given this understanding of the similarities and differences, to provide a continuum of interventions, the MTSS team then generates interventions from this perspective, as we saw in Table 11.2. Special education and ESL/bilingual professionals both contribute their experience and knowledge to this discussion. Just as with multilingual learner specialists generating support strategies based on their experience with linguistic and cultural diversity, special educators can generate interventions employing appropriate mediational techniques and beneficial strategies that will best meet the needs of these students if intrinsic difficulties exist (e.g., Cloud, 1994; Dunaway, 2004; Kouzlin & Gindis, 2007; Paradis et al., 2021; Westby & Vining, 2002). They can lend their experience to the MTSS team by working with students' disabilities, while ESL/bilingual educators continue to remind the team that because multilingual learners have valuable resources from their home languages and cultures they can benefit from continued interventions in those languages and those cultural contexts. All too often, once a disability perspective is taken in meeting student needs, the home language is viewed as unnecessary or even as a barrier to progress in the second language, despite strong evidence to the contrary (Martin, 2009; Paradis et al., 2021).

Using the template available in Online Resources titled "Generating Special Education Interventions: Listening, Speaking, Reading, and Writing," the MTSS team works together to generate a set of special education interventions for each possible explanation that was suggested earlier, and fills in the empty cells with these interventions. Questions of who is to implement the strategies, in what contexts, toward what goals, and according to what timelines are also determined by the team. Precise documentation of the interventions, their implementation, and the results can add qualitative information to the assessment data for diagnostic purposes.

A Forum for Crafting and Evaluating Interventions

Our collaborative solution-seeking approach can be a potential catalyst for change and growth in addressing the diverse needs of students. The MTSS team could become the structure within a school that promotes creative programming, fosters innovative collaboration, suggests professional learning opportunities, and provides a forum for crafting both specific and general interventions for multilingual learners and for all students. This means that when systemic interventions are implemented, general education students could also benefit by being exposed to the same good practices designed for multilingual learners (Chalfant & Pysh, 1989; Friend & Cook, 1996; Maeroff, 1993; Sánchez-López & Young, 2018). The approach to teaching and learning in these schools will broaden, and the teachers will be better able to accommodate the diverse linguistic and cultural backgrounds and academic needs of students who enter through their doors every day.

The success of this approach would be drastically diminished, however, if MTSS teams relied on one-size-fits-all programming. Taking a "cookbook" approach to crafting interventions can only lead to failure because it would not take into account each multilingual learner's different set of circumstances, which warrant careful consideration. The process described in this guide requires significant creativity: It requires MTSS teams to assess students' and teachers' needs, generate reasonable explanations for a host of observable behaviors, elicit ideas, and devise interventions and programming. For this process to work, MTSS team members should consider a few key principles.

Key Principles for Crafting and Evaluating Interventions

Often, the interventions suggested and implemented for multilingual learners are those that have traditionally worked for monolingual English speakers. In the school, staff members who are unfamiliar with multilingual learner education assume that these interventions work similarly with multilingual learners. However, some strategies that were designed for native speakers of English are ineffective for multilingual learners. Sometimes the intervention proves successful in the short term but not in the long term. Lack of success can also lead the team to erroneously assume that the difficulties are related to intrinsic disabilities. Adapting evidence-based interventions developed for one population for use by another ignores the learning principles known to be true for the second population. Although no one solution can address the needs of all multilingual learners, some key principles should be followed in designing interventions and support services. The key principles discussed in this section have been derived from research in general and bilingual education, sociolinguistics, second language acquisition, natural learning theory, and social action theory. MTSS teams that allow these principles to guide the creation of interventions for multilingual learners rather than imposing prepackaged programs will have more success.

Principle 1: Second language input must be made comprehensible for proficiency to develop.   The language (both oral and written) that surrounds a multilingual learner must be contextualized and presented with a physical or visual referent so that it is meaningful; this is a necessary requirement for successful language acquisition (Flege, 2019; Krashen, 1982). This principle, often referred to as the *comprehensible input hypothesis*, should remind the MTSS team that disconnected discourse in a nonproficient language is incomprehensible noise, and whatever interventions the team devises should work toward making meaning out of this noise. Thus, interventions in English should always be set in a clear context. For example, a lesson in science that is being taught in the monolingual English classroom should be accompanied by a visual or physical clue, such as graphic representations, pictures, photographs, physical models, manipulatives, or realia, to help multilingual learners make sense of the words or the text (Hill & Flynn, 2006; Janzen, 2008).

Principle 2: A second or additional language develops more easily when learners are actively engaged in authentic use of the language.   When learners are focused on using the second language for meaningful communication, proficiency in that language develops more efficiently (P. Smith, 2012). Multilingual learners need authentic reasons to communicate. They need to listen to understand, say things they want to say, read to gather information (we hope about something they are interested in), and they need to write about things they want to write about. When communication is authentic, learners also become actively involved in the interaction and use of language, and this helps push the language learning forward significantly. The implication of this principle for MTSS teams is that the interventions they recommend must have authentic communication at their base. Classroom tasks must require listening for understanding, speaking for communicating ideas and thoughts, reading to collect information, and writing to inform others.

A source of difficulty in some RtI/MTSS models is that the materials or strategies used in interventions are designed to be very controlled and often contrived and reductionist so that students work on a particular grammatical form or a specific literacy skill (Klingner et al., 2007; Pacheco, 2010; S. G. Paris, 2005; van Kraayenoord, 2010). What we have seen in schools that use these types of materials or approaches with multilingual learners is that the students may show improvement in a superficial way on the targeted skill so long as the student is in the contrived and controlled context. Once the child is put into an authentic learning environment and asked to do real reading, writing, speaking, and listening, there is little to no transfer of the skills taught under such a controlled and inauthentic setting. We recommend that teams attend very carefully to the context of the interventions and supports so that they are authentic and represent real communication contexts from the beginning to ensure the transition and transfer of skills from one learning environment to another. This planning by the MTSS team will also ensure that the multilingual learner experiences cohesion throughout the day rather than a fragmented day of instruction.

Principle 3: Because of a common underlying proficiency, concepts and structures that are learned in one language have the potential to transfer to the other language.   There is a **common underlying proficiency** that is the basis for learning and producing any language (Cummins, 2000). This underlying proficiency allows for development of strong cross-language connections that help the learner. This principle suggests using the home language (through listening and speaking as well as reading and writing) as a resource for developing the new language and for strengthening the home language of multilingual learners, as well as a means for learning new concepts in either or both languages (Beeman & Urow, 2013; O Garcia & Woodley, 2015; O. Garcia et al., 2016). For example, concepts can be previewed and learned in multilingual learners' home languages first, to facilitate learning in the new language (Calderón et al., 2011). Concepts that are taught in the home language can then be reinforced during instruction in English. Concepts do not have to be re-taught in one language if they have been established in the other language. Interventions should be implemented in both languages as a way to check for understanding and progress.

Consistent with recent developments in bilingualism and education, we recognize that a bilingual person's languages are not two separate entities, but rather a dynamic intermeshed system that is constantly evolving. The two languages feed one another and serve as resources for comprehension and production during various kinds of activities, both social and academic, in either or both languages. Making cross-linguistic connections reflects "a process of making meaning, shaping experiences, gaining understanding and knowledge" (Baker 2011, p. 288). Bridges and connections made between the student's two languages can be planned in a lesson or unit to assist in formulating and understanding a message so that not only can social and academic interactions (literacy and learning) occur successfully, but the learning of new concepts can be strengthened by leveraging students' bilingualism for learning (N. Flores & Schissel, 2014). The instructional approaches currently referred to as *bridging*, or bringing the two languages together for contrastive analysis (Beeman & Urow, 2013) and *translanguaging*, or drawing on the dynamic language practices of multilingual learners (O. Garcia et al., 2016), have continued to gain influence over the last decade (Lewis et al., 2012). There are a number of applications of these cross-linguistic connections in assessment (e.g., Antón et al., 2016; Ascenzi-Moreno, 2018), literacy (e.g., Beeman & Urow, 2013; Hornberger & Link, 2012), general education (e.g., Creese & Blackledge, 2010; O. Garcia et al., 2016; O. Garcia & Wei, 2014; Lewis et al., 2013), and specific learning venues (Licona & Kelly, 2020; Ryu, 2019; Tavares, 2015).

Principle 4: Multilingual learners' home languages are resources for learning and for developing their multilingual/multicultural identities. In an additive bilingual situation, an individual adds proficiency in a new language without losing proficiency in the home language. Learning in additive bilingual environments will support optimal language and literacy development in both languages. In contrast, in a subtractive learning situation, as the individual becomes more proficient in the new language, proficiency in the home language diminishes, or worse, is lost altogether (Lambert, 1974). In addition, the second language may not develop to an optimal level of proficiency. Multilingual learners' loss of the home language in the course of acquiring English can have severe social, cognitive, and academic consequences for the students and their families. For this and other reasons, team members should never implement an intervention or programming that causes multilingual learners to lose their home language, identity, or culture or cuts them off from their families and communities. On the contrary, schools should actively seek ways to create an environment in which students' languages and cultures are viewed as resources and become an integral and natural part of everyday learning and interacting for multilingual learners as well as for all students (O. Garcia et al., 2016; Hamayan et al., 2013; Medina 2010; Soltero-González 2009). Multilingualism and cross-cultural experiences will become the norm in these school settings. Cultural and linguistic resources of any kind are not left on the steps outside school. Chronicle 11.1 offers an example of a simple strategy that brings in students' home languages and helps make the classroom more effective for both multilingual learners and monolingual English-speaking students, even when there are numerous languages represented in the classroom.

Principle 5: Second language acquisition occurs in predictable stages.   The stages of second language acquisition are generally defined as preproduction, early production, speech emergence, intermediate fluency, and fluency. Although there is little consistency in the time it takes individual learners to go through the stages, the order is quite well defined. This has some implications for what to expect from learners in different stages (Hamayan & Freeman Field, 2012). There is emerging evidence that multilingual learners' rate of linguistic growth in the new language at the early stages of proficiency is fast and then slows down at the intermediate to advanced stages (G. Cook et al., 2012; H. G. Cook et al., 2011; Sahakyan, 2013). The linguistic demands, in terms of the complexity of the language at the later stages of proficiency, are greater than they are at the earlier levels (Hakuta et al., 2000). Because the process of learning a second language academically is developmental, overall it still takes students 5 to 7 years or more to reach full academic proficiency in their second language. We caution against assuming that the quick growth and subsequent slower growth is an indication of learning disabilities (Cardenas-Hagan et al., 2007; Carhill et al., 2008). This rate of growth in academic language appears to represent a typical pattern. It also means that the interventions devised must be appropriate for each particular stage of second language acquisition. An intervention is more likely to be effective if it is in accordance with the particular stage of second language acquisition that the learner is passing through. Multilingual learners may well need continued and intense support to meet the demands of the higher levels of proficiency.

Principle 6: It is important to plan for the language demands of the school curriculum and to support multilingual learners in their development of language proficiency in academic and social contexts across a range of discourses.   Although it is important for students to develop effective conversational skills in English and their home languages, academic proficiency is key to academic achievement (A. L. Bailey, 2006; Cummins, 2012; Gibbons, 2015; Hadjioannou, 2007; Schleppegrell, 2004; Schussler, 2009). Students need to know the aspects of language at the discourse, sentence, and word/phrase level that are essential for learning new concepts in academic content areas (WIDA, 2020). For example, students need to master the past tense in order to process concepts in history, or *more than/less than* in mathematics. This

Chronicle 11.1

Viewing Students' Languages as Resources

By a Monolingual English-Speaking Speech–Language Pathologist

I co-teach a kindergarten classroom with a general education kindergarten teacher. In our class, we have children from many different language backgrounds, including English, and for a while I felt the need to incorporate the students' home languages into classroom work. I thought it would help the students, some of whom seemed to be having significant language difficulties. I had read about the academic advantages for multilingual learners when they continue to use and develop their home languages while learning English, even when they may have specific language impairments. So it seemed logical to use all the students' linguistic and cultural resources in school.

There were already two strategies in place to help multilingual learners: During the intake process, parents were interviewed about their child's home language use and we used multilingual greetings as part of our daily entry process with the children. Both practices provided a great deal of insight into the children's languages and cultures and allowed us to connect with the families of these students even though we didn't speak their languages. Our students' families appreciated the fact that we wanted to know about their cultural and linguistic backgrounds.

When we started using the multilingual greetings at school, some children found it strange to hear their language in that context. Somehow these very young children had already gotten the message that school was the English domain and that their home languages were not welcome there. I even heard one 5-year-old advising another child against using her home language in class. We continued to remind the children that we wanted to learn about their languages and that they were welcome to speak their other languages in our classroom. I would tell them how fortunate they were for knowing how to speak many languages. Eventually, with all the encouragement, the greetings began to take off, with the students participating more freely and using different languages. Monolingual English speakers were encouraged to try others' greetings, and everyone seemed to like using Dora the Explorer's "hola" on a regular basis!

I felt it was time to extend the use of students' home languages in class. I did this by taking the step of previewing important vocabulary for each unit in their home languages before reading the related stories In English. The Family and Friends unit was next, so I made up a homework assignment for students to do with family members (the assignment that follows). I wrote out some of the important vocabulary that the students would be hearing in English over the next weeks. Those words were listed in the first column. In the next two columns, parents were asked to write the name of their language and how each word is written in that language. Examples of a couple of words were provided.

Homework: Family and Friends

We are collecting different ways of saying these words in English and in other languages. Please help your child teach us how you say these words at home in your language.

Example:

Word	Language	How you write it	How you say it (i.e., how it sounds)
Mother	Arabic	أمي	'ummi
Father	English	daddy	dadi

Name: _____   Home language: _____

Word	Language	How you write it	How you say it (i.e., how it sounds)
Mother			
Father			
Sister			
Brother			
Grandmother			
Grandfather			
Aunt			
Uncle			
Friend			

(continued)

continued

By a Monolingual English-Speaking Speech–Language Pathologist

The results were amazing! Every student brought the homework back! I put the completed list on the computer with links to audio recordings of the children saying their word so that we could share them with everyone. Students from other grades could go into the school library and listen to the different languages! That year we had approximately 17 languages represented in the class, and it was beautiful to see all these written out and to hear how they sounded. The students were very proud to share the homework they had completed with their parents and to help us pronounce the words we couldn't say very well. Even students who had previously indicated they didn't speak another language willingly demonstrated what they knew in their language for this activity.

We all gained a great deal of linguistic and cultural knowledge from this simple activity. The students began seeing similarities and differences among their languages. We also learned that in some languages different words are used when referring to an aunt who is your mother's sister and one who is your father's sister; the same was true for grandparents and cousins. We learned that in some languages there are different words to indicate you are referring to older or younger siblings. What fascinated children the most was learning that some languages are written from right to left, unlike English and many other languages, which are written from left to right. When reading a story that featured a grandfather, we made a word web with all the different ways we knew to say *grandfather*.

For children who experience challenges in both languages, it was encouraging to continue to find ways to incorporate students' home languages into instruction, even at this young age.

Questions for Discussion

1. What knowledge and beliefs were required to implement these home language activities and practices? What are some potential long-term benefits of these practices?

2. How could teachers at other grade levels adapt these strategies and routines for use in their classroom instruction?

3. How could the MTSS team support English-speaking teachers who want to begin incorporating multilingual learners' home languages into their instruction?

principle reminds MTSS team members that multilingual learners may sound proficient in English in social settings but may need more time and instruction in the academic language skills necessary for success in school. Thus, any assessment of multilingual learners' second language proficiency must address all aspects of language, and students' needs in either social or academic language proficiency must be addressed with specific interventions. The team must advocate for the learning environment that would best promote the development of academic proficiency among multilingual learners.

Principle 7: Although many multilingual learners may reach academic parity with their monolingual English-speaking peers in 5 years of instruction, some multilingual learners may take more than 5 years to develop a high enough level of academic proficiency to effectively access content in a classroom where abstract concepts are taught in English.   Although many multilingual learners develop fluency in social English, they may take 5 to 7 years to catch up to average monolingual English-speaking peers in academic English (Cummins, 2012). Most multilingual learners are not given this long to develop the language skills they need to flourish in an academic setting where English is the medium of instruction. Multilingual learners must have repeated opportunities to use language in a variety of meaningful contexts (Cardenas-Hagan et al., 2007; Carhill et al., 2008). The MTSS team must pay close attention to the opportunities that a multilingual learner has had to develop social and academic language proficiency.

> **MTSS TEAM ACTIVITY**
>
> Using Table 11.1, generate discussion among team members regarding which of the principles for crafting interventions discussed in this chapter (and summarized in Table 11.1) is represented in each of the interventions suggested. Assign one of three roles to team members: (1) *critic*: examines the intervention(s) critically, identifying how the principles are supported in each intervention; (2) *supporter*: comes up with ideas to support how and why the interventions would be effective for multilingual learners; and (3) *interventions developer*: finds additional multilingual learner interventions that apply one or more of the principles. The three groups develop their ideas and suggestions and return to the whole group to discuss them.

Validating Difficulties and Intervening across Contexts

By observing the seven principles just described, MTSS teams can design interventions based on the hypothesized explanations of specific behaviors. It is critical that these interventions be implemented across contexts and in all of the multilingual learners' languages (Goldstein, 2011; K. Kohnert & Goldstein, 2005; D. Martin, 2009; Schall-Leckrone, 2018). By monitoring the progress of multilingual learners in both (or all) of their languages, the team can identify the contexts in which difficulties occur. Expanding on the hypothesis of a common underlying language proficiency that gives rise to all meaning-making manifestations, including language, cognition, memory, and intelligence, we think it unlikely that an individual with a true disability would express that disability in one language but not another (Cummins, 1984: Kay-Raining Bird et al., 2016). If the difficulty is intrinsic to the individual, it would be expected to manifest in all of the multilingual learner's languages and in all the contexts that lead to its use. Here is another excellent reason to maintain learning in both the home language and English: Once multilingual learners begin to lose their home languages, as may occur in a subtractive school environment, it is very difficult to uncover an intrinsic disability as the explanation for the students' difficulties (Cummins, 2000, 2008), or more important, to provide the appropriate support.

> **MTSS TEAM ACTIVITY**
>
> Discuss the seven principles during an MTSS team meeting by posing the question, "What evidence of the application of these principles do we see in our school?" If evidence of the use of a principle seems to be lacking, then ask the question, "What needs to be done for this principle to be put into effect in our practice?"

An Example of Validating the Source of Difficulties

In the example we have used throughout this book, a student experiences difficulties retelling a story that has just been read. A possible multilingual learner explanation for this observed behavior is that the student is in the early stages of second language acquisition. If so, there are a number of ways that the emerging English proficiency may become manifest (e.g., Altman et al., 2016; Gagarina et al., 2016; Kang, 2012). For example, the student may understand a story read in English or a procedure presented in class, but may not have developed enough oral English to provide a sufficiently well-organized, coherent narrative about the story or procedure. Further, the student may not have much experience with narratives, so the problem becomes one of experiential diversity in addition to linguistic diversity (Dyson & Ginishi, 1994; C. J. Flores & Delgado, 2012; McCabe, 1989; Uccelli & Paez, 2007; Washington et al., 2021). To understand this complex situation, MTSS team members need to come up with possible explanations for the particular challenge the student is experiencing, first from the perspective of the second language development process. Can the challenge be explained by the student's developing English proficiency, and hence the limited comprehension of the story told in English? Does the student understand the story because the teacher has made it highly comprehensible, but has not yet developed sufficient proficiency in oral English to supply a coherent and appropriate narrative in English in front of the teacher or peers? Has the student not had enough experience using the English narrative storytelling form? This form may vary significantly from narratives in the student's home language. Has the student not been exposed to different types of narratives orally and in writing during instruction?

The ESL teacher on the team suggests that the team help the classroom teachers provide contextualized models, demonstrations, and mini-lessons on the uses of narratives during story time and storytelling activities (Paley, 1994), in critical literacy activities (Edelsky, 1999), and during writing workshops (Y. Freeman & Freeman, 2002). The team will want to know whether the student can employ narratives in any circumstance and whether the student can benefit from various types of cross-modality scaffolds when attempting to create a narrative (Alvermann, 1991). The MTSS team will also ask the teacher to provide contextualized assignments using dialogue journals (Bode, 1989) and by making narrative construction the focus of that week's homework for everyone (McEwan & Egan, 1995). The teacher may ask students to narrate the events of the day to an adult at home throughout the week. With young children, teachers may engage parents in the process by giving each child a sticker to take home (written in the child's home language) that reads, "Ask me what I did in science class today." Older students may have to practice narrating the events of a procedure in their home language to an adult or volunteer in the room before retelling and reporting it to the class (Wells, 1998). Teachers can use technology to help students create podcasts, digital stories, or biographies.

After a couple of weeks of using this practice and after receiving support in hearing and employing various types of narratives across languages and contexts, the team reconvenes to discuss how multilingual learners responded to the interventions. It is important for the team to contrast what happened in various language contexts as well as in nonverbal settings. It is also important to note whether the students were able to use their social language to construct narratives in either language, but were unable to use their academic language to narrate more abstract concepts. With the recommended interventions implemented, multilingual learners who do not have underlying difficulties with comprehension, topical organization, expressive language, or memory should be able to show progress in at least one of the contexts and languages and typically would benefit from use of various contextual and interactional scaffolds (Gibbons, 2015; Kheirkhah & Cekaite, 2018; Schall-Leckrone, 2018; Trousdale, 1990; Wells, 1998, 2003). With multilingual learners who show the same difficulties across contexts and in all their languages, even in enriched, highly contextualized and focused learning environments, we must intensify the intervention, have them work in smaller groups or pairs with a teacher, and use meaning-making strategies more often. This process of validating difficulties emphasizes the need to look at multilingual learners' performance in as many contexts as possible. If teams looked only at multilingual learners' performance in English (such as work samples, oral or written output, or performance on standardized measures), they would never develop a complete profile of the students and would not be able to help the student, regardless of the source of the students' difficulties (Goldstein, 2011; Sánchez-López, 2012; Sánchez-López & Young, 2018).

Home Language and Culture as Resources

Valuing and strategically integrating students' home languages and cultures as resources is a key precept for the MTSS team in planning and implementing interventions for multilingual learners. The team can help teachers invite students' home languages and cultures into their classrooms. This not only enriches the learning environment, it also provides teachers with valuable information on how students complete tasks in both of their languages and helps in building skills that the student finds challenging. First, assessment that captures multilingual learners' skills and knowledge in both or all of their languages across contexts provides invaluable diagnostic information, as it is generally accepted that difficulties resulting from intrinsic disabilities would be evident in both languages and in multiple contexts. If a multilingual learner's difficulties are evident only in English and are not present in similar activities when the student is using the home language, it is likely that they are simply manifestations of second language learning. If the observed behaviors appear in both languages and across various social and academic contexts, however, the special educators on the MTSS team would offer suggestions for strategies that the teachers may try that would support the student's challenges if these could be explained by intrinsic learning or processing difficulties.

Second, the home language and culture serve as bases for learning new concepts, as well as for developing proficiency in the second language. It is much easier to acquire language forms when contextual scaffolding is available and background information or experiences can be accessed to aid in processing novel information (Bachman et al., 2020; Bruner, 2006; B. A. Collins et al., 2014; Creese, 2009; DaSilva Iddings, 2009; Kalil, 2015; Menard-Warwick, 2007; Reese & Goldenberg, 2006; F. Smith, 2004; Wells, 2003).

Bilingualism and Special Education Needs

In many academic settings, once it has been determined that a multilingual learner does indeed have a learning disability, use of the home language often falls by the wayside, owing to the common misconception that students having significant difficulties should use their "limited language learning" resources to focus on one language. As principles 3 and 4 suggest, however, research shows exactly the opposite: Maintenance of multilingual learners' home languages is beneficial for psychosocial, cognitive, educational reasons; skills in two or more languages need to be nurtured and viewed as personal, social, educational, vocational assets" (Genesee et al., 2005; Martin, 2009).

A growing body of evidence supports the hypothesis that resources used in the student's home language help second language development. For example, when typically developing bilingual preschoolers were taught one set of words in their home language followed by the same words in their second language and another set of words only in their second language, they demonstrated understanding of words in the first condition with fewer trials (Kiernan & Swisher, 1990). The results of similar studies have shown that the home language supports learning a second language, even among children with specific language impairment (Perozzi & Sanchez, 1992). Evidence continues to emerge which indicates that the capacity for bilingualism is adequately strong and that more than one language can be learned even under conditions of language impairment (Kay-Raining Bird et al., 2016; K. Kohnert et al., 2005; Martin, 2009; Paradis et al., 2003, 2021).

If the possibility of having intrinsic learning disabilities exists, these students should receive all the interventions and support at the multilingual learner end of the continuum, as well as the specialized support that special education can provide in both of the multilingual learner's languages. In practice, this means that although many of the same meaning-based and contextualized activities and teaching approaches may be employed, the mediational techniques, contextual scaffolds, and strategies and contexts within which interventions occur will be carefully planned and implemented (e.g., Allington, 2009; Crowe, 2003; H. L. Damico et al., 2021; H. L. Damico et al., 2017; Keene, 2008; Norris, 1988; Sánchez-López & Young, 2018). In this way, students with exceptionalities gain the benefits of the principles of meaning-making while still getting the appropriate accommodations for their specific levels of disability.

Monolingual Educators in Multilingual Settings

It is a major challenge to create an effective bilingual intervention environment when there are multilingual student populations in a school with monolingual-oriented infrastructures: monolingual staff members; scarce multilingual resources for instruction, assessment, and technology; and a monolingual mindset among practitioners and administrators. The obvious solution is for administrators to try to fill positions with personnel who speak and have literacy in the languages of their multilingual learner populations. The goal in a multilingual school should be an additive environment for all multilingual learners, regardless of their language background. Given the increasing range of linguistic and cultural diversity found in schools, however, this is not always possible, and more often than not, monolingual educators and service providers must somehow provide support in languages they do not know. Some publications address general issues of interference of one language with another (e.g., Babatsouli, 2021; Babatsouli, et al., 2017; Swan & Smith, 2001) that could provide useful information to speech pathologists and special educators.

Innovative digital projects and materials available on the web can provide models and resources in just such a situation. Some of the linguistic and cultural resources that educators, students, and families can use to actively promote bilingualism in multilingual schools have been discussed. More extensive examples of how these resources have been used across grade levels are discussed throughout the book.

Even with these resources in place, monolingual teachers need to forge alliances with speakers of their students' home languages in the community and partner on a regular basis with trained interpreters. They may be fortunate enough to work with bilingual educators or teaching assistants who speak some of these languages. Educators need to enlist parents, university students, older students, and volunteers as resources to support the home language and to provide cultural information relevant to multilingual learners in the classroom.

If the assessment of the learning environment reveals a school that does not seem to provide multilingual learners with the best possible opportunity to learn, then perhaps it is time to modify or even overhaul some of the aspects of schooling there so that multilingual learners are better served and less likely to face unnecessary challenges in their learning journey.

A Sample Process

The following is a description of the process of developing the continuum of services framework in two districts that we call District A and District B. In District A, the development process began when the ESL and special education directors brainstormed ideas for how they could better support multilingual learners in their district who were experiencing significant academic challenges. One of the first steps they took was to start a district think tank.

The ESL director and a speech–language pathologist from the district, who is enthusiastic about collaborating on this project, led the think tank. This group included participants from various fields in the district who were asked to review the literature in the field of both ESL and special education. The group discussed the learning environment created for multilingual learners, as described in Chapter 3, and made some recommendations based on a quick assessment of the various aspects of instruction and programming offered to multilingual learners. The think tank made some recommendations at the district level for professional learning opportunities and suggested ideas for how to proceed.

The ESL and special education directors arranged a day for special education and ESL staff in the district to become familiar with the six integral factors. There were representatives from each school at this larger meeting. Participants engaged in different activities that facilitated cross-professional conversations. The participants shared some of their concerns and questions in this large group and made further suggestions to the district personnel, who worked with building administrators to improve the program and other aspects of the learning environment for multilingual learners. These representatives returned to their schools and shared what they learned with their home schools. School administrators scheduled short meetings at their schools during which information about their assessments of the learning environment for multilingual learners in the district as well as the six integral factors was shared so that all staff would have a common base of knowledge with regard to multilingual learners.

District A then brought the professionals together again for a day to go through the solution-seeking process described in this chapter and in the previous one, using examples of specific observable behaviors that multilingual learners exhibited in their schools. In this district, after reviewing their instruction and programming for multilingual learners and the six integral factors, the schools identified very specific areas that should be improved to help improve multilingual learners' academic progress.

District B was in a different situation when it began the process. District B scheduled an evaluation of its instructional program for multilingual learners every couple of years and had a very-well-established infrastructure for addressing the needs of multilingual learners in all six areas. What they had not done was to establish regularly scheduled conversations between multilingual learner and special education professionals. Over a 3-year period, teams representing multiple perspectives met to review information related to the learning environment and each of the six integral factors. This served to remind everyone of the areas that had to be addressed to prevent a wide range of multilingual learner difficulties. On two occasions, teams met to go through a sample process of crafting interventions. The emphasis in those meetings was on professional bridge building, collaborative problem-solving, and listening to each other's perspective. Today, the bilingual/ESL and special education directors are in frequent communication about their individual program needs and responsibilities and the areas in which they can collaborate and share services by using this new approach to address and prevent difficulties for all students. Both the bilingual/ESL program and the special education program have undergone dramatic changes to implement innovative programming for multilingual learners.

Questions for Reflection and Action

1. Many schools cannot seem to take the proactive approach espoused in this book; how could a group of teachers/administrators get a school community to see the tremendous benefits of providing support to multilingual learners using this proactive way?

2. What are some benefits that you have experienced by collaborating with another professional who comes from a very different background than your own?

3. If you have an RtI/MTSS system in place, how would the framework presented in this book work in conjunction with it? What would have to change?

4. How well do the interventions and instructional strategies that are presently used in your school adhere to the principles described in this chapter?

5. How do interventions currently recommended by your team align with the seven principles outlined in this chapter to better craft/evaluate interventions? If alignment is limited, detail what needs to be done to foster use of these principles. If alignment is sufficient, detail what should be done to maintain and/or strengthen the alignment.

Putting It All Together

Key Concepts. *Establishing a system whereby a continuum of services is provided to multilingual learners who seem to be facing significant challenges in school is no small feat, but one that is worth doing. By moving the focus away from trying to decide whether the challenges are the result of second language learning or disability, we can concentrate on creating a linguistically and culturally sustaining learning environment from the outset as we keep multilingual learners in mind. Implementing learning support strategies and specific intervention approaches developed from the language-learner's perspective, after gathering extensive information about individual and groups of multilingual learners, as suggested in this book, will benefit all students—not only multilingual learners, but all students.*

Throughout this guide we have described a process that helps school districts identify and address the varied needs of multilingual learners who are experiencing significant challenges in school. For this process to be effective, it must be proactive. School solution-seeking teams, such as multi-tiered system of supports (MTSS) teams, can use the process described in this handbook to identify early and support multilingual learners who are encountering more than the expected number of challenges in school. In fact, if implemented collaboratively and systematically, this process can help teams to anticipate and even prevent those challenges that can be explained by factors extrinsic to the learner. Teachers and other school staff need not wait for students to fail before giving them the enriched and intensive support they need to begin experiencing success in school.

In this chapter, we review the elements of the process that help to ensure that schools provide a continuum of effective services for all multilingual learners, including those with special education needs. Even if a process is available and in place, it is still necessary to determine when and in what instances the process should be implemented. This requires a kind of circumspection on the part of the individual schools. In the first section of this chapter, we discuss a primary way that such circumspection may occur: how the schools or district can determine how well they are doing with regard to the appropriate placement of multilingual learners and how the continuum of services process can help them improve the learning environment for these students. Toward that end, the first section focuses on the need for the individual school to examine its process of service delivery to multilingual learners, especially how it identifies those multilingual learners who are not making the progress expected. The rest of the chapter focuses on the services provided to multilingual learners.

Identification of Multilingual Learners Who Experience Significant Challenges

Because the identification of multilingual learners experiencing significant challenges in school is attended by numerous difficulties, schools should check whether the extent to which multilingual learners are identified as having special education needs is commensurate with other student populations. Schools can also assess the way that multilingual learners who are facing significant challenges are identified. This review assists in preventing the two undesirable outcomes too often seen in public schools: overrepresentation and underrepresentation of multilingual learners in special education.

Checking the Proportion of Multilingual Learners in Special Education

One measure that schools can use to ensure that they are appropriately supporting multilingual learners, both those with and those without exceptionalities, is the proportion of students who are placed in special education. If the number of multilingual learners in special education is disproportionate (overrepresentation or underrepresentation) to the number of other students in special education, there may be problems with the process of identification and placement. There are two ways to make this determination. The first method entails a cross-student group comparison. With this method, the number of multilingual learners placed in special education programs in the school or district is divided by the total number of multilingual learners in that school or district, to derive a percentage of multilingual learners placed in special education. Then the number of monolingual learners placed in special education programs in the school or district is divided by the total number of monolingual learners in that school or district to derive a percentage of monolingual learners placed in special education. A comparison of the two figures should show approximately the same percentage of each group placed in special education. A second method for determining the proportion of multilingual learners in special education placement uses within-group comparisons. With this method the percentage of multilingual learners in the school or district is compared with the percentage of multilingual learners in the entire special education population. The proportion of multilingual learners in the total population of the school or district should be the same as the proportion placed in special education.

These methods are useful but they ignore the concept of intersectionality: Students typically belong to more than one subgroup (Crenshaw, 2022). In addition, some caveats must be kept in mind when a school begins looking at the over- or underrepresentation of multilingual learners in special education placement (Artiles et al., 2010; Waitoller et al., 2010). First, the percentage comparisons are only approximate. Students from lower socioeconomic backgrounds who have received fewer healthcare services and perhaps had poorer nutrition may have a slightly greater need for special education services. This difference, however, is generally not large. Second, the disproportionality seen in special education (if it exists) is often noted in categories of exceptionality that require clinical judgment: categories like primary language impairment, specific learning disability, mild emotional disturbance, mild behavior disorder, mild developmental delay, speech impairment, and other health-related issues most often show the disproportionality. Finally, schools should check for underrepresentation of multilingual learners in special education programs. Providing no services when they are needed is just as problematic as inappropriately providing services that are not needed. Both scenarios exacerbate the challenges faced by multilingual learners.

By gathering information from year to year on the number and percentage of multilingual learners served in their special education programs, schools can see whether they are moving toward a more accurate identification of multilingual learners with intrinsic learning difficulties. Unless the school is a specific destination for students with challenges (i.e., a side-by-side program or a special education center), the percentages of all subgroups in a school should coincide. The proportion of multilingual learners in special education programs with respect to the general population should not be significantly higher or lower than the proportion of other groups in the school or school district (N. Flores et al., 2015; Klingner et al., 2007).

Research suggests that the magnitude of disproportionality of multilingual learners in special education classes changes depending on whether the analysis is conducted at the national, state, district, or school level. Overrepresentation at the national level applies only to African Americans and Native Americans. Although Latinos are not overrepresented nationally, this group is affected in some states and districts. Other factors that can mediate the magnitude of overrepresentation include the size of the district, the proportion of an ethnic group in the district population, the indicators used to measure the challenges that students are experiencing, and the availability of specialized programs such as bilingual education (Artiles et al., 2005; Zirkel, 2006). Regardless of the level of analysis, the proportion of multilingual learners in special education should be no different than the proportion of any other subgroup.

Investigating Misidentification

Once a problem with identification and placement into special education has been acknowledged, how identification and placement occurred should be carefully reviewed to determine possible breakdowns in the methods that are currently being used to make these determinations. There are typically four areas in which breakdown may occur: the assessment instruments or processes used, the interpretations applied to the collected data, placement pressures because of funding issues, and insufficient resources for multilingual learners.

With regard to the assessment instruments (psychological assessments, screening tools, assessments for monitoring student progress, language assessments, among others) and how they are employed, many problems may arise. Although this issue has been addressed in previous chapters, it is important to revisit some of the concerns in light of the present solution-seeking discussion. Many assessment instruments, especially norm-referenced and standardized tests, are not up to the task of validly and effectively addressing the complexity of human meaning-making (Afflerbach, 2007; J. S. Damico, 2019a, 2019b; Geva & Wiener, 2014; McDermott & Varenne, 1995; van Kraayenoord, 2010). These tools may focus on superficial indices of proficiency or may be too decontextualized to give an authentic view of a student's strengths and those areas in need of support. Some assessments are too narrow or superficial in their focus, and consequently they either overidentify multilingual learners as having disabilities of some sort or completely miss students who truly are experiencing difficulties because of intrinsic causes. These problems are being increasingly recognized, and more authentic and descriptive assessment procedures are being used (Andrade & Heritage, 2017; Artiles & Ortiz, 2002; J. S. Damico, 2019a; Goodman, 2005; Gottlieb, 2021; Gottlieb & Hamayan, 2006; Johnston & Costello, 2005; Leslie & Caldwell, 2009; Stahl, 2009).

This growing awareness of the problems of using standardized testing approaches in English is one of the reasons why in 2004 the Individuals with Disabilities Education Act (IDEA) was reauthorized as IDEA (Individuals with Disabilities Education Improvement Act) and moved away from relying on such tools for assessment purposes (Zirkel, 2006). To ensure the best assessments possible, the assessment tools and procedures used with the multilingual learner population should be carefully analyzed. If assessment instruments are employed, the following questions should be asked of each procedure:

- Does the instrument directly collect relevant and actual behaviors in the authentic classroom context?

- Are the actual behaviors focused on and the procedures employed for data collection appropriate, given the multilingual learners' linguistic, cultural, and experiential diversity?

- If norms or some other kind of referencing procedure is employed, is it appropriate to this multilingual learner population?

- Is some flexibility built into the assessment procedure to account for the dynamic nature of multilingual learners' bilingualism and biculturalism during interpretation?

MTSS teams must shift toward a solution-seeking process that looks for possible underlying factors as indices of difficulty, and begin to gather performance data that are more revealing than norm-referenced, standardized test scores. As advocated through the reauthorization of IDEA and by various researchers (Allington & Walmsley, 1995, 2007; Clay & Tuck, 1991; Milner, 2010; Palmer & Martínez, 2013; van Kraayenoord, 2010), the use of early support services, wherein some type of learning support is undertaken before a final assessment is made, may be the best option to avoid the problems inherent in using formalized tests.

The second area of difficulty implicated in the potential misidentification of multilingual learners involves interpretation of data that have been collected. Even if the information obtained is authentic, descriptive, and performance based, once data are collected, they must be carefully analyzed to determine what the patterns of performance actually mean. Do the data show what particular strengths and weaknesses the multilingual learner has? Do these patterns of performance help or hinder classroom or communicative effectiveness? Why do the patterns of weakness or challenges exist? Can these challenges be explained by considering differences that result from the dynamic nature of bilingualism and biculturalism or by considering disability issues? How would a multilingual learner be affected by one kind of remedial placement versus another? What kind of programming can we offer for multilingual learners who benefit most from an enrichment approach to education that sees bilingualism as an added value? Each of these questions should be a routine part of the interpretive process when focusing on the assessment data. As discussed earlier, these questions are necessary to complete the explanatory phase of the bi-level analysis paradigm (J. S. Damico et al., 2021). When employed systematically and completely, these questions enable appropriate data interpretation so that accurate identification and placement may occur. If these interpretive issues are not addressed, however, the result may be insufficient; inaccurate interpretations may lead to misidentification and, subsequently, to inappropriate support services. With regard to addressing these questions, it is critical that as many of those involved in teaching and assessing multilingual learners as possible build a solid knowledge base in the areas of bilingualism, second language learning, and delivering **culturally sustaining pedagogy** so that they can apply this knowledge to interpreting the performance of these students. The continuum-of-services approach is designed to accomplish this objective.

One specific interpretive issue that often results in misidentification of multilingual learners is the use of discrepancy formulas. Current legislation and regulations prohibit state departments of education from requiring that districts apply discrepancy formulas (Zirkel, 2006). If school districts abandon these discrepancy formulas, which are riddled with ethical, procedural, and cultural problems, they will move toward more authentic assessments and more accurate interpretation of performance.

When addressing misidentification of multilingual learners, the third area of concern involves an institutional variable. School districts must examine biases that are created or reinforced because of the funding structure associated with multilingual learner education and special education. A legitimate (if difficult) question must be asked: Is the school still making decisions about programming based primarily on funding availability or funding categories? For both ethical reasons and issues of equity, school districts must seek to support students' needs, whether those needs fall within the realm of funding labels or not. Students should not be placed in special education when they need other services that are more appropriate (such as language support, dual language education, English-as-second language [ESL]) just because special education funding is available (J. E. Brown & Dolittle, 2008; D. J. Connor & Ferri, 2005; J. S. Damico, 2019c; J. S. Damico et al., 2021; O'Connor & Fernandez, 2006).

Finally, the district and the individual schools must determine whether they have sufficient quality services available for multilingual learners. A frequent cause of multilingual learners' difficulties in the monolingual English or special education classroom is that they are not receiving appropriate language learning opportunities and comprehensible academic content instruction in the first place. Because special educators are known for being able to reach a wide range of learners, their classrooms become the first option for students who experience significant challenges, even though these students may not have impairment of any sort. Rather than relying on special education services as a first choice, investing in building robust bilingual, multilingual, and ESL programs allows teams to more readily find those multilingual learners who do have special education needs and support all other multilingual learners in a more timely manner. Therefore, if there is misidentification of multilingual learners with regard to special education, this lack of appropriate services must be considered.

The reality of teaching and supporting multilingual learners is that each student's experience is unique, and thus more creativity and flexibility are needed when designing and funding programming for these students. Multilingual learners should have access to core curriculum instruction that is culturally and linguistically sustaining and then, in addition, have access to more intensive support and intervention via an RtI/MTSS system already in place in their school. It is the school's responsibility to find ways to intervene in a timely and effective manner, even if the instruction and intervention being suggested for a student or group of students has never been implemented in that school before.

Anticipating and Addressing Predictable Challenges

Once the MTSS team begins gathering information about a multilingual learner or group of multilingual learners, the team members engage in a collaborative process to evaluate the quality of the learning environment that has been set up for multilingual learners, suggesting improvements to multilingual learner instruction and programming, interpreting the information, proposing hypotheses to account for multilingual learners' observed behaviors, and creating specific learning support strategies and interventions. The team also provides support in implementing these strategies and interventions. The responsibilities of gathering information and implementing learning support strategies and interventions must be shared so that the process does not become so cumbersome and draining that it falls apart. It is also possible that the decision-making and solution-seeking processes may become stale and fall into a routine that keeps team members from looking at each case with fresh eyes. MTSS team members must strike a balance between delegating these responsibilities and supporting those who carry them out.

Identifying Exceptionalities in Diverse Settings

The first step in applying a creative approach to supporting the needs of multilingual learners is to shift the orientation from prematurely identifying a student as having an intrinsic difficulty ("he is low" or "she is doing poorly in math") to requiring a description of the student's behavior coupled with evidence of that behavior and, when possible, data on any learning support strategies or interventions that have been attempted with the student. The more specific teachers, parents, and others are in describing multilingual learners' observable behaviors and reactions to support strategies or interventions, the better able the team is to hypothesize possible explanations and to further intervene in a timely and appropriate manner.

When gathering assessment information, the MTSS team must insist on qualitative assessment information (including attempts at support, student bilingual oral language and writing samples over time, across content areas, and contexts). Rubrics and checklists that enhance reliability and validity and provide a more comprehensive profile of these students' strengths and areas of difficulty should accompany this qualitative information. MTSS teams should seek out teacher recommendations for multilingual learners who are not performing as well as would be expected, coordinate the gathering of historical and contemporary data on these students, and assist teachers in some initial attempts at providing support as an aspect of the assessment process. Once specific challenges are identified, teams must validate students' performance across various content areas as well as in diverse settings, including those that are extracurricular or that occur in multilingual learners' communities and homes.

As soon as concerns arise, it is crucial to engage the multilingual learner's parents as collaborators in the information-gathering process through interviews and conversations. When addressing the needs of multilingual learners, it is vital to collaborate with a cultural liaison who can provide an appropriate context for interpreting the information that is collected. The cultural liaison must be equipped to understand the cultural and linguistic nuances of both the multilingual learner's community and the school culture in order to mediate discussions and explain the nature of the concerns as well as the solution-seeking process.

We have suggested that the first place to look at is the learning environment created for multilingual learners to ensure that it gives these students the best opportunity to learn. At the same time information needs to be gathered about six integral factors present in students' lives: personal and family issues, physical and psychological factors, previous schooling, oral language and literacy development, academic performance, and cultural differences.

These six integral factors provide a rich context for understanding learning and achievement among multilingual learners and influence how and what data are collected, evaluated, and interpreted. The information gathered in relation to these six factors provides an important context within which instruction in general, and more specific support strategies and interventions are suggested, implemented, and monitored. Addressing the six integral factors at the same time that a critical look is taken at the learning environment and programming for multilingual learners helps to remove many of the obstacles that have traditionally kept multilingual learners from reaching their optimal levels of performance and their families from gaining access to the school system. Over time, with practice and additional professional learning opportunities, the MTSS team will be in a position to address situations proactively, before students experience difficulty, rather than intervening only once difficulties arise.

Rejecting Common Myths

For schools to take a proactive approach, staff must reflect on their beliefs on bilingualism, academic performance, and how multilingual learners learn. Several commonly held misconceptions stand in the way of providing support to multilingual learners in the most efficient way, and these myths must be explicitly recognized and challenged. Recall that one such myth is that multilingual learners must be fully proficient in English before being considered for special education support. Another myth takes the opposite stance and suggests that multilingual learners facing academic difficulties must be placed immediately into special education programming because it is a funded program of support. The last myth is that multilingual learners who are facing challenges must be instructed only in English so that they do not get more confused. The research and examples presented in this guide show that multilingual learners' home languages and cultures are resources that should be used to help these students develop optimal levels of language proficiency in English, bilingualism, academic achievement, and emotional well-being. In the process of questioning misconceptions and myths, MTSS teams begin to reflect on the principles on which the instruction of multilingual learners is based. Beyond the MTSS team, all professionals who work closely with multilingual learners can begin to consider the six integral factors discussed in this guide as a way to provide more culturally and linguistically sustaining support systems for these students. Any learning support strategies or interventions implemented without consideration of these factors may be perceived as educational malpractice, especially if greater care is provided to other student subgroups in the school.

Creating a Supportive and Enriching Learning Environment

A learning environment that has a sound theoretical base that espouses instructional strategies and programming shown to be effective for multilingual learners will result in an enriched rather than a compensatory educational program. An enriched educational environment sees the value of the diverse resources that multilingual learners bring and the added value of bilingualism and biculturalism as essential elements for optimal learning and growth. Many factors contribute to creating an enriched learning environment.

Teachers and Resources

Essential to an enriched learning environment is the involvement of expert teachers in the field of bilingualism and ESL/bilingual education. Recruiting and hiring qualified teachers who know the languages and cultures of the multilingual learner population in the school is a priority. When this is not possible, professional learning opportunities should be supported for existing teachers (Janzen, 2007; Palmer & Martínez, 2013; Rodríguez-Mojica et al., 2019) on issues of second- language acquisition, bilingualism, delivering culturally and linguistically sustaining instruction, differentiation for multilingual learners, and multicultural education.

When MTSS team members work together in the solution-seeking process proposed in our framework, their professional perspectives expand, and they find they are better able to address the new and diverse needs of the students in their schools. Collectively, they represent an extraordinary amount of knowledge and experiences that, ideally, increase over time. One important function of the MTSS team is to build professional bridges within the team and within the school as a way to share and expand professional knowledge. By working together with ESL/bilingual teachers, the classroom and special education teachers in the school expand their expertise in the instruction of multilingual learners and they begin to explore the various factors that impact multilingual learners' performance as well as consider various ways to support learning. With proper guidance, these teachers can implement authentic, performance-based assessment. Throughout this process, teachers also develop more effective ways to communicate with multilingual learner parents and to ensure that they become integral members of the school community.

With the help of special education teachers, ESL/bilingual teachers, in turn, can begin to develop a sense of how disabilities affect the learning process and what can be expected of multilingual learners who are developing in a typical manner. These teachers also develop confidence in their ability to function as cultural interpreters for other staff members and for families. The professional growth that brings together these various areas of expertise is not just limited to the teachers who work with multilingual learners but extends to all staff, including administrators. By collaborating with teachers in their classrooms and planning for general professional learning, the MTSS team assists in making the school a place that offers the best opportunity to learn, not just for students but for staff as well.

In addition to skilled teachers, an enriched learning environment for multilingual learners includes an abundance of high-quality, age-appropriate academic content-area instructional and supplemental materials at a variety of language proficiency and reading levels. These materials should reflect the languages and cultures of the students and can include student-created texts as well as purchased resources. In addition to high-quality materials, multilingual learner classrooms must be highly interactive to ensure multiple opportunities exist for students to practice newly learned language skills. There is no reason for multilingual learners or their teachers to be isolated from the rest of the school population. Collaboration among staff allows multilingual learners to be fully integrated in academic and nonacademic classes as well as other school activities, even as we seek to give them the specific programming that they require (Dove & Honigsfeld, 2018).

Program and Instructional Issues

If the core instructional programming that has been developed for multilingual learners fails to meet the needs of these students, it should be rectified immediately to create a more effective learning environment. Schools should not be limited by existing programs; rather, schools must provide the range of services multilingual learners need, in terms of both duration and frequency, even if this means creating innovative programs. The MTSS team and school administrators must work together to ensure that classroom instruction includes practices that are based on comprehensibility, increased interaction, and promotion of higher-order thinking. Assessment practices that are used must include formative, summative, quantitative, qualitative, and performance-based information so that all those who work with multilingual learners, as well as the students themselves, have a realistic understanding of what the students know and can do. The most effective and informative assessments are embedded in instruction, include all four language domains, come from all content areas, include self-review and peer review, are in the students' home languages and English, and are judged against clear criteria.

All aspects of an enriched learning environment for multilingual learners should work together to help these students gain access to the academic concepts and skills and learn the language necessary to become successful in these classes. Appropriate assessment of the learning that occurs in these enriched environments should allow students to show what they know, not just what they are having difficulty learning. When the learning environment is enriched in this way, it is easier to find children who may be experiencing difficulties stemming from more intrinsic causes. When the learning environment is depressed and lacks substance and appropriate methods and materials, many multilingual learners may appear to have learning disabilities and are not making the progress that is expected.

Adopting a Culturally and Linguistically Appropriate Approach

By adopting a culturally and linguistically appropriate RtI/MTSS approach in which both systemic and specific learning support strategies or interventions are implemented, schools are better able to assess multilingual learners' special needs and to provide support to students who seem to be facing significant academic challenges. However, it is essential to avoid the pitfalls and problems that have accompanied various approaches to RtI. The MTSS team can provide leadership for this shift to more performance-based, authentic assessment of multilingual learners' strengths and areas of difficulty. The MTSS team engages in a solution-seeking process that includes proactive information gathering and culturally appropriate interpretation of this information. The team should encourage and support timely application of enhanced instruction that is high quality, effective, consistent, research-based, and tailored to the needs of multilingual learners, as well as facilitating collaboration across disciplines. It is essential to recognize that the application of RtI/MTSS may be innovative or deceptively stale. Although the overall multi-tiered system of support and systematic intervention to determine learning ability and potential are quite promising, if the support strategies or interventions employed within them are decontextualized and fragmented, if they represent strategies employed far too long in some aspects of special education and remedial reading programs, then nothing changes. If the assessment to determine the RtI or MTSS is based on artificial tasks in contrived situations that only tangentially focus on real meaning-making activities, then nothing changes. It is the obligation of the MTSS team to ensure that any innovation is truly innovative, rather than doing the same things as before under the guise of a new acronym.

The MTSS team also periodically implements needs assessments and surveys as a way of assessing current practice and monitoring progress in these new endeavors. In order to assess the effectiveness of the changes that have been institutionalized and the strategies and interventions that are being implemented with multilingual learners, it is critical to collect multilingual learner performance data (quantitative and qualitative information on academic language development and academic performance), along with evidence of systemic and specific strategies and interventions, and to schedule periodic data-review retreats to scrutinize and interpret the data and evaluate the success rate of interventions, as well as to make short- and long-term recommendations.

Monitoring the Effectiveness of Learning Support Strategies and Interventions

As the MTSS team works with individual teachers or groups of teachers, it should meet frequently to monitor the effectiveness of its work. Continual monitoring on an intermittent basis is important, because progress over time is often the criterion used to determine the effectiveness of methods and the multilingual learner's developing proficiency and performance. Especially if a kind of RtI/MTSS is employed, it is necessary to determine which support strategies or interventions are being used, whether they are appropriate to the needs of the student, whether they are appropriately and effectively implemented, and whether the intervention resulted in some change or progress in the desirable (and targeted) student behaviors. Only if all of these conditions are met can we comment on the learning capacity of the multilingual learner and use the data to help determine the best placement and learning

Case 1

A 12-year-old boy whose home language is Spanish has been placed in an English-only sixth- grade classroom. The teacher has expressed concern about how much he understands during social studies lectures and discussions. If this multilingual learner exhibits difficulty comprehending classroom instruction, then observable and documented data should be collected and learning support strategies formulated and monitored.

Observable Behaviors

With that objective in mind, it has been observed and documented that the student does not attend to the actual lectures and the teacher's notes placed on the chalkboard. Rather, his attention is directed elsewhere, and he often draws in his notebook rather than take notes. In three 30-minute class sessions, the student raised his hand to respond to only three of 35 opportunities (8.5% of the time), compared with a response rate of 63% by three randomly chosen class peers. In addition, he was unable to respond accurately or appropriately when questions were directed to him during these three sessions. On 14 requests for responses, he responded appropriately in only two instances (both closed-ended questions). This response rate of 14% compares unfavorably with the response rates of three randomly chosen class peers, who responded appropriately to direct questions 79%, 95%, and 100% of the time.

Information Gathered

- The student has been in the United States only 3 months.
- He seems quite engaged in the science class, and according to his parents, he excelled in biology during the previous school year in his home country, Mexico.
- He has a collection of seashells that he took great trouble bringing with him to the United States.
- The family seems to be quite unified and strong despite the expected hurdles for new arrivals from a lower socioeconomic background.
- The student does not seem to have any unusual health problems.
- When asked about the history of Mexico in Spanish, he was able to list major events accurately.

Possible Multilingual Learner Explanations

Because he has been in the English language classroom only 5 weeks and in the United States 3 months, and since he speaks primarily conversational English, it is anticipated that the student does not yet have sufficient comprehension of English grammar or the vocabulary of social studies to participate in class. Moreover, the academic discourse and expectations of how to be an active learner in this classroom are unfamiliar to him.

Support Strategies

Once the behaviors were documented, several strategies were tried. First a bilingual aide sat with the student during a 15-minute homeroom session to introduce a list of vocabulary words that would be used during the social studies lesson. She exposed him to the vocabulary and previewed additional information in Spanish so that he would understand the context of the upcoming lesson in English and could recognize the English words when they were used and understand their meaning. Second, with a peer tutor, he jointly prepared a short outline (based on the textbook headings and subheadings) to organize the structure of the social studies lecture. This was done at the end of the previous day's social studies class. Third, the teacher was instructed in several effective **sheltered instruction** techniques to help increase his comprehension in her classroom (Echevarria et al., 2017; Gibbons, 2015). In addition, he was asked to prepare, with the help of the peer tutor, a short bilingual digital presentation for his class on the geographic regions where different kinds of seashells can be found around the world, with references as to where he obtained the shells in his collection.

Monitoring

The aide and the teacher were asked to keep a journal that required several one- to two- line entries every other day regarding how well they believed their specific teaching strategies were implemented that day and how well the multilingual learner did in class that day. They were asked to provide some description of behavior rather than just an overall evaluative statement. In addition, once a week, a member of the MTSS team observed the class for 10 to 15 minutes during social studies to monitor both the teacher and the multilingual learner. Finally, every 2 weeks the peer tutor, the aide, and the teacher met with a member of the MTSS team to discuss progress and concerns. This meeting lasts approximately 15 minutes.

Outcomes

Outcomes were determined by comparing the student's performances across the first three sessions (with regard to attending, bids for a turn, and correct responses) with three other sessions that occurred approximately 12 weeks later. In addition, the information written in the journals of the teacher and the aide was used to triangulate the observational data. The student was found to have made substantial progress (as had the social studies teacher with her strategies), and he was not referred for special education assessment.

Case 2

A 6-year-old girl whose family is from the Philippines was referred to the MTSS team because of her limited English proficiency and for poor reading ability. Her teacher reported that she could not effectively recognize her letters and that she had little or no phonemic awareness in English. In addition, it was reported that she was not a reader and that she shied away from invitations to read aloud in English.

Observable Behaviors

Observations made during two round-robin reading sessions documented that the student was only able to read 45% of the words on her three assigned pages (compared with 88%, 94%, and 96% of words read by other members of her heterogeneous reading group). Also, she tended to guess at unknown words based on their first letters (81% of the time) and often did not even employ the correct first sounds. When given a familiar book that she had been reading with a room-parent, she did try to read. A running record found that she was able to read only 62% of the words correctly and that she either guessed at the others or skipped the words (or whole lines) if she did not know the words or sounds.

Information Gathered

- Student's family has been in the United States for 1 year.
- The father works in a restaurant.
- Student has had no prior schooling.
- She is a very gregarious child and seems to love socializing with other children.
- She has a fascination with photographs (books illustrated with photos are particularly interesting to her).
- According to her mother, her development has been as expected.
- She seems to have no unusual health problems.
- She seems to enjoy listening to stories in Tagalog.

Possible Multilingual Learner Explanations

Given her limited experience with literacy in the Philippines (no prior schooling) and her developing English language skills, the approaches used to teach reading were not appropriate. Rather than decontextualized phonemic awareness and a round-robin reading approach that provided little mediation while she was learning, more contextualization and assistance based on more meaningful materials should be used.

Support Strategies

Consistent with a modification of reading recovery techniques (Chapman et al., 2015; Clay, 1985; Pinnell, 1989), three approaches were suggested. First, an older multilingual learner student (a fifth-grader) read aloud to her every day on topics that interested the younger student. This was a component of both of their reading programs. Second, with a student teacher, she engaged in a joint reading activity for 20 minutes each day. The student teacher was instructed in using Clay's "roaming around the known" strategy to assist the multilingual learner's motivation and confidence. That is, during authentic reading with the child, the teacher stays within what the child already knows rather than introducing new items of learning. However, teachers can employ and review what the child knows in different ways until their ingenuity runs out, and until the student seems comfortable in the familiar environment (Clay, 1993). This strategy requires the teacher to work from the child's responses rather than simply from the teacher's preconceived ideas and strategies. Such individualization is never a bad idea. Finally, the teacher engaged in a small-group shared reading activity with this student and two other struggling readers. Alphabetics and the graphophonemic system were not an explicit focus. Rather, the book and the inherent meaning of the story were stressed as the multilingual learner and the other children read with the teacher. The student was also asked to reflect on topics that interested her, and her oral narratives were encoded onto pages in a small notebook. The teacher periodically asked the young student to read back her dictated narrative. Each entry into the notebook was dated so the student and the team could see progress over time. In addition, the parents were urged to read as much as possible to the child, and the librarian was able to find some bilingual children's storybooks in Tagalog and English that she sent home. Another support was put in place when a high school student volunteered to record podcasts of dual language books in English and Tagalog at the elementary library media center for younger students to use. This idea caught on with other high school students as their school decided to issue credit for service and volunteer hours.

Monitoring

The student teacher kept a running record of literacy performance (Clay, 1985) during her daily sessions with the student and also observed the teacher with the student once a week during the shared reading time and collected similar running records of those sessions. Running records were conducted on the students' oral reading of her dictated stories.

Outcomes

Outcomes were determined by comparing the student's reading performance from the first two round-robin sessions with her reading performances during three shared reading sessions 10 weeks later. Evaluations focused on how many words she could read on the pages, how her fluency had changed, and what meaning-based strategies she exhibited during the shared reading.

environment for this student. For this purpose, monitoring is required. The following case examples illustrate how this system may work.

There are many ways that various support strategies and interventions may be employed and monitored to determine their effectiveness. The MTSS team and individual teachers are limited only by their own experience and creativity. It is important, however, to follow a consistent format from which measurements may be taken and comparisons made with descriptions of the observable behaviors, the possible multilingual learner and disability explanations for those behaviors, the support strategies and interventions being used in both the home language and English, and the observed outcomes.

Building Capacity to Anticipate New Challenges

In time, as MTSS team members work together to build capacity, use of a creative process that generates innovative programming and interventions becomes the norm. Capacity building occurs mainly as teachers and other school professionals learn from each other. As this learning occurs, all team members find that they incorporate the knowledge sets and skills found in another's specialization into their own repertoire. Role flexibility comes from the full implementation of the MTSS team, as members pair up in nontraditional ways to address the needs of students in their schools. This collaboration fosters dynamic conversations leading to innovative suggestions for both systemic and specific changes in instruction.

With the ever-growing expectations and responsibilities laid on educators, the MTSS team can serve to support the students facing challenges and the teachers who have these students in their classrooms. It is clear that encouraging teamwork and collaboration throughout the school is a principal role for the MTSS team because no one individual or program can meet the needs of all students. In these ways the MTSS team can function as a catalyst for change, providing valuable impetus for the more equitable distribution of human, physical, and fiscal resources in schools.

Creating a Context for Assessment

The process and contexts we have been describing in this guide have been discussed and implemented in part or in alternative versions in various school settings. Discussed as versions of the flexible delivery model, a multi-tiered system of supports, the Iowa model, or the RtI model, these methods are all oriented toward school-based problem-solving and are consistent with our continuum of services framework. Any model that has been developed primarily with monolingual speakers of English in mind must be adapted to be beneficial to multilingual learners. Models used for multilingual learners should be broader in design and in implementation. In particular, they should stress the innovations necessary to create strong contextualized strategies that respect the authenticity of the concepts involved and are meaningful to the student. These strategies and interventions and should focus on outcomes that truly reflect authentic classroom performance rather than on splinter skills or abilities only tangentially related to the classroom. This focus is demonstrated in the two case studies just presented.

Whether implementing an RtI/MTSS approach that is somewhat narrow in scope or a flexible delivery model that broadly attempts to create methods to provide prompt services to different kinds of learners within the limits of the school's resources, it is essential to focus on the learning environment established for multilingual learners, the value of getting to know these students, the assessment principles described, and the framework discussed extensively in this guide. To address the needs of the multilingual learners, all possible innovations and research-supported practices should be considered as potential sources of implementation.

When an MTSS team embraces an RtI/MTSS approach or uses the broader flexible delivery model, a forum is established for contextualized assessment that is appropriate for multilingual learners and other learners in the school. When the team works on creating the most effective learning environment for multilingual learners, on learning support strategies and information gathering pertaining to the six integral factors, this is analogous to Tier 1 strategies in the RtI/MTSS model. Preparing the inventory of specific observable behaviors, brainstorming possible explanations, and then creating and implementing interventions that address both extrinsic and intrinsic possible explanations corresponds to Tier 2 of the RtI/MTSS model. When more intensive interventions are required for a group of students above and beyond all of those mentioned, the MTSS team is addressing Tier 3 of the model.

In Tier 3, it is likely that some of the students require further assessment as part of a full case study. The MTSS team and the processes we have suggested in this guidebook ensure a flexible model is used for further assessment through its cycle of brainstorming, implementing, assessing, and reflecting. Traditionally, multilingual learners have been given psychological and other assessments out of context and in a language they were still in the process of learning. We hope that the information we have presented has shed light on why this practice is unacceptable. Schools must engage all of the students' linguistic, cultural, and cognitive resources when administering any sort of assessment and must accept that the best results can be obtained with flexible assessment, interpretation, and intervention based on extensive knowledge about multilingual learners and the learning environment that we have created for them.

After Tier 3, those students who are still not making the progress that would be expected go on to have a case study evaluation. Case study assessments must be carried out bilingually, dynamically, and in a meaningful context; that is, strategies that have been suggested so far apply to this phase of the process as well. Multilingual learners who go on to a full case study evaluation take with them all the documentation collected throughout Tier 1, 2, and 3 interventions, as well as information on the six integral elements. This information provides a rich context for these case study assessments. If at this point students are found to need more intensive special education support, all the interventions implemented in students' home languages and English and the other information gathered allow staff to create programming that addresses the multilingual learner's unique linguistic and cultural needs while providing specialized support for the student's particular disabilities.

Benefits for All Learners

Many educators assert that understanding how multilingual learners learn and the application of such information to a broader student population will have positive effects on the achievement of all students. After all, a school that gives equally effective opportunities to all types of students is a school that offers an enriched education to every child and family. What is advocated in this guide is based on sound theory and practice and these principles and procedures are defensible, logical, and effective for all learners. The same six integral factors tend to apply to all learners, regardless of their language background. Rather than modifying an existing school system infrastructure to try to fit multilingual learner populations, it may be beneficial to look at recreating our schools so that all teachers emphasize elements such as academic language and literacy development across the curriculum, access to academic concepts and ideas, authentic assessment practices, culturally sustaining pedagogy, and school and community links that seek out families' funds of knowledge (González et al., 2005; Moll et al., 1992). Developing school environments that support educators by not only seeking out their expertise and perspectives, but also encouraging them to use their professional judgment, allows a school to anticipate and address potential difficulties while encouraging collaboration among professionals. This sort of environment benefits all students, not just multilingual learners.

Advocating to Change the System

The traditional method used in most schools to identify and serve multilingual learners with disabilities is rife with problems. In the past, multilingual learners had to wait to become proficient in English before being considered for any sort of learning support or they had to wait to fail before their difficulties were considered serious enough to require additional assistance. On the other hand, many multilingual learners were inappropriately placed in special education programs as a way to "get them some help." Neither approach has been successful in helping multilingual learners whose challenges do not fall neatly into preset categories. Supporting multilingual learners who are experiencing significant challenges in school is a complex process that requires that a continuum of both systemic and specific learning support strategies and interventions be employed, not simplistic or short-sighted one-size-fits-all approaches.

Advocacy to change the present system becomes an important activity for the MTSS team as well as all stakeholders. All staff who work with multilingual learners, including ESL and bilingual teachers, must build advocacy into their role as educators and their work as liaisons to multilingual learners' families and communities. Classroom teachers and special education staff members must also take on advocacy roles as they learn more about multilingual learners and become more flexible in providing support to these students through collaboration with ESL and bilingual teachers. It is clear that schools are becoming increasingly diverse, and the number of multilingual learners is growing every year. Because all educators have a moral and ethical responsibility to ensure an effective educational program for all multilingual learners and to secure appropriate methods of intervention for students who are experiencing academic difficulty, advocacy for change must come from all areas of the educational system.

Advocacy may take the form of fellow educators supporting one another. It may also involve constituents working with policy makers and those who allocate resources in the system to make certain that multilingual learners receive equitable learning experiences, as well as high-quality services and resources that allow them to dream and to make their dreams a reality. We hope that this guidebook is a useful resource in advocating for innovative and creative changes in school systems and promotes optimal learning opportunities for multilingual learners and indeed for all students.

Questions for Reflection and Action

1. Examine the RtI/MTSS framework used in your school or district in relation to the framework presented in this text. To what extent does the existing framework correspond to the framework advocated here?
2. Create a plan to validate and celebrate the pieces of the frameworks that do align and address those aspects of the existing framework that do not fit within the advocated framework.
3. How can you follow up on this plan to assess whether or not the strategy created to address the aspects needing improvement is successful?

Glossary

This glossary contains definitions of terms used in specialized ways in the text according to the usage understood in linguistics and education. Words appearing in bold italics in the glossary entries are defined in this glossary.

Academic language   The language found in a variety of academic texts; the language used in debates, poetry, and a wide range of oral discourse; the language of formal writing and discipline-specific discourse, vocabulary, and syntax found in math, literature, science, and social studies.

Acculturation process   A model of cultural adaptation that suggests that the individual moves through stages that may lead to choosing between the two cultures or adapting to find a balance between the two cultures.

Authentic assessment   Performance-based assessment of what students know and can do with content and language during actual tasks in authentic classroom-based contexts. Authentic assessments often stand in contrast to *norm-referenced* standardized *tests*.

Bi-level analysis paradigm   An operational framework for implementing *authentic assessment* that consists of an initial phase of descriptive analysis of the difficulties exhibited by a *multilingual learner*, followed by a detailed explanatory-analysis phase. This dual-phase process requires users to describe the language difficulties observed in the learner before determining why the student experiences these difficulties.

Bilingual education   An educational program in which instruction is provided in two languages. There are three prototypical kinds of bilingual education: (1) *transitional bilingual education*, (2) *maintenance* or one-way developmental *bilingual education*, and (3) *dual language education*, or two-way immersion. These types of bilingual education programs differ in their target populations, goals, program structures, and anticipated outcomes.

Code-mixing   Sometimes referred to as code-switching or code-meshing, the process of alternating use of two languages during the same conversational event. Although language learners may switch languages when a word or phrase is not immediately available, code switching typically shows more proficient use of both languages among bilingual speakers.

Common underlying proficiency (CUP) Within a model of language abilities, this refers to the deepest level of human processing attributes or capacity, which gives rise to all cognitive and linguistic abilities within an individual regardless of the language(s) used. This proposed attribute accounts for the fact that knowledge or skills that have been learned in one language may readily *transfer* to the second language.

Continuum of services framework A framework used to assess the learning challenges of multilingual learners that identifies appropriate systemic and specific support strategies and interventions to address those challenges, and monitors the learner's response to those interventions. This approach advocates *descriptive analysis* before *explanatory analysis* and the immediate provision of services independent of a formal categorization of the student as having a special education need.

Culturally sustaining pedagogy Instructional practices that sustain students' cultural and linguistic ways of being, especially for those groups who historically have been marginalized or erased. Incorporating students' home languages and cultures positively influences academic achievement and leads to deeper student engagement and connection to their schooling experience.

Descriptive analysis The first stage of analysis in the *continuum of services framework*. During this stage, the *multi-tiered system of supports (MTSS) team* collects information on the specific challenges exhibited by the *multilingual learner* to determine specific behaviors and tasks that are problems in the classroom. This step of the descriptive analysis yields an *inventory of specific observable behaviors (ISOB)*. At the same time, information is collected about characteristics of the student's home and school lives.

Discrepancy model A statistical approach to diagnosis that defines a *learning disability* as a specific discrepancy between intellectual ability (as measured by intelligence tests) and achievement as determined by a *norm-referenced test*. This traditional model stands in contrast to the *response to intervention (RtI)/multi-tiered system of supports (MTSS) model*, also known as the *dual discrepancy model* as well as the *continuum of services framework*.

Dual discrepancy model A description of the process that determines whether the child responds to scientific, research-based intervention; an example is the *response to intervention/multi-tiered system of supports model*. This alternative model stands in contrast to the traditional *discrepancy model*.

Dual language education A model or type of *bilingual education* that targets *multilingual learners* and English speakers who learn through two languages in integrated classes for at least 5 years. The goals are bilingualism, biliteracy, academic achievement through two languages, and cross-cultural competence. When multilingual learners and English-speaking students are in the program together these programs are referred to as *two-way immersion programs*.

Dynamic bilingualism The notion that a bilingual or multilingual person's languages interact continually so that the individual has constant access to their languages as they are used with different people in different contexts and for different purposes.

Early intervention services   Phrase used in the 2004 reauthorization of the *Individuals with Disabilities Education Improvement Act (IDEA)* that refers to addressing the needs of students and determining the need and eligibility for services on the basis of pre-referral interventions. This service model stands in contrast to *discrepancy models* used to place students into special education.

English language learners (ELLs)   Students in the United States who are learning English in addition to their home language or other languages they may speak. Also referred to as *English learners (ELs), bilingual learners, and multilingual learners (MLs)*. Previously referred to as *limited English proficient (LEP)*.

English as a second language (ESL)   Referring to programs or classes that target students identified as *multilingual learners*, with the goal of promoting the language development and social integration of these students. These programs are also referred to as *English as an additional language (EAL), English as a new language (ENL), and English for speakers of other languages (ESOL)*.

Explanatory analysis   The second stage of analysis in the *continuum of services framework*. In this stage the evaluator seeks to determine explanations for the challenges during the *descriptive analysis*.

Extrinsic   Refers to causal variables or factors located outside of the child. Generally accounted for, for example, by one of the six integral factors influencing *multilingual learners* at school (personal and family factors, physical and psychological factors, previous schooling, oral language and literacy development, academic performance, and cross-cultural factors). Extrinsic factors are to be contrasted with *intrinsic* factors.

Funds of knowledge   Areas of expertise that families, communities, or cultural groups have developed outside of school (for example, about professional or cultural practices). Educators can integrate and build on these areas of expertise in order to provide access to and make relevant the academic content that students are learning.

Individualized Education Program (IEP)   Federally mandated plan for school-based services provided to children with exceptionalities. These services must be developed jointly by the student's family and professional interventionists, based upon multidisciplinary assessment of the student, and include services to enhance the academic development of the student.

Individuals with Disabilities Education Improvement Act (IDEA)   Federal legislation enacted to ensure the rights and to provide appropriate and necessary public educational services to students with exceptionalities. Also known as the *Individuals with Disabilities Education Act (IDEA)*. First passed in 1975 as the Education Act for All Handicapped (PL 94-142) with subsequent re-authorizations (including 2004).

Intersectionality   The interconnected and overlapping nature of a person's identity that stems from various individual characteristics such as race, age, ethnicity, socioeconomic status, and gender. The reality of intersectionality results in certain groups of people being impacted by multiple social justice and human rights issues simultaneously.

Interventions Strategies   Used to address a student's observed learning difficulty. See *Tier 2 interventions, Tier 3 interventions, specific interventions, systemic interventions*.

Intrinsic   Refers to causal variables or factors located within the child. Generally accounted for by semiotic, processing, cognitive, or linguistic impairments. Intrinsic factors are to be contrasted with *extrinsic* factors.

Inventory of specific observable behaviors (ISOB)   A compiled list of all the specific challenges that a given student seems to be facing at school. This list can be generated from scratch based on *MTSS team* observations, or it can be based on a previously generated list and revised according to MTSS team observations.

Learning disability   Any of a variety of cognitive, perceptual, language, or mathematical disabilities that lead to difficulties in learning in an academic setting.

Multilingual learners (MLs)   Students in the United States who are learning English in addition to their home language or other languages they may speak. Also referred to as *English language learners (ELLs)*, *English learners (ELs)*, and *bilingual learners*. Previously referred to as *limited English proficient (LEP)*.

Multi-tiered system of supports (MTSS) team   A team of four or five individuals with expertise in *ESL/bilingual education*, monolingual English education, and special education. This team collaborates to gather information, interpret information, suggest support strategies and interventions (a *continuum of services*), and monitor the progress of the *multilingual learners* experiencing challenges at school.

Norm-referenced test   Standardized test designed to measure a particular skill or knowledge base wherein student scores are ranked by performance and distributed along a bell curve expressed in percentages, percentiles, or stanines.

Resistant to instruction/intervention   Designation, according to RtI/MTSS, for students who do not respond to instruction in the form of *Tier 2 interventions*. These students' *response to intervention* is assessed, and new interventions within the *continuum of services framework* are identified by the *MTSS team* and implemented in practice.

Response to intervention (RtI)/Multi-tiered system of supports (MTSS) model   A three-tiered framework that seeks to improve the learning environment for all students within the classroom by supporting both teachers and students and keeping track of the students who resist *interventions*. RtI/MTSS stands in contrast to the *discrepancy model*.

Sheltered instruction   Educational services that offer *English language learners* access to grade-level core content courses taught in English using instructional strategies designed to make the content concepts comprehensible while students are acquiring English. Such programs/classes are sometimes referred to as *sheltered English immersion (SEI)* or *specially designed academic instruction in English (SDAIE)*. The term *sheltered* *instruction* may also be used to describe actual instructional strategies (such as those designed to make content comprehensible to MLs in the academic mainstream) rather than to a program design.

Social language   Language used in highly contextualized situations during everyday conversation in face-to-face communication and in a variety of genres. This type of language may develop quickly and students will use it to engage with peers, on social media, and in academic and problem-solving tasks.

Specific interventions   Teaching designed to assist an individual student to overcome or cope with specific identified challenges in school.

Systemic interventions   Interventions designed to most appropriately address the challenges *multilingual learners* encounter in school. These interventions are generally applied systemwide, at the school or district level. It is possible that these systemic interventions may lead to policy changes that affect education at an even more extensive level.

Teacher Assistance Team   School-based problem-solving team designed to combine the knowledge and expertise of the team members in a collaborative fashion to meet the needs of students in general education who are experiencing academic difficulties. Also known as *student support teams* or *student services teams*, they are intended to be a general education initiative for problem-solving prior to special education alternatives. We refer to these teams as **MTSS teams** in this book.

Tier 1   In the RTI/MTSS approach, Tier 1 or core instructional learning environments, should be accessible to all students and include large- and small-group instruction.

Tier 2 interventions   Within the *response to intervention (RtI)/multi-tiered system of supports (MTSS)* approach. A Tier 2 small-group intervention is provided to students in addition to their core instruction. Tier 2 support may be temporary and resolve the difficulties students experience and allow them to function successfully in the core instructional environment.

Tier 3 interventions   Within the *response to intervention (RtI)/multi-tiered system of supports (MTSS)* approach. A Tier 3 intervention may be composed of specialized individualized interventions for students with significant needs. This level of support is the most intensive and occurs in addition to core instruction and Tier 2 support. It is often offered as a one-on-one intervention.

Transfer   Process wherein knowledge and skills learned in one language are applied in the other language. Learners may do this naturally, by themselves, or the teacher can point out similarities and differences between learners' two languages. Transfer can be positive and help the learner (as in the area of cognates), or transfer can be negative and result in errors or interference, as in incorrect word order, or false cognates in the new language.

Universal Design for Learning (UDL)   An educational framework that combines theories of pedagogy, neuroscience, and developmental psychology in order to create flexible learning environments to accommodate individual learning differences and improve and optimize teaching and learning for all.

References

Abedi, J., Hofstetter, C. H., & Lord, C. (2004). Assessment accommodations for English language learners: Implications for policy-based empirical research. *Review of Educational Research, 74*, 1–28.

Afflerbach, P. (2007). *Understanding and using reading assessment, K–12*. Newark, DE: International Reading Association.

Afflerbach, P., Pearson, P. D., & Paris, S. G. (2008). Clarifying differences between reading skills and reading strategies. *Reading Teacher, 61*, 364–373.

Agar, M. (2013). *The lively science. Remodeling human social research*. Minneapolis, MN: Mill City Press.

Ahlsén, E. (2005). Argumentation with restricted linguistic ability: Performing a role play with aphasia or in a second language. *Clinical Linguistics & Phonetics, 19*(5), 433–451.

Alami, A., Khosravan, S.,Moghadam, L. S., Pakravan, F & Hosseini, F. (2014). Adolescent self-esteem in single and two-parent families NCBI-NIH (Electronic version). International Journal of Community Based Nursing and Midwifery, 2(2), 69.

Aldana, U. S. & Martinez, D. C. (2018). The development of a community of practice for educators working with newcomer, Spanish-speaking students. *Theory Into Practice, 57*(2), 137–146.

Allington, R. L. (2002a). Research on reading/learning disability interventions. In A. E. Farstrup & S. J. Samuels (Eds.), *What research says about reading instruction* (3rd ed., pp. 261–290). Newark, DE: International Reading Association.

Allington, R. L. (2002b). *Big brother and the national reading curriculum: How ideology trumped evidence*. Portsmouth, NH: Heinemann.

Allington, R. L. (2006). *What really matters for struggling readers: Designing research-based programs* (2nd ed.). Portsmouth, NH: Heinemann.

Allington, R. L. (2009). *What really matters in response to intervention*. Boston: Pearson.

Allington, R. L., & Nowak, R. (2004). "Proven programs" and other unscientific ideas. In C. C. Block, D. Lapp, E. J. Cooper, J. Flood, N. Roser, & J. V. Tinajero (Eds.), *Teaching all the children: Strategies for developing literacy in an urban setting* (pp. 93–102). New York: Guilford.

Allington, R. L., & Walmsley, S. A. (1995). *No quick fix: Rethinking literacy programs in America's elementary schools*. New York: Teachers College Press.

Allington, R. L., & Walmsley, S. A. (2007). *No quick fix: Rethinking literacy programs in America's elementary schools. The RtI edition*. New York: Teachers College Press.

Alsop, P., & McCaffrey, T. (Eds.). (1993). *How to cope with childhood stress: A practical guide for teachers*. Harlow, UK: Longman.

Altman, C., Armon-Lotem, S., Fichman, S., & Walters, J. (2016). Macrostructure, microstructure and mental state terms in the narratives on English–Hebrew bilingual preschool children with and without specific language impairment. *Applied Psycholinguistics, 37*(1), 165–193.

Alvermann, D. (1991). The discussion web: A graphic aid for learning across the curriculum. *Reading Teacher, 45*, 92–99.

Alves, D.C. (2019). Oral language. In J. S. Damico & M. J. Ball (Eds.), *The SAGE encyclopedia of human communicative sciences and disorders* (pp. 1285–1289). Thousand Oaks, CA: Sage.

American Psychiatric Association. (2013). *Diagnostic and statistical manual of mental disorders* (5th ed.). Washington, DC: American Psychiatric Press.

Anastasi, A., & Urbiba, S. (1997). *Psychological testing* (7th ed.). Englewood Cliffs, NJ: Prentice–Hall.

Anderson-Levitt, K. M. (2003). *Local meanings, global schooling: Anthropology and world culture theory*. New York: Palgrave Macmillan.

Andrade, H. L., & Heritage, M. (2017). *Using formative assessment to enhance learning, achievement, and academic self-regulation*. New York: Routledge, Taylor & Francis Group.

Antón, E., Thierry, G., Goborov, A., Anasagasti, J., & Duñabeitia, J. A. (2016). Testing bilingual educational methods: A plea to end the language-mixing taboo. *Language Learning, 66*(S2), 29–50.

Archibald, L. (2017). SLP-educator classroom collaboration: A review to inform reason-based practice. *Autism & Developmental Language Impairments, 2*, 1–17.

Archibald, L., & Vollebregt, M. (2019). Collaboration in speech–language therapy. In J. S. Damico & M. J. Ball (Eds.), *The SAGE encyclopedia of human communicative sciences and disorders* (pp 417–422). Thousand Oaks, CA: Sage.

Armstrong, E. (2005). Language disorder: A functional linguistic perspective. *Clinical Linguistics & Phonetics, 19*(3), 137–153.

Arnold, D. H., & Doctoroff, G. L. (2003). The early education of socioeconomically disadvantaged children. *Annual Review of Psychology, 54*, 517–545.

Arrow, A. W., Chapman, J. W., & Greaney, K. T. (2015). Meeting the needs of beginning readers through differentiated instruction. In W. E. Tunmer & J. W. Chapman (Eds.), *Excellence and equity in literacy education: The case of New Zealand* (pp. 171–193). London, UK: Palgrave MacMillan.

Artiles, A., Dorn, S., & Bal, A. (2016). Objects of protection, enduring nodes of difference: Disability intersections with "other" differences, 1916-2016. *Review of Research in Education, 40*(1), 277–820.

Artiles, A. J. (2015). Beyond responsiveness to identity badges: Future research on culture in disability and implications for response to intervention. *Educational Review, 67*, 1–22.

Artiles, A. J. (2019). Understanding practice and intersectionality in teacher education in the age of diversity and inequality. *Teachers College Record, 121*(6), 1–6. Retrieved from http://www.tcrecord.org/Content.asp?ContentId=22682

Artiles, A. J., Kozleski, E, B., Trent, S. C., Osher, D. & Ortiz, A. (2010). Justifying and Explaining Disproportionality, 1968–2008: A Critique of Underlying Views of Culture. *Exceptional Children, 76* (3), 279-299.

Artiles, A. J., & Ortiz, A. A. (2002). *English language learners with special education needs: Identification, assessment and instruction.* McHenry, IL: Delta Systems.

Ascenzi-Moreno, L. (2018). Translanguaging and responsive assessment adaptations: Emergent bilingual readers through the lens of possibility. *Language Arts, 95*, 355–369.

Asgedom, M. (2002). *Of beetles and angels: A boy's remarkable journey from a refugee camp to Harvard.* New York: Little, Brown.

Asgedom, M. (2003). *The code: The five secrets of teen success.* New York: Little, Brown.

Asher, N. (2007). Made in the (multicultural) U.S.A.: Unpacking tensions of race, culture, gender, and sexuality in education. *Educational Researcher, 36*(2), 65–73.

August, D. (2012). How does first language literacy relate to second language literacy development? In E. Hamayan & R. Freeman Field (Eds.), *English language learners at school: A guide for administrators* (2nd ed., pp. 56–57). Philadelphia, PA: Caslon.

August, D. & Shanahan, T. (2008). *Developing reading and writing in second-language learners: Lessons from the Report of the National Literacy Panel on Minority-Language Children and Youth.* New York: Routledge.

August, L. R., & Gianola. B. A. (1987). Symptoms of war trauma-induced psychiatric disorders: Southeast Asian refugees and Vietnam veterans. *International Migration Review, 21*, 820–832.

Babatsouli, E. (2021). Diversity considerations in speech and language disorders: A focus on training. In J. S. Damico, N. Müller, & M. J. Ball (Eds), *The Handbook of Language and Speech Disorders.* (2nd ed., pp. 33–52). Oxford, UK: Wiley-Blackwell.

Babatsouli, E., Ingram, D., & Müller, N. (Eds.). (2017). *Crosslinguistic encounters in language acquisition: Typical and atypical development.* Bristol, UK: Multilingual Matters.

Bachman, H. J., Elliott, L., Scott, P. W., & Navarro, M. G. (2020). Latino children's academic and behavioral trajectories in early elementary school: Examining home language differences within preschool types. *Early Childhood Research Quarterly, 52*, Part A, 138–153.

Bahr, M., Fuchs, D., & Fuchs, L. S. (1999). Mainstream assistance teams: A consultation-based approach to prereferral intervention. In S. Graham & K. Harris (Eds.), *Working together* (pp. 87–116). Cambridge, MA: Brookline Books.

Bailey, A. L. (2006). From lambie to lambaste: The conceptualization, operationalization and use of academic language in the assessment of ELL students. In K. Rolstad (Ed.), *Rethinking school language.* Mahwah, NJ: Lawrence Erlbaum.

Bailey, A. L. (Ed.). (2007). *The language demands of school: Putting academic English to the test.* New Haven, CT: Yale University Press.

Bailey, F., & Pransky, K. (2005). Are "other people's children" constructivist learners too? *Theory into Practice, 44*(1), 19–26.

Bak, T. H. (2016). Cooking pasta in La Paz: Bilingualism, bias and the replication crisis. *Linguistic Approaches to Bilingualism,* 1–19.

Baker, C. (2011). *Foundations of bilingual education and bilingualism* (5th ed.). Clevedon, UK: Multilingual Matters.

Bakhtin, M. M. (1981). *The dialogic imagination: Four essays* (M. Holquist, Trans.). Austin: University of Texas Press.

Baltaci, A. (2017). Relations between prejudice, cultural intelligence and level of entrepreneurship: A study of school principals. *International Electronic Journal of Elementary Education, 9*(3), 645–666.

Banks, J. (2001). *Multicultural education: Issues and perspectives.* New York: John Wiley & Sons.

Banks, J. (2005). *Cultural diversity and education: Foundations, curriculum, and teaching* (5th ed.). Boston: Pearson.

Barac, R., Bialystok, E., Castro, D. C., & Sanchez, M. (2014). The cognitive development of young dual language learners: A critical review. *Early Childhood Research Quarterly, 29*(4), 699–714.

Barnes, A. C., & Harlacher, J. E. (2008). Clearing the confusion: Response-to-intervention as a set of principles. *Education and Treatment of Children, 31,* 417–431.

Bartolo, P. A., Dockrell, J., & Lunt, I. (2001). Naturalistic decision-making task processes in multiprofessional assessment of disability. *Journal of School Psychology, 39*(4), 499–519.

Bassok, D., Finch, J. E., Soonchunhyang R., Reardon, S. F., & Waldfogel, J. (2016). Socioeconomic gaps in early childhood experiences: 1998 to 2010. *AERA Open, 2* (3), 1–22.

Bassok, D., & Galdo, E. (2016). Inequality in preschool quality? Community-level disparities in access to high-quality learning environments. *Early Education and Development, 27*(1), 128–144.

Bedore, L. M., Peña, E. D., García, M., & Cortez, C. (2005). Conceptual versus monolingual scoring: When does it make a difference? *Language, Speech, and Hearing in Schools, 36,* 188–120.

Beeman, K., & Urow, C. (2013). *Teaching for biliteracy: Strengthening bridges between languages.* Philadelphia, PA: Caslon.

Bennett, C. (2011). *Comprehensive multicultural education: Theory and practice* (7th ed.). Boston, MA: Pearson.

Berliner, D. C., & Biddle, B. J. (1995). *The manufactured crisis: Myth, fraud and the attack on America's public schools.* Reading, MA: Perseus Books.

Berquist, E. (2017). *UDL: Moving from exploration to integration.* Wakefield, MA: CAST Professional Publishing.

Berry, J. W., Poortinga, Y. H., Segall, M. H., & Dasen, P. R. (2002). *Cross-cultural psychology: Research and applications.* New York: Cambridge University Press.

Bettini, E., & Park, Y. (2021). Novice teachers' experiences in high-poverty schools: An integrative literature review. *Urban Education, 56,* 3–31.

Bhat, P., Rapport, M. J. K., & Griffin, C. C. (2000). A legal perspective on the use of specific reading methods for students with learning disabilities. *Learning Disability Quarterly, 23,* 283–297.

Bialystock, E. (2001). *Bilingualism in development: Language, literacy and cognition.* Cambridge, UK: Cambridge University Press.

Bialystok, E. (2015). Bilingualism and the development of executive function: The role of attention. *Child Development Perspectives, 9*(2), 117–121.

Bialystok, E. (2018). Bilingual education for young children: Review of the effects and consequences. *International Journal of Bilingual Education and Bilingualism, 21,* 666–679.

Bialystok, E., Luk, G., Peets, K. F., & Yang, S. (2010). Receptive vocabulary differences in monolingual and bilingual children. *Bilingualism: Language and Cognition, 13*(4), 525–531.

Bialystok, E., Peets, K. F., & Moreno, S. (2014). Producing bilinguals through immersion education: Development of metalinguistic awareness. *Applied Psycholinguistics 35,* 177–191.

Blackburn, C. (1991). *Poverty and health: Working with families.* Buckingham, UK: Open University Press.

Blitz, L. V., Yull, D., & Clauhs, M. (2016). Bringing sanctuary to school: Assessing school climate as a foundation for culturally responsive trauma-informed approaches for urban schools. *Urban Education, 55*(1), 95–124.

Blosser, J. L. (1990). A strategic planning process for service delivery changes. *Best Practices in School Speech-Language Pathology, 1,* 81–88.

Bode, B. A. (1989). Dialogue journal writing. *Reading Teacher, 42*(8), 568–571.

Boerma, T., & Blom, E. (2017). Assessment of bilingual children: What if testing both languages is not possible? *Journal of Communication Disorders, 66,* 65–76.

Bolger, K. E., Patterson, C. J., Thomson, W. W. M., & Kuper-smidt, J. B. (1995). Psychosocial adjustment among children experiencing persistent and intermittent family economic hardship. *Child Development, 66,* 1107–1129.

Bower, J. M., van Kraayenoord, C., & Carroll, A. (2015). Building social connectedness in schools: Australian teachers' perspectives. *International Journal of Educational Research, 70,* 101–109.

Boyd, J. K., & Goldberg, A. E. (2009). Input effects within a constructionist framework. *Modern Language Journal, 93*(3), 418–429.

Bradley, R. H., & Corwyn, R. F. (2002). Socioeconomic status and child development. *Annual Review of Psychology, 53*, 371–399.

Bransford, J. D., Brown, A. L., & Cocking, R. R. (Eds.). (2000). *How people learn: Brain, mind, experience, and school.* Washington, DC: National Academy Press.

Brantlinger, E. (1997). Using ideology: Cases of nonrecognition of the politics of research and practice in special education. *Review of Educational Research, 64*, 425–459.

Brinton, B., & Fujiki, M. (1994). Ways to teach conversation. In J. Duchan, L. Hewitt, & R. Sonnenmeier (Eds.), *Pragmatics: From theory to practice* (pp. 59–71). Englewood Cliffs, NJ: Prentice-Hall.

Brinton, B., & Fujiki, M. (2010). Principles of assessment and intervention. In J. S. Damico, N. Müller, & M. J. Ball (Eds.), *The handbook of language and speech disorders* (pp. 131–150). Chichester, UK: Wiley-Blackwell.

Bronfenbrenner, U. (1979). *The ecology of human development.* Cambridge, MA: Harvard University Press.

Brown, J. E., & Doolittle, J. (2008). A cultural, linguistic, and ecological framework for Response to Intervention with English Language Learners. *Teaching Exceptional Children, 41*(3), 66–72.

Brown, P. (1995). Naming and framing: The social construction of diagnosis and illness. *Journal of Health and Social Behavior 35*, 34–52.

Brown, R. W. (1973). *A first language: The early stages.* Cambridge, MA: Harvard University Press.

Brown, S., & Souto-Manning, M. 2008. Culture is the way they live here: Young Latinos and parents navigate linguistic and cultural borderlands in U.S. Schools. *Journal of Latinos and Education 7*(1), 25–42.

Brown-Jeffy, S., & Cooper, J. E. (2012). Toward a conceptual framework of culturally relevant pedagogy: An overview of the conceptual and theoretical literature. *Teacher Education Quarterly, 38*(1), 65-84.

Bruner, J. S. (1981). The social context of language acquisition. *Language and Communication, 1*, 155–178.

Bruner, J. S. (1983). *In search of mind: Essays in autobiography.* New York NY: Harper-Row.

Bruner, J. S. (1996). *The culture of education.* Cambridge, UK: Blackwell.

Bruner, J. S. (Ed.). (2006). The selected works of Jerome S. Bruner. *In search of pedagogy* (Vol. I). New York, NY: Routledge.

Bruner, J. S. (2008). Culture and mind: Their fruitful incommensurability. *Ethos, 36*(1), 29–45.

Brunzell, T., Stokes, H., & Waters, L. (2019). Shifting teacher practice in trauma-affected classrooms: Practice pedagogy strategies within a trauma-informed positive education model. *School Mental health, 11*(3), 600–614.

Bunce, B. (2003). Children with culturally diverse backgrounds. In L. McCormick, D. F. Loeb, & R. L. Schiefelbusch (Eds.), *Supporting children with communication difficulties in inclusive settings* (2nd ed., pp. 367–408). Boston: Pearson Education.

Bussing, R., Schoenberg, N. E., & Perwien, A. R. (1998). Knowledge and information about ADHD: Evidence of cultural differences among African-American and white parents. *Social Science and Medicine, 64*, 919–928.

Cabrera, N. L., Milem, J. F., Jaquette, O., & Marx, R. W. (2014). Missing the (student achievement) forest for all the (political) trees: Empiricism and the 34 Mexican American studies controversy in Tucson. *American Educational Research Journal, 51*(6), 1084–1118.

Caesar, L. G., & Kohler, P. D. (2007). The state of school-based bilingual assessment: Actual practice versus recommended guidelines. *Language, Speech, and Hearing Services in Schools, 38*(3), 190–200.

Calderón, M., Slavin, R., & Sánchez, M. (2011). Effective instruction for English learners. *Future of Children, 21*(1), 103–127.

Calkins, S.D. (Ed.). (2015). *Handbook of infant biopsychosocial development.* New York, NY: Guilford.

Callahan, R.M. (2005). Tracking and high school English learners: Limiting opportunity to learn. *American Educational Research Journal, 42*(2), 305–328.

Callahan, R. M., & Gándara, P. C. (2014). *The bilingual advantage: Language, literacy and the U.S. labor market.* Tonawanda, NY: Multilingual Matters.

Cambourne, B. (2002). Conditions for literacy learning. Is learning natural? *Reading Teacher, 55*, 758–762.

Cambourne, B., & Turbill, J. (Eds.). (1994). *Responsive evaluation: Making judgments about student literacy.* Portsmouth, NH: Heinemann.

Capp, R., Fix, M., Murray, J., Ost, J., Passel, J., & Herwantoro, S. (2005). *The new demography of America's school immigration and the no child left behind act.* Washington, DC: The Urban Institute. Retrieved from http://www.urban.org/UploadedPDF/311230_new_demography.pdf

Cardenas-Hagan, E., Carlson, C. D., & Pollard-Durodola, S. D. (2007). The cross-linguistic transfer of early literacy skills: The role of initial L1 and L2 skills and language of instruction. *Language, Speech, and Hearing Services in Schools, 38*(3), 249–259.

Carhill, A., Suárez-Orozco, C., & Páez, M. (2008). Explaining English language proficiency among adolescent immigrant students. *American Educational Research Journal, 45*(4), 1155–1179.

Carlson, V. J., & Harwood, R. L. (1999). Understanding and negotiating cultural differences concerning early developmental competence: The sixth raisin solution. *Zero to Three, 20,* 20–23.

Carneiro, R. (2007). The big picture: Understanding learning and meta-learning challenges. *European Journal of Education, 42*(2), 151–172.

Carroll, J. B. (1997). Psychometrics, intelligence and public perception. *Intelligence, 24,* 25–52.

Carter, P. L. (2003). "Black" cultural capital, status positioning, and schooling conflicts for low-income African American youth. *Social Problems, 50,* 136–155.

Carter, P. L. (2006). Straddling boundaries: Identity, culture, and school. *Sociology of Education, 79*(4), 304–328.

CASEL. (2017). *Key insights from the Collaborating Districts Initiative.* Chicago, IL: CASEL.

CAST. (2018). Universal Design for Learning Guidelines version 2.2. Retrieved from http://udlguidelines.cast.org

Centers for Disease Control (CDC). (2012). Minority health, United States. Retrieved from http://www.cdc.gov/

Chaikind, S., Danielson, L. C., & Brauen, M. L. (1993). What do we know about the costs of special education? A selected review. *Journal of Special Education, 26,* 344–370.

Chakrabarti, S., & Fombonne, E. (2001). Pervasive developmental disorders in preschool children. *Journal of the American Medical Association, 285,* 3093–3099.

Chalfant, J., & Pysh, M. (1989). Teacher assistance teams: Five descriptive studies on 96 teams. *Remedial & Special Education, 10*(6), 49–58.

Chalfant, J. C., Pysh, M. V., & Moultrie, R. (1979). Teacher assistance teams: A model for within building problem solving. *Learning Disability Quarterly, 2,* 85–95.

Chandler, M. K., Dunaway, C., Levine, D., & Damico, J. (2005, November). *Serving students with language learning disorders collaboratively: A transdisciplinary model.* A mini-seminar presented at the annual meeting of the American Speech–Language–Hearing Association, San Diego, CA.

Chapman, J. W., Greaney, K. T., & Tunmer, W. E. (2015). Is Reading Recovery an effective early intervention programme for those who need literacy supports? In W. E. Tunmer & J. W. Chapman (Eds.), *Excellence and equity in literacy education: The case of New Zealand* (pp. 41–70). London, UK: Palgrave Macmillan.

Chappell, S. V., & Faltis, C. J. (2013). *The arts and emergent bilingual youth: Building culturally responsive, critical and creative education in school and community contexts.* New York, NY: Routledge.

Chappuis, J., Stiggins, R., Chappuis, S., & Arter, J. (2012). *Classroom assessment for student learning: Doing it right—using it well.* Boston, MA: Pearson

Charles, M. (2008). Culture and inequality: Identity, ideology, and difference in "postascriptive society." *Annals of the American Academy of Political and Social Science, 619,* 41–58.

Cheadle, J. E. (2008). Educational investment, family context, and children's math and reading growth from kindergarten through the third grade. *Sociology of Education, 81*(1), 1–31.

Chhuon, V., & Hudley, C. (2010). Asian American ethnic options: How Cambodian students negotiate ethnic identities in a U.S. urban school. *Anthropology and Education Quarterly, 41,* 341–359.

Chiang, M. (2016). Effects of varying text difficulty levels on second language (L2) reading attitudes and reading comprehension. *Journal of Research in Reading, 39,* 448-468.

Cho, H. (2016). Formal and informal academic language socialization of a bilingual child, *International Journal of Bilingual Education and Bilingualism, 19*(4), 387–407.

Chow, P., & Cummins, J. (2005). Affirming identity in multi-lingual classrooms. *Educational Leadership: Whole Child, 63*(1), 38–43.

Christiansen, M. H., Chater, N., & Culicover, P. W. (2016). *Creating language: Integrating evolution, acquisition, and processing.* Cambridge, MA: MIT Press.

Chudgar, A., & Luschei, T. F. (2009). National income, income inequality, and the importance of schools: A hierarchical cross-national comparison. *American Educational Research Journal, 46*(3), 626–658.

Cirino, P. T., Vaughn, S., Linan-Thompson, S., Cardenas-Hagan, E., Fletcher, J. M., & Francis, D. J. (2009). One-year follow-up outcomes of Spanish and English interventions for English language learners at risk for reading problems. *American Educational Research Journal, 46*(3), 744–781. Retrieved from https://doi.org/10.3102/0002831208330214

Clay, M. (1985). *Early detection of reading difficulties.* Portsmouth, NH: Heinemann.

Clay, M. (1991). *Becoming literate: The construction of inner control.* Portsmouth, NH: Heinemann.

Clay, M. (1993). *Reading recovery: A guidebook for teachers in training.* Auckland, NZ: Heinemann.

Clay, M. M., & Tuck, B. (1991). *A study of reading recovery subgroups: Including outcomes for children who did not satisfy discontinuing criteria.* Auckland, NZ: University of Auckland.

Cloud, N. (1994). Special education needs of second language students. In F. Genesee (Ed.), *Educating second language children: The whole child, the whole curriculum, the whole community* (pp. 243–277). New York, NY: Cambridge University Press.

Cloud, N. (2012). How can we best serve English language learners who do have special needs, such as a disability? In E. Hamayan & R. Freeman Field (Eds.), *English language learners at school: A guide for administrators* (2nd ed., pp. 205–207). Philadelphia, PA: Caslon.

Cloud, N., Genesee, F., & Hamayan, E. (2009). *Literacy instruction for English language learners. A teacher's guide to research-based practices.* Portsmouth, NH: Heinemann.

Cloud, N., Lakin, J., Leininger, E., & Maxwell, L. (2010). *Teaching adolescent English language learners. Essential strategies for middle and high school.* Philadelphia, PA: Caslon.

Coelho, E. (1994). *Learning together in the multicultural classroom.* Markham, Canada: Pippin.

Collier, C. (2010). *RtI for diverse learners.* Thousand Oaks, CA: Corwin.

Collier, V., & Thomas, W. (2017a). *Why dual language schooling.* Albuquerque, NM: Fuente Press.

Collier, V. P., & Thomas, W.P. (2017b). Validating the power of bilingual schooling: Thirty-two years of large-scale, longitudinal research. *Annual Review of Applied Linguistics, 37,* 1–15.

Collins, B. A., O'Connor, E. E., Suárez-Orozco, C., Nieto-Castañon, A., & Toppelberg, C. O. (2014). Dual language profiles of Latino children of immigrants: Stability and change over the early school years. *Applied Psycholinguistics, 35*(3), 581–620.

Collins, H. M. (1998). Socialness and the undersocialized conception of society. *Science, Technology, & Human Values, 23,* 494–516.

Collins, P. H., & Bilge, S. (2016). *Intersectionality.* Cambridge, UK: Polity Press.

Commeyras, M. (2007). Scripted reading instruction? What's a teacher educator to do? *Phi Delta Kappan, 88,* 404–407.

Commins, N. (2012). What are defining features of effective programs for English language learners? In E. Hamayan & R. Freeman Field (Eds.), *English language learners at school: A guide for administrators* (2nd ed., pp. 98–100). Philadelphia, PA: Caslon.

Commins, N. L., & Miramontes, O. B. (2005). *Linguistic diversity and teaching.* Mahwah, NJ: Lawrence Erlbaum.

Connor, C. M., Piasta, S. B., Fishman, B., Glasney, S., Schatschneider, C., Crowe, E., Underwood, P., & Morrison, F. J. (2009). Individualizing student instruction precisely: Effects of child × instruction interactions on first graders' literacy development. *Child Development, 80*(1), 77–100.

Connor, D. J., & Ferri, B. A. (2005). Integration and inclusion: A troubling nexus: Race, disability, and special education. *Journal of African American History, 90*(1/2), 107–127.

Conrad, P. (2007). *The medicalization of society.* Baltimore, MD: The Johns Hopkins University.

Cook, G., Linquanti, R., Chinen, M., & Jung, H. (2012). *National evaluation of Title III implementation supplemental report: Exploring approaches to setting English language proficiency performance criteria and monitoring English learner progress.* Washington, DC: U.S. Department of Education, Office of Planning, Evaluation and Policy Development.

Cook, G. I., Marsh, R. L., & Hicks, J. L. (2003). Halo and devil effects demonstrate valenced-based influences on source-monitoring decisions. *Conscious Cognition, 12*(2), 257–278.

Cook, H. G., Boals, T., & Lundberg, T. (2011). Academic achievement for English learners: What can we reasonably expect? *Phi Delta Kappan, 93*(3), 66–69. Retrieved from: https://doi.org/10.1177/003172171109300316

Corsaro, W. A., & Nelson, E. (2003). Children's collective activities and peer culture in early literacy in American and Italian preschools. *Sociology of Education, 76,* 209–227.

Cousins, J. H., Power, T. G., & Olvera-Ezzell, N. (1993). Mexican-American mothers' socialization strategies: Effects of education, acculturation, and health locus of control. *Journal of Experimental Child Psychology, 55,* 258–276.

Cowie, H. (2019). *From birth to sixteen: Children's health, social, emotional and linguistic development* (2nd ed.). New York, NY: Routledge.

Cox, B. E., & Hopkins, C. J. (2006). Theory and research into practice: Building on theoretical principles gleaned from reading recovery to reform classroom practice. *Reading Research Quarterly, 41,* 245–267.

Crago, M., & Paradis, J. (2003). Two of a kind? Commonalities and variation in languages and language learners. In Y. Levy & J. Schaeffer (Eds.), *Language competence across populations: Towards a definition of specific language impairment* (pp. 97–110). Mahwah, NJ: Lawrence Erlbaum.

Crandall, J., with Stein, H., & Nelson, J. (2012). What kinds of knowledge and skills do general education teachers, English as a second language teachers, bilingual teachers, and support staff need to implement an effective program for English language learners? In E. Hamayan & R. Freeman Field (Eds.), *English language learners at school: A guide for administrators* (2nd ed., pp. 9–17). Philadelphia, PA: Caslon.

Creese, A. (2009). Building on young people's linguistic and cultural continuity: Complementary schools in the United Kingdom. *Theory into Practice, 48*(4), 267–273.

Creese, A., & Blackledge, A. (2010). Translanguaging in the bilingual classroom: A pedagogy for learning and teaching? *Modern Language Journal, 94*(1), 103–115.

Crenshaw, K. W. (1989). Demarginalizing the intersection of race and sex: A Black feminist critique of antidiscrimination doctrine, feminist theory, and antiracist politics. *University of Chicago Legal Forum, 139,* 139–167.

Crenshaw, K. (2022). On Intersectionality: Essential Writings. New York: The New Press.

Cronbach, L. J. (1957). The two disciplines of scientific psychology. *American Psychologist, 12,* 671–684.

Cronbach, L. J. (1975). Beyond the two disciplines of scientific psychology. *American Psychologist, 30,* 116–127.

Crowe, L. (2003). Comparison of two reading feedback strategies in improving the oral and written language performance of children with language-learning disabilities. *American Journal of Speech–Language Pathology, 12,* 16–27.

Cuero, K. K. (2010). Artisan with words: Transnational funds of knowledge in a bilingual Latina's stories. *Language Arts, 87*(6), 427–436.

Culotta, B. (1994). Representational play and story enactments: Formats for language intervention. In J. Duchan, L. Hewitt, & R. Sonnenmeier (Eds.), *Pragmatics: From theory to practice* (pp. 105–119). Englewood Cliffs, NJ: Prentice-Hall.

Cummins, J. (1984). *Bilingualism and special education: Issues in assessment and pedagogy.* Clevedon, UK: Multilingual Matters.

Cummins, J. (1996). *Negotiating identities: Education for empowerment in a diverse society.* Sacramento, CA: California Association for Bilingual Education.

Cummins, J. (2000). *Language, power and pedagogy: Bilingual children in the crossfire.* Clevedon, UK: Multilingual Matters.

Cummins, J. (2007). Pedagogies for the poor? Realigning reading instruction for low-income students with scientifically based reading research. *Educational Researcher, 36,* 564–572.

Cummins, J. (2008). Teaching for transfer: Challenging the two solitudes assumption in bilingual education. In J. Cummins & N. H. Hornberger (Eds.), *Encyclopedia of language and education*, Volume 5: Bilingual Education (2nd ed., pp. 65–76). New York, NY: Springer.

Cummins, J. (2012). How long does it take for an English language learner to become proficient in a second language? In E. Hamayan & R. Freeman Field (Eds.), *English language learners at school: A guide for administrators* (2nd ed., pp. 37–39). Philadelphia, PA: Caslon.

Cummins, J. & Early, M. (2011). Identity texts: The collaborative creation of power in multilingual schools. London: Trentham Books.

Cunningham, P. M., & Allington, R.L. (2011). *Classrooms that work. They can all read and write.* Boston, MA: Pearson.

Dahl, K. L., Scharer, P. L., Lawson, L. L., & Grogan, P. R. (1999). Phonics instruction and student achievement in whole language first-grade classrooms. *Reading Research Quarterly, 34,* 312–341.

Damico, H. L., Damico, J. S., & Nelson, R. L. (2021). Literacy and literacy disorders. In J. S. Damico, N. Müller, & M. J. Ball (Eds.), *The handbook of language and speech disorders* (2nd ed., pp. 237–265). Oxford, UK: Wiley-Blackwell.

Damico, H. L., Damico, J. S., Nelson, R. L., Weill, C., & Maxwell, J. (2017). Infusing meaning and joy back into books: Reclaiming literacy in the treatment of young children with autism spectrum disorder. In R. J. Meyer & K. F. Whitmore (Eds.), *Reclaiming early childhood literacies: Narratives of hope, power, and vision* (pp. 109–119). New York, NY: Routledge.

Damico, J. S. (1987). Addressing language concerns in the schools: The SLP as consultant. *Journal of Childhood Communication Disorders, 11*(1), 17–40.

Damico, J. S. (1991). Descriptive assessment of communicative ability in limited English proficient students. In E. V. Hamayan & J. S. Damico (Eds.), *Limiting bias in the assessment of bilingual students* (pp. 157–218). Austin, TX: PRO-ED.

Damico, J. S. (2003). The role of theory in clinical practice: Reflections on model building. *Advances in Speech–Language Pathology, 5,* 57–60.

Damico, J. S. (2006). *Shared reading with the exceptional child.* Portland, OR: National CEU. Retrieved from http://modavox.com/nationalceu

Damico, J. S. (2019a). Descriptive assessment. In J. S. Damico & M. J. Ball (Eds.)., *The SAGE encyclopedia of human communicative sciences and disorders* (pp. 566–572). Thousand Oaks, CA: Sage.

Damico, J. S. (2019b). Anchored assessment. In J. S. Damico & M. J. Ball (Eds.), *The SAGE encyclopedia of human communicative sciences and disorders.* (pp 135–139). Thousand Oaks, CA: Sage.

Damico, J. S. (2019c). Labeling of communicative disorders. In J. S. Damico & M. J. Ball (Eds.), *The SAGE encyclopedia of human communicative sciences and disorders* (pp. 975–978). Thousand Oaks, CA: Sage.

Damico, J. S. (2019d). Observation. In J. S. Damico & M. J. Ball (Eds.), *The SAGE encyclopedia of human communicative sciences and disorders* (pp. 1273–1276). Thousand Oaks, CA: Sage.

Damico, J. S. (2019e). Constructivism. In J. S. Damico & M. J. Ball (Eds.), *The SAGE encyclopedia of human communicative sciences and disorders* (pp. 478–484). Thousand Oaks, CA: Sage.

Damico, J. S. (2019f). Reading and reading disorders. In J. S. Damico & M. J. Ball (Eds.), *The SAGE encyclopedia of human communicative sciences and disorders* (pp. 1561–1566). Thousand Oaks, CA: Sage.

Damico, J. S., & Ball, M. J. (2010). Prolegomenon: Addressing the tyranny of old ideas. *Journal of Interactional Research in Communication Disorders 1*, 1–29.

Damico, J. S., Damico, H., & Nelson, R. (2003, November). *Impact of mixed instruction on meaning making in literacy.* Poster presented at the annual meeting of the American Speech–Language–Hearing Association, Chicago.

Damico, J. S., & Damico, S. K. (1993a). Language and social skills from a diversity perspective: Considerations for the speech-language pathologist. *Language, Speech, and Hearing Services in Schools, 24*, 236–243.

Damico, J. S., & Damico, S. K. (1993b). Mapping a course over different roads: Language teaching with special populations. In J. W. Oller, Jr. (Ed.), *Methods that work: A smorgasbord of language teaching ideas* (2nd ed., pp. 320–331). New York, NY: Newbury House.

Damico, J. S., Müller, N., & Ball, M. J (2021). Labeling as a sociocultural process in communicative disorders. In J. S. Damico, N. Müller, & M. J. Ball (Eds.), *The handbook of language and speech disorders* (2nd ed., pp. 2–32). Oxford, UK: Wiley-Blackwell.

Damico, J. S., & Nelson, R. L. (2005). Interpreting problematic behavior: Systematic compensatory adaptations as emergent phenomena in autism. *Clinical Linguistics and Phonetics, 19*(4), 405–418.

Damico, J. S., & Nelson, R. L. (2010). Reading and reading impairments. In J. S. Damico, N. Müller, & M. J. Ball (Eds.), *The handbook of language and speech disorders* (pp. 267–295). Chichester, UK: Wiley-Blackwell.

Damico, J. S., & Nelson, R. L. (2012). How can we ensure that response to intervention (RtI) is appropriate for English language learners? In E. Hamayan & R. Freeman Field (Eds.), *English language learners at school: A guide for administrators* (2nd ed., pp. 207–208). Philadelphia, PA: Caslon.

Damico, J. S., Nelson, R. L., & Bryan, L. (2005). Literacy as a sociocultural process. In M. Ball (Ed.), *Clinical sociolinguistics* (pp. 242–249). Oxford, UK: Blackwell.

Damico, J. S., & Nye, C. (1990). Collaborative issues in multicultural populations. *Best Practices in School Speech-Language Pathology, 1*, 127–139.

Damico, J. S. & Oller, J. W. (1985). *Spotting Language Problems: A manual for the use of pragmatic criteria in language screening.* San Diego: Los Amigos.

Damico, J. S., Oller, J. W., & Storey, M. E. (1983). The diagnosis of language disorders in bilingual children: Pragmatic and surface–oriented criteria. *Journal of Speech and Hearing Disorders, 48*, 285–294.

Damico, J. S., & Simmons-Mackie, N. N. (2003). Qualitative research and speech–language pathology: Impact and promise in the clinical realm. *American Journal of Speech Language Pathology, 12*, 131–143.

Damico, J. S., Smith, M., & Augustine, L. L. (1996). Multicultural populations and childhood language disorders. In M. Smith & J. S. Damico (Eds.), *Childhood language disorders* (pp. 272–299). New York, NY: Thieme Medical.

Danzak, R. L. (2011). The interface of language proficiency and identity: A profile analysis of bilingual adolescents and their writing. *Language, Speech, and Hearing Services in Schools, 42*, 506–519.

Darling-Hammond, L. (2013). Inequality and school resources: What it will take to close the opportunity gap. In P. L. Carter & K. G. Welner (Eds.), *Closing the opportunity gap: What America must do to give every child an even chance* (pp. 77–97). New York, NY: Oxford University Press.

DaSilva Iddings, A. C. (2009). Bridging home and school literacy practices: Empowering families of recent immigrant children. *Theory into Practice, 48*(4), 304–311.

DaSilva Iddings, A. C., Haught, J., & Devlin, R. (2005). Multi-modal representations of self and meaning for second-language learners in English-dominant classrooms. In J. K. Hall, G. Vitanova, & L. Marchenkova, (Eds.), *Dialogue with Bakhtin on second and foreign language learning: New perspectives* (pp. 33–53). Mahwah, NJ: Lawrence Erlbaum.

Davidson, A. L. (1996). *Making and molding identity in schools: Student narratives on race, gender, and academic engagement.* Albany, NY: State University of New York Press.

Day, J., Ji, P., DuBois, D. L., Silverthorn, N., & Flay, B. (2016). Cumulative social–environmental adversity exposure as predictor of psychological distress and risk behavior in urban youth. *Child and Adolescent Social Work Journal, 33*, 219–235.

De Brigard, F. (2010). "If you like it, does it matter if it's real?" *Philosophical Psychology, 23*, 43–57.

de Jong, E. J. (2011). *Foundations for multilingualism in education. From principles to practice.* Philadelphia, PA: Caslon.

de Jong, E. (2012). How do we decide what kind of program for English language learners is appropriate for our school? In E. Hamayan & R. Freeman Field (Eds.), *English language learners at school: A guide for administrators* (2nd ed., pp. 115–117). Philadelphia, PA: Caslon.

Dee, T., & Penner, E. (2016). *The causal effects of cultural relevance: Evidence from an ethnic studies curriculum* (CEPA Working Paper No.16-01). Retrieved from Stanford Center for Education Policy Analysis: http://cepa.stanford.edu/wp16-01

Dee, T. S., Jacob, B. A., Hoxby, C. M., & Ladd, H. F. (2010). The impact of No Child Left Behind on students, teachers, and schools. *Brookings Papers on Economic Activity, 149–207.*

Degloma, T. (2009). Expanding trauma through space and time: Mapping the rhetorical strategies of trauma carrier groups. *Social Psychology Quarterly, 72*(2), 105–122.

Deming, D. (2009). Early childhood intervention and life-cycle skill development: Evidence from Head Start. *American Economic Journal: Applied Economics, 1*(3), 111–134.

Denton, C. A., Vaughn, S., & Fletcher, J. M. (2003). Bringing research-based practice in reading intervention to scale. *Learning Disabilities Research and Practice, 18,* 201–211.

Dirksen, D.J. (2011). Hitting the rest button: Using Formative Assessment to guide Instruction. *Phi Delta Kappan, 92*(7), 26–31.

Dombo, E. A. & Sabatino, C. A. (2019). Creating trauma-informed schools: A guide for school social workers and educators. Oxford, UK: Oxford Scholarship online.

Dove, M., & Honigsfeld, A. (2010). ESL co-teaching and collaborations: Opportunities to develop teacher leadership and enhance student learning. *TESOL Journal, 1,* 1–22.

Dove M. G., & Honigsfeld, A. (2018). *Co-teaching for English learners: A guide to collaborative planning, instruction, assessment, and reflection.* Thousand Oaks, CA: Corwin.

Duchan, J. F., Hewitt, L. E., & Sonnenmeirer, R. M. (Eds.). (1994). *Pragmatics: From theory to practice.* Englewood Cliffs, NJ: Prentice-Hall.

Dudley-Marling, C. (2000). *A family affair: When school troubles come home.* Portsmouth, NH: Heinemann.

Dudley-Marling, C., & Paugh, P. (2004). *A classroom teacher's guide to struggling readers.* Portsmouth, NH: Heinemann.

DuFour, R. (2004). What is a "professional learning community?" *Schools as Learning Communities, 61*(8), 6–11.

Dufva, H., & Alanen, R. (2005). Metalinguistic awareness in dialogue: Bakhtinian considerations. In J. K. Hall, G. Vitanova, & L. Marchenkova (Eds.), *Dialogue with Bakhtin on second and foreign language learning* (pp. 99–118). Mahwah, NJ: Lawrence Erlbaum.

Dunaway, C. (2004). Attention deficit hyperactivity disorder: An authentic story in the schools and its implications. *Seminars in Speech and Language, 25*(3), 271–275.

Dunaway, C. (2021). *Collaborative academic conversation assessment manual: Qualitative measures for assessment and progress monitoring.* Available at: <https://www.thinkspeaksuccess.com>

Durán-Cerda, D. (2008). Strengthening "la identidad" in the heritage learner classroom: Pedagogical approaches. *Hispania, 91*(1), 42–51.

Durkheim, E., & Coser, L. A. (1984). *The division of labor in society.* New York, NY: Free Press.

Dyson, A. H., & Genishi, C. (Eds.). (1994). *The need for story. Cultural diversity in classroom and community.* Urbana, IL: National Council of Teachers of English.

Echevarria, J., & Short, D. (2003). *The effects of sheltered instruction on the achievement of limited English proficient students.* Washington, DC: Center for Applied Linguistics. Retrieved from www.cal.org/crede/si.htm

Echevarria, J., Vogt, M. E., & Short, D. (2017). *Making content comprehensible for English learners: The SIOP model* (4th ed.). Boston, MA: Pearson.

Edelsky, C. (1999). On critical whole language practice: Why, what, and a bit of how. In C. Edelsky (Ed.), *Making justice our project* (p. 736). Urbana, IL: National Council of Teachers of English.

Edmonds, M. S., Vaughn, S., Wexler, J., Reutebuch, C., Cable, A., Klingler Tackett, K., & Wick Schnakenberg, J. (2009). A synthesis of reading interventions and effects on reading comprehension outcomes for older struggling readers. *Review of Educational Research, 79,* 262–300.

Education Alliance at Brown University. (2006). *The knowledge loom.* Providence, RI: Brown University.

Ehren, B. J., & Nelson, N. W. (2005). The responsiveness to intervention approach and language impairment. *Topics in Language Disorders, 25,* 120–131.

Ehri, L. C., Dreyer, L. G., Flugman, B., & Gross, A. (2007). Reading rescue: An effective tutoring intervention model for language-minority students who are struggling readers in first grade. *American Educational Research Journal, 44*(2), 414–448.

Elias, M. J., & Dilworth, J. E. (2003). Ecological/developmental theory, context-based best practice, and school-based action research: Cornerstones of school psychology training and policy. *Journal of School Psychology, 41*(3), 293–297.

Elo, I. T. (2009). Social class differentials in health and mortality: Patterns and explanations in comparative perspective. *Annual Review of Sociology, 35,* 553–572.

Entwisle, D. R., Alexander, K. L., & Olson, L. S. (1997). *Children, schools, and inequality.* Boulder, CO: Westview Press.

Epstein, J. (2001). *School, family, and community partnerships: Preparing educators and improving schools.* Boulder, CO: Westview Press.

Escamilla, K., & Hopewell, S. (2010). Transitions to biliteracy: Creating positive academic trajectories for emerging bilinguals in the United States. In J. Petrovic (Ed.), *International perspectives on bilingual education: Policy, practice, controversy* (pp. 69–93). Charlotte, NC: Information Age Publishing.

Escamilla, K., Hopewell, S., Butvilofsky, S., Sparrow, W., Soltero-González, L., Ruiz-Figueroa, O., & Escamilla, M. (2014). *Biliteracy from the start: Literacy squared in action.* Philadelphia, PA: Caslon.

Evans, G. W., & Kim, P. (2013). Childhood poverty, chronic stress, self-regulation, and coping. *Child Development Perspectives, 7*(1), 43–48.

Fadiman, A. (1997). *The spirit catches you and you fall down. A Hmong child, her American doctors, and the collision of two cultures.* New York: Noonday Press.

Fairbairn, S. & Jones-Vo, S. (2019). *Differentiating instruction and assessment for ELLs with differentiator flip chart: A guide for K–12 teachers* (2nd ed.). Philadelphia, PA: Caslon.

Fan, W., & Wolters, C. A. (2014). School motivation and high school dropout: The mediating role of educational expectation. *British Journal of Educational Psychology, 84,* 22-39.

Feeley, T. H. (2002). Comment on halo effects in rating and evaluation research. *Human Communication Research, 28*(4), 578–586.

Fennacy, J. (1998). Becoming readers and writers over time. In C. Weaver (Ed.), *Practicing what we know: Informed reading instruction* (pp. 462–478). Urbana, IL: National Council of Teachers of English.

Fielding, N. G., & Fielding, J. L. (1986). *Linking data.* Beverly Hills, CA: Sage.

Fine, M., Jaffe-Walter, R., Pedraza, P., Futch, V., & Stoudt, B. (2007). Swimming: On oxygen, resistance, and possibility for immigrant youth under siege. *Anthropology and Education Quarterly, 38,* 76–96.

Five, C. L. (1995). Ownership for the special needs child: Individual and educational dilemmas. In C. Dudley-Marling & D. Searle (Eds.), *Who owns learning? Questions of autonomy, choice, and control* (pp. 113–127). Portsmouth, NH: Heinemann.

Flege, J. E. (2019). Give input a chance! In T. Piske & M. Young-Scholten (Eds.), *Input matters in SLA* (175–190). Buffalo, NY: Multilingual Matters.

Fletcher, J. M., Denton, C. A., Fuchs, L. S., & Vaughn, S. R. (2005). Multi-tiered reading instruction: Linking general education and special education. In S. O. Richardson & J. W. Gilger (Eds.), *Research-based education and intervention: What we need to know* (pp. 21–44). Baltimore, MD: International Dyslexia Association.

Flick, U. (1992). Triangulation revisited: Strategy of validation or alternative? *Journal for the Theory of Social Behavior, 27,* 175–198.

Flores C. J., & Delgado, B. D. (2012). Oral histories in the classroom: The Latina/o home as a pedagogical site. In C. E. Sleeter & E. Soriano Ayala (Eds.), *Building solidarity between schools and marginalized communities: International perspectives.* New York, NY: Teachers College Press.

Flores, N., Kleyn, T., & Menken, K. (2015) Looking holistically in a climate of partiality: Identities of students labeled long-term English language learners. *Journal of Language, Identity & Education,* 14:2, 113-132.

Flores, N., & Schissel, J. L. (2014). Dynamic bilingualism as the norm: Envisioning a heteroglossic approach to standards-based reform. *TESOL Quarterly, 48*(3), 454–479.

Flynn, J. R. (2000). The hidden history of IQ and special education: Can the problems be solved? *Psychology, Public Policy, and Law, 6*(2), 191–198.

Fozdar, F., & Torezani, S. (2008). Discrimination and well-being: Perceptions of refugees in western Australia. *International Migration Review, 42*(1), 30–63.

Frank, C. L., & Richards, S. B. (2020). *Essentials of special education: What educators need to know* (1st ed.). New York, NY: Routledge.

Freedman, K. L. (2006). The epistemological significance of psychic trauma. *Hypatia, 21*(2), 104–125.

Freeman, D., & Freeman, Y. (2003). Teaching English learners to read: Learning or acquisition? In G. G. García (Ed.), *English learners reaching the highest level of English proficiency* (pp. 34–54). Newark, NJ: International Reading Association.

Freeman, D. E., & Freeman, Y. S. (2001). *Between worlds: Access to second language acquisition* (2nd ed.). Portsmouth, NH: Heinemann.

Freeman, Y., & Freeman, D. (2002). *Closing the achievement gap: How to reach limited formal schooling and long-term English learners.* Portsmouth, NH: Heinemann.

Freiberg, H. J. (1998). Measuring school climate: Let me count the ways. *Educational Leadership, 56*(1), 22–26.

Freiberg, H. J. (Ed.). (1999). *School climate: Measuring, improving and sustaining healthy learning environments*. London, UK: Falmer Press.

Freire, J.A. (2014). *Spanish-English dual language teacher beliefs and practices on culturally relevant pedagogy in a collaborative action research process*. An unpublished dissertation from the University of Utah. Salt Lake City, UT.

Friend, M., & Cook, L. (1996). *Interactions: Collaboration skills for school professionals*. White Plains, NY: Longman.

Fuchs, D., & Fuchs, L. S. (2006). Introduction to response to intervention: What, why, and how valid is it? *Reading Research Quarterly, 41*, 93–99.

Fuchs, D., Fuchs, L. S., & Compton, D. L. (2004). Identifying reading disabilities by responsiveness to instruction: Specifying measures and criteria. *Learning Disabilities Quarterly, 27*, 216–228.

Fuchs, D., Mock, D., Morgan, P. L., & Young, C. (2003). Responsiveness-to-intervention: Definitions, evidence, and implications for the learning disabilities construct. *Learning Disabilities Research & Practice, 18*, 157–171.

Fuchs, L. S. (2002). Three conceptualizations of "treatment" in a responsiveness-to-treatment framework for LD identification. In R. Bradley, L. Danielson, & D. P. Hallahan (Eds.), *Identification of learning disabilities: Research to practice* (pp. 521–529). Mahwah, NJ: Lawrence Erlbaum.

Fuchs, L. S. (2003). Assessing intervention responsiveness: Conceptual and technical issues. *Learning Disabilities Research & Practice, 18*, 172–186.

Fuchs, L. S. (2004). The past, present, and future of curriculum-based measurement research. *School Psychology Review, 33*, 188–192.

Fuchs, L. S., & Fuchs, D. (2008). The role of assessment within the RtI Framework. In D. Fuchs, L. S. Fuchs, & S. Vaughn (Eds.), *Response to intervention. A Framework for reading educators* (pp. 27–50). Newark, DE: International Reading Association.

Fullan, M. (2019). *Nuance: Why some leaders succeed and others fail*. Thousand Oaks, CA: Corwin.

Fullan, M., & Quinn, J. (2016). *Coherence: The right drivers in action for schools, districts, and systems*. Thousand Oaks, CA: Corwin.

Gagarina, N., Klop, D., Tsimpli, D. L., & Walters, J. (2016). Narrative abilities in bilingual children. *Applied Psycholinguistics, 37*(1), 11–17.

Garbarino, J., Kostelny, K., & Dubrow, N. (1991). *No place to be a child*. San Francisco, CA: Jossey-Bass.

García, E. (2005). *Teaching and learning in two languages: Bilingualism and schooling in the United States*. New York, NY: Teachers College Press.

Garcia, E., & Miller, L. (2008). Findings and recommendations of the National Task Force on Early Childhood Education for Hispanics. *Child Development Perspectives. 2*, 53–58.

García, G. G. (Ed.). (2003). *English learners: Reaching the highest level of English literacy*. Newark, DE: International Reading Association.

García, O., Johnson, S. I., & Seltzer, K. (2016). *The translanguaging classroom: Leveraging student bilingualism for learning*. Philadelphia, PA: Caslon.

García, O., & Kleifgen, J. A. (2010). *Educating emergent bilinguals: Policies, programs and practices for English language learners*. New York: Teachers College Press.

García, O., & Wei, L. (2014). *Translanguaging: Language, bilingualism and education*. Hampshire, UK: Palgrave MacMillan.

García, O., & Woodley, H. H. (2015). Bilingual education. In M. Bigelow & J. Ennser-Kananen (eds.), *The Routledge handbook of educational linguistics*. New York: Routledge.

Garmezy, N. (1991). Resiliency and vulnerability to adverse developmental outcomes associated with poverty. *American Behavioral Scientist, 34*, 416–430.

Gee, J. P. (2008). Sociocultural perspective on opportunity to learn. In Moss, P. (Ed.), *Assessment, equity and opportunity to learn*. New York, NY: Cambridge University Press.

Geekie, P., Cambourne, B., & Fitzsimmons, P. (1999). *Understanding literacy development*. Staffordshire, UK: Trentham Books.

Genesee, F. (2003). Rethinking bilingual acquisition. In J. M. deWaele (Ed.), *Bilingualism: Challenges and directions for future research* (pp. 158–182). Clevedon, UK: Multilingual Matters.

Genesee, F. (2012). How do English language learners acquire a second language at school? In E. Hamayan & R. Freeman Field (Eds.), *English language learners at school: A guide for administrators* (2nd ed., pp. 65–66). Philadelphia, PA: Caslon.

Genesee, F., & Hamayan, E. (2016). *CLIL in context: Practical guide for educators*. Cambridge, UK: Cambridge University Press

Genesee, F., Lindholm-Leary, K., Saunders, W., & Christian, D. (2005.) English language learners in U.S. schools: An overview of research findings. *Journal for Education for Students Placed at Risk, 10*(4), 365–385.

Genesee, F., Lindholm-Leary, K. J., Saunders, W., & Christian, D. (2006). *Educating English language learners: A synthesis of empirical evidence*. New York, NY: Cambridge University Press.

Gerber, S. B., Finn, J. D., Achilles, C. M., & Boyd-Zaharias, J. (2001). Teacher aides and students' academic achievement. *Educational Evaluation and Policy Analysis, 23*, 123–143.

Gergen, K. J. (2015). *An invitation to Social Constructivism* (3rd ed.). Thousand Oaks, CA: Sage.

Gernsbacher, M. A., Dawson, M., & Goldsmith, H. H. (2005). Three reasons not to believe in an autism epidemic. *Current Directions in Psychological Science, 14*(2), 55–58.

Gersten, R., & Edomono, J. A. (2006). RtI (response to intervention): Rethinking special education for students with reading difficulties (yet again). *Reading Research Quarterly, 41*, 99–108.

Geva, E., & Wiener, J. (2014). *Psychological assessment of culturally and linguistically diverse children and adolescents: A practitioner's guide*. New York, NY: Springer Publishing Company.

Giangreco, M. F. (2000). Related services research for students with low-incidence disabilities: Implications for speech-language pathologists in inclusive classrooms. *Language, Speech, and Hearing Services in Schools, 13*(3), 230–239.

Gibbons, P. (2015). *Scaffolding language, scaffolding learning: Teaching second language learners in the mainstream classroom* (2nd ed.) Portsmouth, NH: Heinemann.

Gibbs, S., & Elliot, J. (2015). The differential effects of labelling: How do "dyslexia" and "reading difficulties" affect teachers' beliefs. *European Journal of Special Needs Education, 30*, 323–337.

Gilbert, J. K. (2005). *Constructing worlds through science education*. New York, NY: Routledge.

Gillam, S. L., & Gillam, R. B. (2006). Making evidence-based decisions about child language intervention in schools. *Language, Speech, and Hearing Services in Schools, 37*(4), 304–315.

Goffman, E. (1964). *Stigma: Notes on the management of spoiled identity*. New York, NY: Simon & Schuster.

Goh, S. K. Y, Yang, H., Tsotsi, S., Qiu, A., Chong, Y-S., Tan, K. H., Pei-Chi, L. S., Broekman, B. F. P., Rifkin-Graboi, A. (2020). Mitigation of a prospective association between early language delay at toddlerhood and ADHD among bilingual preschoolers: Evidence from the GUSTO cohort. *Journal of Abnormal Child Psychology, 48*, 511–523.

Goldstein, B. (2011). *Bilingual language development and disorders in Spanish-English speakers* (2nd ed.). Baltimore, MD: Paul H. Brookes Publishing Co.

Goldstein, B. A., & Horton-Ikard, R. (2010). Diversity considerations in speech and language disorders. In J. S. Damico, N. Müller, & M. J. Ball (Eds.), *The handbook of language and speech disorders* (pp. 38–56). Chichester, UK: Wiley-Blackwell.

González, N., Moll, L. C., & Amanti, C. (2005). *Funds of knowledge: Theorizing practices in households, communities, and classrooms*. Mahwah, NJ: Lawrence Erlbaum Associates.

Gonzalez, T., & Artiles, A. J. (2015). Reframing venerable standpoints about language and learning differences: The need for research on the literate lives of Latina/o language minority students. *The Journal of Multilingual Educational Research, 6*, 9-34.

Gonzalez-Barrero, A. M., & Nadig, A. S. (2017). Can bilingualism mitigate set-shifting difficulties in children with autism spectrum disorders? *Child Development, 90(4)*, 1043–1060.

Gonzalez-Barrero, A. M., & Nadig, A. (2018). Bilingual children with autism spectrum disorders: The impact of amount of language exposure on vocabulary and morphological skills at school age. *Autism Research, 11*(12), 1667–1678.

Goodman, K. (Ed.). (2006). *Examining DIBELS: What it is and what it does*. Brandon, VT: Vermont Society for the Study of Education.

Goodman, K. (2014). *What's whole in whole language in the 21st Century?* New York, NY: Garn Press.

Goodman, K., Fries, P. H., & Strauss, S. L. (2016). *Reading. The Grand Illusion. How and Why People Make Sense of Print*. New York, NY: Routledge.

Goodman, K. S. (2005). The perfect literacy test. *Language Magazine, 5*(4), 24–27.

Goodman, K. S. & Goodman, Y. M. (2014). *Making sense of learners making sense of written language: The selected works of Kenneth S. Goodman and Yetta M. Goodman*. New York, NY: Routledge.

Gordon, R. G., Jr. (Ed.). (2005). *Ethnologue: Languages of the world* (15th ed.). Dallas, TX: Summer Institute of Languages International.

Gottlieb, M. (2012). How should we assess the language proficiency of English language learners? In E. Hamayan & R. Freeman Field (Eds.), *English language learners at school: A guide for administrators* (2nd ed., pp. 155–157). Philadelphia, PA: Caslon.

Gottlieb, M. (2016). *Assessing English language learners: Bridges from language proficiency to academic achievement* (2nd ed.) Thousand Oaks, CA: Corwin.

Gottlieb, M. (2021). *Classroom assessment in multiple languages*. Thousand Oaks, CA: Corwin.

Gottlieb, M., & Ernst-Slavit, G. (2014). *Academic language in diverse classrooms: Definitions and contexts*. Thousand Oaks, CA: Corwin.

Gottlieb, M., & Hamayan, E. (2006). Assessing oral and written language proficiency: A guide for psychologists and teachers. In G. B. Esquivel, E. Lopez, S. Nahari, & A. Brice (Eds.), *Handbook of multicultural school psychology*. Mahwah, NJ: Lawrence Erlbaum.

Grant, C. A. & Gillette, M. (2006). A candid talk to teacher educators about effectively preparing teachers who can teach everyone's children. *Journal of Teacher Education, 57*, 292–299.

Graves, D. H. (2002). *Testing is not teaching: What should count in education.* Portsmouth, NH: Heinemann.

Graves, M. F., & Fitzgerald, J. (2003). Scaffolding reading experiences for multilingual classrooms. In G. G. García (Ed.), *English learners reaching the highest level of English proficiency* (pp. 96–124). Newark, NJ: International Reading Association.

Gray, C., McCoy, S., Dunbar, C., Dunn, J., Mitchell, D., & Ferguson, J. (2007). Added value or a familiar face: The impact of learning assistants on young readers. *Journal of Early Childhood Research, 5,* 285–300.

Grigorenko, E. L. (2009). Dynamic assessment and response to intervention. Two sides of one coin. *Journal of Learning Disabilities, 42,* 111–132.

Grosjean, F. (1998). Studying bilinguals: Methodological and conceptual issues. *Bilingualism: Language and Cognition, 1* (1), 131–149.

Grosjean, F. (2010). *Bilingual: Life and reality.* Cambridge, MA: Harvard University Press.

Grosjean, F. (2015a). *Bilingual: Life and reality.* Cambridge, MA: Harvard University Press.

Grosjean, F. (2015b). Bicultural bilinguals. *International Journal of Bilingualism, 19*(5), 572–586.

Grzadzinski, R., Huerta, M. & Lord, C. (2013). DSM-5 and autism spectrum disorders (ASDs): an opportunity for identifying ASD subtypes. *Molecular autism, 4* (1), 1–6.

Guendouzi, J. (2014). Qualitative research revisited. In M. J. Ball, N. Müller, & R. L. Nelson (Eds.), *Handbook of qualitative research communication disorders* (pp. 331–342). New York, NY: Psychology Press.

Gunderson, L., & Siegel, L. S. (2001). The evils of the use of IQ tests to define learning disabilities in first- and second-language learners. *Reading Teacher, 55*(1), 48–55.

Gursoy, E., & Ozcan, E. N. (2018). Perceptions and linguistic actions of bilingual speakers of Turkish and English: An explanatory study. *Advances in Language and Literary Studies, 9,* 212–222.

Gutierrez, K., & Rogoff, B. (2003). Cultural ways of learning: Individual traits or repertoires of practice. *Educational Researcher, 32*(5), 19–25.

Gutiérrez, K. D., & Larson, J. (2007). Discussing expanded spaces for learning. *Language Arts: ProQuest Research Library, 85*(1), 69–77.

Gutierrez-Clellen, V., Simon-Cereijido, G., & Sweet, M. (2012). Predictors of second language acquisition in Latino children with specific language impairment. *American Journal of Speech–Language Pathology, 21*(1), 64–77.

Gutiérrez-Clellen, V. F., & Peña, E. (2001). Dynamic assessment of diverse children: A tutorial. *Language, Speech, and Hearing Services in Schools, 32,* 212–224.

Gutkin, T. B. (1990). Consultative speech–language services in the schools: A view through the looking glass of school psychology. *Best Practices in School Speech–Language Pathology, 1,* 57–65.

Gutkin, T. B., & Nemeth, C. (1997). Selected factors impacting decision making in prereferral intervention and other school-based teams: Exploring the intersection between school and social psychology. *Journal of School Psychology, 35*(2), 195–216.

Haager, D., Klingner, J. K., & Vaughn, S. (Eds.). (2007). *Evidence-based reading practices for response to intervention.* Baltimore, MD: Paul H. Brookes Publishing Co.

Hadjioannou, X. (2007). Bringing the background to the foreground: What do classroom environments that support authentic discussions look like? *American Educational Research Journal, 44,* 370–399.

Hakuta, K. (1986). *Mirror of language: The debate on bilingualism.* New York, NY: Basic Books.

Hakuta, K., Butler, Y., & Witt, D. (2000). How long does it take English learners to attain proficiency? *University of California Linguistic Minority Research Institute Policy Report 2000–1.* Berkeley: University of California Linguistic Minority Research Institute.

Hall, E. T. (2001). *The hidden dimension.* New York, NY: Double Day.

Halligan, F. R. (2009). Youth and trauma: Terror, war, murder, incest, rape, and suicide. *Journal of Religion and Health, 48*(3), 342–352.

Halls, G., Cooper, P. J., & Creswell, C. (2014). Social communication deficits: Specific associations with Social Anxiety Disorder. *Journal of Affective Disorders, 172,* 38–42.

Hamayan, E. (1994). Language development of low-literacy students. In F. Genesee (Ed.), *Educating second language children: The whole child, the whole curriculum, the whole community* (pp. 278–300). New York, NY: Cambridge University Press.

Hamayan, E. (2012). What is the role of culture in language learning? In E. Hamayan & R. Freeman Field (Eds.), *English language learners at school: A guide for administrators* (2nd ed., pp. 47–49). Philadelphia, PA: Caslon.

Hamayan, E., & Damico, J. (Eds.). (1991). *Limiting bias in the assessment of bilingual students.* Austin, TX: PRO-ED.

Hamayan, E., & Freeman Field, R. (2012). How do English language learners acquire a second language at school? In E. Hamayan & R. Freeman Field (Eds.), *English language learners at school: A guide for administrators* (2nd ed., pp. 53–56). Philadelphia, PA: Caslon.

Hamayan, E., Genesee, F., & Cloud, N. (2013). *Dual language education: From A to Z*. Portsmouth, NH: Heinemann.

Hammer, C. S., Komaroff, E., Rodriguez, B. L., Lopez, L. M., Scarpino, S. E., & Goldstein, B. (2012). Predicting Spanish-English bilingual children's language abilities. *Journal of Speech, Language, and Hearing Research, 55*(5), 1251–1264.

Hammer, C. S., Lawrence, F. R., & Miccio, A. W. (2007). Bilingual children's language abilities and early reading outcomes in Head Start and kindergarten. *Language, Speech, and Hearing Services in Schools, 38*(3), 237–248.

Hammond, Z. (2014). *Culturally responsive teaching and the brain*. Thousand Oaks, CA: Corwin.

Harding-Esch, E., & Riley, P. (2012). *The bilingual family. A handbook for parents* (10th ed.). Cambridge, UK: Cambridge University Press.

Harris, A., & Leonardo, Z. (2018). Intersectionality, race–gender subordination and education. *Review of Research in Education, 42*(1), 1–27. https://doi.org/10.3102/0091732X18759071.

Harris, A. L., Jamison, K. M., & Trujillo, M. H. (2008). Disparities in the educational success of immigrants: An assessment of the immigrant effect for Asians and Latinos. *Annals of the American Academy of Political and Social Science, 620*, 90–114.

Harry, B., Kalyanpur, M., & Day, M. (1999). *The posture of cultural reciprocity: A practical approach to collaborative relationships with families from culturally diverse backgrounds*. Baltimore, MD: Paul H. Brookes Publishing Co.

Harry, B., & Klingner, J. (2014). *Why are so many minority students in special education? Understanding race and disability in schools*. New York, NY: Teachers College Press.

Hart, B., & Risley, T. R. (2003). *Meaningful differences in the everyday experience of young American children*. Baltimore, MD: Paul H. Brookes Publishing Co.

Haycock, K. (1998). *Good teaching matters*. Washington, DC: Education Trust.

Heath, C., & Heath, D. (2010). *Switch: How to change things when change is hard*. New York, NY: Crown.

Heath, S. B., & McLaughlin, M. (1993). *Identity and inner city youth: Beyond ethnicity and gender*. New York, NY: Teachers College Press.

Heider, F. (1958). *The psychology of interpersonal relations*. New York, NY: John Wiley & Sons.

Henry, D. (2006). Violence and the body: Somatic expressions of trauma and vulnerability during war. *Medical Anthropology Quarterly, 20*(3), 379–398.

Heritage, M. (2010). *Formative assessment: Making it happen in the classroom* (3rd ed). Thousand Oaks, CA: Corwin.

Heritage, M. & Harrison, C. (2019). The Power of Assessment for Learning. Thousand Oaks, CA: Corwin.

Heritage, M., & Wylie, E. C. (2020). *Formative assessment in the disciplines. Framing a continuum of professional learning*. Cambridge, MA: Harvard Education Press.

Herrera, S. G., Murry, K. G., & Cabral, R. M. (2012). *Assessment accommodations for classroom teachers of culturally and linguistically diverse students*. Boston, MA: Pearson/Allyn & Bacon.

Hill, J., & Flynn, K. (2006). *Classroom instruction that works: Research-based strategies for increasing student achievement*. Alexandria, VA: Association for Supervision and Curriculum Development.

Hilliard, J., & Hamayan, E. (2012). How do you plan for language development? In E. Hamayan & R. Freeman Field (Eds.), *English language learners at school: A guide for administrators* (2nd ed., pp. 121–123). Philadelphia, PA: Caslon.

Hodgson, A., Steer, R., Spours, K., Edward, S., Coffield, F., Finlay, I., & Gregson M. (2007). Learners in the English learning and skills sector: The implications of half-right policy assumptions. *Oxford Review of Education, 33*(3), 315–330.

Hoff, E., Core, C., Place, S., Rumiche, R., Señor, M., & Parra, M. (2012). Dual language exposure and early bilingual development. *Journal of Child Language, 39*(1), 1–27.

Hoffman, D. M. (1999). Culture and comparative education: Toward decentering and recentering the discourse. *Comparative Education Review, 43*, 464–488.

Hornberger, N. H. & Link, H. (2012). Translanguaging and transnational literacies in multilingual classrooms: A biliteracy lens. *International Journal of Bilingual Education and Bilingualism, 15, 261–278*.

Horton-Ikard, R., & Ellis Weismer, S. (2007). A preliminary examination of vocabulary and word learning in African American toddlers from middle and low socioeconomic status homes. *American Journal of Speech-Language Pathology, 16*(4), 381–392.

Howard, M. (2009). *RTI from all sides. What every teacher needs to know*. Portsmouth, NH: Heinemann.

Howard, M. (2012). *Good to great teaching. Focusing on the literacy work that matters*. Portsmouth, NH: Heinemann.

Individuals with Disabilities Education Improvement Act, PL 108-466. (2004). 20 USC 1400.

International Literacy Association. (2019). *The role of bilingualism in improving literacy achievement [Literacy Leadership Brief]*. Newark, DE: Author.

Isaacs, J. B. (2012). *Starting school at a disadvantage: The school readiness of poor children. The Social Genome Project*. Washington, DC: Center on Children and Families at Brookings.

Ivey, G., & Broaddus, K. (2007). A formative experiment investigating literacy engagement among adolescent Latina/o students just beginning to read, write, and speak English. *Reading Research Quarterly, 42*, 512–545.

Jack, G. (2000). Ecological influences on parenting and child development. *British Journal of Social Work, 30*, 703–720.

Jacobson, P. F., & Schwartz, R. G. (2005). English past tense use in bilingual children with language impairment. *American Journal of Speech–Language Pathology, 14*(4), 313–323.

Jaeger, E.L. (2019). Response to intervention (Rtl). In J. S. Damico & M. J. Ball (Eds.). *The SAGE encyclopedia of human communicative sciences and disorders* (pp. 1615–1619). Thousand Oaks, CA: Sage.

Janzen, J. (2007). Preparing teachers of second language reading. *TESOL Quarterly, 41*, 707–729.

Janzen, J. (2008). Teaching English language learners in the content areas. *Review of Educational Research, 78*(4), 1010–1038.

Jen, G. (1997, April 21). Who's to judge? *New Republic*, 18–19.

Jerald, C. D. (2003). *All talk no action: Putting an end to out-of-field teaching*. Washington, DC: Education Trust.

Jia, G., & Fuse, A. (2007). Acquisition of English grammatical morphology by native Mandarin-speaking children and adolescents: Age-related differences. *Journal of Speech, Language, and Hearing Research, 50*(5), 1280–1299.

Jiménez, R. T., Smith, P. H., & Teague, B. L. (2009). Transnational and community literacies for teachers. *Journal of Adolescent & Adult Literacy, 53*(1), 16–26.

Johnson, B., & Stevens, J. (2006). Student achievement and elementary teachers' perceptions of school climate. *Learning Environments Research, 9*, 111–122.

Johnson, G. M. (2004). Constructivist remediation: Correction in context. *International Journal of Special Education, 19*, 72–88.

Johnston, P., & Costello, P. (2005). Principles for literacy assessment. *Reading Research Quarterly, 40*, 256–267.

Jones, K. D., Young, T., & Leppma, M. (2010). Mild traumatic brain injury and posttraumatic stress disorder in returning Iraq and Afghanistan war veterans: Implications for assessment and diagnosis. *Journal for Counseling and Development, 88*, 372–376.

Joyce, B., & Showers, B. (2002). *Designing training and peer coaching: Our needs for learning*. Alexandria, VA: ASCD.

Jurado, B. C., & Garcia, C. M. (2018). Students' attitude and motivation in bilingual education. *International Journal of Educational Psychology, 7*, 317–342.

Justice, L. M. (2006). Evidence-based practice, response-to-intervention, and the prevention of reading difficulties. *Language, Speech, and Hearing Services in Schools, 37*, 284–297.

Kagan, J. (2013). *The human spark. The science of human development*. New York, NY: Basic Books.

Kalil, A. (2015). Inequality begins at home: The role of parenting in the diverging destinies of rich and poor children. In P. R. Amato, A. Booth, S. M. McHale, & J. V. Hook (Eds.), *Families in an era of increasing inequality* (pp. 63–82). Cham, Switzerland: Springer International Publishing.

Kalil, A., & Mayer, S. E. (2016). Understanding the importance of parental time with children: Comment on Milkie, Nomaguchi, and Denny (2015). *Journal of Marriage and Family, 78*(1), 262–265.

Kalyanpur, M. (2019). Challenges in implementing Response to Intervention with culturally and linguistically diverse students. *International Journal of Diversity in Education, 19*(2), 45–56.

Kalyanpur, M., & Harry, B. (1999). *Culture in special education: Building a posture of reciprocity in parent-professional relationships*. Baltimore, MD: Paul H. Brookes Publishing Co.

Kalyanpur, M., & Harry, B. (2012). *Cultural reciprocity in special education: Building family–professional relationships*. Baltimore, MD: Paul H. Brookes Publishing Co.

Kame'enui, E., Fuchs, L. S., Good, R., Francis, D., O'Connor, R., & Simmons, D. (2006). The adequacy of tools for assessing reading competence in primary grades: A decision-making framework and review of prominently used tests. *Educational Researchers, 35*, 3–11.

Kaminski, R. A., & Good, R. H. (1998). Assessing early literacy skills in a problem-solving model: Dynamic indicators of basic early literacy skills. In M. S. Shinn (Ed.), *Advanced applications of curriculum-based measurement* (pp. 113–142). New York: Guilford.

Kang, J. Y. (2012). How do narrative and language skills relate to each other?: Investigation of young Korean EFL learners' oral narratives. *Narrative Inquiry, 22*, 307–331.

Kao, G., & Thompson, J. S. (2003). Racial and ethnic stratification in educational achievement and attainment. *Annual Review of Sociology, 29*, 417–442.

Kapantzoglou, M., Restrepo, M. A., & Thompson, M. S. (2012). Dynamic Assessment of Word Learning Skills: Identifying Language Impairment in Bilingual Children. *Language, Speech, and Hearing Services in Schools, 43*, 81–96.

Kaplan, S., & Leckie, A. (2009). The impact of English-only legislation on teacher professional development: Shifting perspectives in Arizona. *Theory into Practice, 48*(4), 297–303.

Kašćelan, D., Katsos, N., & Gibson, J. L. (2019). Relations between bilingualism and autistic-like traits in a general population sample of primary school children. *Journal of Autism and Developmental Disorders, 49*, 2509–2523.

Katz, S. R. (1999). Teaching in tensions: Latino immigrant youth, their teachers and the structures of schooling. *Teachers' College Record, 100*(4), 809–840.

Kauffman, J. M., Hallahan, D. P., Pullen, P. C., & Badar, J. (2018). *Special education: What it is and why we need it.* New York, NY: Routledge.

Kay-Raining Bird, E., Cleave, P. L., Trudeau, N., Thordardottir, E., Sutton, A., & Thorpe, A. (2005). The language abilities of bilingual children with Down syndrome. *American Journal of Speech-Language Pathology, 14*, 187–199.

Kay-Raining Bird, E., Genesee, F., & Verhoeven, L. (2016). Bilingualism in children with developmental disorders: A narrative review. *Journal of Communication Disorders, 63*, 1–14.

Keene, E. O. (2008). *To understand: New horizons in reading comprehension.* Portsmouth, NH: Heinemann.

Keene, E. O. (2012). *Talk about understanding: Rethinking classroom talk to enhance comprehension.* Portsmouth, NH: Heinemann.

Kelly, B., & Gates, T. (2017). Strengths-based approaches: An interdisciplinary historical account. In J. Edwards, A. Young, & H. Nikels (Eds.), *Handbook of strengths-based clinical practices finding common practices* (pp. 19–32). New York, NY: Routledge.

Kendall, J., & Khuon, O. (2005). *Making sense. Small-group comprehension lessons for English language learners.* Portland, ME: Stenhouse.

Kheirkhah, M., & Cekaite, A. (2018.) Siblings as language socialization agents in bilingual families. *International Multilingual Research Journal, 12*(4), 255–272.

Kibler, J. (2005). How does one develop an intercultural perspective? *International Forum of Teaching and Studies, 1*(1), 9–12.

Kiernan, B., & Swisher, L. (1990). The initial learning of novel English words: Two single-subject experiments with minority-language children. *Journal of Speech, Language, and Hearing Research, 33*, 707–716.

King, K. A., & Fogle, L. (2013). Family language policy and bilingual parenting. *Language Teaching, 46*, 172–194.

Klasen, H. (2000). A name, what's in a name? The medicalization of hyperactivity revisited. *Harvard Review of Psychiatry, 7*(3), 334–344.

Klingner, J., & Vaughn, S. (2000) The helping behaviors of fifth graders while using collaborative strategic reading during ESL content classes. *TESOL Quarterly, 34*, 69–98.

Klingner, J., & Vaughn, S. (1999). Promoting reading comprehension, content learning and English acquisition through Collaborative Strategic Reading (CSR). *The Reading Teacher, 52*, 738–747.

Klingner, J., Vaughn, S., Arguelles, M. E., Tejero Hughes, M., & Ahwee Leftwich, S. (2004). Collaborative strategic reading: "Real worlds": Lessons from classroom teachers. *Remedial and Special Education, 25*, 291–302.

Klingner, J. K. (2014). *Distinguishing language acquisition from learning disabilities.* New York, NY: Division of English Language Learners and Student Support, New York City Department of Education.

Klingner, J. K., & Edwards, P. A. (2006). Cultural considerations with response to intervention models. *Reading Research Quarterly, 41*, 108–117.

Klingner, J. K., Sorrells, A. R., & Barrera, M. T. (2007). Considerations when implementing response to intervention with culturally and linguistically diverse students. In D. Haager, J. K. Klingner, & S. Vaughn (Eds.), *Evidence-based reading practices for response to intervention* (pp. 223–244). Baltimore, MD: Paul H. Brookes Publishing Co.

Kohn, A. (2000). *The case against standardized testing. Raising the test scores, ruining the schools.* Portsmouth, NH: Heinemann.

Kohnert, K., & Goldstein, B. (2005). Speech, language, and hearing in developing bilingual children: From practice to research. *Language, Speech, and Hearing Services in Schools, 36*(3), 169–171.

Kohnert, K., Yim, D., Nett, K., Kan, P. F., & Duran, L. (2005). Intervention with linguistically diverse preschool children: A focus on developing home language(s). *Language, Speech, and Hearing Services in Schools, 36*, 251–263.

Kohnert, Y. (2004). Processing skills in early sequential bilinguals. In B. Goldstein (Ed.), *Bilingual language development and disorders in Spanish-English speakers* (pp. 53–76). Baltimore, MD: Paul H. Brookes Publishing Co.

Kokkinos, C. M., Kakarani, S., & Kolovou, D. (2016). Relationships among shyness, social competence, peer relations, and theory of mind among pre-adolescents. *Social Psychology of Education, 19*, 117–133.

Koskinen, P. S., Gambrell, L. B., Kapinus, B., & Heathington, B. S. (1988). Retelling: A strategy for enhancing students' reading comprehension. *Reading Teacher, 41*, 892–897.

Koth, C. W., Bradshaw, C. P. & Leaf, P. J. (2008). A multilevel study of predictors of student perceptions of school climate: The effect of classroom-level factors. *Journal of Educational Psychology, 100 (1),* 96–104.

Kozol, J. (1988). *Rachel and her children: Homeless families in America.* New York, NY: Random House.

Kozulin, A., & Gindis, B. (2007). Sociocultural theory and education of children with special needs: From defectology to remedial pedagogy. In H. Daniels, M. Cole, & J. V. Wertsch (Eds.), *The Cambridge companion to Vygotsky* (pp. 332–362). Cambridge, UK: Cambridge University Press.

Krashen, S. (1982). *Principles and practices in second language acquisition.* Oxford, UK: Pergamon Press.

Krashen, S. (2001). Does "pure" phonemic awareness training affect reading comprehension? *Perceptual and Motor Skills, 93,* 356–358.

Krashen, S. (2003). Three roles for reading for minority-language children. In G. G. Garcia (Ed.), *English learners reaching the highest level of English literacy* (pp. 55–70). Newark, DE: International Reading Association.

Krashen, S. D. (1985). *The input hypothesis: Issues and Implications.* London, UK: Longman.

Krashen, S. D. (2004). *The power of reading. Insights from the Research* (2nd ed.). Portsmouth, NH: Heinemann

Kritikos, E. P. (2003). Speech–language pathologists' beliefs about language assessment of bilingual/bicultural individuals. *American Journal of Speech–Language Pathology, 12,* 73–91.

Kroska, A., & Harkness, S. K. (2008). Exploring the role of diagnosis in the modified labeling theory of mental illness. *Social Psychology Quarterly, 71*(2), 193–208.

Kuder, S. J. (2013). *Teaching students with language and communication disabilities* (4th ed.). Upper Saddle River, NJ: Pearson.

Kuhl, P. K. (2010). *Brain mechanisms in early language acquisition.* Retrieved from http://life-slc.org/docs/Kuhl-brainmechanisms2010.pdf

Ladd, H. (2012). Education and poverty: Confronting the evidence. *Journal of Policy Analysis and Management, 31,* 203–227.

Ladson-Billings, G. (2006). It's not the culture of poverty, it's the poverty of culture: The problem with teacher education. *Anthropology and Education Quarterly, 37,* 104–109.

Ladson-Billings, G. (2014). Culturally relevant pedagogy 2.0: a.k.a. the remix. *Harvard Educational Review, 84*(1), 74–84.

Lai, M. K., McNaughton, S., Amituanai-Toloa, M., Turner, R., & Hsiao, S. (2009). Sustained acceleration of achievement in reading comprehension: The New Zealand experience. *Reading Research Quarterly, 44*(1), 30–56.

Lai, M.C., Lombardo, M.V., Chakrabarti, B., Baron-Cohen, S. (2013) Subgrouping the Autism "Spectrum": Reflections on DSM-5. PLOS Biology 11(4): e1001544. https://doi.org/10.1371/journal.pbio.1001544

Laing, S. P., & Kamhi, A. (2003). Alternative assessment of language and literacy in culturally and linguistically diverse populations. *Language, Speech, and Hearing Services in Schools, 34,* 44–55.

Lambert, W. E. (1974). Culture and language as factors in learning and education. In F. E. Aboud & R. D. Mead (Eds.), *Cultural factors in learning and education* (pp. 91–122). *Proceedings of the Fifth Western Washington Symposium on Learning.* Bellingham, WA: Western Washington University.

Langer, J. A. (2001). Beating the odds: Teaching middle and high school students to read and write well. *American Educational Research Journal, 38,* 837–880.

Lantolf, J. P., & Thorne, S. L. (2006). *Sociocultural theory and the genesis of second language development.* New York, NY: Oxford University Press.

Lareau, A. (2011). *Unequal childhoods: Class, race, and family life, 2nd edition with an update a decade Later.* Berkeley, CA: University of California Press.

Lareau, A., & Conley, D. (Eds.). (2008). *Social class. How does it work?* New York, NY: Russell Sage Foundation.

Lau, R. R. (1982). Origins of health locus of control beliefs. *Journal of Personality and Social Psychology, 31,* 322–334.

Lave, J. (1988). *Cognition in practice: Mind, mathematics, and culture in everyday life.* Cambridge, UK: Cambridge University Press.

Leary, M. R. (1990). Anxiety, cognition and behavior: In search of a broader perspective. In M. Booth-Butterfield (Ed.), *Communication, cognition, and anxiety* (pp. 39–44). Newbury Park, CA: Sage.

Lee, C. D. (2008). The centrality of culture to the scientific study of learning and development: How an ecological framework in education research facilitates civic responsibility. *Educational Researcher, 37*(5), 267–279.

Lee, E., Menkart, D. & Okazawa-Rey, M. (2008). *Beyond heroes and holidays: A practical guide to K-12 anti-racist, multicultural education and staff development* (2nd ed.). Washington, DC: Teaching for Change.

Lee, S. (1996). *Unraveling the "model minority stereotype": Listening to Asian American students.* New York: Teachers College Press.

Lee, V. E., & Burkhan, D. T. (2002). *Inequality at the starting gate.* Washington, DC: Economic Policy Institute.

Lesaux, N. K., & Harris, J. R. (2015). *Cultivating knowledge, building language: Literacy instruction for English learners in elementary school.* Portsmouth, NH: Heinemann.

Leslie, L., & Caldwell, J. (2009). Formal and informal measures of reading comprehension. In S. E. Israel & G. G. Duffy (Eds.), *Handbook on research on reading comprehension* (pp. 403–427). New York, NY: Routledge.

Levitt, E. E. (1980). *The psychology of anxiety.* Hillsdale, NJ: Erlbaum.

Lewis, G., Jones, B., & Baker, C. (2012). Translanguaging: Origins and development from school to street and beyond. *Educational Research and Evaluation, 18, 641-654.*

Lewis, G., Jones, B., & Baker, C. (2013). 100 bilingual lessons: Distributing two languages in classrooms. In C. Abello-Contesse, P. M. Chandler, M. D. Lopez-Jemenez, & R. Chacon Beltran (Eds.), *Bilingual and multilingual education in the 21st century: Building on experience.* Bristol, UK: Multilingual Matters.

Li, J. (2006). Self in learning: Chinese adolescents' goals and sense of agency. *Child Development, 77*(2), 482–501.

Licona, P. R. & Kelly, G. J. (2020). Translanguaging in a middle school science classroom: Constructing scientific arguments in English and Spanish. *Cultural Studies of Science Education, 15,* 485–510.

Lightbown, P., & Spada, N. (2006). *How languages are learned* (3rd ed.). Oxford, UK: Oxford University Press.

Linan-Thompson, S., Cirino, P. T., & Vaughn, S. (2007). Determining English language learners' response to intervention: Questions and some answers. *Learning Disability Quarterly, 30*(3), 185–195.

Lindholm-Leary, K. (2012). What are the most effective kinds of programs for English language learners? In E. Hamayan & R. Freeman Field (Eds.), *English language learners at school: A guide for administrators* (2nd ed., pp. 105–106). Philadelphia, PA: Caslon.

Lubinski, D. (2000). Scientific and social significance of assessing individual differences: Sinking shafts at a few critical points. *Annual Review of Psychology, 51,* 405–444.

Luby, J., Belden, A., Botteron, K., Marrus, N., Harms, M. P., Babb, C., Nishino, T., & Barch, D. (2013). The effects of poverty on childhood brain development: The mediating effect of caregiving and stressful life events. *JAMA Pediatrics, 167*(12), 1135–1142.

Lucariello, J. M., Nastasi, B. K., Dwyer, C., Skiba, R., DeMarie, D., & Anderman, E. M. (2016). Top 20 Psychological Principles for PK-12 Education. *Theory into Practice, 55,* 86–93.

Lucas, T., Henze, R., & Donato, R. (1990). Promoting success of Latino language minority students: An exploratory study of six high schools. *Harvard Educational Review, 60,* 315–340.

Lum, C. (2002). *Scientific thinking in speech and language therapy.* Mahwah, NJ: Lawrence Erlbaum.

MacIntyre, P. D., & Gardner, R. C. (1991). Methods and results in the study of foreign language anxiety: A review of the literature. *Language Learning, 41,* 85–117.

Macksoud, M. S., & Aber, J. L. (1996). The war experiences and psychosocial development of children in Lebanon. *Child Development, 67,* 70–88.

Maeroff, G. I. (1993). *Team building for school change.* New York, NY: Teachers College Press.

Magid, B. & Boothby, N. (2013). Promoting resilience in children of war. In C. Fernando & M. Ferrari, (Eds.), *Handbook of Resilience in children of War* (pp. 39–49). New York: Springer Publishing.

Magnuson, K. A., & Waldfogel, J. (2005). Early childhood care and education: Effects on ethnic and racial gaps in school readiness. *Future of Children, 15,* 169–196.

Manning, M., Kamii, C., & Kato, T. (2005). Dynamic indicators of basic early literacy skills (DIBELS): A tool for evaluating student learning? *Journal of Research in Childhood Education, 20,* 81–96.

Manuck, S. B., & McCaffrey, J. M. (2014). Gene–environment interaction. *Annual Review of Psychology, 65,* 41–70.

Marchman, V., & Martínez-Sussman, C. (2002). Concurrent validity of caregiver/parent report measures of language for children who are learning both English and Spanish. *Journal of Speech, Language, and Hearing Research, 45*(5), 983–997.

Marler, B. (2012). How can we best serve students who come with interrupted formal education (SIFE) or limited formal schooling? In E. Hamayan & R. Freeman Field (Eds.), *English language learners at school: A guide for administrators* (2nd ed., pp. 213–214). Philadelphia, PA: Caslon.

Marshall, E., & Toohey, K. (2010). Representing family: Community funds of knowledge, bilingualism, and multimodality. *Harvard Educational Review, 80*(2), 221–241.

Martin, D. (2009). *Language disabilities in cultural and linguistic diversity.* Bristol, UK: Multilingual Matters.

Marvin, C. (1990). Problems in school-based speech-language consultation and collaboration services: Defining the terms and improving the process. *Best Practices in School Speech–Language Pathology, 1,* 37–48.

Marzano, R. (2003). *What works in schools: Translating research into action.* Alexandria, VA: Association for Supervision and Curriculum Development.

Marzano, R. J., Water, T., & McNulty, B. A. (2005). *School leadership that works: From research to results.* Alexandria, VA: Association for Supervision and Curriculum Development and Denver, CO: Mid-continent Research for Education and Learning.

Maslow, A., & Lowery, R. (Eds.). (1998). *Toward a psychology of being* (3rd ed.). New York, NY: John Wiley & Sons.

Matson, J. L., Matheis, M., Burns, C. O., . . . Goldin, R. L. (2017). Examining cross-cultural differences in autism spectrum disorder: A multinational comparison from Greece, Italy, Japan, Poland, and the United States. *European Psychiatry, 42,* 70–76.

Mattingly, C. (2008). Reading minds and telling tales in a cultural borderland. *Ethos, 36*(1), 136–154.

Maxwell, J., Nelson, R. L., Damico, H. L., Damico, J. S., & Weill, C. (2020). Reclaiming the socio-cultural power of recontextualizing: "I put my name with lots of names." In K. F. Whitmore & R. J. Meyer (Eds.), *Reclaiming literacies as meaning-making: Manifestations of values, identities, relationships, and knowledge.* New York, NY: Routledge.

Maxwell, J., Weill, C., & Damico, J. S. (2017). Investigating the use of appropriation in the writing of a child with autism: A case study. *Journal of Communication Disorders, 65,* 10–21.

McCabe, A. (1989). Differential language learning styles in young children: The importance of context. *Developmental Review, 9,* 1–20.

McCall, L. (2005). The complexity of intersectionality. *Signs, 30,* 1771–1800.

McCormick, T. W. (1988). *Theories of reading in dialogue: An interdisciplinary study.* New York, NY: University Press of America.

McDermott, R. (1997). Achieving school failure: An anthropological approach to illiteracy and social stratification. In G. D. Spindler (Ed.), *Education and cultural process. Anthropological approaches* (2nd ed., pp. 173–209). Prospect, IL: Waveland Press.

McDermott, R. (1999). Culture is not an environment of the mind. *Journal of Learning Sciences, 8,* 157–169.

McDermott, R., & Varenne, H. (1995). Culture as disability. *Anthropology & Education Quarterly, 26*(3), 324–348.

McEneaney, J. E., Lose, M. K., & Schwartz, R. M. (2006). A transactional perspective on reading difficulties and Response to Intervention. *Reading Research Quarterly, 41,* 117–128.

McEwan, H., & Egan, K. (Eds.). (1995). *Narrative in teaching learning, and research.* New York, NY: Teachers College Press.

McGill-Franzen, A. (2006). *Kindergarten literacy. Matching assessment and instruction in kindergarten.* New York, NY: Scholastic.

McLaughlin, B., & McLeod, B. (1996). Educating all our children: Improving education for children from culturally and linguistically diverse backgrounds. Impact statement/final report on the accomplishments of the National Center for Research on Cultural Diversity and Second Language Learning. Unpublished manuscript.

McMaster, K. L., Fuchs, D., & Fuchs, L. S. (2006). Research on peer-assisted learning strategies: Peer mediation's promise and limitations. *Reading and Writing Quarterly, 22,* 5–25.

McNeil, L. M. (2000). *Contradictions of school reform: Economic costs of standardized testing.* New York, NY: Routledge.

Medina, C. (2010). "Reading across communities" in biliteracy practices: Examining translocal discourses and cultural flows in literature discussions. *Reading Research Quarterly, 45*(1), 40–60.

Mehisto, P., Marsh, D. & Frigols, M. J. (2008). *Uncovering CLIL: Content and language integrated learning in bilingual and multilingual education.* Oxford, UK: Macmillan.

Meisuri, Sinar, T. S., Gurning, B., & Zein, T. T. (2018). The classroom interaction patterns in a bilingual classroom at a junior high school in Medan City. *Advances in Language and Literary Studies, 9,* 31–36.

Mellard, D. F., Byrd, S. E., Johnson, E., Tollefson, J. M., & Boesche, L. (2004). Foundations and research on identifying model responsiveness-to-intervention sites. *Learning Disability Quarterly, 27,* 243–256.

Menard-Warwick, J. (2007). Biliteracy and schooling in an extended-family Nicaraguan immigrant household: The sociohistorical construction of parental involvement. *Anthropology and Education Quarterly, 38,* 119–137.

Menken, K. (2008). *English language learners left behind: Standardized testing as language policy.* Clevedon, UK: Multilingual Matters.

Menken, K., & Garcia, O. (Eds.) (2010). *Negotiating Language Policies in Schools: Educators as Policymakers.* New York, NY: Routledge.

Mesmer, E. R., & Mesmer, H. A. E. (2008). Response to intervention (RtI): What teachers of reading need to know. *Reading Teacher, 62,* 280–290.

Mesmer, H. A. E. (2007). *Tools for matching readers to texts. Research-based practices.* New York, NY: Guilford.

Miech, R., Essex, M. J., & Goldsmith, H. H. (2001). Socioeconomic status and the adjustment to school: The role of self-regulation during early childhood. *Sociology of Education, 74,* 102–120.

Miller, D. (2009). *The Book Whisperer.* San Francisco: Jossey-Bass.

Milner, H. R. (2007). Race, culture, and researcher positionality: Working through dangers seen, unseen, and unforeseen. *Educational Researcher, 36*(7), 388–400.

Milner, H. R. IV (2010). *Understanding diversity, opportunity gaps, and teaching in today's classrooms: Start where you are, but don't stay there.* Cambridge, MA: Harvard Education Press.

Miramontes, O., Nadeau, A., & Commins, N. (2011). *Restructuring schools for linguistic diversity: Linking decision making to effective programs* (2nd ed.). New York, NY: Teachers College Press.

Moll, L., Amanti, C., Neff, D., & Gonzalez, N. (1992). Funds of knowledge for teaching: using a qualitative approach to connect homes and classrooms. *Theory into Practice, 31*(1), 132–141.

Möller, V. (2018): Promoting bilingualism at the primary and secondary level: The role of intelligence, motivation and anxiety. *International Journal of Bilingual Education and Bilingualism.* doi: 10.1080/13670050.2018.1559795

Montgomery, J. K. (1990). Building administrative support for service delivery changes. *Best Practices in School Speech-Language Pathology, 1,* 75–80.

Monz, L. D., & Rueda, R. (2009). Passing for English fluent: Latino immigrant children masking language proficiency. *Anthropology & Education Quarterly, 40*(1), 20–40.

Morita, N. (2004). Negotiating participation and identity in second language academic communities. *TESOL Quarterly, 38,* 573–603.

Müller, N. (2003). Multilingual communication disorders: Exempla et desiderata. *Journal of Multilingual Communication Disorders, 1* (1), 1–12.

Myhill, D., & Jones, S. (2009). How talk becomes text: Investigating the concept of oral rehearsal in early years' classrooms. *British Journal of Educational Studies, 57*(3), 265–284.

Nagy, W. E., McClure, E. E., & Mir, M. (1997). Linguistic transfer and the use of context by Spanish-English bilinguals. *Applied Psycholinguistics, 18*(4), 431–452.

Nakatani, Y. (2010). Identifying strategies that facilitate EFL learners' oral communication: A classroom study using multiple data collection procedures. *Modern Language Journal, 94*(1), 116–136.

Nasir, N. (2002). Identity, goals, and learning: Mathematics in cultural practice. *Mathematical Thinking and Learning, 4,* 211–247.

National Academies of Sciences, Engineering, and Medicine. (2017). *Promoting the educational success of children and youth learning English: Promising futures.* Washington, DC: The National Academies Press.

National Academies of Sciences, Engineering, and Medicine (2018). *How people Learn II. Learners, Contexts, and Cultures.* Washington, DC: National Academies Press.

National Institutes of Health. (2017). *Rates of new diagnosed cases of type 1 and type 2 diabetes on the rise among children, teens.* Retrieved from https://www.nih.gov/news-events/news-releases /rates-new-diagnosed-cases-type-1-type-2-diabetes-rise-among-children-teens

Neill, M. (2012). What are the problems with standardized testing for English language learners? In E. Hamayan & R. Freeman Field (Eds.), *English language learners at school: A guide for administrators* (2nd ed., pp. 69–70). Philadelphia, PA: Caslon.

Nelson, K. (2007). *Young minds in social worlds: Experience, meaning, and memory.* Cambridge, MA: Harvard University Press.

Neokleous, G., Krulatz, A., & Farrelly, R. (2020). *Handbook of research on cultivating literacy in diverse and multilingual classrooms.* Hershey, PA: IGI Global.

Nessel, D. D., & Jones, M. B. (1981). *The language experience approach to reading: A handbook for teachers.* New York, NY: Teachers College Press.

Ngo, B. (2008). Beyond "culture clash": Understandings of immigrant experiences. *Theory into Practice, 47*(1), 4–11.

Ngo, B., & Lee, S. J. (2007). Complicating the image of model minority success: A review of Southeast Asian American education. *Review of Educational Research, 77*(4), 415–453.

Nguyen, D. (2012a). How do we decide what kind of program for English language learners is appropriate for our school? In E. Hamayan & R. Freeman Field (Eds.), *English language learners at school: A guide for administrators* (2nd ed., pp. 117–118). Philadelphia, PA: Caslon.

Nguyen, D. (2012b). How do we use data on student performance to make decisions about the implementation of our program for English language learners? In E. Hamayan & R. Freeman Field (Eds.), *English language learners at school: A guide for administrators* (2nd ed., pp. 162–164). Philadelphia, PA: Caslon.

Niazifar, A., & Shakibaei, G. (2019). Effects of different text difficulty levels on Iranian EFL learners' foreign language reading motivation and reading comprehension. *Asian-Pacific Journal of Second and Foreign Language Education, 4*(1), 1–18.

Nieto, S. (1999). *The light in their eyes: Creating multicultural learning communities.* New York, NY: Teachers College Press.

Nieto, S. (2002). *Language, culture and teaching: Critical perspectives for teacher education.* 26th Annual Charles DeGarmo Lecture. Presented at the AERA meeting, New Orleans. Kennesaw, GA: Society of Professors of Education.

Nieto, S. (2010). *The light in their eyes: Creating multicultural learning communities.* New York, NY: Teachers College Press.

No Child Left Behind Act of 2001 (H.R.1). (2002). Washington, DC: 107th Congress.

Noble, G. (2017). Asian fails and the problem of bad Korean boys: Multiculturalism and the construction of an educational problem. *Journal of Ethnic and Migration Studies, 43,* 2456–2471.

Noble, K. G., Tottenham, N., & Casey, B. J. (2005). Neuroscience perspectives on disparities in school readiness and cognitive achievement. *Future of Children, 15*(1), 71–89.

Norris, J. A. (1988). Using communicative reading strategies to enhance reading strategies. *Reading Teacher, 47,* 668–673.

O'Connor, R. E., Bell, K. R., Larkin, L. K., Sackor, S. M., & Zigmond, N. (2002). Teaching reading to poor readers in the intermediate grades: A comparison of text difficulty. *Journal of Educational Psychology, 94,* 474–485.

Ollendick, T. H., Weist, M. D., Borden, M. C., & Greene, R. W. (1992). Sociometric status and academic, behavioral, and psychological adjustment: A five year longitudinal study. *Journal of Clinical Psychology, 60,* 80–87.

Oller, D. K. (2008). Sequence of reading acquisition in bilinguals. *Encyclopedia of language and literacy development* (pp. 1–7). London, ON: Canadian Language and Literacy Research Network.

Oller, D. K., & Eilers, R. E. (2002). *Language and literacy in bilingual children.* Clevedon, UK: Multilingual Matters.

Ontario Association of Speech–Language Pathologists and Audiologists. (2005). *Effective collaborative practices for speech-language pathologists: A resource guide.* Toronto, Canada: Author.

Opitz, M. F., Ford, M. P., & Erekson, J. A. (2011). *Accessible assessment: How nine sensible techniques can power data-driven reading instruction.* Portsmouth, NH: Heinemann.

Orelove, F. P., & Sobsey, D. (1996). *Educating children with multiple disabilities: A transdisciplinary approach* (3rd ed.). Baltimore, MD: Paul H. Brookes Publishing Co.

Ortiz, A. A., & Artiles, A. J. (2010). Meeting the needs of ELLs with disabilities: A linguistically and culturally responsive model. In G. Li & P. A. Edwards (Eds.), *Best practices in ELL instruction* (pp. 247–272). New York: Guilford.

Ortiz, A. A., García, S. B., Wheeler, D., & Maldonado–Colon, E. (1986). *Characteristics of English language learners served in programs for the speech and language disabled: Implications for policy, practice and research.* Austin, TX: University of Texas, Disabled Minority Research Institute on Language Proficiency.

Oxley, J., Gunhan, E., Kaniamattam, M., & Damico, J. S. (2017). Multilingual issues in qualitative research. *Clinical Linguistics and Phonetics, 7-9,* 612–630. doi: 10.1080/02699206.2017.1302512

Ozfidan, B., & Toprak, M. (2020). Cultural awareness on a bilingual education: A mixed method study. *Multicultural Learning and Teaching, 14,* 1–10. DOI:10.1515/mlt-2017-0019

Pacheco, M. (2010). English-language learners' reading achievement: Dialectical relationships between policy and practices in meaning-making opportunities. *Reading Research Quarterly, 45*(3), 292–317.

Paley, V. G. (1994). Every child a storyteller. In J. F. Duchan, L. E. Hewitt, & R. M. Sonnenmeier (Eds.), *Pragmatics: From theory to practice* (pp. 10–19). Englewood Cliffs, NJ: Prentice-Hall.

Palmer, D., & Martínez, R. A. (2013). Teacher agency in bilingual spaces: A fresh look at preparing teachers to educate Latina/o bilingual children. *Review of Research in Education, 37,* 269-297.

Paradis, J. (2005). Grammatical morphology in children learning English as a second language: Implications of similarities with specific language impairment. *Language, Speech and Hearing Services in Schools, 36,* 172–187.

Paradis, J., Crago, M., Genesee, F., & Rice, M. (2003). Bilingual children with specific language impairment: How do they compare to their monolingual peers? *Journal of Speech, Language and Hearing Research, 46,* 1–15.

Paradis, J., Genesee, F., & Crago, M. (2021). *Dual language development and disorders: A handbook on bilingualism and second language learning* (3rd ed.). Baltimore, MD: Paul H. Brookes Publishing Co.

Paradise, R., & Rogoff, B. (2009). Side by side: Learning by observing and pitching in. *Ethos, 37*(1), 102–138.

Paris, D. (2012). Culturally sustaining pedagogy: A needed change in stance, terminology, and practice. *Educational Researcher, 41*(3), 93–97.

Paris, D., & Alim, H. S. (Eds.). (2017). *Culturally sustaining pedagogies: Teaching and learning for justice in a changing world.* New York, NY: Teachers College Press.

Paris, D., & Alim, H. S. (2014). What are we seeking to sustain through culturally sustaining pedagogy? A loving critique forward. *Harvard Educational Review, 84*(1), 85–100.

Paris, S. G. (2005). Reinterpreting the development of reading skills. *Reading Research Quarterly, 40,* 184–202.

Parmar, S., Roseman, M.J., Siegrist, S. & Sowa, T. (2010). *Children and transitional justice: Truth-telling, accountability and reconciliation.* Cambridge, MA: Human Rights Program Harvard Law School and the UNICEF Innocenti Research Centre.

Pearson, B. Z., Fernánez, S., & Oller, D. K. (1995). Cross-language synonyms in the lexicons of bilingual infants: One language or two? *Journal of Child Language, 22*(2), 345–368.

Pearson, P. D., & Samuels, S. J. (1980). Editorial. *Reading Research Quarterly, 15,* 429–430.

Peña, E., Bedore, L., & Baron, A. (2017). Bilingualism in child language disorders. In R. G. Schwartz (Ed.), *Handbook of child language disorders.* New York, NY: Psychology Press.

Penn, C. (2014). Intercultural health communication: Why qualitative methods matter. In M. J. Ball, N. Müller, & R. L. Nelson (Eds.), *Handbook of qualitative research in communication disorders* (pp. 219–244). New York, NY: Psychology Press.

Perkins, M. R. (2005). Pragmatic ability and disability as emergent phenomena. *Clinical Linguistics and Phonetics, 19,* 367–378.

Perozzi, A. J., & Sanchez, M. L. C. (1992). The effect of instruction in L1 on receptive acquisition of L2 for bilingual children. *Language, Speech and Hearing Services in Schools, 23,* 348–352.

Pesco, D., MacLeod, A. A. N., Kay-Raining Bird, E., Cleave, P., Trudeau, N., de Valenzuela, J. S., Cain, K., Marinova-Todd, S. H., Colozzo, P., Stahl, H., Segers, E., & Verhoeven, L. (2016). A multi-site review of policies affecting opportunities for children with developmental disabilities to become bilingual. *Journal of Communication Disorders, 63,* 15–31.

Peyton, J. K., & Stanton, J. (1993). *Dialogue journals in the multilingual classroom: Building language fluency and writing skills through written interaction.* Norwood, NJ: Ablex.

Phelan, P., & Davidson, A.L. (Eds.). (1993). *Renegotiating cultural diversity in American schools.* New York, NY: Teachers College Press.

Phelan, P., Davidson, A. L., & Yu, H. C. (1993). Students' multiple worlds: Navigating the borders of family, peer, and school cultures. In P. Phelan & A. L. Davidson (Eds.), *Renegotiating cultural diversity in American schools* (pp. 52–88). New York, NY: Teachers College Press.

Philips, S. (1983). *The invisible culture.* New York, NY: Longman.

Piasta, S. B., & Wagner, R. K. (2010). Developing early literacy skills: A meta-analysis of alphabet learning and instruction. *Reading Research Quarterly, 45*(1), 8–38.

Pieretti, R. A. & Roseberry-McKibbin, C. (2016). Assessment and intervention for English language learners with primary language impairment: Research-based best practices. *Communication Disorders Quarterly, 37,* 117–128.

Pietarinen, J., Soini, T., & Pyhältö, K. (2014). Students' emotional and cognitive engagement as the determinants of wellbeing and achievement in school. *International Journal of Educational Research, 67,* 40–51.

Pinker, S. (1994). *The language instinct: How the mind creates language.* New York, NY: Harper Collins.

Pinnell, G. S. (1989). Reading recovery: Helping at-risk children learn to read. *Elementary School Journal, 90,* 160–183.

Pipher, M. (2002). *The middle of everywhere: Helping refugees enter the American community.* San Diego, CA: Harvest Book/Harcourt.

Poehner, M. E. (2007). Beyond the test: L2 dynamic assessment and the transcendence of mediated learning. *Modern Language Journal, 91,* 323–340.

Poplak, S. (1980). "Sometimes I'll start a sentence in English y termino en español": Toward a typology of code switching. *Linguistics, 18,* 581–618.

Portes, A., & Fernández-Kelly, P. (2008). No margin for error: Educational and occupational achievement among disadvantaged children of immigrants. *Annals of the American Academy of Political and Social Science, 620,* 12–36.

Portes, P. R. (1999). Social and psychological factors in the academic achievement of children of immigrants: A cultural history puzzle. *American Educational Research Journal, 36*(3), 489–507.

Potocky-Tripodi, M. (2002). *Best practices for social work with refugees and immigrants.* New York, NY: Columbia University Press.

Poveda, D. (2003). Literature socialization in a kindergarten classroom. *Journal of Folklore Research, 40*(3), 233–272.

Pransky, K., & Bailey, E. (2002). To meet your students where they are, first you have to find them: Working with culturally and linguistically diverse at-risk students. *The Reading Teacher, 56,* 370–383.

Prelock, P. A. (2000). Multiple perspectives for determining the roles of speech–language pathologists in inclusionary classrooms. *Language, Speech and Hearing Services in Schools, 31*(3), 213–218.

Pressley, M., Allington, R. L., Wharton-McDonald, R., Block, C. C., & Morrow, L. M. (2001). *Learning to read: Lessons from exemplary first-grade classrooms*. New York: Guilford.

Purcell-Gates, V., Duke, N. K., & Martineau, J. A. (2007). Learning to read and write genre-specific text: Roles of authentic experience and explicit teaching. *Reading Research Quarterly, 42*(1), 8–45.

Quinn, A. E. (2001). Moving marginalized students inside the lines: Cultural differences in classrooms. *English Journal, 90*(4), 44–50.

Ramirez, N. R., & Kuhl, P. K. (2016). *Bilingual language learning in children*. Institute for Learning & Brain Sciences. University of Washington. http://ilabs.washington.edu/sites/default/files/Ramirez_WhiteHouse_Paper.pdf

Rapley, M. (2004). *The social construction of intellectual disability*. Cambridge, UK: Cambridge University Press.

Reese, L., Garnier, H., Gallimore, R., & Goldenberg, C. (2000). Longitudinal analysis of the antecedents of emergent Spanish literacy and middle-school English reading achievement of Spanish-speaking students. *American Educational Research Journal, 37*(3), 633–662.

Reese, L., & Goldenberg, C. (2006). Community contexts for literacy development of Latina/o children: Contrasting case studies. *Anthropology and Education Quarterly, 37*, 42–61.

Reid, B. M., Secord, W. A., & Damico, J. S. (1993). Strategies for the integration of collaborative theory into practice. *NSSLHA Journal, 20*, 32–42.

Reutebuch, C. K. (2008). Succeed with a response-to-intervention model. *Intervention in School and Clinic, 44*, 126–128.

Reyes, I., & Azuara, A. (2008). Emergent biliteracy in young Mexican immigrant children. *Reading Research Quarterly, 43*, 374–398.

Rinaldi, C., & Sampson, J. (2008). English language learners and response to intervention. Referral considerations. *Teaching Exceptional Children 40*, 6–14.

Roberts, T. A. (2008). Home storybook reading in primary or second language with preschool children: Evidence of equal effectiveness for second-language vocabulary acquisition. *Reading Research Quarterly, 43*, 103–130.

Rodgers, C. (2002). Seeing student learning: Teacher change and the role of reflection. *Harvard Educational Review, 72*, 230–253.

Rodríguez-Mojica, C., Briceño, A., & Muñoz-Muñoz, E. (2019). Combating linguistic hegemony: Preparing and sustaining bilingual teacher educators in the United States. *Teacher Education Quarterly, 46*(3), 57–78.

Roessell, J., Schoell, C., & Stahlberg, D. (2020). Modern notions of accent-ism: Findings, conceptualizations, and implications for interventions and research on nonnative accents. *Journal of Language and Social Psychology, 39*, 87–111.

Rogoff, B. (2003). *The cultural nature of human development*. New York, NY: Oxford University Press.

Rolstad, K., Mahoney, K., & Glass, G. (2005). Weighing the evidence: A meta-analysis of bilingual education in Arizona. *Bilingual Research Journal, 29*, 1.

Roseberry-McKibbin, C. (2014). *Multicultural students with special language needs: Practical strategies for assessment and intervention* (4th ed.). Oceanside, CA: Academic Communication Associates.

Roseberry-McKibbin, C., Brice, A., & O'Hanlon, L. (2005). Serving English language learners in public school settings: A national survey. *Language, Speech, and Hearing Services in Schools, 36*, 48–61.

Routman, R. (2003). *Reading essentials: The specifics you need to teach reading well*. Portsmouth, NH: Heinemann.

Rueda, R., & Windmueller, M. (2006). English language learners, LD, and overrepresentation: A multiple-level analysis. *Journal of Learning Disabilities, 39* (2), 99–107.

Ruiz-de-Velasco, J., & Fix, M. (2000). *Overlooked and underserved: Immigrant students in U.S. secondary schools*. Washington, DC: Urban Institute.

Ryu, M. (2019). Mixing languages for science learning and participation: An examination of Korean-English bilingual learners in an after-school science-learning programme. *International Journal of Science Education, 41*(10), 1303–1323.

Sacks, P. (1999). *Standardized minds: The high price of America's testing culture and what we can do to change it*. Cambridge, MA: Perseus.

Saenz, L., Fuchs, L. D., & Fuchs, D. (2005). Effects of peer-assisted learning strategies on English language learners: A randomized controlled study. *Exceptional Children, 71*, 231–247.

Sahakyan, N. (2013). *District-level analysis of ELL growth*. Madison WI: Wisconsin Center for Education Research. Retrieved from: https://wida.wisc.edu/sites/default/files/resource/Report-DistrictLevelAnalysisOfELLGrowth.pdf

Sahlins, M. (1999). Two or three things that I know about culture. *Journal of the Royal Anthropology Institute, 5*, 399–421.

Salameh, E., Håkansson, G., & Nettelbladt, U. (2004). Developmental perspectives on bilingual Swedish-Arabic children with and without language impairment: A longitudinal study. *International Journal of Language and Communication Disorders, 39*(1), 65–92.

Samson, J. F., & Lesaux, N. K. (2009). Language-minority learners in special education: Rates and predictors of identification for services. *Journal of Learning Disabilities, 42,* 148–162.

Sánchez-López, C. (2012). How can we distinguish between a language difficulty and a learning disability? In E. Hamayan & R. Freeman Field (Eds.), *English language learners at school: A guide for administrators* (2nd ed., pp. 204–205). Philadelphia, PA: Caslon.

Sánchez-López, C., & Young, T. (2003, December). *Continuum of interventions for English language learners experiencing difficulties.* Paper presented at the 27th Annual Statewide Conference for Teachers of Linguistically and Culturally Diverse Students, Oak Brook, IL.

Sánchez-López, C., & Young, T. (2018). *Focus on special educational needs.* Oxford, UK: Oxford University Press.

Schall-Leckrone, L. (2018). Coursework to classroom. *Teacher Education Quarterly, 45,* 31–56.

Schecter, S. R., & Cummins, J. (Eds.). (2003). *Multilingual education in practice: Using diversity as a resource.* Portsmouth, NH: Heinemann.

Schiller, B. (2001). *The economics of poverty and discrimination.* Englewood Cliffs, NJ: Prentice Hall.

Schleppegrell, M. (2004). *The language of schooling: A functional linguistics perspective.* Mahwah, NJ: Lawrence Erlbaum.

Schön, D. (1991) *The reflective practitioner.* Farnham, UK: Ashgate.

Schussler, D. L. (2009). Beyond content: How teachers manage classrooms to facilitate intellectual engagement for disengaged students. *Theory into Practice, 48*(2), 114–121.

Schütze, U. (2017). *Language learning and the brain: Lexical processing in second language acquisition.* Cambridge, UK: Cambridge University Press.

Seccombe, K. (2002). "Beating the odds" versus "changing the odds": Poverty, resilience, and family policy. *Journal of Marriage and Family, 64,* 384–394.

Shea, M., Murray, R., & Harlin, R. (2005). *Drowning in data? How to collect, organize, and document student performance.* Portsmouth, NH: Heinemann.

Sheng, L., Peña, E. D., Bedore, L. M. & Fiestas, C. E. (2012). Semantic deficits in Spanish-English bilingual children with language impairment. *Journal of Speech, Language, and Hearing Research, 55*(1), 1–15.

Simmons-Mackie, N. N., & Damico, J.S. (2003). Contributions of qualitative research to the knowledge base of normal communication. *American Journal of Speech–Language Pathology, 12,* 144–154.

Sims, M., Ellis, E. M., & Knox, V. (2017). Parental plurilingual capital in a monolingual context: Investigating strengths to support young children in early childhood settings. *Early Childhood Education Journal, 45,* 777–787.

Sirin, S. R. (2005). Socioeconomic status and academic achievement: A meta-analytic review of research. *Review of Educational Research, 75*(3), 417–453.

Skrentny, J. D. (2008). Culture and race/ethnicity: Bolder, deeper, and broader. *Annals of the American Academy of Political and Social Science, 619,* 59–77.

Skrtic, T. M. (1991a). The special education paradox. *Harvard Educational Review, 6*(2), 148–206.

Slavin, R., & Cheung, A. (2003). *Effective reading programs for English language learners: A best evidence synthesis.* Baltimore, MD: Johns Hopkins University, Center for Research on the Education of Students Placed at Risk.

Sleeter, C. E. (2012). Confronting the marginalization of culturally responsive pedagogy. *Urban Education, 47*(3), 562-584.

Sloan, K. (2007). High-stakes accountability, minority youth, and ethnography: Assessing the multiple effects. *Anthropology and Education Quarterly, 38,* 24–41.

Smaje, C. (1995). *Health, "race" and ethnicity: Making sense of the evidence.* London: King's Fund Institute.

Smeeding, T. M. (2005). Public policy, economic inequality, and poverty. The United States in comparative perspective. *Social Science Quarterly, 86,* 955–983.

Smith, F. (1998). *The book of learning and forgetting.* New York, NY: Teachers College Press.

Smith, F. (2003). *Unspeakable acts, unnatural practices: Flaws and fallacies in scientific reading instruction.* Portsmouth, NH: Heinemann.

Smith, F. (2004). *Understanding reading* (6th ed.). Mahwah, NJ: Lawrence Erlbaum.

Smith, F. (2015). *Landmarks in literacy. The Selected works of Frank Smith.* New York, NY: Routledge.

Smith, K. P., & Christakis, N. A. (2008). Social networks and health. *Annual Review of Sociology, 34,* 405–429.

Smith, P. (2012). How do English language learners acquire a second language at school? In E. Hamayan & R. Freeman Field (Eds.), *English language learners at school: A guide for administrators* (2nd ed., pp. 52–53). Philadelphia, PA: Caslon.

Snow, M. A., Met, M., & Genesee, F. (1989). A conceptual framework for the integration of language and content in second/foreign language instruction. *TESOL Quarterly, 23,* 201–217.

Soltero-González, L. (2009). Preschool Latino immigrant children: Using the home language as a resource for literacy learning. *Theory into Practice, 48*(4), 283–289.

Soltero-González, L., Sparrow, W., Butvilofsky, S., Escamilla, K., & Hopewell, S. (2016). Effects of a paired literacy program on emerging bilingual children's biliteracy outcomes in third grade. *Journal of Literacy Research, 48*(1), 80–104. Retrieved from https://doi.org/10.1177/1086296X16653842

Sox, A. K. (2009). Latino immigrant students in southern schools: What we know and still need to learn. *Theory into Practice, 48*(4), 312–318.

Spandel, V., & Stiggins, J. J. (1997). *Creating writers. Linking writing assessment and instruction* (2nd ed.). New York, NY: Longman.

Speece, D. L., & Walker, C. Y. (2007). What are the issues in response to intervention research? In D. Haager, J. K. Klingner, & S. Vaughn (Eds.), *Evidence-based reading practices for response to intervention* (pp. 287–302). Baltimore, MD: Paul H. Brookes Publishing Co.

Spindler, G. D. D. (1997). *Education and cultural process: Anthropological approaches*. Prospect Heights, IL: Waveland Press.

Spindler, G. D. D. & Spindler, L. (1994). *Pathways to cultural awareness: Cultural therapy with teachers and students*. Thousand Oaks, CA: Sage.

Stahl, K. A. D. (2009). Assessing comprehension of young children. In S. E. Israel & G. G. Duffy (Eds.), *Handbook of research on reading comprehension* (pp. 428–448). New York, NY: Routledge.

Stanton-Salazar, R. D. (1997). A social capital framework for understanding the socialization of racial minority children and youths. *Harvard Education Review, 67*, 1–40.

Stecker, P. M., Fuchs, L. S., & Fuchs, D. (2005). Using curriculum-based measurement to improve student achievement: Review of research. *Psychology in the Schools, 42*, 795–820.

Steele, C. M. (2004). A threat in the air: How stereotypes shape intellectual identity and performance. In J. Banks & C. Banks (Eds.), *Handbook of research on multicultural education* (2nd ed., pp. 682–698). San Francisco, CA: Jossey-Bass.

Stern, M. P., Pugh, J. A., Gaskill, S. P., & Hazuda, H. (1982). Knowledge, attitudes, and behavior related to obesity and dieting in Mexican Americans and Anglos: The San Antonio Heart Study. *American Journal of Epidemiology, 115*, 917–928.

Sternberg, R. J. (2007a). Culture, instruction, and assessment. *Comparative Education, 43*(1), 5–22.

Sternberg, R. J. (2007b). Who are the bright children? The cultural context of being and acting intelligent. *Educational Researcher, 36*(3), 148–155.

Sternberg, R. J., & Grigorenko, E. L. (2002). Difference scores in the identification of children with learning disabilities: It's time to use a different method. *Journal of School Psychology, 40* (1), 65–83.

Stevens, L.C. (2019). Advocacy. In J. S. Damico & M. J. Ball (Eds.), *The SAGE encyclopedia of human communicative sciences and disorders* (pp. 55–56). Thousand Oaks, CA: Sage.

Stevenson, M. (1995). The power of influence: Effecting change by developing ownership. In C. Dudley-Marling & D. Searle (Eds.), *Who owns learning? Questions of autonomy, choice, and control* (pp. 128–141). Portsmouth, NH: Heinemann.

Stow, C., & Dodd, B. (2005). A survey of bilingual children referred for investigation of communication disorders: A comparison with monolingual children referred in one area in England. *Journal of Multilingual Communication Disorders, 3*(1), 1–24.

Strauss, S. L. (2001). An open letter to Reid Lyon. *Educational Researcher, 30*(5) 26–33.

Street, B. (2009). Ethnography of reading and writing. In D. R. Olson & N. Torrance (Eds.), *The Cambridge handbook of literacy* (pp. 329–345). Cambridge, UK: Cambridge University Press.

Suárez-Orozco, M., Darbes, T., Dias, S. I. & Sutin, M. (2011). Migrations and schooling. *Annual Review of Anthropology, 40*, 311–328.

Suarez-Orozco, M. M. (1995). The cultural patterning of achievement motivation: A comparative study of Mexican, Mexican immigrant, and non-Latino white American youths in schools. *International Migration Review, 28*, 748–794.

Suleman, S., McFarlane, L.A., Pollock, K. Schneider, P., Leroy, C., & Skoczylas, M. (2014). Collaboration: More than "working together" – An exploratory study to determine effect of interprofessional education on awareness and application of models of specialized service delivery by student speech-language pathologists and teachers. *Canadian Journal of Speech–Language Pathology & Audiology, 37*, 298-307.

Sundqvist, P., & Sylvén, L. S. (2014). Language-related computer use: Focus on young L2 English learners in Sweden. *ReCALL, 26*(1), 3–20.

Swain, M. (2006). Languaging, agency and collaboration in advanced second language learning. In H. Byrnes (Ed.), *Advanced language learning: the contribution of Halliday and Vygotsky* (pp. 95–108). London, UK: Continuum.

Swain, M., & Deters, P. (2007). "New" mainstream SLA theory: Expanded and enriched. *Modern Language Journal, 91*, 820–836.

Swan, M., & Smith, B. (Eds.). (2001). *Learner English: A teacher's guide to interference and other problems* (2nd ed.). Cambridge, New York: Cambridge Handbooks for Language Teachers.

Swanson, H., & Hoskyn, M. (1998). Experimental intervention research on students with learning disabilities: A meta-analysis of treatment outcomes. *Review of Educational Research, 68*, 277–321.

Swenson, N. C., & Williams, V. (2015). How to collaborate: Five steps for success. *SIG 16 Perspectives on School-Based Issues. 16*(4), 122–130.

Taberski, S. (2000). *On solid ground: Strategies for teaching reading K–3.* Portsmouth, NH: Heinemann.

Tavares, N.J. (2015). How strategic use of L1 in an L2-medium mathematics classroom facilitates L2 interaction and comprehension, *International Journal of Bilingual Education and Bilingualism, 18*, 319–335.

Taylor, B. M., Pearson, P. D., Clark, K., & Sharon, W. (2000). Effective schools and accomplished teachers: Lessons about primary-grade reading instruction in low-income schools. *Elementary School Journal, 101*(2), 121–165.

Taylor, D. (1983). *Family literacy. Young children learning to read and write.* Portsmouth, NH: Heinemann.

Taylor, D. (1993). *From a child's point of view.* Portsmouth, NH: Heinemann.

Taylor-Leech, K. (2013). Finding space for non-dominant languages in education: Language policy and medium of instruction in Timor-Leste 2000–2012. *Current Issues in Language Planning, 14*(1), 109–126.

TESOL International Association. (2006). *PreK–12 English language proficiency standards.* Alexandria, VA: Author.

TESOL International Association. (2020). *The 6 Principles for Exemplary Teaching of English Learners.* Alexandria, VA: Author.

Tedick, D. J. (2009). K–12 language teacher preparation: Problems and possibilities. *Modern Language Journal, 93*(2), 263–267.

TenHouten, W.D. (2016), Normlessness, anomie, and the emotions. *Sociological Forum, 31*, 465–486.

Tetnowski, J. A., & Franklin, T. C. (2003). Qualitative research: Implications for description and assessment. *American Journal of Speech–Language Pathology, 12*(2), 155–165.

Tharp, R. (1999). *The five standards for effective pedagogy.* Santa Cruz: University of California, Center for Research on Education, Diversity and Excellence.

Thomas, W., & Collier, V. (2002). *A national study of school effectiveness for language minority students' long term academic achievement.* Santa Cruz: University of California, Center for Research in Education, Diversity and Excellence.

Thomas, W.P., & Collier, V. P. (2017). Why dual language schooling. Albuquerque, NM: Dual Language Education of New Mexico-Fuente Press.

Thorndike, E. L. (1920). A constant error on psychological rating. *Journal of Applied Psychology, 4*, 469–477.

Tizard, J., Schofield, W. N., & Hewison, J. (1982). The Haringey shared reading project. *British Journal of Educational Psychology, 52*, 1–15.

Tomczak, E., & Jaworska-Pasterska, D. (2017). Affective language processing and bilingualism: Complementary perspectives. *Poznań Studies in Contemporary Linguistics, 53*, 1–16.

Toohey, K. (1996). Learning English as a second language in kindergarten: A community of practice perspective. *Canadian Modern Language Review, 52*, 549–576.

Trelease, J. (2001). *The read-aloud handbook* (5th ed.). New York, NY: Penguin Books.

Troia, G.A. (2005). Responsiveness to intervention: Roles for speech–language pathologists in the prevention and identification of learning disabilities. *Topics in Language Disorders, 25*, 106–119.

Trousdale, A. M. (1990). Interactive storytelling: Scaffolding children's early narratives. *Language Arts, 67*, 164–173.

Trueba, H. T. (1988). Culturally based explanations of minority students' academic achievement. *Anthropology & Education Quarterly, 19*, 270–287.

Trueba, H. T. (1993). Cultural therapy in action. In H. T. Trueba, C. Rodriguez, Y. Zou, & J. Cintron (Eds.), *Healing multi-cultural America: Mexican immigrants rise to power in rural California* (pp. 155–168). London, UK: Falmer Press.

Tsybina, I., & Eriks-Brophy, A. (2010). Bilingual dialogic book-reading intervention for preschoolers with slow expressive vocabulary development. *Journal of Communication Disorders. 43*, 538–556.

Uccelli, P., & Paez, M. M. (2007). Narrative and vocabulary development of bilingual children from kindergarten to first grade: Developmental changes and associations among English and Spanish skills. *Language, Speech, and Hearing Services in Schools, 38*(3), 225–236.

Uchendu, E. (2007). Recollections of childhood experiences during the Nigerian Civil War. *Africa: Journal of the International African Institute, 77*(3), 393–418.

Ukrainetz, T. A. (2006). The implications of TRI and EBP for SLPs: Commentary on L. M. Justice. *Language, Speech, and Hearing Services in Schools, 37*, 298–303.

Ullucci, K., & Howard, T. (2015) Pathologizing the poor: Implications for preparing teachers to work in high-poverty schools. *Urban Education, 50,* 170–193.

Understanding Special Education. (2012). *Special education funding.* Retrieved from http://www.understandingspecialeducation.com/special-education-funding.html

United Nations Children's Fund. (2011). *The state of the world's children: Adolescence, an age of opportunity.* Retrieved from http://www.unicef.org/sowc2011/pdfs/SOWC-2011-Main-Report_EN_02092011.pdf

United Nations Educational. Scientific and Cultural Organization. (2012). *Family literacy programme.* UNESCO Institute for Lifelong Learning. Retrieved from http://www.unesco.org/uil/litbase/?menu=4&programme=105

U.S. Department of Veterans Affairs. (2006). *Facts about PTSD.* Washington, DC: National Center for Post-traumatic Stress Disorder. Retrieved from www.ncptsd.va.gov/facts/index.html

Vadeboncoeur, J. A. (2006). Engaging young people: Learning in unformal contexts. *Review of Research in Education, 30,* 239–278.

Valencia, S. W., Smith, A. T., Reece, A. M., Li, M., Wixson, K. K., & Newman, H. (2010). Oral reading fluency assessment: Issues of construct, criterion, and consequential validity. *Reading Research Quarterly, 45*(3), 270–291.

Valenzuela, A., Prieto, L., & Hamilton, M. P. (2007). Introduction to the Special Issue: No Child Left Behind (NCLB) and minority youth: What the qualitative evidence suggests. *Anthropology & Education Quarterly, 38*(1), 1–8.

van der Putten, S.J. (2017). Are motivational theories too general to be applied in education [Special issue]? *SFU Educational Review, 10,* 1–12.

van Kraayenoord, C. E. (2009) What really works in special and inclusive education: Using evidence-based teaching strategies, *International Journal of Disability, Development and Education, 56*(3), 308–310.

van Kraayenoord, C. E. (2010). Review: Response to intervention: New ways and wariness. *Reading Research Quarterly, 45,* 363–376.

van Kraayenoord, C. E., & Chapman, J.W. (2016). Learning disabilities in Australia and New Zealand. *Learning Disabilities: A Contemporary Journal, 14,* 1–6.

van Kraayenoord, C. E., Honan, E., & Moni, K. B. (2011) Negotiating knowledge in a researcher and teacher collaborative research partnership, *Teacher Development, 15*(4), 403–420.

Van Lier, L. (2004). *The ecology and semiotics of language learning: A sociocultural perspective.* Boston, MA: Kluwer Academic.

Varenne, H. (2008). Culture, education, anthropology. *Anthropology & Education Quarterly, 39*(4), 356–368.

Vaughn, S., & Denton, C. A. (2008). Tier 2: The role of intervention. In D. Fuchs, L. S. Fuchs, & S. Vaughn (Eds.), *Response to intervention. A framework for reading educators* (pp. 51–70). Newark, DE: International Reading Association.

Vaughn, S., & Klingner, J. K. (2007). Overview of the three-tier model of reading intervention. In D. Haager, J. K. Klingner, & S. Vaughn (Eds.), *Evidence-based reading practices for response to intervention* (pp. 3–10). Baltimore, MD: Paul H. Brookes Publishing Co.

Vaughn, S., Linan-Thompson, S., Kouzekanani, K., Bryant, D. P., Dickson, S., & Blozis, S. A. (2003). Reading instruction grouping for students with reading difficulties. *Remedial and Special Education, 24,* 301–315.

Vaughn, S. R., & Fuchs, L. S. (2003). Redefining learning disabilities as inadequate response to treatment: Rationale and assumptions. *Learning Disabilities Research and Practice, 18,* 137–146.

Verdon, S., McLeod, S., & Winsler, A. (2014). Language maintenance and loss in a population study of young Australian children. *Early Childhood Research Quarterly, 29*(2), 168–181.

Vitanova, G. (2005). Authoring the self in a non-native language: A dialogic approach to agency and subjectivity. In J. K. Hall, G. Vitanova, & L. Marchenkova (Eds.), *Dialogue with Bakhtin on second and foreign language learning: New perspectives* (pp. 149–169). Mahwah, NJ: Lawrence Erlbaum.

Vurdien, R., & Puranen, P. (2018). Development of critical thinking skills and intercultural awareness in bilingual telecollaborative projects. In P. Taalas, J. Jalkanen, L. Bradley & S. Thouësny (Eds), *Future-proof CALL: Language learning as exploration and encounters—short papers from EUROCALL 2018* (pp. 307-312). https://doi.org/10.14705/rpnet.2018.26.9782490057221

Vygotsky, L. S. (1978). *Mind in society: The development of higher psychological processes.* Cambridge, MA: Harvard University Press. [Originally published in Russian in 1930]

Wagner, T., Kegan, R., Lahey, L. L., Lemons, R. W., Garnier, J., Helsing, D., Howell, A. & Rasmussen, H. T. (2006). *Change leadership: A practical guide to transforming our schools.* San Francisco, CA: Jossey-Basse.

Waitoller, F. R., Artiles, A. J. & Cheney, D. A. (2010). The Miner's Canary: A Review of Overrepresentation Research and Explanations. *The Journal of Special Education, 44* (1), 29-49.

Wang, M.-T., & Degol, J. L. (2016). School climate: A review of the construct, measurement, and impact on student outcomes. *Educational Psychology Review. 28*(2), 315–352.

Washington, K. N., Westby, C., Fritz, F., Crowe, K., Karem, R. W., & Basinger, M. (2021). The narrative competence of bilingual Jamaican Creole– and English-speaking preschoolers. *Language, Speech, and Hearing Services in Schools, 52*, 317–334.

Watson-Gegeo, K. A. (2004). Mind, language, and epistemology: Toward a language socialization paradigm for SLA. *Modern Language Journal, 88*, 331–350.

Watters, E. (2010). *Crazy like us: The globalization of the American psyche.* New York, NY: Free Press.

Wax, M. (1993). How culture misdirects multiculturalism. *Anthropology and Education Quarterly, 24*, 99–115.

Weaver, C. (1996). Teaching grammar in the context of writing. *English Journal, 85*, 15–24.

Weininger, E. B., Lareau, A., & LaRossa, R. (2009). Paradoxical pathways: An ethnographic extension of Kohn's findings on class and childrearing. *Journal of Marriage and Family, 71*(3), 680–695.

Weisner, T. S. (2009). Culture, development, and diversity: Expectable pluralism, conflict, and similarity. *Ethos, 37*(2), 181–196.

Weissbourd, R. (1996). *The vulnerable child: What really hurts America's children and what we can do about it.* Reading, MA: Addison-Wesley.

Welch, M., Sheridan, S. M., Wilson, B., Colton, D., & Mayhew, J. C. (1996). Site-based transdisciplinary educational partnerships: Development, implementation, and outcomes of a collaborative professional preparation program. *Journal of Educational and Psychological Consultation, 7*(3), 223–249.

Wells, G. (1986). *The meaning makers: Children learning language and using language to learn.* Portsmouth, NH: Heinemann

Wells, G. (1994). The complementary contributions of Halliday and Vygotsky to a "language-based theory of learning." *Linguistics and Education, 6*, 41–90.

Wells, G. (1998). Some questions about direct instruction: Why? to whom? how? and when? *Language Arts, 76*, 27–35.

Wells, G. (2003). *Dialogic inquiry: Toward a sociocultural practice and theory of education.* Cambridge: Cambridge University Press.

Wentzel, K. R., & Wigfield, A. (1998). Academic and social motivational influences on students' academic performance. *Educational Psychology Review, 10*(2), 155–175.

Werner, E., & Smith, R. (1992). *Overcoming the odds: High-risk children from birth to adulthood.* Ithaca, NY: Cornell University Press.

Westby, C., & Vining, C. B. (2002). Living in harmony: Providing services to Native American children and families. In D. E. Battle (Ed.), *Communication disorders in multicultural populations* (3rd ed., pp. 135–178). Woburn, MA: Butterworth-Heinemann.

Westernoff, F. (2019). Cultural and Linguistic Informants. In J. S. Damico. & M. J. Ball (Eds.). *The SAGE encyclopedia of human communicative sciences and disorders* (pp. 531–536). Thousand Oaks, CA: Sage.

Westernoff, F., Jones-Vo, S. & Markus, P. (2021). *Powerful Practices for Supporting English Learners.* Thousand Oaks, CA: Corwin Press.

Whitehurst, G. J., Falco, F. L., Lonigan, C. J., Fischel, J. E., DeBaryshe, B. D. & Valdez-Menchaca, M. C. (1988). Accelerating language development through picture book reading. *Developmental Psychology, 24*, 552–559.

Whiting, J. W. M. (1990). Adolescent rituals and identity conflicts. In J. W. Stigler, R. A. Shweder, & G. Herdt (Eds.), *Cultural psychology: Essays on comparative human development* (pp. 357–365). Cambridge, UK: Cambridge University Press.

Whitmore, R. (1987). *Living with stress and anxiety.* Manchester, UK: Manchester University Press.

WIDA (2020). *The WIDA English Language Development Standards, 2020 Edition Kindergarten – Grade 12.* Retrieved from wida.wisc.edu/2020standards,

WIDA (2015). *SLIFE: Students with limited or interrupted formal education.* Retrieved from https://wida.wisc.edu/sites/default/files/resource/FocusOn-SLIFE.pdf

WIDA (2012). D*eveloping a culturally and linguistically responsive approach to response to instruction & intervention (RtI²) for English language learners.* Madison: Board of Regents of the University of Wisconsin System

WIDA (2006). *English language proficiency standards.* Madison: University of Wisconsin–Madison, Wisconsin Center for Education Research.

Wiener, J., & Davidson, I. (1990). The in-school team: A preventive model of service delivery in special education. *Canadian Journal of Education, 15*(4), 427–444.

Wiggins, G., & McTighe, J. (2004) *Understanding by design: Professional development workbook.* Alexandria, VA: Association for Supervision and Curriculum Development.

Wilding, L., & Griffey, S. (2015). The strength-based approach to educational psychology practice: A critique from social constructionist and systemic perspectives. *Educational Psychology in Practice, 31.* 43–55.

Wiley, T., & Wright, W. (2004). Against the undertow: Language-minority education policy and politics in the "age of accountability." *Educational Policy, 18*(1), 142–168.

Wilkinson, C.Y. & Ortiz, A.A. (1986). *Characteristics of limited English proficient learning disabled Hispanic students at initial assessment and at reevaluation.* Austin, TX: Handicapped Minority Research Institute on Language Proficiency.

Willingham, W. W., & Jones, M. B. (1958). On the identification of halo through analysis of variance. *Educational and Psychological Measurement, 18,* 403–407.

Wine, J. D. (1980). Cognitive-attentional theory of test anxiety. In I. G. Sarason (Ed.), *Test anxiety: Theory, research, and applications* (pp. 349–385). Hillsdale, NJ: Erlbaum.

Winter, K. (1999). Speech and language therapy provision for bilingual children: Aspects of the current service. *International Journal of Language and Communication Disorders, 34*(1), 85–98.

Winter, K. (2001). Number of bilingual children in speech and language therapy: Theory and practice of measuring their representation. *International Journal of Bilingualism, 5*(4), 465–495.

Woodward, H. (1994). *Negotiated evaluation: Involving children and parents in the process.* Portsmouth, NH: Heinemann.

World Health Organization. (2002). *International classification of diseases* (ICD–10). Geneva, Switzerland: Author.

Wright, J. (2005). Five interventions that work. *NAESP [National Association of Elementary School Principals] Leadership Compass, 2*(4), 1, 6.

Xu, Y., & Drame, E. (2008). Culturally appropriate context: Unlocking the potential of response to intervention for English language learners. *Early Childhood Education Journal, 35,* 305–311.

York-Barr, J., & Rainforth, B. (1997). *Collaborative teams for students with severe disabilities: Integrating therapy and educational services* (2nd ed.). Baltimore, MD: Paul H. Brookes Publishing Co.

Young, T., & Westernoff, F. (1999). Reflections of speech and language pathologists and audiologists on practices in a multicultural, multilingual society. *Journal of Speech–Language Pathology and Audiology, 23*(1), 24–30.

Youngs, P., Jones, N., & Low, M. (2011). How beginning special and general education elementary teachers negotiate role expectations and access to professional resources. *Teachers College Record, 113,* 1506–1540.

Yturriago, J. (2012a). What can you can tell parents of English language learners about language use at home? In E. Hamayan & R. Freeman Field (Eds.), *English language learners at school: A guide for administrators.* Philadelphia, PA: Caslon. Retrieved from casloncommunity.com/resources/161

Yturriago, J. (2012b). How do we use evidence on program effectiveness to inform policy? In E. Hamayan, & R. Freeman Field (Eds.) *English language learners at school: A guide for administrators* (2nd ed., pp. 87–90). Philadelphia, PA: Caslon.

Zirkel, P. A. (2006). *SLD eligibility: A user's guide to the new regulations.* Lawrence, KS: National Research Center on Learning Disabilities.

Index

Page numbers followed by *f*, *b*, and *t* indicate figures, boxes, and tables, respectively.